The Wooden Horse of Gallipoli

The Wooden Horse of Gallipoli

Stephen Snelling

Frontline Books

THE WOODEN HORSE OF GALLIPOLI
The Heroic Saga of SS River Clyde, a WW1 Icon, Told Through the
Accounts of Those Who Were There

First published in 2017 by Frontline Books,
an imprint of Pen & Sword Books Ltd,
47 Church Street, Barnsley, S. Yorkshire, S70 2AS.

ISBN: 978-1-84832-852-5

CIP data records for this title are available from the British Library

For more information on our books, please visit
www.frontline-books.com
email info@frontline-books.com
or write to us at the above address.

Printed and bound by Gutenberg Press in Malta.
Typeset in 10.5/12.5 point Palatino

To my grandchildren, Pippin, Quinn and Francis, in the sincere hope that they never have to endure anything on a par with the ordeal suffered by those who landed at V Beach, Gallipoli, on 25 April 1915.

Contents

Acknowledgements

Many books have long gestations. This one, I suspect, has longer than most. From my earliest encounter with the *River Clyde*, via the fifteen speech bubble-filled illustrations on the cover of *The Victor* comic, to my biographical study of the Victoria Cross recipients of the Gallipoli campaign, I have lived with the story for very nearly half a century. Of course, I cannot pretend I have devoted all of that time to planning this particular work. The thought that here was a book waiting to be written occurred to me some fifteen years ago. It might have remained no more than a vague idea but for a telephone call 'out of the blue' in the autumn of 2014. It came from Martin Mace, newly established publisher of Frontline Books, as he sought to continue a happy and rewarding association that had begun during his editorship of *Britain at War* Magazine. For better or worse, that conversation proved the catalyst for a two-year historical odyssey that has culminated in *The Wooden Horse of Gallipoli*.

When asked if I had any subjects I would like to develop into book form, I found myself drawn inexorably back by that fifteen-year-old nagging thought to the story of the *River Clyde*. Here was my opportunity to make the idea a reality and turn a few biographical sketches into a comprehensive examination of one of the most extraordinary operations not just of the First World War, but of any conflict in the history of British arms. Without thinking where the research would take me, or, more to the point, how long it would take to complete, I took my chance. Two years on, it is fair to say I under-estimated by some considerable margin the scale of the challenge I had set myself. I am, therefore, most grateful to Martin and his team at Frontline for their patience and understanding in allowing me the time and space required to produce a book that I hope does justice to the memory of all those connected with the 'wooden horse', whether they be British, Irish or Turkish.

ACKNOWLEDGEMENTS

As with any book of this nature, there are many people to thank. With the passing of that generation that experienced the 1914–18 conflict first-hand, writers such as myself have come to depend on the nation's great depositories of letters, diaries and tape-recorded interviews with those who were there. Indeed, without the National Archives, the Imperial War Museum, the National Army Museum, the Liddell Hart Centre for Military Archives at King's College, London, the Churchill Archives Centre at Churchill College, Cambridge, and the Liddle Collection at Leeds University Library, this book would not exist. The staffs of all these historical treasure houses have, as ever, been unfailingly courteous and helpful in answering all questions and in furnishing me with the wealth of eyewitness accounts that are at the heart of this retelling of the *River Clyde* story. I am also grateful to Rachel Holmes, assistant curator of The Royal Hampshire Regimental Museum; Anne Pedley, regimental archivist of the Royal Welch Fusiliers Museum; Christine Hiskey, archivist at the Holkham Hall estate; and Anne Rainsbury, curator of Chepstow Museum, for their assistance with enquiries and information over the course of a number of years.

Other individuals who have knowingly, and in some instances unknowingly, contributed to this latest book include fellow writers and 'Gallipoli hands' Nigel Steel, Peter Hart and Stephen Chambers. Both Nigel and Peter were of great assistance to me during my initial research in the 1990s, which pre-dated the 'Wooden Horse' project. As well as pointing me in the direction of key witnesses and archival collections, they offered their own insights on aspects of the struggle at V Beach that were based on their own detailed research. Stephen's support has been no less important. The author of no fewer than five books on Gallipoli and an acknowledged authority on the involvement of naval armoured car units in the campaign, he has generously allowed access to papers and photographs gathered during his own researches. I am particularly thankful for his kind permission to quote from the letters of Douglas Illingworth and the eloquent diary compiled by David Fyffe, both of them members of Josiah Wedgwood's volunteer machine gun party aboard the *River Clyde*. My record of the 'Wooden Horse' at V Beach would have been much the poorer without their vivid commentaries.

Others who have helped with diaries, letters and all manner of historical information include a large number of relatives of men who played a prominent role in the landings from the *River Clyde* and the fighting to secure a toehold on the peninsula. I am particularly grateful to the following: Edward Dix-Perkin and Johanna Dix-Perkin (family of Edward Unwin); Hugh St A Malleson and Jane McWilliams (family of Wilfrid Malleson); Carole Macdonald, Norma Samson Kogut and Maureen Samson Robertson (family of George Samson); and Heather Thorne (family of George Drewry).

I would also like to thank those people who responded to my appeal for assistance published in *The Gallipolian*, the journal of the Gallipoli Association, and to those people, including Jon Toohey, Stephen Beaumont and Michael D. Robson, for the loan of books, papers and photographs connected with my research.

Of course, any author of an historical work owes a debt to all those writers who have ploughed a similar furrow and I am no different. I am particularly indebted to veterans of the campaign who either wrote their own memoirs or whose personal accounts enlivened other writers' studies of the operations at Cape Helles. Such books have been a source of inspiration as well as information and you will find them listed in the bibliography and cited in the footnotes that accompany the narrative.

As with all my work, however, the greatest thanks of all are reserved for my wife, Sandra. I have long been aware of her remarkable tolerance when it comes to my incurable and inexplicable fascination with the events of a century or more ago, but with this book her stoical forbearance and support were challenged as never before. In the course of the two years' spent on the book, during which she has acted as editor, proof-reader, sounding board and chief critic, she has been with me every step of the way. As a result, I have no hesitation in stating that *The Wooden Horse of Gallipoli* owes as much to her perseverance as to my own and I shall forever be grateful for her willingness to accept with such good grace an historical odyssey that has spanned nearly forty years and shows little sign of ending.

Foreword

My interest in military history was kindled during my childhood when reading boys' own adventure novels and war stories in comics such as *Battle* and *Victor*. Feats of British military perseverance, heroism and sacrifice were made vivid by classic films such as *Zulu* and *The Charge of the Light Brigade*. Similarly to Stephen, it was the front cover of a *Victor* summer special depicting the *River Clyde* in all its glory that really sparked my Gallipoli interest. The films *Tell England* (1931) and *Gallipoli* (1981) only fuelled it.

When Stephen asked me to write a foreword for this book the similarities between the semi-mythological Trojan War and Gallipoli sprung to mind. Gallipoli, and the immediate area, is rich in other stories of conflict: the Trojan Wars, King Xerxes and his mighty Persian army crossing the Hellespont, Alexander the Great roaming through Thrace, and the place where Attila the Hun destroyed the mighty Roman Eastern Army. The First World War is but a pin-prick on the historical timeline of this region. Gallipoli and Troy are sites of strategic importance that have made the area a target for attack throughout history. While one campaign may have been fought over a woman named Helen, the other to knock Turkey out of the First World War, the goal for both was the control of the Dardanelles; the only maritime route between the Aegean and Black Sea.

The symbolism of the *River Clyde* as the 1915 'Wooden Horse' is, therefore, not lost on us, nor the irony of another ship's participation – HMS *Agamemnon*, whose namesake was the commander-in-chief of the Greeks during the Trojan Wars. Several of those who wrote of their Gallipoli experiences found a common bond in the Homeric heroes of mythical times as they walked in the footsteps of warriors such as Hector and Achilles. They were merely fighting in a tragedy of a modern kind. The poet and Royal Naval Division officer, Rupert

Brooke, wrote 'the winds of history will follow me all the way' and made reference in one of his poems to the guns stirring Achilles and waking Priam, the last king of Troy.

At Gallipoli, a modern-day 'Wooden Horse', the converted tramp steamer *River Clyde* which was the product of Captain Edward Unwin's creative genius, would not become a symbol of victory nor even a stratagem to outsmart the enemy. Yet, even though this high-risk method of landing sufficient men on V Beach failed, it succeeded in cementing itself into history as one of the most recognisable images of the campaign. To this day, it characterises the countless deeds of heroism and endurance in a struggle that was flawed from the very beginning and which would become little more than a forlorn hope.

What can often seem a confused action to read about is here brought alive beautifully by Stephen Snelling through a masterly collation of personal accounts. Many have written about the V Beach landings, but never before has so much been written about the *River Clyde*. The accounts add an important human layer to this story, all of which are chronologically presented and exquisitely stitched together into this excellent narrative.

Where the story of Troy has endured for thirty centuries, the saga of Gallipoli is but one century old. It is thanks to books such as this one that the legacy and lessons of that campaign continue to be studied and that all those who fought and died there are not forgotten.

Stephen Chambers,
Gallipoli Association Historian,
January 2017.

Author's Note

As with many a furious struggle, the fight for V Beach was confused and protracted. Understandably, given the intensity of the action and the exhaustion that set in soon after, few who were there had either the time or the inclination to make detailed notes until days after. It is hardly surprising, therefore, that eyewitness accounts from men standing sometimes as little as a few yards apart should on occasions seem so different. The precise timing of events is a particular problem in dealing with key events during the main landing at Sedd-el-Bahr. I have tried to navigate as accurate a course as possible through 'the fog of war', while acknowledging either in the text or in footnotes varying perspectives and discrepancies in chronology. In such matters I beg readers' forbearance with what might be described as conflicts within a conflict.

List of Maps and Drawings

Introduction

'The Rusted Bulk'

Novelist, raconteur and newly 'regularised' intelligence officer Compton Mackenzie found himself unexpectedly at a loose end on the morning of Whit Sunday, 23 May 1915. Too late for Mass and far too early for lunch, he decided to fill his time by exploring France's toehold on Gallipoli around Cape Helles.

The first time he had seen the southernmost tip of the peninsula had been from the deck of a ship carrying him across the Aegean. Huddled along the shore, the village and fort of Sedd-el-Bahr, 'with its cracked domes and crumbled walls',[1] had reminded him of an 'old-fashioned print of Paradise in a tattered family Bible'. Closer inspection appeared only to confirm his initial impression. 'The medieval village was a picturesque place,' he wrote, 'and though the cypresses round the mosque had been shorn and pollarded by the guns of the *Queen Elizabeth*, there were still many fruit-trees untouched, figs and pomegranates in high-walled Turkish gardens which cast their shade over narrow entries and winding secluded ways.'[2]

Far more incongruous than the 'gun-slashed cypresses', however, was the strange addition to the shoreline below. Only four weeks before, V Beach, as it was officially styled, had been the most bitterly contested of all the Allied landing points in Turkey. Now, as he wandered across what had so recently been a bloody battleground, the writer who would be best-remembered for a beguiling comic novel about a whisky-loaded cargo vessel run aground on a remote Hebridean island was transfixed by another ship grounded beneath the ruins of Sedd-el-Bahr. Her partially camouflaged hull, rising sheer and steep from the shallows, was slashed with regular doorway-like openings, while her decks displayed the haphazard wounds of more violent treatment. Otherwise there was little in her drabness to distinguish her from a thousand other workaday tramp steamers. Appearances, however, can be deceptive. As the thirty-two-year-old recently commissioned Royal Marines lieutenant 'looked with awe at the rusted bulk of the *River Clyde*,[3] her fame, unlikely and unfettered, was already assured.

A century on, she remains one of history's most instantly recognisable ships. A myriad of paintings and photographs showing her hard aground and troops spilling from her gangways on to a clutter of barges are among the most iconic images not only of the First World War, but of any conflict before or since. In a peculiarly British way, this most unwarlike of vessels has become synonymous with a campaign doomed to failure with all its folly and futility, sacrifice and squandered heroism.

As the emblem of the world-renowned Gallipoli Association, an organisation dedicated to honouring the memory of the men who fought on the peninsula and to educating future generations about their forlorn endeavours, it has featured on the cover of every one of its journals spanning more than forty years. Variously known as 'the Dun Cow', 'the Wreck Ship', 'the Iron Horse', 'the Horse of Troy' and 'the Wooden Horse', she has, over time, acquired an aura touching on reverence that makes a nonsense of the short-sighted failure to preserve her as a 'living' memorial in 1919 and then again in 1965.

This book sets out to tell how so humble a ship as the *River Clyde* came to achieve legendary status and to show why men such as Compton Mackenzie and thousands more like him came to view her with such awe. It is a saga of tragedy and triumph against the odds on both sides and of almost superhuman courage in the face of unbelievable carnage that helped to turn near defeat into costly victory on the blood-drenched shores of Sedd-el-Bahr.

It is a study born, in part, out of two earlier works, biographical studies of the Naval recipients of the First World War and of all those men who earned the country's highest award for valour during the course of the 8½-month long campaign waged on and around the Gallipoli peninsula. My fascination with the *River Clyde*, however, goes back much further: to 1967 and a boyhood encounter with the collier-cum-landing ship on the front and back cover of my favourite comic, *The Victor*. Titled 'Landing at Gallipoli', issue number 315 featured a crude reworking of Charles Dixon's magnificent painting of troops storming ashore from the collier. Through speech bubbles and vivid illustrations, it related the extraordinary exploits of Edward Unwin, captain of the *River Clyde* and originator of 'the Wooden Horse' scheme. The drama of its telling could hardly fail to stir the imagination of an adventure-mad ten-year-old. Looking again at those yellowing pages with rather more objectivity than I did then I am struck not so much by the inaccuracies as their ability to capture the essential spirit of what I now regard as one of the most outstanding feats of heroism performed in the 160-year history of the Victoria Cross. For what moved me then, moves me even more now after years of reading and researching in search of the truth behind a comic-strip hero.

As an object lesson in leadership by example and in trying to rescue a plan teetering on the brink of disaster, Unwin's performance at V Beach rivals explorer Ernest Shackleton's Herculean efforts to save the men of the *Endurance* trapped on the South Polar ice cap even as the *River Clyde* was making her own rendezvous with history. Yet, towering though his presence is in this story of gallant endeavour, he is only one among a cast of heroes that is as long as it is varied.

In this first full-length study devoted entirely to the *River Clyde* and the men who sailed in her to Gallipoli, we follow boy midshipmen and 'red-tab' staff officers, rank amateurs and thorough-going professionals, aristocratic volunteers and lowly rankers plucked straight from the pages of Kipling as they make their way aboard a landing ship like no other on a mission fraught with hazard.

From its Heath Robinson-like conversion to its audacious assault barely a fortnight later and its miraculous survival thereafter on the peninsula, the book charts the collier's epic course from the genesis of her ingenious improvisation to her unceremonious end half a century later. It also seeks to examine how the desperate gallantry displayed by a volunteer ship's company and the thousands of British and Irish soldiers carried in her holds helped obscure the flawed thinking and muddled direction that consigned so many men to unnecessary deaths with dire consequences for the rest of the campaign.

Above all, it is a saga of unsurpassed valour deserving of a better outcome by a disparate band of men who contrived to make 'the Wooden Horse' of Gallipoli one of the most highly honoured ships in the history of modern warfare.

This, then, is their story, told, so far as possible, in the words of the men who, in the judgement of their commanders, achieved the seemingly impossible over the course of two astonishing days in April 1915.

Stephen Snelling,
Thorpe St Andrew, Norwich,
September, 2016.

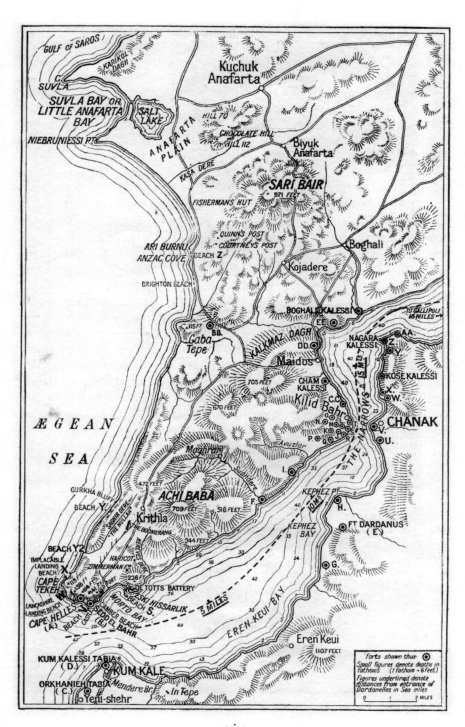

xix

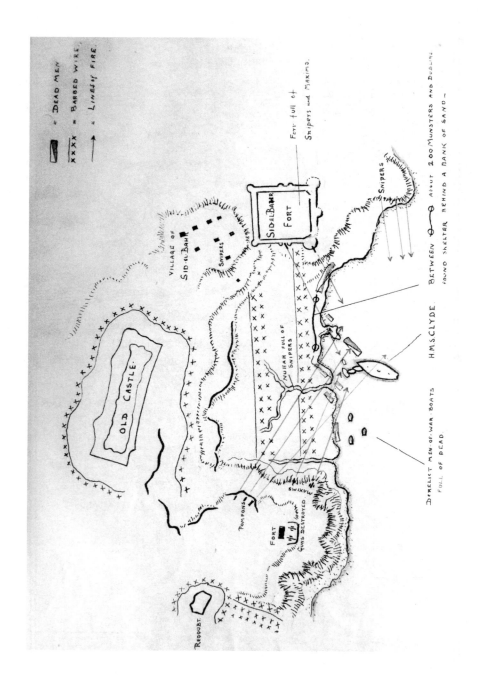

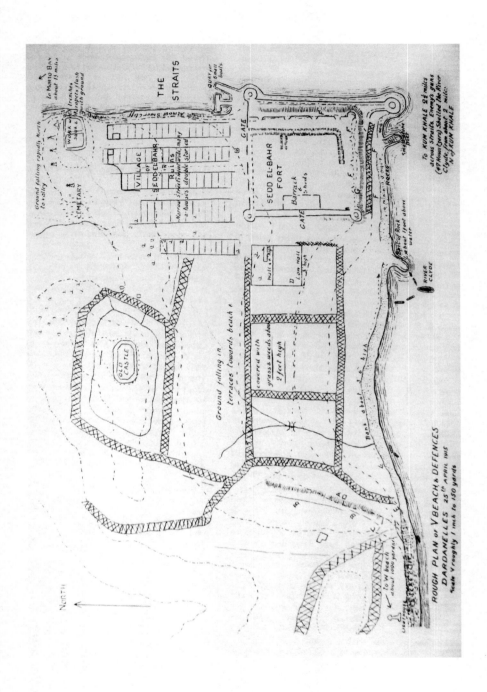

ROUGH PLAN OF V BEACH & DEFENCES
DARDANELLES 25th APRIL 1915
Scale Vroughly 1 inch to 150 yards

NORTH

THE STRAITS

VILLAGE OF SEDD-EL-BAHR

Ruins

Narrow Street, Sea wall walk, many 1-4 ways double store

CEMETARY

Ground falling rapidly north to valley

Wall with trenches above & loop holes flush with ground

To MORTO BAY about 1½ miles

GATE

Quay for small boats

SEDD EL-BAHR FORT

Barrack & sheds

GATE

Wire 3 feet

Wire 3 feet high

ROCKS

Spit of Rock about 1 foot above water

RIVER CLYDE

To KUM KHALE 2½ miles across straits (4 Hows guns) shelled the River Clyde from about 2 miles N of KUM KHALE

OLD CASTLE

Ground falling in terraces towards beach &

Wall 2 high

D 10 wall 5 high

covered with grass & weeds about 3 feet high

Beach about 5 to 8 yds

ARIVED

to W beach about 1000 yards

xxi

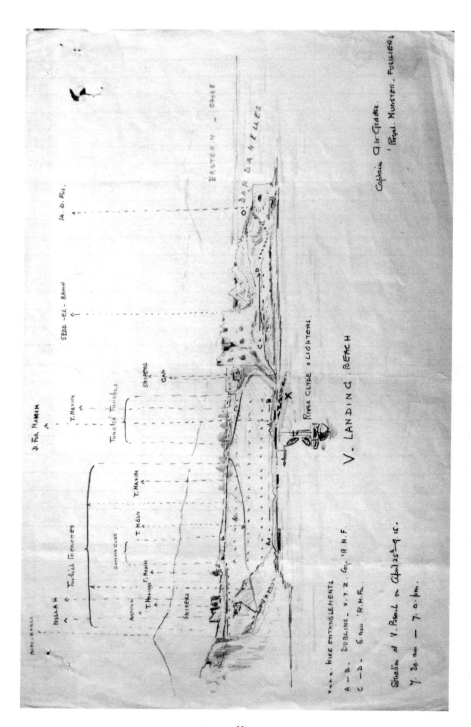

V. LANDING BEACH

Situation of V. Beach on April 25th 1915.
7.30 a.m — 7.0 p.m.

····· wire entanglements

A — B. DUBLINE - x.y.z. Coy. 'R.N.F.
C — D. 6th R.M.F.

Captain Geiger.
'Royal Munster Fusiliers.

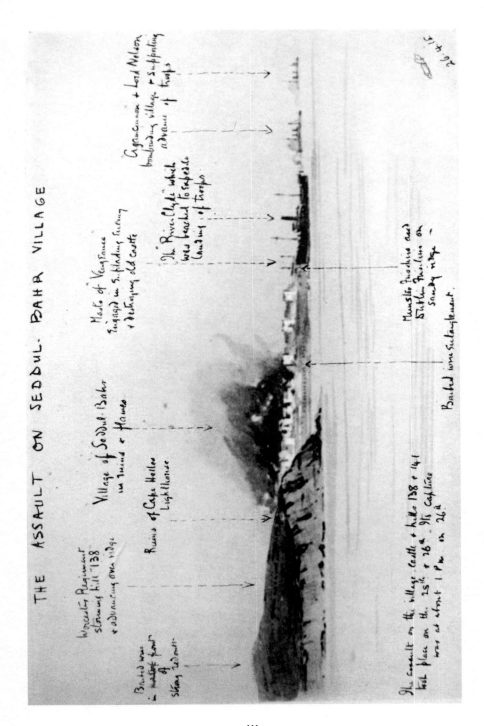

THE ASSAULT ON SEDDUL-BAHR VILLAGE

Worcester Regiment storming Hill 138 & advancing over ridge

Boats were made fast of strong current

Ruins of Cape Helles Lighthouse

Village of Seddul-Bahr in ruins & flames

Mole of Vengeance engaged in shelling enemy & destroying old castle

The "River Clyde" which was beached to enable landing of troops

Agamemnon & Lord Nelson bombarding village & advance of troops

Maxim machine and Nordenfelt gun on sandy ridge —

Beached men sheltering

The assault on the village, castle & hills 138 & 141 took place on the 25th & 26th. 9th Captured was at about 1 P.M. on 26th.

Chapter 1

'We Shall Have to Land'

The first glimpse of the peninsula was an unforgettable one. Rising from the sea 'like the glacis of a giant's fortress',[1] it shimmered and sparkled in the fierce light of a brilliant sun. From the deck of HMS *Phaeton*, a general without an army but with an abundance of imagination was in dreamy thrall to an ancient world aglow with myth and legend.

Sir Ian Hamilton, the sixty-two-year-old slight, sprite and enigmatic commander of a multi-national expeditionary force that had yet to muster, was transfixed by the beguiling beauty of a panorama beyond compare. From the rocky headland past the battered remains of Sedd-el-Bahr and the sun-bleached fortress, tumbling down the slopes to touch the sea, he was drawn towards the mouth of the Dardanelles, the fabled Hellespont, that most 'enchanted' of backdrops to a conflict resonant of another titanic struggle 5,000 years earlier.

'There,' he mused, 'Hero trimmed her little lamp; yonder the amorous breath of Leander changed to soft sea form. Far away to the Eastwards, painted in dim and lovely hues, lies Mount Ida. Just so, on the far horizon line she lay fair and still, when Hector fell and smoke from burning Troy blackened the midday sun …'[2]

The vision of ancient glory did not last long on 18 March 1915. As afternoon faded into evening, reality blotted out fanciful idyll. Steaming south along the western coast of the peninsula, one of Hamilton's junior staff officers, Captain Guy Dawnay, observed 'a great browny-black column of smoke'.[3] Billowing above the higher ridges of undulating country, it stretched, a fusion of brown, green, olive and white, 'as far as one could see'.[4] The pall that smeared the cloud-flecked sky came not from Troy but from a thunderous naval battle that was destined to change the entire complexion of the 4½-month old war against Turkey and recast its most distinguished spectator into the campaign's leading player.

* * *

1

Ever since Turkey entered the war on Germany's side, hostilities in the Aegean had been almost exclusively the preserve of the Admiralty. In many ways, it was apt that it should be so. After all, it was Winston Churchill, the firebrand First Lord of the Admiralty, who had outraged Ottoman opinion by seizing two Dreadnought battleships that were being built in Britain for the Turkish navy. Tensions between the two countries were then further ratcheted up by the Turkish decision to allow safe passage through the Dardanelles of the German battlecruiser *Goeben* and light cruiser *Breslau* following an audacious and, so far as the Royal Navy was concerned, humiliating dash through the Mediterranean.

The ships' appearance in the Golden Horn at the end of the first week of the war triggered an inevitable response. In September, a British squadron was dispatched to blockade the mouth of the Dardanelles. Although Britain and Turkey were not yet at war, the orders given to its commander, Vice-Admiral Sackville Carden, were unequivocal. He was to 'sink the *Goeben* and the *Breslau*, no matter what flag they fly',[5] if they tried to break out. At the same time, he was given discretionary powers to deal with any Turkish vessels venturing out, either turning them back or, if he saw fit, letting them pass.

The posturing ended on 1 November when the stand-off gave way to a declaration of war. Two days later, following instructions from Churchill, British and French ships sallied forth to bombard the shore batteries at Sedd-el-Bahr and Kum Kale guarding the entrance to the Dardanelles. The battlecruisers *Indomitable* and *Indefatigable* fired forty-six rounds of 12in shells into the ancient castle and modern fort on the European shore, while the battleships *Suffren* and *Vérité* directed their fire against the Asian side. A number of Turkish guns were put out of action, particularly at Sedd-el-Bahr, where a single lucky shot that detonated a magazine was responsible for considerable damage and loss of life. Hailed an allied victory, the attack, followed by a swift withdrawal, achieved nothing beyond galvanising Turkish commanders into redoubling their efforts to strengthen the aged and weak defences protecting a strategic waterway many observers had long considered invulnerable to seaborne attack.

Since the last successful opposed passage of the Straits more than a century earlier, advances in shore-based gunnery appeared to have rendered any repetition highly improbable, if not impossible. Writing in 1836, the distinguished German military theorist, Helmuth von Moltke, declared: 'If the artillery material in the Dardanelles were set in proper order I do not believe that any Fleet in the world would dare to enter the Straits.'[6] Nothing much had happened to alter opinion by the turn of the century. Sir John Fisher, before and after becoming First Sea Lord in 1904, had considered the matter closely and concluded that such an operation, even in conjunction with land forces, was liable to prove 'mightily hazardous'.[7] Two years later a joint military and naval investigation thought that while a force of the Navy's 'least valuable ships' might be capable of 'rushing' the Straits, the attempt was 'much to be deprecated'.[8] By 1911, all thoughts of breaking through the defences appeared to have sunk without trace. A Cabinet memorandum stated: 'It should be remembered that it is no longer possible to force the Dardanelles, and nobody would expose a modern fleet to such peril.'[9] Its author was Winston Churchill.

The first hint that the First Lord of the Admiralty had had a change of heart came less than a month after Britain and Turkey went to war. At the first meeting of the newly constituted War Council on 25 November, Churchill proposed a joint military and naval attack on the Dardanelles as a means of nullifying Turkish designs on Egypt. The idea was rejected on the grounds that there were insufficient troops available, as was the suggestion of assembling an armada of ships in readiness for such a strike. But it was not the end of the matter. A few weeks later, with the opposing armies deadlocked on the Western Front, a memorandum written by the Secretary of the War Council, Lieutenant Colonel Maurice Hankey, reopened the debate. It proposed an attack on Turkey as a means not just of forcing one of Germany's key allies out of the conflict but of opening a vital sea route into Russia and of pushing wavering Balkan powers into the Entente camp.

Coming as it did less than a week before a Russian appeal for help to thwart a strong Turkish thrust into the Caucasus, it served to re-focus attention on the Aegean. For as the Secretary of State for War, Lord Kitchener, pointed out:

> The only place that a demonstration might have some effect in stopping reinforcements going East would be the Dardanelles – particularly if, as the Grand Duke says, reports could be spread at the same time that Constantinople is threatened.[10]

In the absence of troops, Kitchener and Churchill agreed that such 'a demonstration', based on bluff and feint, might be effectively staged by naval power alone. Thus were the seeds for disaster sewn.

Events then moved quickly. A vast and fantastical plan conceived by Fisher involving landings on the Gallipoli peninsula and in Asia Minor, the employment of 75,000 British and Indian troops and the intervention of as yet neutral Bulgaria, Greece and Romania was distilled by

Churchill to its single-most practical element, a charge through the Dardanelles by a force of outmoded pre-dreadnought battleships deemed to be expendable. On 3 January he asked Carden if he thought such an operation could work. His question was weighted with the caveat 'importance of the result would justify severe loss'. Two days later came the reply. 'I do not consider Dardanelles can be rushed,' wrote Carden. 'They might be forced by extended operations with large number of ships.'[11]

Carden's plan for a three-stage advance, employing naval gunfire to methodically demolish first the outer, then the intermediate and finally, having swept the sea clear of mines, the inner defences before entering the Sea of Marmora was duly presented to the War Council on 13 January and, in spite of a melodramatic denunciation by Fisher, approved on 28 January. Orders to launch the campaign by mid-February if possible were issued on 5 February.

Carden would quickly discover that the Turks had not been idle since his last ill-considered strike. As well as significant reinforcements of men and weaponry on land and sea, the defences had undergone fundamental change since the November bombardment. Following a study by senior German officers, a fourth defensive zone had been established under German command, consisting of batteries of howitzers designed to direct plunging fire on to attacking ships' weaker deck armour. More crucially, the mines that laced the narrow waters had multiplied alarmingly. Since the first minefield was laid in August 1914, ten more lines, comprising more than 400 mines, were added over the course of the next six months.

The strengthening of defences that, in some cases, dated back to the seventeenth century went hand-in-hand with a relentless build-up in guns and troops. Between the bombardment of 3 November and the opening of the new campaign on 19 February, the number of troops available to the Turkish Fortress Command and III Corps had grown from 40,000 to 50,000 men armed with 34,500 rifles, sixteen machine guns and 313 artillery pieces. These numbers would continue to rise as a part of a co-ordinated Turkish programme to counter any amphibious invasion of the Gallipoli peninsula. Under the plan, potential landing beaches were identified and work undertaken to defend them with entrenched infantry whose job was to delay any assault long enough for reserves, sited further back in protected positions, to be brought up and drive the invaders back into the sea.

By comparison with such intense preparations, the allied military build-up was positively ad hoc. In the space of five weeks what began as a limited effort confined to an Anglo–French fleet composed mainly of elderly warships would metamorphose into a combined operation without an overall plan. The first troops despatched were two battalions of marines, ordered out on 6 February. They were followed twelve days later by the rest of the Royal Naval Division. 'Winston's Little Army', as it was sometimes disparagingly referred to, was a barely trained force of reservists and new recruits surplus to fleet requirements whose first active employment had been an unmitigated disaster. Sent hurriedly to Belgium to protect the port of Antwerp in October 1914, the division was swiftly forced into headlong retreat. In the confusion that followed almost 1,500 men ended up in neutral Holland with years of internment ahead of them. Their new task was to help garrison the fortresses and territory that the Navy's methodical bombardment was expected to deliver into allied hands. It was a role they were to share with the Australian and New Zealand Army Corps under Lieutenant General Sir William Birdwood and the specially formed French Corps Expéditionnaire d'Orient commanded by General Albert d'Amade.

The Anzacs, then in the process of completing their training, were sent from Egypt, initially as replacements for the British 29th Division, which was promised and refused by Kitchener before finally being committed all within the space of a month. Together they would make up a Mediterranean Expeditionary Force that Kitchener still believed, or at least hoped, would be spared any serious active involvement and be required only for garrison or small-scale landing purposes. His choice for commander, announced just two days after confirming that the 29th Division would go to the Aegean after all, was Sir Ian Hamilton.

In hindsight, the speed of events in that mad and maddening March of 1915 would scarcely seem credible. But even in the midst of it all, it hardly seemed possible that so much could have happened in so short a span. From his appointment on 12 March to his arrival off the coast of Gallipoli six days later, Hamilton scarcely had time to draw breath. Everything about the mission appeared rushed, its complexities barely understood and its objectives only dimly conceived. One moment, he had been working at his desk in Horse Guards, the commander-in-chief of Home Forces guarding the nation against German invasion, the next he had been summoned by Kitchener and told matter-of-factly: 'We are sending a military force to support the Fleet now at the Dardanelles, and you are to have Command.'[12]

The news came as a bolt from the blue. Hardly a day had passed over the previous six months when the two men had not spoken and not once in all that time had the Dardanelles been mentioned. The nearest they came, geographically speaking, was the suggestion that Hamilton might be sent to command a force in Salonika. By his own admission, he knew as little about the Dardanelles as he did about the Turks, which was precisely nothing.

There was little by way of explanation. Hamilton thought the meeting might have ended there and then with Kitchener's abrupt statement but for his desire to ask some pertinent questions about the scale and composition of his force, the plan for its employment, the enemy's strength and, not least, the overall objective. Hamilton later recalled:

> K frowned; shrugged his shoulders; I thought he was going to be impatient, but although he gave curt answers at first he slowly broadened out, until, at the end, no one else could get a word in edgeways.[13]

Hamilton learned that his expeditionary force was to be as cosmopolitan as it was well scattered. Of them all, only a brigade of Australians had, as yet, reached the Aegean. The Royal Naval Division was still en route, as were the French, while the bulk of Birdwood's command was still in Egypt and the 29th Division had yet to leave England. All told, they amounted to a little under 80,000 men, with a fighting strength of about 50,000 men. Of these, Hamilton regarded the 29th as his *division de luxe*, even though Kitchener stressed that its participation in the expedition was to be temporary and that it was to be returned for employment in France 'the moment they can be spared'.[14]

At that point General Charles Callwell, the Director of Military Operations, joined the discussion. Hamilton later wrote:

> We moved to the map in the window and Callwell took us through a plan of attack upon the Forts at the Dardanelles, worked out by the Greek General Staff. The Greeks had meant to employ (as far as I can remember) 150,000 men. Their landing was to have taken place on the North-west coast of the Southern part of the Peninsula, opposite Kilid Bahr. 'But,' said K, 'half that number of men will do you handsomely; the Turks are busy elsewhere; I hope you will not have to land at all; if you do have to land, why then the powerful Fleet at your back will be the prime factor in your choice of time and place.'[15]

Hamilton then suggested that the Admiralty might be encouraged to send 'a submarine or two' through the Straits in order to disrupt the flow of reinforcements and supplies reaching the Narrows and its screen of fortresses. Kitchener's reply, as remembered by Hamilton, betrayed an arrogant contempt for Turkish resolve. 'Supposing,' he said, 'one submarine pops up opposite the town of Gallipoli and waves a Union Jack three times, the whole Turkish garrison on the Peninsula will take to their heels and make a bee line for Bulair.'[16]

The following day Hamilton boarded a specially chartered train at Charing Cross on the first leg of a journey that would carry him, via Dover and a fog-blanketed English Channel to Calais and on, by rail to Marseilles, where he arrived at 9 pm on 14 March. Accompanying him was a motley entourage of staff officers, clerks and servants assembled at short notice to form the nucleus of a headquarters that was still short of key personnel.

They were a strange crowd, numbering just twenty-nine officers and men. The most senior among them was Major General Walter Braithwaite, the expeditionary force's chief of staff and a Kitchener appointee in place of Hamilton's preferred choice, Major General Gerald Ellison. According to Hamilton, they bore 'the bewildered look of men who have hurriedly been snatched from desks to do some extraordinary turn on some unheard-of theatre'.[17]

Making light of their discomfiture, he noted: 'One or two of them put on uniform for the first time in their lives an hour ago. Leggings awry, spurs upside down, belts over shoulder straps! I haven't a notion of who they all are.'[18]

Not all, however, were total strangers. One of the more colourful recruits was Major John Strange Spencer Churchill, younger brother of Winston Churchill, a great friend and ally of Hamilton's and, as First Lord of the Admiralty, the prime mover behind Britain's intervention in the Dardanelles. Like so much else to do with the mission, 'Jack' Churchill's role was vague and ill-defined, and his presence as 'camp commandant' seemed to some to owe more than a little to nepotism and political string-pulling. Whatever the truth, his military credentials were not in question. A battle-scarred veteran of the South African War, in which he was wounded and mentioned in despatches, he was the only member of Hamilton's headquarters with active experience in the present war. As though to prove the point, he had arrived at Charing Cross carrying 'a vicious bludgeon', with a large revolver sticking out of his belt and the look of 'the hardened warrior'.[19]

Others in the party were less warlike in appearance. Orlando 'Orlo' Williams had been a highly respected Clerk of the House of Commons just forty-eight hours before stepping aboard the special train in London. Now, he was Hamilton's personal cipher officer with a brand new uniform bearing the rank of captain. Yet, far from being in any way disconcerted, he appeared struck only by the high spirits that attended their journey overseas. There was, he noted, 'a sense of boyish enthusiasm for adventure ... in the air'[20] which he felt emanated from their commander's exuberance.

Hamilton, 'that most friendly and accessible of men' as Williams called him, was buoyed both by his appointment and the apparent faith shown in him by Lord Kitchener. It had evoked proud memories of their service together, defeating the Boers in South Africa. On that occasion, Hamilton had departed, 'uninstructed and unaccredited',[21] for the front with nothing more than a single ADC, two horses, a couple of mules and a buggy. Not much, it seemed, had changed in fifteen years. According to Hamilton, a search of the intelligence branch in the hours before leaving England had yielded little information about the Turkish Army or the strength of its defences in the Dardanelles, this in spite of the fact that successive military attaches in Constantinople and minor diplomats based at Chanak had been filing detailed reports on Turkish military preparedness since 1911. In his diary-style memoir, he later noted: 'The Dardanelles and Bosphorus might be in the moon for all the military information I have got to go upon.'[22] His observation was echoed by another of his staff officers. Captain Cecil Aspinall, who was destined to become the campaign's official historian, had been given a day to organise Hamilton's headquarters and the transport and supply arrangements for an expeditionary force without any idea of its intended employment. Only after he had boarded the train did he have an inkling as to their objective:

> I shall never forget the dismay and foreboding with which I learnt that apart from Lord Kitchener's very brief instructions, a pre-war Admiralty report on the Dardanelles defences and an out-of-date map, Sir Ian had been given practically no information whatever.[23]

Hamilton's chief of staff was none the wiser. Apart from an outdated text book on the Turkish Army and a couple of guide books on western Turkey – 'travellers' tales' as Hamilton called them – Braithwaite had little else to go on when he eventually sat down with Hamilton, en route to Marseilles, to set out a 'doctrine' for the expedition. Among a few 'hurried jottings' scribbled out by Braithwaite were a diagrammatic plan of the general staff with half the spaces still unfilled and an outline for an as yet non-existent Q branch. The scraps of notes continued in similar vein:

> Only 1600 rounds for the 4.5 Howitzers!!! High explosive essential. Who is to be CRE? Engineer Stores? French are to remain at Tunis

until the day comes that they are required. Egyptian troops also remain in Egypt till last moment. Everything we want by 30th (it is hoped). Await arrival of 29th Division before undertaking anything big ...[24]

As far as Braithwaite and, indeed, Hamilton understood it, the effort in the Dardanelles was primarily a naval-led operation. If the Navy required military help, it was, observed Braithwaite, 'for Sir Ian's consideration whether to give or to withhold it'.[25]

Braithwaite was not the only one trying to bring order to chaos. While the expeditionary force's chief of staff was making plans on the hoof, or more accurately in the cramped confines of a railway carriage rattling through France, a few hundred miles to the south-east a senior naval officer was wrestling with a mission every bit as confused and poorly resourced as Hamilton's own somewhat nebulous operation.

Like Hamilton, Rear-Admiral Rosslyn Erskine Wemyss' appointment to a critical leadership role in the newly opened Aegean theatre of operations had been unexpected. Having been passed over for command of the Mediterranean Cruiser Squadron, the fifty-year-old protégé of Admiral Lord Charles Beresford had started the war in charge of a force of clapped out ships guarding the entrance to the English Channel against an enemy reluctant to show his face. Desperate for a more active command, 'Rosy', as he was widely known to his many friends and admirers, was poised to lead naval operations along the East African post only to have his appointment cancelled at the eleventh hour. Enraged, he had stormed to the Admiralty on 16 February to demand a meeting with Churchill. He eventually cornered the Navy's political chief in a corridor and, determined to have it out with him, followed him into his office where Churchill pre-empted his fury:

Before I could open my mouth he informed me ... that it had that morning been decided to force the Dardanelles, that the island of Lemnos was to be made the base of the operations, that he wished me to proceed out there at once – the next day in fact – that I should probably be the Governor of the island and that further orders were to follow immediately, which by the way they never did![26]

'Rosy' Wemyss, the incurable optimist with an infectious laugh, did not appreciate the enormity of the task awaiting him nor the extent of Admiralty ignorance about what it entailed until he reached Mudros on Lemnos on 24 February. Writing home to his 'beloved' wife, the 'Puss cat' to his 'Tom cat' as he affectionately called her in his letters, he noted:

> Everybody, ie, Admirals etc, a little embarrassed about my position because since I left England the Greek Government had written to say that they did not mean the whole Island to be turned over to England, but only the port and surrounding district, as much in fact as I required for my necessities and no more …[27]

Five days had passed since the Navy had commenced its bombardment of the outer forts as a preliminary to forcing the Dardanelles. Eight days had gone by since military and political leaders, including Churchill and Kitchener, had agreed to send British and Anzac troops to Lemnos to prepare for small-scale military operations in support of the Navy. And with Hamilton's appointment still more than a fortnight off the muddle was only just beginning.

Most concerning of all was the realisation that Mudros, notwithstanding its immense natural harbour, was utterly unprepared for its role as a major military base. Until then used only by a few Greek fishermen, it possessed neither quays nor wharves and was served by a solitary wooden pier. As for Lemnos itself, the island had little in the way of buildings or natural resources to accommodate let alone sustain the thousands upon thousands of men headed its way. 'Rosy' Wemyss was reminded by a remark made by Jacky Fisher, the First Sea Lord, before his departure. 'Fisher said it was a big thing they were sending me out to,' he wrote. 'I think he little imagined how big.'[28]

As early as 3 March, he admitted: 'I am beginning to feel the want of many things.'[29] It was hardly surprising. Still uncertain as to either his or the island's political status, still less to his country's strategic imperatives, he had no depot ship, no shore base and no flagship from which to direct operations. In fact, the newly arrived governor and senior naval officer of Mudros was devoid of almost everything bar an innate faith in his own ability to conjure something from nothing and render the seemingly impossible into a miraculous reality. Writing to his wife on 7 March, he observed:

> The work piles up, but not the means to cope with it. I have innumerable matters to see to – landing of troops, provisioning them, providing stores of all manner and kind of vessels, work on shore in connection with the village – water, telegraph and so on. Something cropping up every moment and I have neither officers nor men to cope with it all. Truly the Admiralty are marvellous. Luckily for them and for the nation they are marvellously served …[30]

A day later he returned to his theme:

> My work seems to increase each day. Of course difficulties arise …
> but the real trouble, as usual emanates from the Authorities at home.
> They will not say what they want, nor give me any idea of what their
> ultimate goal is. Now with 40,000 men, and no knowledge of how
> they are to be used you can imagine that it is not easy for me out
> here to foresee what may be required, especially as I don't know
> what they are bringing.[31]

A meeting with Vice-Admiral Sackville Carden left Wemyss none the
wiser. As he put it, the commander of the Eastern Mediterranean
Squadron

> was completely ignorant of any plans for combined naval and
> military operations – 10,000 troops, he said, were expected shortly,
> and there was a brigade of Marines … in two transports in Mudros
> Bay ready to demolish the forts. That was all he knew.[32]

Undaunted, Wemyss decided to take 'the Bull by the horns' by
preparing for 'all eventualities'. To his wife, he wrote: 'It is amusing
going our own way, and I am ignoring the Admiralty to a great degree
and, so to speak, helping myself to all I want without asking them.'[33]
Summoning all his reserves of energy and enthusiasm, he threw
himself into his work with all his customary verve. Ever the born
diplomat, he quickly charmed the local Greek population into giving
him their full support. Within weeks of his arrival, he claimed to have
the mayor, who doubled as banker, shopkeeper, publican and 'general
Pooh Bah', in his 'pocket'. And, bit by bit, his efforts began to produce
results, though there were moments when the sometimes competing
demands of his twin roles as civil administrator and man o' war left
him feeling that 'a Solomon would have been more fit for this business
than I'.[34]

His work was, as he put it, 'as all-embracing as it is perpetual'. As
the days turned to weeks, he explained to his wife:

> From allocating land, adjudging compensation for damage, landing
> armies, supplying water, urging lazy Frenchmen to do some work
> and organising defences down to the ordinary Squadron work,
> nothing seems to pass me by. Telegrams pouring in, in basketfuls,
> messages by wireless telegraphy, orders from England, requests

11

from all parts of the world, demands for the possible and impossible from every quarter ...[35]

As if that wasn't daunting enough, there came, on 16 March, an added complication. Under pressure from Churchill to hasten the naval operations, Vice-Admiral Carden collapsed under the 'accumulation of strain and worry', leaving Wemyss and Carden's second in command, Vice-Admiral John de Robeck, with a dilemma. Wemyss, who was on a visit to the squadron's advanced base at Tenedos when Carden went sick, informed his wife:

> The predicament was somewhat curious. I became the Senior Officer. The Senior Officer by all the rules of the game should be with the Fleet, but it was quite impossible for me to give up this job. It is in much too complicated a state at present to be lightly handed over to anyone else. The same thing applied to de Robeck. It would have been madness to swap horses whilst crossing the stream. He had the strings in his fingers there as I had here. I took the Bull by the horns and ordered him to carry on and informed the Admiralty ...[36]

Written on 18 March, the letter made brief mention of Hamilton's arrival in theatre and continued with a vague and tantalising reference to events that would alter the course of the campaign:

> There has been much fighting today, and I fear that some of the ships have been badly damaged – but up to now I have no direct information.[37]

In fact, the consequences of the Navy's attempt to 'rush' the Dardanelles were even worse than he had imagined. Under de Robeck's direction, a combined Anglo–French fleet had been roundly defeated, its three waves of battleships repulsed by a combination of mines and shore batteries. All told, three battleships – the *Bouvet*, *Irresistible* and *Ocean* – had been sunk and three more crippled with a loss of nearly 700 men. In return, they had inflicted damage on only eight out of more than 170 coastal guns. The reverse was more than a mere setback. It signalled a shift away from a naval to an Army-led operation requiring new plans and new priorities all pointed towards a full-scale invasion against an enemy buoyed by its success and all too alert to the prospect of imminent landings on the Gallipoli peninsula.

During the course of his impromptu inspection of the coast from beyond Bulair to Cape Helles, Hamilton had ventured sufficiently near to land as to be able to see 'not only the regular spider's-web of entrenchments facing each possible landing place, but the glistening of the barbed wire entanglements covering them'.[38] Entering the Straits in the midst of the Navy's mauling, he had also seen enough of the enemy's fire and of the fleet's retreat to convince him of two things. Firstly, the idea of the shores having been cleared of guns was 'illusory' and, secondly, the Straits could not be forced by ships alone.

Writing on 19 March to his old friend and Commander-in-Chief of the British Expeditionary Force, Sir John French, he admitted:

> My mind is hardening to the idea that this will be a case of the Army helping the Navy through rather than of the Navy helping the Army through. We shall have to land and storm the bloody trenches – that's about the long and short of it. Naturally, I would infinitely prefer to see the thing done by Naval means, if this could succeed, supplemented by a few landing parties under fire of their guns, but after yesterday I greatly doubt so easy a solution.[39]

Three days later his thoughts had crystallised into certainty. At a joint naval and military conference held aboard de Robeck's flagship *Queen Elizabeth*, the admiral, who had oscillated between outrageous optimism and gloom-laden pessimism in the wake of an action he described as a 'disaster', effectively passed the baton to Hamilton. According to Lieutenant General William Birdwood, the commander of the Australian and New Zealand Army Corps, de Robeck 'told us he did not consider [the] fleet could get through without co-operation of [the] army …'[40]

The Navy having declared its hand, 'there was no discussion', observed Hamilton. 'At once,' he added, 'we turned our faces to the land scheme.'[41]

Even Wemyss, the most indefatigable of optimists, bowed to the inevitable. Just eight days earlier, he had 'every reason to hope' that Turkish resistance 'will not be very great' and would 'slacken'[42] every day under the Navy's relentless pressure. But the events of 18 March had led him to reassess. Following his 'council of war' with Hamilton and de Robeck on 22 March, he told his wife:

> If the public in England think that the Dardanelles are going to be won in one big fight they are very much mistaken. From the nature

of things it must be a long job – a regular siege … but we shall get there.[43]

Together with his revised expectations came the gradual realisation that a change of plan would entail having to shoulder a still greater responsibility, namely the landing of an army on a hostile shore in the face of an enemy growing daily in strength and self-belief. In the absence of suitable boats and equipment, it would call for another conjuring trick on a par with that employed to transform Mudros from fishing port to a springboard for invasion and an as yet unimagined innovation that would become forever synonymous with the struggle to come.

All of that lay in the future. There were hurried plans to be laid and an invasion force to be mustered. Eager as he was to push on, Hamilton could not contemplate nor countenance any move without his force's *'pièce de résistance'*. To go off 'half-cock' was to risk disaster. As he wrote: 'I must wait for the 29th Division.'[44]

Chapter 2

'My British Division from India'

O n a nondescript March morning a train slowed to a halt amid a cloud of steam in the small Warwickshire village of Dunchurch. There were no crowds and no fanfare as a familiar-looking gentleman in general's uniform stepped on to the platform. He was accompanied by a small retinue of military figures.

Scarcely pausing, they passed through the station to find their horses already saddled and waiting for them. A few moments later, they were off, a vice-admiral, a lieutenant colonel and a major trotting a respectful distance behind the smaller man, his slight frame protected from the cold by a thick, thigh-length coat. King George V had come to the chilly heart of England to inspect and to bid farewell to a force he addressed, with an unmistakeable note of pride, 'my British Division from India'.[1]

The 'splendid spectacle'[2] that followed a little after midday on 12 March 1915 represented the first and last occasion on home soil that the 29th Division came together in a single formation before being deployed overseas. It was, by all accounts, a display fit for a king. The last-formed 'Regular' Division in the British Army, its units drawn mostly from imperial garrisons in far-flung corners of the empire, stretched as far as the eye could see beneath a canopy of elms. Thousand upon thousand of men, comprising twelve battalions of infantry, brigades of horse-limbered artillery and myriad ancillary units, came to attention along two miles of the London Road as the King rode slowly by before taking up position close to the Fosse Way intersection near Stretton-on-Dunsmore.

Many of those lining the route were already tired and foot-weary from hours of marching on roads that were 'beastly hard'.[3] But few who saw them that day would have realised it. To divisional staff officer Captain Clement Milward, a thirty-seven-year-old Indian Army veteran of five North West Frontier campaigns and future aide-de-camp to the King, the parade bordered on perfection, with 'guns and horses in beautiful condition and the infantry incomparable'.[4] Oswin Creighton, newly appointed chaplain to the 86th Infantry Brigade, was no less impressed by the sheer scale of the march past that followed. Breaking away from the leading regiment, he mingled among a little crowd of onlookers that had gathered and later wrote:

> It was wonderful seeing the long line of silver bayonets winding through the trees like a stream. It seemed quite endless watching 12,000 infantry pass. Unfortunately, I missed the artillery and other divisional troops, as they had passed ahead of us. There must have been 18,000 men altogether. It seemed vast, and the men were magnificent.[5]

The 29th Division was still very much in its infancy. Mobilised as recently as 18 January, it drew its infantry units, contrary to the King's descriptions, from a wide area of the country's extensive empire. The 1st Royal Dublin Fusiliers were shipped back from Madras after more than four years in the Sub-Continent. The 2nd Hampshires were ordered home from Mhow, where they had been stationed for just eight months. And other battalions were plucked from garrison duty in Burma, Malta, Mauritius and South Africa, with another taken from the northern Chinese treaty port of Tientsin following its involvement in the Japanese-led assault on the German colony at Tsingtao.

Typical of the Regular Army units relieved of their imperial responsibilities was the 1st Royal Munster Fusiliers. A southern Irish battalion with long associations with the Sub-Continent dating back to the days of the old East India Company, the Munsters had spent almost a decade in India, during which it took part in another of the interminable frontier wars, before being transferred to Burma in 1912. The battalion was still there when war broke out in Europe in August 1914: five companies in Rangoon, two more at Thayetmyo and another at Port Blair in the Andaman Islands. After battling the worst of the monsoon to improve the capital's defences against the threat of the German light cruiser *Emden*, the Munsters were finally relieved in November. The following month, by which time it had been reorganised on the four-company model, the battalion departed India, reaching England on 10 January. An overnight train carried them on to Coventry, their arrival signalling the beginning of an influx of units into Warwickshire and North Oxfordshire that would eventually come together as the 'Incomparable 29th'.

Major General Frederick Shaw was given the task of forming the division, having been promoted from brigadier general following 'magnificent work' with the British Expeditionary Force. By mid-February the structure of its infantry and artillery components was in place and its principal officers appointed with divisional headquarters established in the Manor House Hotel, Leamington. For all the much-vaunted professionalism of the Regular units placed at their disposal, the challenges facing Shaw and his subordinates were considerable. Not the least of the difficulties to be overcome was the widespread dispersal of the division, which hampered efforts to forge a cohesive force even out of such high quality material. The three infantry brigades, the 86th, 87th and 88th, and their constituent battalions were spread across a swathe of the Midlands with brigade headquarters in Nuneaton, Rugby and Stratford-upon-Avon. The 86th 'Fusiliers Brigade' alone had its units variously billeted in Coventry (1st Royal Munster Fusiliers), Nuneaton (1st Royal Dublin Fusiliers and 1st Lancashire Fusiliers) and Stockingford (2nd Royal Fusiliers). Such arrangements seriously restricted the amount of brigade, let along divisional, exercises that could be conducted. Even battalion schemes presented staff with organisational headaches, as reflected in an entry in the 86th Brigade's war diary. Major Thomas Frankland, the Brigade Major, observed towards the end of February:

> As regards billeting generally … men have been very well fed and are very fit. On the other hand, billets are very scattered and for training purposes and discipline the system is extremely inconvenient. It takes a long time to collect men and [it] is difficult to turn out in short notice. COs will all be glad to get their men together again …[6]

As well as re-equipping and welcoming fresh drafts of men to bring them up to strength, the battalions were, out of necessity, compelled to focus mostly on fitness and shooting practice on platoon and company scale. What the brigade war diary euphemistically referred to as 'regular training', consisted mostly of 'route marches, digging and other exercises'.[7]

It was much the same story in other brigades. Second Lieutenant Reginald Gillett, who joined the 2nd Hampshires from the 3rd (Reserve) Battalion in the last week of February, kept a short diary in which he mentions church parades and route marches but only one divisional 'scheme'. Even then, Gillett, a subaltern of seven months who was still a schoolboy when the war began, found the going tough among so many veterans with a wealth of experience to fall back on. He had been with his new battalion at Stratford for fewer than three weeks when he had to be 'excused' parade as his feet 'were rather bad'. He later admitted:

> I felt completely out of my depth … a young officer with no experience whatsoever, very little training as most of my time had been spent drilling recruits. I had no real field practice and only one field day and there I was, landed with a Battalion of hardened regulars … I felt completely inadequate and I had a major battle with my Company Commander … The training was, for me, appalling. We never did less than a 16-mile route march a day or a day in the country on extra field work. The training ground on that occasion was 5 or 6 miles away. So we had to march out that distance. A long day in the field and march back again, all in full marching order, and I found that a great trial.[8]

While new recruits such as Gillett were struggling to meet expectations, more senior officers were left to try and mould a force that was not yet fully formed. Fresh units continued to arrive throughout February: including the 4th Worcestershire Regiment, which arrived at Banbury on the 2nd by way of Avonmouth and Burma, and the 1st West Riding Field Company, Royal Engineers, which reached Kineton four days later. The last significant addition, the 5th Royal Scots, only arrived in the billeting area on 11 March, twenty-four hours after Lord Kitchener's fateful decision to send the 29th Division to join the Mediterranean Expeditionary Force. There was a limit to what could be achieved in such a short time, whether the troops were professionals or, as in the case of the last two named units, part-timers from the Territorial Army.

In the circumstances, Shaw and his staff worked minor miracles in creating a common *esprit de corps*. Taking their lead from the fine military bearing and sheer professionalism of the Regulars, the 'Terriers' took particular pride in being associated with famous units filled with so many long service men. One man recalled being 'very impressed – nay overawed – by the discipline and smartness of the Regular soldiers'.[9] Oswin Creighton was of much the same opinion. Having joined the division from a New Army unit, he was struck by the differences between them:

> They seem exceedingly smart and seasoned troops, and have an air that there is nothing they don't know about soldiering. Of course one feels that they have inherited an ancient army tradition, and there is not the feeling of new ground to be broken there was with

Kitchener's Army. It makes so much difference, feeling they are so absolutely ready for the front ... There seems nothing they are not prepared to do ...[10]

Creighton found most of the officers 'friendly and agreeable' if, at times, a little insouciant. Overall, though, they were extremely companionable. He recalled an encounter with Lieutenant Colonel Richard Rooth, the Dublins' forty-nine-year-old, Sandhurst-trained commanding officer whose twenty years of service had been spent mainly in the east. On a 12-mile route march during which 'the Colonel rode part of the way, but walked a good deal', he was 'very pleasant, and talked away quite a lot'. Even more surprising, however, was the demeanour of the men. On the whole, they were 'very well-behaved' as well as being 'charming ... civil and clean and orderly'. Following another route march, he remarked in his diary: 'I ... made friends with a number of the men. They are very easy to get on with, and are always cheery and laughing.'[11]

A case of wishful thinking or naivety it may have been, but Creighton was not entirely blind to their shortcomings. He recognised soon enough that those same men he so admired were also programmed to obey without question the orders passed down to them. As he noted:

They all seem to have had any individuality crushed out of them by army discipline. They confess this, and say themselves that it is useless ever calling for volunteers to do anything. They must always be detailed.[12]

Rightly or wrongly, it was a mindset and military philosophy that would reach its appalling apotheosis just a few weeks later. For now, though, the impression made by the men who made up the bulk of the 29th Division was overwhelmingly positive. Local newspapers were positively panegyric in their descriptions of the soldiers townspeople were proud to claim as their own. One described the new arrivals as 'a fine stalwart lot of fellows'.[13] Another recorded how the men 'looked in splendid trim',[14] their prowess on the march presenting onlookers with a 'spectacle' that was 'dazzling'[15] in its martial precision. When the Dublins left Nuneaton for their final billets in Kenilworth during the first week of March, they were already akin to folk heroes in the eyes of many. They had become, in the words of one journalist, 'these large-hearted, happy soldiers who have filled the town with good-humoured merriment' and, in the process, 'endeared themselves to the inhabitants'.[16]

By then rumours of their impending move overseas were rife, with the smart money on a voyage to the Aegean. Lieutenant Guy Nightingale of the Munsters was among those convinced that their days in the Midlands were numbered. Aged twenty-four and a product of nearby Rugby School and the military academy at Sandhurst, Nightingale was not sorry about the prospect of leaving behind the snow and sleet of a 'perfectly frightful' English winter. Writing to his mother from Coventry on 1 March, the second in command of Y Company commented:

> Very busy day today … We are off to the Dardanelles I think. We ought to have sailed last Thursday – transports and everything ready for the whole Divn but Kitchener stopped it at the last moment. Now we are ready to move at 2 hours' notice and have to have everything ready packed, though I daresay we won't go for ages yet …[17]

Further clues in the coming days would show the barrack-room gossip to be correct in substance if not in detail. On 6 March, with a number of units in the process of switching billets for the sake of 'training convenience', the 86th Brigade received orders to 'send in a return of sizes of caps, boots and service dress' which were correctly interpreted by the war diarist as 'indicating equipping for another theatre of war'.[18] Three days later, Nightingale informed his mother:

> It is quite definite that we are going to the Dardanelles. It was in the Midland Telegraph last night in fact … The men are being fitted out with Helmets again and new clothes. The Rugby lot have already got slouch hats issued to them. It is an awful scrum as you can imagine. No date yet as to when we go. It will take a little time getting our new kit and helmets etc, but the chief thing is that we are going there and not to France …[19]

The excitement was mounting. A 'long Brigade field day', one of the few staged since the division's mobilisation, followed by the King's review served only to fuel speculation. Finally, on 13 March, came the news Nightingale and most others had been eagerly anticipating. Scribbling a brief note home, he confirmed the orders that quashed any hope of a last leave. 'I hear we will be off any minute,' he wrote, 'so won't be home again.'[20] Later that same day, he wrote more fully and excitedly:

20

Now we have got our definite orders. I can't tell you the exact time as it is all confidential, but by the time you get this we will be out to sea. We have a ripping boat – the sister-ship to a boat which was in our convoy coming home. We share her with the Dublins … The scrum is awful here. Everyone packing up and trying to settle things before leaving. Even the Coventry people don't know what trains we are going by, or the Port we sail from … It's ripping to think we are really off at last and sounds almost too good to be true.[21]

It was true enough, although there would be a day's delay before leaving on account, according to Nightingale, of a mix-up over the delivery of rations. If so, it was entirely in keeping with a departure that was far from smooth and which, at times, descended into shambolic farce. The chaotic events in Coventry on 15 March as the Munsters bid an emotional farewell to their hosts were fairly typical. Writing home two days later, Nightingale confessed:

I've never seen such scenes as there were at Coventry when we left. The crowd was terrific – all the men very drunk, and their late land-ladies hanging round their necks. Though our trains were going all through the night – the last one leaving at 4am – the streets were full of Coventry people seeing us off. The police had no control at all over them and it was absolutely impossible to try to march through the town. There were women and children walking about between the ranks and flatly refusing to go away from the men till the very last moment![22]

Captain Guy Geddes was not amused. In fact, the thirty-four-year-old commander of X Company, an officer of fifteen years' continuous service with the Munsters, was incandescent. A terse diary note summed up his mood:

Coy paraded at 4pm. About a quarter of the men there. Awful. Cannot write about the march to station … Awful business entraining men. Station master's conduct scandalous – with the result that I got left behind.[23]

The first of three scheduled trains left at 1800, one of them carrying a bull terrier called Buller bearing the arms of Coventry and Munster on its coat as a parting gift. Refusing to wait for the second train, due shortly before midnight, Geddes joined a contingent of the Royal

Fusiliers aboard the 1940. He arrived in Avonmouth to find all his men 'tucked away'. By 0840 on 16 March, twenty-eight officers, 1,000 men, ninety horses and twenty-four vehicles had reached the port in readiness for sailing aboard the waiting transports, *Ausonia*, *Alaunia*, *Haverford* and *Mercian*. All things considered, Guy Nightingale thought it something of a 'miracle'.[24]

However, the troubles dogging the 29th Division's progress overseas were far from over. Something of the chaos that had marred their departure from the Midlands followed them to the dockside. The 86th Brigade's war diarist reported that stores and vehicles were loaded 'under no particular system',[25] resulting in confusion with some pieces of equipment being misplaced and other items being placed in entirely the wrong ships. One officer complained that 'the arrangements for the embarkation had been made, and the ships taken up, in such a hurry that it was almost impossible to tell in what ships the various stores and vehicles … were situated'.[26] Later departures were little improved. An officer of the 89th (1st Highland) Field Ambulance told how his unit reached Avonmouth only to find their ship absent. 'The men were put up in a cold, draughty shed for the night, where they had little sleep, while the officers took train to Bristol, nine miles off …'[27]

The first ships carrying elements of the 29th Division left in the early evening of 16 March. As they headed out into the Bristol Channel with an escort of two destroyers their destination, though officially undeclared, was an open secret, referenced in letters home, in uncensored newspaper reports and even in signs attached to the sides of Army trucks that brazenly, if light-heartedly, promised a 'Cheap trip to the Dardanelles'. Once at sea the thin pretence was finally dropped. In a letter written aboard the *Ausonia* a day after leaving port, Guy Nightingale stated:

> We were given out maps this morning – six each. All of the Dardanelles and neighbourhood. So there's not much doubt of where we [are] bound for.[28]

Around half the Munsters were sharing the ship with the whole of the Dublins and Brigade Headquarters. And despite his own unit being 'very much split up' Nightingale was in 'cheery' mood on that St Patrick's Day. The Dublins, he noted, were 'a very nice lot' and the generals who commanded them were 'a jolly good crowd'.[29] The latter included one new name. Shortly before embarking, General Shaw had, as Nightingale put it, been 'sent elsewhere' and his place taken as GOC

29th Division by a man whose subsequent performance would become the subject of fierce and enduring debate.

Regarded by many as the epitome of the unfeeling and unimaginative British Army general of the First World War, Major General Aylmer Gould Hunter-Weston has been widely denigrated. Field Marshal Haig later decried him as 'a rank amateur', thus contributing to the popular image of a blundering and blustering incompetent of General Melchett-like proportions forever remembered as the tragicomic 'Hunter-Bunter'. But his resumé to February 1915, when he left Flanders for what he imagined was eight days' leave, told a different story.

The fifty-year-old 27th Laird of Hunterston was an officer with a reputation for dash and daring displayed on battlefields from the mountains of northern India to the plains of northern France. In South Africa, he had distinguished himself at the head of a 'flying column', thrusting deep into enemy territory and spreading sufficient alarm and confusion to prompt the Boer president to flee his own home. And, more recently, as commander of the 11th Infantry Brigade, dubbed the 'Stonewall Brigade' for its resolution in the most trying of circumstances, he had displayed tactical skill, formidable energy and qualities of leadership to match his sometimes reckless courage.

By the time he arrived at Leamington Spa on 13 March 1915, to take command of 29th Division his services in the present war had already been recognised by promotion and two mentions in despatches. Even so, the arrangement by which he succeeded Shaw within twenty-four hours of the King's review was an odd one. Ordered to a meeting with Lord Kitchener at the War Office in February, he learned that the Government was considering sending a military expedition to co-operate with the Navy in the Dardanelles. If that happened, then the only available British Army force to be sent was the still-forming 29th Division, in which case Hunter-Weston discovered, for reasons not made clear, he would supersede Shaw. If, however, the idea of an expeditionary force was rejected, then Shaw would continue in command and, once its training was complete, take it to France, while Hunter-Weston acted as a sub-inspector of the 'New Army' currently being formed until such time as another divisional command became available. The die having been cast, Hunter-Weston was wired on 10 March with instructions to take command 'as soon as possible'.[30] A flurry of meetings followed over the course of the next five days, with the Chief of the General Staff, with Winston Churchill, Lord Kitchener and the King, before boarding the Cunard liner *Andania* on 17 March.

There had been no time to get to know, still less to assess, the force he had inherited. Initial reports, however, were encouraging. Rumour had it that Kitchener had complimented him 'on commanding the finest Division which had left the United Kingdom as yet, both in service and equipment', which Nightingale thought 'pleasing'.[31] It was a feeling echoed by others. Preparing to leave Leamington, Captain Garth Walford, Brigade Major of the 29th's artillery, wrote to his wife:

> This is a very fine Division, the best we have now I think … The 29th
> Div Artillery is a good show; horse, field, garrison and mountain,
> with some heavy guns; the whole regiment represented and it is all
> good of its kind, with one or two exceptions …[32]

Like Hunter-Weston and Shaw before him, Walford was speaking from experience. He had been out in France and Flanders from August through to December 1914, during which he was wounded and narrowly escaped death while serving with a battery of Royal Field Artillery. A thirty-two-year-old Balliol scholar with a reputation for being a tireless worker, Walford was a rare combination of the brave and the intellectual soldier. He was also a doting father and loving husband who took great pains to reassure his family about the dangers he faced. Writing home a month before being called back to help form the 29th Division, he explained, in characteristically light-hearted fashion, the differences between a staff captain and a brigade major, before concluding:

> Neither job is particularly dangerous, in fact, I should think either is
> safer than one with a battery but there have certainly been a good
> number of casualties among staffs lately, but they are usually flukes
> – some shell sent off into the blue.[33]

Whether that was sufficient to ease his wife's fears is questionable, but by the middle of March 1915 Walford was absorbed with matters of far greater significance than his own well-being. Unable to mask his delight at being part of such a splendid body of men as the 29th Division, he insisted, '… we have a very big job to do. If all goes well we ought to do as much towards settling the war as any other part of the British Army. I am very glad … to have such a fine job.'[34]

Six days later, he wrote in similar vein from aboard the SS *Aragon*:

> Off tonight … We ought to have a good show, if we can only get landed
> safely in time to sort ourselves out a bit before being asked to fight …[35]

Such reservation, understandable given the division's rushed deployment and restricted training programme, was shared by others, not least the new GOC. A few weeks later, having had a chance to see his command for himself, Hunter-Weston would shrewdly observe:

> The men are certainly very fine. And the officers all up to the highest peace standard, and up to full strength. The criticism I make is that the Lieutenant Colonels in some instances are too old. And that the Division, not having been trained together as a Division, is not a well-oiled machine as were the old Regular Divisions.[36]

By the time he made his assessment the decision to commit the 29th Division, not only to its first action but to an operation of enormous hazard on which all else depended, had been taken. However, for the first few days at least of his voyage to the Mediterranean Hunter-Weston was able to cast aside such thoughts.

Where Kitchener harboured hopes that the division's employment in the Dardanelles might yet be forestalled by a triumph of naval power alone, Hunter-Weston, for very different reasons, also considered it highly likely that the 29th would not be called upon. His feelings were crystallised in a long letter to his wife sent from Malta on March 24. It was written three days after learning of the Navy's failure to break through the Dardanelles and following a 'long talk' with Vice-Admiral Arthur Limpus, a former naval adviser to Turkey and one of the most knowledgeable of all serving officers on Ottoman military strength:

> I don't want you to say so to anyone, but I should not be surprised if we come home again. As you know, I have always thought that if the Turks are capably directed and have the necessary material of war, they should be able to prevent our ships getting through the Straits, and they should also prevent our landing troops on the Peninsular [sic], for they have had ample warning and they have lots of men. They should by now have made the whole Peninsular into a strongly entrenched camp, with hidden trenches all round the coast, with lots of men to hold them. They should have Howitzers in hidden positions covering every possible landing place. If they have done this, and our folk out there should know by this time, the passage of the Dardanelles is not a feasible operation and we shall have to return home again and be employed elsewhere ...[37]

Of course, there was, as Hunter-Weston acknowledged, a possibility that the Turks might not 'do what I should do in their place', thus enabling the ships to get through and, 'by their fire, make it impossible for the Turks to hold'[38] their ground. But he rather doubted it, adding,

> with so clever an old man as the German general [Field Marshal Colmar von der Goltz] to lead them, I fear that they will not make mistakes; of course they may not have the guns, howitzers and mines; but then I fear they have. It is, as I have said to you always, a big gamble and if there is any chance of pulling off the big stakes it is well worth trying. If I don't see a good chance, I shall counsel caution. If I see a good chance, I shall try and work it out carefully and push it through with determination and vigour. But the decision does not rest with me.[39]

As we have seen, that decision had already been made two days earlier. The following day, 25 March, Hunter-Weston had a further meeting with Vice-Admiral Limpus, picking up what intelligence he could before going on to talk with Lord Methuen, the Governor of Malta. 'Neither,' wrote Hunter-Weston, 'are in favour of Dardanelles operations now.'[40] Perhaps influenced by their own pessimism, his own misgivings continued to mount. A day out of Malta, having studied Hamilton's staff appreciations of the proposed operations, he called a meeting of his divisional headquarters staff and told them to prepare for a landing either at Cape Suvla [sic] or at the southern point of the Gallipoli Peninsular [sic]. At Hamilton's behest, he then set about writing his own appreciation based on the limited information that was available to him 'up to the time of leaving Malta'. It proved 'a long job' and was not completed until 0300 hours on 28 March. It did not make for comfortable reading.

The premature bombardments and landing operations had, he said, resulted in the Turkish Army, 'under German direction', converting the Peninsula into 'an entrenched camp', with the potential landing places covered by 'several' lines of trenches, concealed machine guns, land mines and batteries of artillery. While identifying Suvla Bay as a potential landing zone, he thought, on balance, the southern shore around Cape Helles offered a greater chance of success. However, even there, with the Navy able to provide support from three directions, he forecast a hard struggle with 'no scope for manoeuvre' against an alert enemy in well-sited and heavily fortified positions. His own experience of trying to overcome such defences gave little cause for optimism:

> Throughout this war none of the combatants has ever been successful in breaking quickly through even indifferent

entrenchments. The usual result has been stalemate. Success has only been obtained after long and careful preparation and the expenditure of an enormous amount of High Explosive gun ammunition both from quick-firers and howitzers. We are short of gun ammunition and particularly short of High Explosive Shell. There appears therefore every prospect of getting tied up on an extended line across the Peninsula, in front of the Turkish Kildare [sic] plateau trenches – a second Crimea.[41]

Hunter-Weston recognised that the stakes were high and the prizes for success 'very great'.

If we seriously threaten Constantinople all the Balkan nations are likely to come in at once on our side ... [but] if we land troops and fail, [he noted presciently] the Bulgarians are more than likely to come in against us ...[42]

With a reasonable chance of success, he thought 'the freeing of the Dardanelles should be undertaken whatever the cost'. But without a reasonable chance, he believed 'the operations should go no further than they have'. For the time being at least, he feared the opportunity had passed. In his view, the possibility of a quick victory had been compromised by an untimely assault that had achieved little beyond warning the enemy of the Entente intentions and giving them ample time to build roads, bring up heavy guns and prepare defences. In short, he reckoned:

All that clever German officers under Von der Goltz can design, and hard-working diggers like the Turks can carry out, has been done to make the Peninsula impregnable.[43]

Rather than risk a setback that he felt would be 'a disaster to the Empire', he advised a more patient and cautious approach:

To continue our preparations; to train our troops for a landing, and to get our expedition properly equipped and organised for this difficult operation of war, so as to be ready to take advantage of any opportunity for successful action that may occur.[44]

Hunter-Weston delivered his 'bombshell' to Braithwaite on 29 March shortly after arriving in Alexandria, where the 29th Division had been diverted mid-journey to undergo further training and make final preparations. Hamilton later admitted that his conclusions, set out in 'black and white', came as 'rather a startler'. Though he would later confess to finding his divisional commander 'grasping and tiresome'[45] and a bit of 'a gasbag',[46] he had considered him 'a man of mettle'[47] and 'a slashing man of action'.[48] His caution came as a surprise, particularly since at their last meeting he had seemed so 'keen and sanguine'.[49]

When they met next at the Savoy Hotel on 30 March, Hunter-Weston, according to his diary note, again expressed his 'pessimism'.[50] In his version of the meeting, he reiterated all of his objections, arguing that the 50,000 men then available were too few, the Turkish defences too strong and the Navy's guns 'ill-adapted' to engaging concealed enemy positions. Having thus reiterated his view of the 'inadvisability' of attempting a landing he considered most likely doomed to failure, he 'strongly urged that the disadvantages ... be clearly brought to the notice of the Cabinet'.[51] According to Hunter-Weston, Hamilton remained unmoved and unconvinced. He wrote:

> The Commander-in-Chief ... was of opinion that the Cabinet having decided on the operation it was for him to carry it out and he expressed himself as confident of success.[52]

Hamilton's own recollection, however, presented their 'confab' in a somewhat different light. He claimed that Hunter-Weston had back-pedalled from his initial cautionary appreciation and asked that it be regarded as an 'ad interim paper'. Hamilton added:

> He wrote it, he says now, without the fuller knowledge he is daily acquiring – knowledge which is tending to make him more sanguine.[53]

That Hunter-Weston did come round is irrefutable. However, he did so reluctantly, having been swayed not by superior argument but out of his bounden duty as a professional soldier to carry out the orders handed down to him. Having made his views known to Hamilton, he felt 'there was nothing further left for me to do than to loyally accept whatever plan he thereafter decided on and to do my utmost to bring his plan to a successful issue'.[54] Privately, however, he continued to voice his doubts. In his diary, he noted that General Albert d'Amade, commander of the 1st Division of the *Corps de Expéditionnaire d'Orient*, 'agreed with my views' and that when the Frenchman voiced his opinion on the planned landings Hamilton 'refused to listen'.[55] A few days later, frustrated by the protracted logistical difficulties caused by the division's stores having been loaded 'just anyhow' at Avonmouth, he wrote to his wife:

As you will have gathered from my letter at Malta, I am not at all well pleased with the way the affair is being managed. If it had been carefully thought out beforehand and launched like a thunderbolt without warning, it would not have been at all a difficult matter. As it is, so much warning has been given that what might have been an easy operation has become a very difficult one. I have given my opinion strongly against it, but it has been decided by Hamilton in conjunction with Kitchener to carry on. I am therefore wholeheartedly with them, only one plan can be carried out and the Commander is the man to make the plan … I therefore am doing, and shall do, my very hardest and best for the success of the plan, though it is gambling with too big odds against success, in my opinion.[56]

What little hope there was of converting an 'outside chance', as he called it, into an outrageous success rested wholly on the exceptional quality of his division. They were, he told his wife, 'a very fine lot of men'.[57] Had he the luxury of a further three weeks of training, he felt he could have turned the division into an even better 'fighting machine', but, as it was, he thought it 'uncommonly good' and sure to give 'a very good account of itself'.[58] And on that, at least, he was in complete harmony with his chief. After inspecting the 86th and 87th Brigades at their camp on April 6, Hamilton rhapsodised:

There was a strong wind blowing which tried to spoil the show, but could not – that Infantry was too superb! Alexander, Hannibal, Caesar, Napoleon; not one of them had the handling of legionaries like these … If we don't win, I won't be able to put it on the men.[59]

In the heat and dust of the sand hills around Mex Camp the men of the 29th Division were working flat out to be ready. 'The weather is perfect altogether and everyone is looking very fit with their short stay at home and now the sunburn on top of it,'[60] noted Guy Nightingale. Sweating profusely in their 'home khaki', the troops were put through their paces in a series of 'strenuous field days'. And when they weren't staging mock fights across the desert, they were practising landing operations from boats, often with comical consequences.

On 2 April, a day after a landing exercise 'without boats', the Munsters attempted the real thing for the first time. It was, in Guy Geddes' opinion, 'one of the most amusing afternoons possible'.[61] 'Such landsmen,' he wrote in his diary. 'My boat did nothing but run on reefs and I never partook of the entertainment …'[62]

The Munsters proved fast learners. A day later Geddes found their boat handling much improved, describing it as a 'very good show'. Other units experienced much the same teething problems as boat training was stepped up. The entries in the Hampshires' war diary have a monotonous ring that is echoed in the records of all of the units in the 29th Division:

> April 5: Companies, etc, employed practising landing operations …
> April 7: Battalion practised climbing rope ladders …
> April 8: Battalion practised landing …[63]

And so it went on, day after wearying day, with growing confidence tempered by increasing realism. In the midst of it all, Garth Walford stole a few moments to pen a short note to his eldest daughter and a longer letter to his wife in which he pulled few punches:

> We move on from here this week, but where remains a secret. We have got a difficult job in front of us, so you mustn't expect too much at first. The Turks have had full warning, thanks to the Navy's trying to do things off their own bat before they had any land forces to work with them, and the Germans are said to have sent a lot of guns, officers and men to stiffen the Turkish Army …[64]

The great exodus from Egypt was well under way by the second week of April. Hamilton led the way, returning to Lemnos on April 8. In his last letter to Kitchener before leaving, he wrote:

> All goes well and my chiefest [sic] worry is that my three or four senior officers (excepting Braithwaite) now seem, for the first time, to see all the difficulties with extraordinary perspicacity. In fact, they would each apparently a thousand times sooner do anything else than what we are going to do. But I have no doubt whatever when once they are fairly embarked they will play up for all they are worth …[65]

His faith was not misplaced. By the time Hunter-Weston reboarded the *Andania* in Alexandria on 9 April, he professed to have put any differences between himself and Hamilton well and truly behind him. 'My mind is at rest and I am happy, cheery, contented and very fit and well,' he assured his wife. In the same letter, he stressed: 'I now wholeheartedly accept whatever plan may be decided on by the Commander and shall do my 'damnest' [sic] to bring his (the Government's) plan to a successful issue.'[66]

While he waited for his ship to leave, he instructed the troops on board to fill the time by rehearsing their boat landing drill, little realising that for at least a part of his force such skills were about to be usurped by an unlikely scheme from the unlikeliest of sources.

Chapter 3

'A Sailor out of a Novel'

According to the disparaging euphemism prevalent at the time, Edward Unwin was a 'dug-out', a washed-up old sea dog plucked from comfortable retirement by the exigencies of a world war. And yet, of all the officers labouring day and night on 'Rosy' Wemyss' overworked staff, there were few more impressive figures than the naval commander whose only combat experience had been against African tribesmen almost twenty years earlier.

An Army officer remembered him vividly:

> He stands over 6 feet and is broad in proportion, with the typical clean-shaven face of a sailor, and with a voice that roars orders through a megaphone, causing those who are ordered to jump about a good deal quicker on their jobs than they probably would do otherwise.[1]

Unwin was, indeed, a commanding presence whose restless and relentless energy made a mockery of his fifty-one years. As forceful and forthright as he was reliable and resourceful, he was a man of strong and often original opinion who got things done after his own fashion. To Wemyss' impeccable social graces and political wiles Unwin added bluntness with an occasional show of bluster and a bluff good humour that invariably left loud laughter trailing in his wake. He was, in short, the perfect foil for Wemyss, with whom he forged a formidable partnership.

For his part, Wemyss counted himself 'very fortunate' to have him on a staff willing to 'pull together' and 'to keep their tempers and their heads' under 'the most trying circumstances'.[2] Included among them were his secretary, 'quite first rate … very energetic and agreeable', his chief telegraphist, 'hard-headed and hard-working' and his flag commander, 'not an attractive man, but clear-headed … hard-working and, though not sympathetic, not disagreeable'. And then there was Unwin. Of the redoubtable commander, he wrote that he was 'always cheery, but at his best when there is real hard work. Rather the type of a sailor out of a novel, good at his job, but quite ignorant of anything else'.[3] Luckily for them both, the 'job' was all that mattered.

Unwin's war thus far had been as unspectacular as his earlier career. A product of the brutal regime aboard the training hulk *Conway* moored in the River Mersey, Unwin had spent more than half his life alternating between the Mercantile Service and Royal Navy. He had sailed before the mast aboard Donald Currie's Castle Line clippers and officered ships of the more prestigious Peninsula & Oriental Steam Navigation Company. However, when the Royal Navy was short of deck watch keepers and navigating officers, he was among a hundred officers who exchanged their appointments for commissions in Her Majesty's Navy.

Quite what persuaded him to change tack at the ripe old age of thirty-one is unclear. Unwin left few records. If it was glory or adventure he was after, he would have to wait awhile. Opportunities for distinction were rare. Aside from brief participation in a small-scale punitive expedition in the forests of West Africa and an involvement in the Boer War that was confined to the fringes of the conflict, he saw precious little in the way of military action. His greatest achievement during fourteen years of mostly uneventful service was the introduction of his own new methods for facilitating and speeding up the most onerous of all naval duties in the Edwardian age, coaling ships. And in all that time, he rose but two ranks from lieutenant to commander before drawing down the curtain on his career in 1909 at the age of forty-five.

The threat of war put a temporary end to his retirement. Recalled when the Navy mobilised at the end of July 1914, his past reputation earned him an appointment on Admiral Jellicoe's staff, as Fleet Coaling Officer in the Grand Fleet flagship, *Iron Duke*. For six months he busied himself with the important but monotonous routine of refuelling logistics before requesting a command of his own. His wish granted, he was posted to Malta to take charge of HMS *Hussar*, a venerable gunboat of Victorian vintage that doubled as Admiral's Yacht and sea-borne communications centre for the Commander-in-Chief, Mediterranean Station. Malta, however, offered merely the briefest of pauses en route to the hubbub of Mudros and an enterprise that was destined to transform his life at a single stroke.

True to form, Unwin's unlikely metamorphosis from 'backroom boy' to leading role in one of the greatest dramas of the First World War began inauspiciously. Loaned out to Wemyss in early March, *Hussar's* role was to provide shipboard accommodation on an island all but devoid of facilities. Until her arrival in Mudros, the newly installed Governor of Mudros and his staff had been forced to live and work in the cramped confines of the *Imogene*, formerly the ambassador's yacht at Constantinople. *Hussar's* appearance was, therefore, a welcome one and it was not long before Wemyss made her his home and headquarters while at the same time enlisting her captain to his staff.

On 13 March, it was a buoyed Wemyss who wrote to his wife:

> I am at last settled for good on board here, but since there is no room on board *Hussar* for my numerous and growing staff I have the Imogene lashed alongside, and between us we fill up both ships. I have now a cable from the shore to the ship and have a telegraph office on board and some ET [Eastern Telegraph Company] clerks to run it, so that I am able to save a little time by doing away with transmissions of telegrams by boat.[4]

With *Hussar* the hub of the Navy's efforts to turn Mudros into a working base for the gathering expeditionary force, Unwin soon made himself an indispensable member of the staff. As well as his energy and enthusiasm, qualities his chief both shared and admired, he brought with him skills of particular relevance to the mission in hand. His Mercantile Service background was especially useful in the Navy's dealings with the ships' masters Wemyss found so infuriatingly 'tiresome' with their endless 'silly'[5] questions. However, it was his familiarity with that most unprepossessing of harbour vessels, the lighter, that Unwin came into his own. His knowledge of the capabilities and peculiarities of these unwieldy flat-bottomed workhorses was unrivalled. Indeed, what he did not know about the movement and stowage of these specialised craft was hardly worth knowing. It was not surprising, therefore, that he should have been made Officer-in-Charge of lighters not only in Mudros itself, but for the impending invasion of the Gallipoli peninsula.

The job was a demanding one, even for an expert such as Unwin. The crowded nature of the harbour and the shortage of landing facilities were problem enough, but the appalling weather that battered the island for weeks on end from March into April made things almost impossible. The equinoctial gales struck the island in the wake of the Navy's failed attempt to break through the Dardanelles. They continued to wreak havoc for days with Unwin's fleet of lighters, some of them only recently purchased and delivered from Athens, especially vulnerable to the storm-force winds. It was, as Wemyss remarked, 'the very deuce of a time' in what he called his 'boisterous kingdom'.[6] In a letter to his wife written on 22 March, Wemyss described a scene of gale-blown carnage:

> The transports are so helpless and their captains useless. Their boats have been getting adrift. A torpedo boat has gone ashore – a total wreck, but everybody saved I am glad to say. Also some lighters that I had bought at Athens are somewhere adrift ...[7]

Wemyss was hopeful that Unwin would be able to recover the 'missing' vessels, but after three days, during which 'all boating and communications' were further 'retarded by bad weather',[8] he was forced to admit defeat. His 'cherished lighters'[9] were given up as sunk. The storms continued to hamper preparations for the landings. On 4 April, it was 'again damnable' and within twenty-four hours another 'howling gale' had rendered 'any work impossible'.[10] The daily focus was now on 'preparing for constant operations',[11] as Wemyss put it, and it was with those in mind that Unwin set forth across the harbour one day in April to attend a joint meeting of the Army and naval staffs aboard Sir Ian Hamilton's headquarters ship.

The precise date of the conference aboard the *Arcadian* is not clear. Unwin later placed it 'on or about'[12] 15 April, but in this he was most certainly mistaken. A more likely date is 11 or 12 April, when a series of meetings were held following Hamilton's return to Mudros with the object of turning his draft scheme into a detailed and workable plan. What is not in any doubt is the substance of that crucial meeting or the fateful decision that followed in its wake.

Its main focus was to try to find the most effective means of landing as many men as possible in the initial critical assault on the Cape Helles sector. Until this point, the scope of the attack had been limited by a mixture of geography and logistics: in other words, the size of the beaches and the number of boats available to be towed and rowed ashore. Cecil Aspinall, the future official historian then serving on the GHQ staff, explained the dilemma facing the planners:

> The number of troops that could be thrown ashore in the first rush for the beach was of vital importance, but for the main operation there was only room on the three southern beaches for 18 tows to arrive simultaneously, namely, four at X, eight at W, and six at V; making a total of not more than 2,200 men all told for the first attack.[13]

A new proposal for carrying the remainder of the covering force on fleet sweepers would, he observed, 'increase the speed at which the first troops could be reinforced; but even with this new method at least three-quarters of an hour would probably elapse before the second trip of tows could reach the shore'.[14]

The meeting in *Arcadian* was chaired by George Hope, captain of the *Queen Elizabeth*, and among those present was Captain Douglas Lionel Dent, former captain of the *Irresistible*, which had been crippled and abandoned during the 18 March debacle. Since then, he had been seconded to Wemyss' staff as harbourmaster and captain superintendent. Described by Wemyss as 'quite a good fellow but not thrilling',[15] he had spent only a few days in his new role before being appointed Principal Naval Transport Officer. From a tiny office, established in a part of the *Arcadian*'s saloon pantry, he and his small staff were responsible for working out and co-ordinating all of the arrangements necessary to deliver thousands of men and tons of supplies on to the enemy beaches.

In the absence of any minutes of the meeting we must rely on two slightly differing accounts written years afterwards by Unwin. Both were entirely based on his recollection of events, though, as he pointed out, these remained 'so vividly in my mind that time has no effect on my memory'.[16]

For much of the discussion, Unwin evidently said nothing, but merely listened and made mental notes. As Officer-in-Charge of Lighters, his main purpose was to get a clear idea of the Cape Helles landing plan in order to better understand what he would have to do. He later wrote:

> The whole idea worked on at the meeting was to land troops in the ordinary service boats, the only question being the number of boats in each tow and the various details arising therefrom ...[17]

The conference was drawing to a close when Captain Dent turned to Unwin, who had been unusually quiet throughout. 'What do you think about it, Unwin?' he asked. Unwin later admitted:

> I had come to the meeting without any plans at all. Only on hearing what had been said, it seemed to me that if the beach was properly defended by an enemy at only 200 yards, who reserved their fire till the boats were about 100 yards from the beach, not many would get ashore.[18]

The ghastly vision of a bloody slaughter triggered an outlandish thought in his ever fertile imagination. If the existing plan courted disaster by exposing hundreds of men to a potential death-ride into the beach, then why not consider a radical alternative. The solution came to him quickly. 'My idea,' he declared, 'would be to land the men in a specially prepared ship, right on the beach.'[19]

Though hardly fully formed, he reasoned that his scheme meant that 'the troops would be safe from rifle fire till they tried to leave the ship'.[20] He realised the plan was not without hazard. His greatest fear and only danger that he could foresee was from heavy guns sited on the shore, but, as he understood it, such a threat was not anticipated.

According to Unwin's own account, the proposal caused 'some sensation'.[21] There was a stunned silence during which, according to the commander, the Army officers present were 'waiting to hear what the naval authorities thought about it'.[22] Unwin felt that many were 'impressed' with the suggestion 'but didn't like to express an opinion'.[23]

At last, the hush was broken by Captain Hope. 'I don't like it,' he said. 'I think the ship would be sunk before she got in and there are too many eggs in one basket.'[24]

The risks were self-evident, but Unwin was not a man to give way easily. 'I contended,' he later wrote, 'that before the enemy realised what we were at, we should be ashore.'[25] With that, the scheme was set to one side and further details of the open boat plan were considered. Shortly afterwards, Unwin left the meeting with the impression that his spur-of-the-moment idea had been discarded. And so it almost certainly would have been but for the timely arrival of 'Rosy' Wemyss. On asking what the meeting had decided, he was told of Unwin's extraordinary suggestion and listened intently as the arguments against were laid before him. By the end, he was left in no doubt that 'the Staff did not view the proposal favourably'.[26]

Wemyss, however, thought differently. He liked the idea. It struck him as something 'reminiscent of the wooden horse of Troy'[27] and it appealed both to the pragmatist and the romantic in him. As he later explained:

> I was at once attracted by the promise it held out of overcoming the disadvantage under which we were labouring from, the shortage of boats for landing sufficiently large numbers of men at one time. Further examination convinced me that the risk of the ship being sunk was not so great as it appeared, and I was able to win over the military authorities to my views and the scheme was adopted with their full consent.[28]

Having thoroughly 'embraced' the concept, Wemyss was not slow in turning it into reality. Summoning a no doubt surprised Unwin to his office, he did not beat about the bush. The idea which the joint staffs appeared to scupper just a few hours earlier had, he explained, now been sanctioned at the highest level. And to the man whose brainchild it was, he gave *carte blanche* to 'take any ship I liked in the harbour and fit her out as I liked to carry out my scheme'.[29]

With no time to waste, Unwin immediately went in search of a 'suitable'[30] ship. What may have seemed a simple enough task in a harbour filled with merchant vessels of all shapes and sizes, proved anything but. His quest took him 'all over' before he finally found a ship that matched his particular requirements. It was, as he later remarked, the 'only ship'[31] in Mudros fitted with so-called 'tween decks that were a prerequisite for carrying 'the necessary number' of troops. The ship was British, though under charter to the French.

Her name was *River Clyde*.

Chapter 4

'The Dirtiest Ship I've Seen'

Midshipman George Drewry cast a critical eye over the steam tramp and was far from impressed. In fact, during five years spent cruising the world's oceans, he couldn't recall finding a single vessel in a worse state than the *River Clyde*. 'She was,' as he later wrote, 'the dirtiest ship I've seen.'[1]

Of medium height and powerfully built, Drewry was 'modest and charming'[2] with the kind of boyish good looks that made him seem even younger than his twenty years. Appearances in his case, however, were deceptive. His tender youth belied a rare mental and physical toughness. As an accident-prone youth growing up in Forest Gate, east London, he had survived being knocked over by a car and almost being swallowed up by a swamp. And his brushes with disaster had continued into his career as an apprentice in the Mercantile Service. On one occasion he had been rescued from heavy seas after falling from the main mast. Another time, he had survived among a group of castaways after being shipwrecked and marooned on a remote island off Cape Horn. In 1913, a year after his South Atlantic ordeal, he transferred as a fourth officer to the P&O Line, where his father was a senior manager, and joined the Royal Naval Reserve as a midshipman. The outbreak of war found him in Egypt, serving aboard the passenger ship Isis on the Brindisi–Port Said shuttle run. Called up immediately, he was posted to Malta and appointments aboard the guardship HMS *Egmont* and then the gunboat *Hussar*, where he quickly came under the spell of one Edward Unwin.

According to an officer who came to know him well, Drewry was 'devoted'[3] to his charismatic captain, which was just as well given his latest chore-like assignment. The youngster had been presented with thirty Greek labourers and tasked with the unenviable duty of cleaning out the *River Clyde*. It was a miserable prospect that would provide a different test of his powers of resilience, but for once Drewry had no one to blame but himself. Following the arrival of two new midshipmen in the *Hussar*, he had grown 'tired of doing nothing'.[4] He put up with it for a couple of days before asking Unwin for more work. 'Well,' he told his father, 'I got it with a vengeance.'[5]

Filthy beyond belief, the *River Clyde* also stank to high heaven. In a letter home, the youngster explained:

> She was in ballast and had just brought French mules up from Algiers. They had built boxes and floors in the 'tween decks and carried the mules there without worrying about sanitary arrangements.[6]

Selected by Unwin and formally purchased by the Admiralty on 12 April, the *River Clyde* may have seen better days, but appearances apart she was in sound working order. Built in the Glasgow Kingston yard of Russell & Co ten years earlier, she represented shipbroker Ormond Cook's first venture into ship-owning on behalf of his eponymous new company. There was nothing remotely pretty about her. Nor were there any especially distinguishing features. Weighing in at 3,913 tons gross, she measured a little under 345ft from stem to stern, was almost 50ft wide with a draught of about 18ft, and, on a good day, her engine room staff might coax 10 knots out of her. In short, she was typical of her type, a workaday steel screw tramp; stout, sturdy and built to last, with cavernous holds designed to maximise her cargo-carrying potential. Just the job, in fact, for what Unwin and Wemyss had in mind.

From her first voyage, bound for Yemen, Calcutta and Karachi with a cargo of Welsh coal, she had been steadily plodding the world's shipping lanes in more or less constant gainful employ. Her journey to Mudros was a circuitous one. The outbreak of war had found her in Japan en route to Sydney by way of Newcastle, New South Wales, and Adelaide. Leaving Australia, she then steamed north to Haiphong, a major sea port in what was then French Indochina, to collect a cargo bound for Marseilles, where she arrived, after a forty-two-day voyage, on 11 February. From then, until April, she had plied the Mediterranean, a British merchantman under charter to the French military. She still had around 100 tons of stores on board when Unwin found her and the French were initially reluctant to let her go. According to Unwin, the commissariat officer in charge 'objected to my taking her'[7] and it was only after an urgent appeal to the French admiral, Emile Guépratte, that she was handed over. That same night, under Unwin's direction, the stores were offloaded and at 9 am the following morning he took her alongside the naval repair ship, *Reliance*, 'to have her fitted out for her novel work'.[8]

Depending on your point of view, the conversion Unwin had in mind was either a classic piece of British improvisation or a crude and hurriedly executed bodge. In reality, it was probably a bit of both. The first task was to cut holes in the ship's hull 'large enough for a fully equipped man to pass through'.[9] There were to be eight holes in all, 'four on each side of the 'tween decks'.[10] These were known as 'sally ports' and the idea was that *River Clyde*'s 2,000-strong human cargo would pour out from these openings on to rope-slung platforms not much wider than a single man that Wemyss called 'galleries' and which led towards the bows before sloping down with the intention of joining a makeshift 'bridge of boats', comprising a flat-bottomed steam hopper and, depending on requirements, some specially decked wooden lighters that were to be towed alongside the *River Clyde* prior to being hauled into position in order to link ship to shore.

To Wemyss, Unwin later outlined the plan and the thinking behind it:

> My idea in using a ship was that I was able to fulfil the following very necessary conditions for a successful landing.
>
> 1 Get the men right on to the beach, in a sort of protected fort, with 12 maxims round my bows, able to keep off any rush tactics.
>
> 2 Carry in 700 tons of fresh water for immediate use and able to condense 100 tons a day …
>
> 3 Also [provide a shelter from where] I was able to treat the wounded and protect them till they could be sent off to the Hospital ship.
>
> My scheme for the disembarking was as follows:
>
> To tow in with me a self-propelled hopper and three wooden-decked lighters; the hopper I towed on the port side, the side furthest away from the Fort. She was fitted with a brow forward, to drop … as soon as she took the beach.
>
> She was towed by a 6-inch Manilla rope through a leading block at the derrick head, the derrick being guyed out, and the hopper abreast of No 2 hatch.
>
> The hopper could steam 6 knots and my idea was that when I

took the beach the hopper would continue my line, the acme of perfection being that her stern was under my stem. [However] as this was hardly to be expected I had the lighters to fill up the probable gap.[11]

The last point highlighted just one of a myriad of problems associated with Unwin's plan; namely, the critical shortage of detailed information about the shoreline on which the *River Clyde* was to be run aground. As Wemyss later acknowledged, 'We did not know how the beach shelved'[12] which meant that 'no exact calculations could be made'[13] as to how far short of the shore the so-called 'wreck ship' would strike the bottom. Hence the uncertainty as to how many boats or lighters would be needed to form the necessary landing 'bridge'.

Another difficulty with the conversion was, as Unwin himself admitted, a mistake of his own making. It involved the positioning of the 'sally ports', at least two of which he felt should have been cut 'right in the eyes' of the *River Clyde*, 'with a baulk of timber placed athwartships for the landing brows to rest on'.[14] This, he contended, 'would have saved me a lot of staging, though it would have made no difference to the result'.[15]

Such errors were almost inevitable given the limited resources and pressure of time available. Unwin would later state that in preparing the ship for her unorthodox mission he had been given 'every assistance' and had suffered 'no interference'[16] from senior officers. With the work, in his own words, 'fairly under weigh', he had asked and received Wemyss' permission to 'carry out the job myself'.[17] To architect and project manager of a plan without a template, he had, therefore, added the role of executive commander. But the freedom associated with sole control brought its own stresses. Left entirely alone to 'make or mar' the mission, Unwin had nowhere to hide from 'the awful responsibility'[18] that went with it. 'Any mistakes from beginning to end must be my load to carry,'[19] he wrote.

The strain was telling, as he candidly admitted:

> I have never spent such a time in my life as I did before the landing … for I wasn't just carrying out orders but carrying through a scheme of my own in which if I failed the consequences might be awful.
>
> The thousands of thoughts that flash through one's head at such a time as to what might happen and how to meet them, and top of it all, the wonder as to how one will behave one's self, as I don't believe any man is quite sure of himself.[20]

Self-doubts aside, the work on the *River Clyde* continued at a feverish pace. As naval engineers from the *Reliance* grappled with the heavy duty work, slicing man-sized doorways in the ship's steel hull, Midshipman Drewry and his Greek labourers toiled to make her fit to carry human beings. They broke up the mule boxes and cleared the stinking mess they left behind. The holds satisfactorily cleaned, Drewry then turned his attention to the exterior. 'A large port was cut on each side of each hatch in the 'tween decks,' he wrote, 'and from the No 2 ports I rigged stages right round the bow.'[21] As a final touch, he added his own homage to his and Unwin's old Mercantile Service employers by painting the ship's starboard side 'P&O colour'.[22] But such niceties could not disguise the strangeness of a ship which, with its weird girdle of engineering contraptions, looked more like something out of a Heath Robinson cartoon than the Navy's spearhead for the war's most ambitious amphibious operation.

Appearances were the last thing on Unwin's mind. With the refit well under way, his focus switched to finding a crew for his extraordinary enterprise. Given the likely hazards involved, his first port of call was perhaps a naïve one. He recalled:

> I fell the ship's company of the *River Clyde* in and told them what I was going to do with their ship and asked for volunteers, pointing out to them that they would never get such a chance again and that, as it was their ship, I gave them the first chance. The Captain of the ship immediately said, 'We will do all we can to help you prepare the ship but I don't think you can expect us to be there when the bricks begin to fly about'. There was no reply to this attitude so I went to my own ship and, of course, had plenty of volunteers.[23]

From these, he selected six seamen and six engine-room ratings, to whom Wemyss added some extra petty officers. *Hussar*'s engineer lieutenant, a man by the name of Patterson, was keen to join them, but Unwin, who was 'anxious to convert the *River Clyde*'s condensing plant into use for distilling [water] to the shore'[24] chose instead the ship's warrant engineer, William Rowntree Horend, on account of his experience with this kind of work. He also agreed to take the ship's carpenter together with an Irish naval surgeon by the name of Peter Burrowes Kelly and, as his second in command, he selected the young officer who, aside from himself, had worked longest and hardest to prepare the ship for its remarkable new role.

George Drewry was to share command responsibilities on the bridge during the approach to the peninsula before transferring shortly before the landing operation to the steam hopper *Argyle*, which was to be towed alongside. Normally used for carrying mud out to sea and dumping it in the ocean, this 150ft long, stub-nosed craft had become a key adjunct to the Cape Helles plan. The intention was that she would surge ahead of *River Clyde* the moment she grounded and help form Unwin's 'bridge' to the shore. It was a task for which her shallow draught – she drew barely 8 ft aft and almost nothing beneath her bow – rendered her eminently suitable. To that end engineers from *Reliance* had constructed in her bow a large, hinged drawbridge-like brow in readiness for lowering on to the beach. To assist him, Drewry had a crew of six Greek sailors who, according to Unwin, 'had begged to be allowed to come',[25] although he doubted 'if they quite realised what they were in for',[26] and a single Royal Naval Reserve seaman whose place among the *River Clyde* party had only been secured after the selection process.

George McKenzie Samson was a Scot from Carnoustie in Fife. Known to his friends as 'Geordie', he was, by his own admission, a man of 'a roving disposition'.[27] From working as a 'cowboy' in Argentina to whaling off Greenland, he claimed to have 'touched nearly every country in the world'.[28] In the process, he had managed to cram more adventure into his twenty-six years than most men manage in a lifetime. His last job, following spells in the Army and Merchant Navy, had taken him to Turkey and the port of Smyrna. There, he had been variously employed in a gas works and on the railways, in the course of which he had picked up more than a smattering of Greek and Turkish. In Mudros, where he had arrived in March as a member of *Hussar*'s crew, his linguistic skills had been much in demand. Over the course of the past month, he had served as interpreter to both Wemyss and Unwin in their dealings with the local population. And it was that talent which very nearly cost him a place in *River Clyde*, as he later recounted:

> Of course, it was … well in the wind about the projected landing, and there were many rumours flying about as to what we were going to do. It so happened that on the very evening on which preparations were set in motion for what proved to be one of the greatest enterprises of the war that I was sent ashore to transact certain business for the ship.
>
> I was a good time ashore, and I can assure that I should not have been so long had I known of the important matter that was then being settled on the Hussar, which became a kind of flagship. When I returned there was an unusual buzz of excitement on the ship, and before many moments had elapsed I realised that there was 'something doing'.

'What d'ye think, George?' said one of my pals. 'Commander Unwin has been asking for volunteers to run the *River Clyde* ashore.

''And I've missed a chance,' I said despondently.

'Ay,' responded my chum, 'a good many of us will miss a chance, because every man aboard the *Hussar* volunteered, and you know, George, we can't all go.'

'I suppose men have been picked?' I said.

'Yes, they are all picked,' replied my pal.[29]

Samson, however, was not a man to give up without a fight. Aggrieved at being, as he saw it, unjustly overlooked, he confronted Unwin in his cabin:

I … complained that I had not been given the chance … as I thought, considering the work I had been doing, I should have got the first refusal.

'Who said you weren't going?' asked the Commander.

'I have been told that I could not go, as I was needed by the Admiral,' I replied.

'But who's to talk to the Greeks in the hopper if you don't come? None of us can speak Greek. Let's go and see the Admiral.'

Well, to the Admiral we went. When I was taken before him he asked me if I really wanted to go with *River Clyde*. I said I did, as I thought I should get the [first] refusal after … the work I had been doing.

'Don't forget,' said Rear-Admiral Wemyss, that you are not going on a picnic. There are 18 [*sic*] of my men going on the steamer and if one of them returns alive I shall congratulate myself.'

When I heard them trying to discourage me from going that made me all the more determined … I told them that I wished to go. So I got my way.[30]

In another newspaper interview, Samson gave a different version in which Wemyss barely featured at all. Instead, Unwin, who he said was initially reluctant to let him go on account of his usefulness aboard *Hussar*, had taken the decision alone only after being persuaded that he was 'game for anything'.[31] In this version, Wemyss had then addressed all those 'specially picked'[32] for the operation and told them 'in very plain language that we were not going on a picnic [and] that the man who went through it all would be very lucky'.[33] Even allowing for an understandable embroidering of the yarn, there was no mistaking his resolve. And he was not the only one desperate to play a part.

Like 'Geordie' Samson, William Williams, a thirty-four-year-old reservist from Shropshire was disappointed to find himself ignored by Unwin. A veteran of almost fifteen years' service that included campaigns in South Africa and China, he had found it difficult to settle back into civilian life. He had tried factory work and served as a policeman in the Monmouthshire Constabulary, before going back to sea as a merchant seaman. Recalled to the Royal Navy within a month of the outbreak of war, he was serving as a leading seaman in *Hussar* by the end of September 1914. With all his wealth of experience, he evidently felt better equipped than most for the mission Unwin had in mind and he was not prepared to let the matter rest there.

According to Unwin, Williams

> ... came up to me and asked if he couldn't come. I told him I was full up, and I didn't want any more POs [petty officers], to which he replied, 'I'll chuck my hook if you will let me come' [naval parlance for discarding his badge and accepting a drop in rank]. And I did, to his cost and everlasting glory ...[34]

Even then, *River Clyde*'s complement was not quite complete. A few days later, several members of the original ship's crew approached Unwin and asked if they could join him. They told him that their captain had rejected his call for volunteers 'without consulting them'.[35] Although Unwin accepted they were telling the truth, he said he had no choice but to turn them down. 'It was too late then,' he wrote, 'as I [had] promised my fellows.'[36] Unwin did, however, make one exception. He agreed to take the ship's steward, who, though the brother of the *River Clyde*'s captain, apparently possessed, according to Unwin's harsh remark, 'more guts than his brother'.[37] It was a decision he never regretted. 'We all found him most useful,' he later wrote, 'and nobody stood the shelling better than he did.'[38]

In addition, there were fifty men and four officers from one of the expeditionary force's more eccentric entries on the 'Order of Battle'. Volunteers to a man, they belonged to No 3 Squadron, Royal Naval Armoured Car Division. Their very presence in Mudros represented something of a military absurdity that owed everything to a shameless piece of political string-pulling by their commanding officer, the absentee Member of Parliament for Newcastle-under-Lyme and a man of considerable charm and influence, not to mention great wealth.

Chapter 5

'A Splendid Crowd'

Josiah Clement Wedgwood cut a forlorn and frustrated figure. The opportunity he so desperately craved was tantalisingly close; near enough for him to have heard the dull rumble of gunfire and seen an enemy searchlight making its nightly sweep of the entrance to the Dardanelles. Yet such were the diminishing prospects of being able to lead his armoured cars into action on the shores of Gallipoli, it might as well have been a million miles away. As 13 April dawned in the crowded anchorage of Mudros there was not a ship nor another unit that seemed more out of place or its presence more ridiculous than No 3 Squadron, Royal Naval Armoured Car Division.

A day or so earlier one of his officers, his close friend and fellow MP, the Honourable Francis McLaren, had bumped into Sir Ian Hamilton aboard the *Arcadian*. Ever the lobbyist, he could not resist a personal appeal on Wedgwood's behalf for a part to play in the imminent landings. Hamilton, who was in mellow mood following a walk on the island, 'promised to help us all he could'. However, there was no disguising the difficulty. McLaren noted:

> He pointed out of course what is obvious to everybody and makes us rather a laughing stock – that for the Gallipoli campaign armoured cars are absurd. Conditions are so rough that they cannot even use cavalry, or any form of wheel transport. What then of our fate?[1]

What indeed. So far as McLaren could see there were only two options: to land in Gallipoli 'on our feet and use our machine guns to help the Army' or 'to find another job'.[2] His solution was to try both. Wedgwood, on the other hand, was determined on making one last effort to find a role for him and his men. His plan was to split his force, offering, as

47

McLaren put it, 'some of our men and guns to the General'[3] while leaving the drivers and mechanics with their cars. Preparations were made to present his idea to Sir Ian's Staff and, on 13 April, Wedgwood, McLaren and Sub Lieutenant, the Honourable Arthur Coke, set out in a cutter to deliver his proposal. However, part way across the bay another storm blew in and the sea, in McLaren's words, 'was so rough that we had to turn back'.[4] Even the weather, it seemed, was against him …

Josiah Wedgwood was an unusual commander in charge of an unusual force. Hamilton hardly knew what to make of him. Describing him as 'a mighty queer chap'[5], he was frankly bemused by his apparent contradictions:

> Took active part in the South African War. Afterwards became a pacifist MP; here he is again with war paint and tomahawk. Give me a Pacifist in peace and a Jingo in war. Too often it is the other way about.[6]

At forty-two and a parliamentarian of nine years' standing, Wedgwood was of an age and a position that might have reasonably precluded his active participation in the war. But the notion of standing idly by while his countrymen fought and died was anathema to him. Fourteen years earlier he had volunteered to fight the Boers as a captain in the Royal Field Artillery. Back then, he had been motivated by an 'exasperated patriotism'.[7] Now it was a conviction of a different kind that compelled him to act, as he explained to his North Staffordshire constituents:

> Liberals, like myself, love liberty. It is a passion: I cannot explain it. 'You cannot argue with the choice of the soul' … It has to be done.[8]

Principles apart, the war was also, as he later admitted, a 'blessed distraction'[9] from the pain caused by the break-up of his marriage the previous year. After months spent floundering and rudderless, Wedgwood had a new sense of purpose and a cause into which he could pour himself, life and soul. Within weeks of the outbreak of war, he had, with the connivance of his friend, Churchill, secured a commission as lieutenant commander in the Royal Naval Volunteer Reserve. A fortnight's hurried training then followed before his departure to France en route to Belgium and an ill-starred attempt to forestall the fall of Antwerp. Amid the chaos of defeat and retreat, Wedgwood found himself commanding half a dozen Wolseley armoured cars. Short-lived though it was, the experience lasted long enough to convince him of the vehicles' potential.

Ordered to return to England, he was given the task of raising and training new armoured car squadrons at Wormwood Scrubs. He brought with him fellow MP Francis McLaren, who he had met, by chance, on his way home. McLaren was returning after a spell working as a non-combatant volunteer, ferrying senior officers around in his Rolls-Royce. At Ostend, both MP and automobile were, in Wedgwood's words, 'peacefully annexed'.[10]

Together, they spent the next month recruiting, drilling and organising four new squadrons. Among the volunteers rallying to the cause were a host of friends and relatives, including Wedgwood's eldest son, Charles, who arrived following a spell in the ranks of the 5th North Staffordshire Regiment and a cousin, Charles Murray, together with a contingent from McLaren's Spalding constituency. Another to join them was Arthur Coke. The thirty-two-year-old second son of the 3rd Earl of Leicester, he had served in the Royal Navy as a midshipman and, more recently, as a cavalryman consigned by heavy losses among the infantry to manning the waterlogged trenches around Ypres. There, he had read with envy the newspaper reports extolling the exploits of a force of armoured cars ranging across Belgium. With a spell of leave beckoning and the prospect of prolonged inactivity, he decided to apply for a transfer to the Navy's motorised unit, explaining:

> I hear they have the greatest sport in every way. They get a lot of exciting fighting, which is better than sitting in these infernal trenches. I am afraid all the exciting work of the cavalry is over and I see nothing ahead except trench work and I defy anyone to enjoy that however much he tries.[11]

Coke reached England on leave on 6 December and by the end of the month the cavalry subaltern had become a sub-lieutenant in the Royal Naval Volunteer Reserve, attached to the armoured car division.

By then, Wedgwood's No 3 Squadron was equipped with new, purpose-built Rolls-Royce armoured cars complete with revolving turrets. For the next two months, they 'exercised and experimented'[12] day and night, first at Henley-on-Thames and then, alongside combined forces, in Norfolk, where the 'sham fights ... were always completely upset by the appearance of the cars in impossible places faced by yeomanry mounted in close order'.[13]

For Coke, the posting to Norfolk represented a homecoming that Wedgwood exploited by making the family's Holkham estate his base. Scarcely less at home in their palladian setting was Francis McLaren. The Old Etonian younger son of the 1st Baron Aberconway, McLaren was described by Wedgwood as having 'the manners and bearing of a Prince of the Blood':[14]

> He was Apollo Belvedere in form, and the Earl of Chesterfield in serenity. Always he got what he wanted, and expected to get it as of right. He always behaved to me as a son to an indulgent father ... and I wished he were my son. But he and Coke and Sir Roger Wernher were three most inveterate gamblers, while Francis alone had the means to pay.
>
> 'I took £600 off Edwin (Montagu) last night!' he would say, on being chid for being late on parade. His wife, Barbara, and Hermione Coke came down to stay at Holkham, but that was no restraint.[15]

And to high spirits were added even higher ambition. Thirsting for action and the opportunity to put their training to some use, Wedgwood and McLaren brought their considerable powers of influence to bear on their friends in high places. Wedgwood had urged they be sent to help in the subjugation of German South-West Africa. When that failed, he appealed to Churchill to send them to France. Writing to the First Lord of the Admiralty from Holkham on 19 February 1915, he declared:

> It would be too awful if we lost that chance too and were left here ... Please don't leave me in this country now. The Squadron will mutiny, which I ignore, but I myself should be seriously incommoded – and I do want to get at them again.[16]

Frustratingly for Wedgwood and his junior thrusters, the French venture went the way of his South African proposal, but he did not give up. Together with McLaren, he mounted a two-pronged attack – 'Francis, ever at the Prime Minister ... I, ever at Churchill'. The incessant lobbying paid off. In March, wrote Wedgwood, the Admiralty was 'induced ... to send us to Gallipoli'.[17]

As Wedgwood led his force aboard the SS *Inkosi* at Plymouth, his only orders were to report to Sir Ian Hamilton at Lemnos for further instructions. Rumours, however, abounded. 'According to Francis,' wrote Wedgwood, 'the intention was to send us through the Dardanelles to land at Constantinople, and roll up to Vienna, 'getting at their soft side', as it was expressed.'[18]

Over the course of the next ten days, the 'rascals and comics'[19] of the armoured car squadron whiled away the hours playing card games and deck cricket against the so-called 'flying birds'[20] of No 3 Squadron,

Royal Naval Air Service, who were sharing the ship with them. Reaching Lemnos via Malta on 1 April, Wedgwood went ashore to discover that Sir Ian Hamilton was in Egypt. Having met briefly with Admiral Wemyss, who was 'pink with rage because a German Taube had the cheek to fly over the harbour that morning'[21] he departed for Tenedos to drop off the airmen, still none the wiser as to his mission. A further week was passed uncomfortably, riding out a storm, before returning in search of a role. Even after meeting with Sir Ian, however, the prospects did not appear good, but Wedgwood refused to be defeated. While McLaren worried about being stuck in Lemnos, 'doing nothing and perhaps returning to England without seeing a shot fired',[22] Wedgwood set about preparing his men for working their Maxim guns 'on their flat feet'.[23] The next few days were spent hardening up the men for whatever opportunity might come their way. Whenever the weather permitted, boats ferried the men ashore for route marches and general exercises, but with no obvious sign of employment in sight there remained an air of unreality about it all. As McLaren sought distraction in a local restaurant's 'very wonderful onion omelette and delicious stewed lamb and artichokes'[24] and amused himself watching a fellow officer 'smoking a great bubbly hookah'[25] Wedgwood's son, Charles, was left pondering the natural splendour all around. The magnificent scenes, he told his sister in a letter written from the deck of the *Inkosi* would stay with him as inspiration for paintings when time allowed:

> I am, as I write, facing another beautiful sunset, not red that tells of war, but yellow and gold, a deep blue sea and purple hills that tell of happier time and in the distance is the music from one of the many bands belonging to a transport. The sun has set, it is growing cold and dark and already the ships are flickering Morse to one another.[26]

They had already spent four days 'awaiting our Fate'[27] as Charles put it, and frustration was growing. The aborted attempt by Wedgwood to have his case heard on 13 April was the final straw for McLaren. The day before he had wangled a place on the *Queen Elizabeth* as she undertook 'steam trials' off the peninsula:

> It was the most interesting day I had ever had. The trials were rather a bluff and the real object was to take Sir Ian and his Staff-officers to look at the coast, choose the landing place and settle final plans. We spent the morning in the gun turrets, conning-tower, range finder place, engine-room; all the while the ship dashing through the sea at

24 knots. When we got to the mouth of the Dardanelles all khaki officers had to hide behind canvas screens. The General and the Admiral were on the bridge, and as that seemed the best place, I went there too. I had a good pair of glasses and a man on the Admiral's staff showed me what to look at. We got within 2,000 yards of the round forts and could clearly see two of the knocked-out guns pointing drunkenly up in the air. The masonry is in an awful mess, and the villages on the Asiatic side are in ruins. The Admiral showed us a little mound on the coast which is Achilles' tomb. The Turks mounted an anti-aircraft gun on top of it, and a few days ago we had to destroy it. After nosing a little about the entrance, we set out to have a look for a landing-place on the top side of the Gallipoli coast. We kept extraordinarily close inshore and got an excellent idea of the beach, contour, cover, etc. I could see their trenches without even using glasses. Our guns were cleared for action. There was great excitement when … we saw the smoke of a Turkish steamer. I thought they were going to let off a 15-inch gun at her over the neck of land, but finally they decided that without supporting aircraft the odds against hitting were too great to be worth the cost of the shell. I can at any rate claim, however, that I have been under fire, for on the way back they loosed off three shots at us. The range was perfect, but unluckily for them the 'Queen Elizabeth' was going astern at the time and they had made the allowance for her going ahead, so the shot fell nowhere near. A lucky shell might have wiped out the whole of the Admiral and General Staffs![28]

The sight of enemy trenches and wrecked guns lining the shore was intoxicating and left him more than ever determined to be a participant in an operation which he felt promised to be 'a 'hell' of an affair'.[29] To that end, he persuaded Wedgwood to let him go as an 'observing officer' in HMS *Doris*, which he thought 'certain, as an old second-class cruiser, to cover the landing'.[30] He might have found a berth in the flagship, but aside from being 'unpleasantly crowded', he thought the chances were greater of seeing 'more of the fighting from an old ship than from one so precious as the 'Queen Elizabeth'.'[31] It was, as he admitted, 'all rather a gamble'[32] but the odds of seeing action with his armoured cars seemed a good deal longer. According to McLaren, Wedgwood was now of the opinion that 'our guns won't be used'.[33] His mind made up, he justified his temporary transfer in a letter home written on 13 April:

> The landing of the troops I think will be one of the most exciting events in the whole war, and I wasn't going to be left at Lemnos in charge of a lot of temporarily useless cars while it was going on.[34]

Before departing, Wedgwood further indulged his senior subaltern by promising to send him a message 'if they are landed',[35] so that he might rejoin them.

McLaren's impatience would cost him dear. In one of the campaign's supreme ironies, the unit without a purpose and which was apparently surplus to Sir Ian's requirements was about to be elevated to a leading role in the most dramatic of all the landing operations. Quite how the change of fortune came about is not entirely clear, with witnesses offering conflicting accounts.

According to the unit's Irish medical officer, Peter Burrowes Kelly, it came about as a result of a chance encounter between Arthur Coke and an old shipmate, who was then serving as Admiral Wemyss' flag lieutenant:

> He told us ... how the *River Clyde* was to be run ashore ... We volunteered there and then, but that was no good, as only a doctor and small guns were wanted. I was not on for going without the other two [sic] if it could be helped. We saw Commander Unwin the following day. He looked us up and down, as only he could, asked me who I was, and if I was prepared to go with him to death or glory. I said 'yes'. He asked Arthur ditto and he said, 'I like you, Coke. You look the man for me, come and bring your guns'.[36]

However, Coke's version of events was significantly different and his rendering a good deal less colourful if no less enthusiastic. In a letter to his wife, he explained:

> The day before yesterday the General told us that he did not think he would want us for at least a month, which was very disheartening, so yesterday Wedgwood and myself went to see him again to offer our services in any capacity ... He said he wanted some marines to man the first Troopship [sic] that land[s]. Isn't it splendid, we have got the job.[37]

Through a combination of perseverance and good fortune, Wedgwood had contrived to gain a place for his unit in the vanguard of the assault. Its task, in Coke's succinct account, was 'to cover the landing of the first troops'[38] with machine gun fire from eight sandbag and steel-plated casemates which they were to construct themselves around the forecastle, on the bridge and all along the port side of the *River Clyde*. The precise number of men and guns involved is a matter of some conjecture. Coke wrote of four officers and forty men taking ten Maxims between them. Unwin, meanwhile, referred to twelve guns, with Drewry and Wedgwood's son putting the figure at eleven. Having called for volunteers, Wedgwood, himself, claimed to have selected three officers to accompany him, together with fifty men, amounting to about half the squadron. In addition, he decided to take eighteen motor cycles to enable them to 'run our guns, or other people's ammunition up to Krithia if all goes well'.[39]

In the absence of McLaren, the officers chosen were: Sub Lieutenants Coke, Charles Parkes and Douglas Illingworth. Those in the ranks included Wedgwood's great friend, Chief Petty Officer Jack Little, a master of hounds from Berwickshire who had two sons serving in the Army and was 'rising fifty', his cousin and petty officer, Charles Murray and a nephew of the novelist Erskine Childers. They were to be spread among four gun positions. Marked out on a sketch plan drawn by Coke and sent to his wife, they included a post with three Maxims under Illingworth sited aft, a similar one under Parkes further forward and a solitary gun on the bridge's port wing where Wedgwood was to be stationed. Most prominent of all, however, was the three-gun shelter on the ship's forecastle that, to Coke's great delight, he was to take charge.

The one-time cavalry subaltern and two-times naval officer could hardly contain his excitement. 'This is to be my seat in the stalls,' he told Wedgwood, 'and many a man now in England would give £1,000 for it.'[40] To his wife, he added:

> I believe we can land quite close in, like at the place in Norfolk [a reference to his family's seat at Holkham Hall close to the broad beaches of the north Norfolk coast]. I cannot think of anything more exciting. Also, we shall see the whole thing. We shall have the fleet behind us, so if the Turks do shell us I don't think it will be for long, although she is a pretty big target … I hear that there are to be 102 Transports here before we start and what with the battleships and colliers, etc, it will really be a marvellous sight. I believe we start the landing this week. I think it will be a short but sharp fight to take Gallipoli.[41]

After all the uncertainty, the effect on the 'mechanics' assigned to build and man the shipboard fortifications was electrifying. Morale soared.

According to Wedgwood, his volunteers, busily constructing casemates and lining the bridge 'with boiler plate and leaky sand-bags'[42] were 'as happy as princes at the chances of a hot fight'.[43]

Unwin was no less impressed. Though politically poles apart from Wedgwood, he could not fault him or any of his 'splendid crowd' of men. 'Whatever he may be in the House of Commons,' he wrote, 'he's a very gallant fellow and ran his show splendidly.'[44]

In the midst of it all, Wedgwood also found time to honour the promise made to his subaltern in absentia. His note reached McLaren at Skyros on 16 April, but the news was not enough to convince him to hurry back to Lemnos and the *River Clyde*:

> I think the show I am in will prove to be the best and most dramatic of all. I don't see what good Wedgwood imagines guns will be as they won't have a target, but will be battered by artillery fire.[45]

Misguided or not, the scene was set. Now it was time for the troops, who were to take centre stage, to make their first appearance aboard the ship with which they would forever be associated.

Chapter 6

'A Place I Mayn't Mention'

There was an air of excitement in Mudros harbour as day broke fresh and cloudless on 17 April. Hundreds of troops lined the decks of the closely packed transports in eager anticipation of their first glimpse of the so-called 'wreck ship' that had transformed the landing plan and, perhaps, with it, their chances of survival. Among those patiently waiting on the *Ausonia* for the boats that would ferry them to the *River Clyde* was Lieutenant George Davidson. A medical graduate of the University of Aberdeen, he was in charge of a contingent of Scottish territorial stretcher bearers from B Section, 89th (1st Highland) Field Ambulance. In his diary, he noted:

> Had breakfast at six, paraded at seven and stood on deck till 10.45 waiting our turn to cross to a collier that is to be used in the Gallipoli attack. The intention is to run her ashore at full speed, ploughing into the sands, when her load of 2,000 men are to get overboard as best they can on to floating gangways. By a long circuitous route, we all got into our places, and were packed close on the various decks which have had large square openings cut through the iron plates of the sides of the ship, and from these and the upper deck we have to decamp as quickly as possible ...[1]

Their introduction to the ship that would carry them to the shores of Gallipoli was as momentous as it was welcome and signalled a dramatic end to a week of uncertainty about a mission grown ever more hazardous.

The first transports carrying the troops of the 29th Division had begun arriving in Lemnos from Egypt on 10 April They were led by two ships in which were the bulk of the 86th Brigade: the *Ausonia* with the 1st Royal Dublin Fusiliers (less its horses and transport), 89th Field

Ambulance and 1/1st (West Riding) Field Company and the *Caledonia* with the 1st Royal Munster Fusiliers, 1st Lancashire Fusiliers and Anson Battalion, detached from the Royal Naval Division to provide beach and fatigue parties. A third vessel, the *Aragon*, carrying the 2nd Hampshires, 4th Worcestershires, 88th Field Ambulance and 88th Brigade Headquarters, entered the outer harbour three days later.

The crowded bay and encampments swarming with soldiers combined with the grandeur of the setting to leave a lasting impression. Writing from 'a place I mayn't mention'[2] in a boat that he hoped would 'eventually take us to Constantinople',[3] Lieutenant Guy Nightingale of the Munsters told his mother:

> This place is most extraordinarily interesting. There are about 100 enormous Atlantic liners of every description and the whole Allied Fleet – to say nothing of seaplanes, balloons and submarines. The *Queen Elizabeth* is a magnificent ship. We see a great deal of her as we are working with her. I had no idea she was such a fine ship … The whole place here is full of troops –Australian, Canadian [*sic*], French, Russian and ourselves …[4]

Captain Walford, the gunner turned staff officer, was no less impressed. Writing to his wife from aboard the *Andania* on 13 April, he commented:

> Here we are in … another harbour, waiting to collect ourselves before we make our dart. It is a great big place, surrounded by bare green hills, with one or two little villages scattered about. We came in yesterday morning, a lovely day, with a bright sun on the water and dark shadows on the hills, past rows of battleships lying at anchor, British, French and one Russian. Behind him were rows and rows of transports, our own and the Australians, and outside them, close inshore, was a swarm of small craft, mine-sweepers and so on …[5]

The wide-eyed awe was equalled only by the rush to get ready for the landings that were only a matter of a few days away, days in which the hazards facing the invasion force would only multiply. As Walford remarked:

> We are waiting for the rest of the Force to join up, and meanwhile are very busy discussing schemes and making preparations.
> A great deal depends on what support the Navy can give us from the sea, as owing to their having already given the Turks notice, there will be no chance of a surprise and consequently no possibility

of landing guns or horses until our infantry have made good several miles of ground. The guns of the ships will, therefore, be the only artillery supporting our attack for some time after landing, and it will be interesting to see how they shoot over-land.[6]

The arrival of the advance guard of the 29th Division coincided with the return to Mudros of the Expeditionary Force's GHQ Staff and the beginning of a fevered rush to complete final preparations for the assault on Gallipoli. They were initiated on 10 April by the arrival from Egypt of the first transports laden with troops. Hamilton spent three hours with De Robeck, Keyes and Wemyss, outlining the draft plan he had agreed in principle with his own staff almost three weeks earlier. Buoyed by their enthusiastic approval, Hamilton dictated a letter to Kitchener:

The more I ponder over the map and consider the character, numbers and position of the enemy, the more I am convinced that the very essence of success must lie in upsetting the equilibrium of the Turk by the most rapid deployment of force possible over a fairly wide extent of country, combined with feints where troops and launches cannot be spared for an actual serious landing.

My main reliance will be on the 29th Division, the covering force of which will be landed at dawn at Sedd-el-Bahr, Cape Helles and, DV, in Morto Bay. I put in a special 'DV' to the Morto Bay project because the transports there will be under fire from the other side [Asiatic shore], and whether they can stick it or not is rather a question. Still, they must try. Also, no doubt, they will be under long range fire from field guns and perhaps howitzers from behind Achi Babi [sic]. To help these fellows along, subsidiary landings in boats will be made along the coast in small groups from Tekke Barnu [sic] up to opposite Crithia [sic]. Even a few men able to scramble up these cliffs should shake the first line of defence which stretches from Old Castle northwards to the coast. The Australians meanwhile will make a strong feint which will, I hope, develop into a serious landing operation north of Gaba Tepe. Braithwaite has marked out a good circular holding position, stretching from about Fisherman's Hut round to Gaba Tepe, and if they can maintain themselves there, I should hope later on they may be able to make a push forward to Koja Dere.

Whatever this does, it will tend to raise anxieties in the minds of the men opposed to the 29th Division, and will prevent the plateau being reinforced. I fear one must expect casualties from guns in concealed positions, both on the sea and whilst this is being done. But that is part of the hardness of the nut. Meanwhile, the Naval Division will move up and make a simultaneous feint somewhere opposite Bulair, which will keep the Gallipoli people on tenterhooks at least for a time.

These are my plans in broad outline. I do not want to talk about the difficulties, for I try to keep my mind fixed on my own objective, feeling sure that if I can stick to that and carry it through with vigour, the enemy will not be able to do all the wonderful things which theorists might expect. Anyway, as to that, the result is, in your favourite phrase, on the knees of the Gods ...[7]

Ideally, Hamilton would have preferred to land his entire force in a single 'hammer stroke',

with the fullest violence of its mass effect – as close as I can to my objective, the Kilid Bahr plateau. But, apart from lack of small craft, the thing cannot be done; the beach space is so cramped that the men and their stores could not be put ashore. I have to separate my forces and the effect of momentum, which cannot be produced by cohesion, must be reproduced by the simultaneous nature of the movement.[8]

His object was to wrong foot the enemy, which, though 'fully warned'[9] of their intentions, could not yet be sure as to where they might actually land. By staging a string of landings, some of those diversions that had yet to be fully worked out, he hoped to make sure the German and Turkish commanders were 'unable to concentrate either his mind or his men against us'.[10] Based on the assumption that they 'could not hope to be strong everywhere',[11] Hamilton believed there was 'every prospect of breaking down local opposition and gaining his objectives before the enemy's reserves could intervene'.[12]

Such a bold rush against 'selected points'[13] ought, he thought, 'to rattle the enemy however imperturbable may be his nature and whatever he knows about us'.[14] In a subsequent account of the discussions with De Robeck, Keyes and Wemyss, Hamilton sought to explain his thinking:

Prudence here is entirely out of place. There will be and can be no reconnaissance, no half measures, no tentatives. Several cautious proposals have been set before me but this is neither the time nor the place for paddling about the shore putting one foot on to the beaches with the idea of drawing it back again if it happens to alight upon a land mine. No; we've got to take good run at the Peninsula and jump plump on – both feet together. At a given moment we must plunge and stake everything on the one hazard.[15]

And nowhere did that 'hazard' appear greater than at Sedd-el-Bahr. Any illusions Hamilton may have had for an easy landing on the southernmost tip of the peninsula had been well and truly shattered by the frank assessments passed to him by the leaders of a Royal Marine raiding party that had very nearly been cut off by well-organised Turkish defenders a month earlier. Listening to their verbal accounts in Egypt, he realised for the first time that the notion which might have been gleaned from naval reports of the area around Sedd-el-Bahr being free of enemy troops was 'quite mistaken'.[16] He told Kitchener:

> There are lots of Turks right down within a few yards of the water's edge at the very point itself. Just at the village there, the first houses are empty, being open to the fire of the Fleet, but the others are quite defiladed by the ground and are occupied.[17]

It was against this most daunting of all the enemy beaches that Hamilton planned to employ his best-trained division. The 29th Division was, as he put it, the 'backbone'[18] of his Gallipoli enterprise. It would form the spearhead for the main thrust and at its tip would be a so-called Covering Force made up of regular, territorial and volunteer units. First mention of the 'force' destined to lead the assault at Cape Helles came in a GHQ order to 29th Division on 1 April. It instructed Hunter-Weston,

> to find a Covering Force, to be embarked in three ships, [comprising] of [an] Infantry Brigade, 1 Field Company and 1 Bearer Sub division Field Ambulance, together with a Beach Party of 1 Field Company and about 200 others. These latter with fatigue parties for the beach are to be formed from the Anson Battalion, RN Division which is attached to the Division for this purpose.[19]

The order further stated that the force was to land 'without Transport, carrying by hand all machine guns and entrenching tools together with three days iron rations'.[20] The infantry was to carry '200 rounds per rifle, and a reserve of 150 rounds per rifle and gun landed, together with 7 days rations'.[21] Forage 'for the whole' was to be landed 'as soon as possible'.[22] No blankets or baggage was to be taken in the first wave, nor any supply sections.

Over time, as more landings and feints were added to the initial plan, the size of the Covering Force would come to number more than 8,000 men spread across five separate landings, but the original composition was much smaller. It consisted of three infantry battalions, the 1st Royal Munster Fusiliers, the 1st Royal Dublin Fusiliers and the 1st Lancashire Fusiliers, which made up Brigadier General Steuart Hare's 86th (Fusilier) Brigade, the 1/1st (West Riding) Field Company, Royal Engineers, a section of the 2nd (London) Field Company and three subdivisions of stretcher bearers from 89th Field Ambulance, Royal Army Medical Corps. According to Guy Nightingale, the infantry battalions selected to be 'the first 3 regiments to [in] the British Force to land on Turkish soil' had been deliberately chosen as 'being the senior Brigade'.[23] If true, it was an honour that would prove a mixed blessing.

With his misplaced faith in the effectiveness of naval support, Brigadier General Hare was possibly alone among his force in believing the Turkish beach defences on the peninsula would be easily overcome:

> They have made it very strong all-round the extreme end but I don't see how they can hold it in the face of the bombardment. Here the sailors will be shooting at what they can see. I do not anticipate much opposition to the actual landing except from long range artillery fire. It will be in our further advance that we shall catch it.[24]

Even Hunter-Weston appeared to have thrown all caution to the wind. As the plans took shape, the executive commander of the southernmost landings seemed to Hamilton a man 'transformed'.[25] Following a meeting on board *Arcadian* on 14 April, Hamilton thought he had 'become the most sanguine of us all', adding:

> He has great hopes that we shall have Achi Baba in our hands by sunset on the day of landing. If so he thinks we need have no fear for the future.[26]

However, not all among the Covering Force shared their commanders' confidence. The historian of the 2nd Hampshires, a unit from the 88th Brigade that was added to the Cape Helles Order of Battle, regarded the plan as hopelessly 'over-optimistic'.[27] In an highly critical appraisal of Hamilton's landing scheme, C. T. Atkinson stated:

> The covering force could hardly be expected both to secure the necessary foothold ashore and to play a major part in the subsequent advance; too small a reserve was left to exploit any opening that

might be made; while the probability of serious casualties in getting ashore, a difficult task even in face of quite slight opposition, had hardly been appreciated; open boats crowded with men afford machine guns and riflemen ideal targets and even a few well-placed and well-concealed defenders might do incalculable damage.[28]

Atkinson considered such flaws 'should have been foreseen'[29] by the expedition's leaders. They certainly were by members of the Covering Force, many of whom came to view the initial landing plan with a morbid pessimism. As they rehearsed being towed and rowed towards a hostile shore, men spoke of the coming trial as likely to be 'a most bloody affair'[30] or a 'bloody errand'.[31] And their bleak predictions were given extra weight by a message from Lord Kitchener warning them to expect 'great hardships and great sacrifices'.[32]

Most troubling of all the landing operations was the Cape Helles enterprise. There, where the enemy's defences were strongest and an assault most certainly anticipated, Hamilton had favoured a pre-dawn strike under cover of darkness. But, following further discussions, he had bowed to Hunter-Weston, who, backed by the Navy, was 'clear and strong'[33] for a daylight landing. Reasoning that the current around the point was very strong and the lie of the beaches not precisely known, Hunter-Weston said he would 'rather face the losses the men in boats must suffer from aimed fire'[34] than risk the aggravated confusion of a night landing.

Particularly concerning was the forest of barbed wire sprouting up along the landing beaches and on the ground between. Writing to Lord Kitchener on 15 April, three days after a further survey of the shoreline from the bridge of the *Queen Elizabeth*, Hamilton reported how the whole of the terrain from half a mile north-east of Tekke Burnu to the walls of the Old Castle was 'a network of successive lines of 6 foot high entanglements',[35] most of which had only recently been constructed. Given that a number of officers from the Covering Force had travelled aboard *Queen Elizabeth* and seen the scale of enemy preparedness with their own eyes, it was not surprising that talk of a bloodbath should have spread.

Aboard the *Ausonia*, George Davidson gathered from listening to officers of the Dublins that 'a very warm reception … is expected'.[36] In his diary entry for 12 April, he noted:

> Several of the officers on our ship visited the *Queen Elizabeth* yesterday and returned with very alarming reports. This boat, having many times taken part in bombarding the Dardanelles Forts, has a good idea of what awaits us. They say the whole of Gallipoli

swarms with Turks, and the whole coast is covered with trenches and barbed wire entanglements 6 feet high. They talk as if it meant absolute annihilation of our small covering force of about 5,000 … It is very evident every man I have spoken to has practically no hope of ever returning. They expect our landing cutters to be well peppered with shot and shell, and in our practice today we had to appear with the straps of all our equipment outside our shoulder straps, and the ends of our belts free, ready to whip open and get rid of it at a moment's notice. I noticed that all our officers were unusually quiet and serious last night …[37]

To some the mood was beyond sombre. The Rev Henry Foster, serving as a chaplain in the Royal Naval Division, recalled two subalterns from the Dublins speaking openly about how they 'expected to be 'wiped out'.'[38] Theirs was a fatalism about the landings that was shared by the battalion's Roman Catholic chaplain. Father William Finn confessed that he 'did not expect to live through it'.[39] He told Foster: 'If you find my body, bury me simply, and say a prayer for my soul, old chap; and if you find any of my boys dying, get them to repeat a short act of contrition.'[40] Then, before parting he scribbled a note in Foster's prayer book. It read: 'O! my God, I am sorry that I have sinned against Thee, because Thou are so good, and I will not sin again.'[41]

Reports from air and sea reconnaissance sorties would have done little to alter the grim forecasts. The surveys carried out on 14 and 15 April 14 showed a number of new guns and emplacements. From aerial photographs, it was 'only too clear' to Hamilton that the Turks had not let 'the grass grow under their feet since the first bombardment':[42]

Broadly speaking, a line of trench and barbed wire entanglement stretches along the Achi Baba ridge, then turns northeast and runs along to Maghram; thence across the Kilid Bahr plateau, and across the next valley and down the Kalkmaz Dagh ridge to the sea. There is about a Division of infantry in the gully between '706', northern point of Kilid Bahr plateau and the main part of the plateau … From 'Fisherman's Hut' right down to the coast, the whole way as far as the end of the cliffs, which run northeast from Tekke Burnu, there is a practically continuous line of trench and entanglement.[43]

Hunter-Weston embarked on the cruiser *Dartmouth* on 14 April for an inspection of the southern end of the peninsula where his division was to land. Leaving Tenedos before light in order for the 'low sun to show up the valleys', he was treated to a 'capital morning view'[44] of the beaches from Tekke Burnu around to Morto Bay that left him with plenty to contemplate:

> Saw no enemy but some smoke from camps behind N spur of Achi Baba, near Krithia and also further South. The South end of the Peninsular [sic] showed heavy entrenchments and much wire.[45]

The thickening beach defences were a constant worry. On 15 April, Hamilton was a spectator on board HMS *Dublin* for an experiment aimed at testing the effectiveness of naval gunnery against 'big wire entanglements'. The results were not encouraging. Returning from Sedd-el-Bahr, Hamilton reported to Kitchener:

> 12 rounds were fired in one instance and 7 in another, without producing any visible effect whatever. I fear an enormous expenditure of ammunition will be necessary to smash these wire entanglements, and we have not got it.'[46]

It was against this backdrop that preparations for the landings continued unabated. In the crowded anchorage of Mudros, soldiers in full kit could be found day and night clambering down rope ladders attached to ships' sides or awkwardly weaving between huge men o' war as they endlessly practised what one officer of the Munsters called 'this hazardous means of disembarkation'.[47] The wearying routine was carried out amid a swirl of rumours and speculation as George Davidson's diary makes clear:

> April 12: Orders were issued yesterday that we were to practise disembarking today in preparation for the landing on Gallipoli. The different units had to line up in the stations allotted to them, ours luckily being on the saloon deck where we will get use of the accommodation ladder instead of the rope ladder as first proposed. Except for our rations, which had not been issued, we had on our full marching order loads – revolver, water-bottle, ammunition, haversack, field glasses, map case, Burberry and ground sheet. When we land we will have about 5lbs of rations in addition ...

> April 13: Orders have come through to us today about our landing. We are warned to keep our equipment dry as we'll be waist-deep in water on leaving the tow boats. Rumour had it yesterday that Thursday night had been definitely fixed, but this afternoon it is said that the landing is likely to take place tomorrow ...

April 14: Had a very slow day on board … No attack to be made today, that is evident, and I doubt if we are ready for it tomorrow. Orders are out for the usual drill tomorrow which now always consists of boating, landing and climbing rope ladders swinging about in mid air.

After dinner I had a long talk with one of the ship's officers who had been in the navy for years, and is now attached to this boat to look after things naval. 'The charge ashore' of the covering party he considers a vast mistake, and his idea is that the authorities have just discovered this too, and are reconsidering its advisability. A few machine guns could wipe us all out before we get ashore. We are to be covered by the navy, but what is the use of big guns against individuals planted everywhere in trenches. However, it is not for us 'to reason why'. My informant had been talking yesterday to the Brigade Major, and on asking him if we were still going to Gallipoli he said 'Oh, I think so'.

April 15: Just returned from a five mile sail in a rowing boat … and while enjoying a cup of tea at a table of Engineer officers, we heard what is evidently the latest proposal about the invasion of Gallipoli. Instead of landing us from troopships we all go on battleships, which seems to be an improvement. We are also likely to land at three if not four different points at the same time. This new plan will likely take a few more days to develop, so that we may expect a few days' grace yet …[48]

Among those burning the midnight oil on the amended plans was Garth Walford. As a member of Hunter-Weston's staff, he had been 'frantically busy … preparing for the landing'.[49] In a letter written to his wife on 21 April, he apologised for the lack of correspondence:

Simply haven't had time to write a line here; full up digesting schemes, writing orders and being bucketed about the harbour in small boats by incompetent oarsmen.[50]

Until then, Walford had only alluded to his location, but now, with the operation only days away, he dropped all pretence at secrecy, writing: 'It doesn't matter your knowing now … as it will all be settled one way or the other before you get this.'[51]

Walford was among the same group of officers that included Francis McLaren who took part in the sea-borne reconnaissance of the peninsula aboard *Queen Elizabeth* on 12 April. Previously, he had only distantly glimpsed the Turkish shore from a hilltop above Mudros. In his letter home, he was understandably guarded about what he saw of 'our future objective'.[52] Describing the trip as 'most interesting',[53] he gave a disarmingly light-hearted account of the foray in which he merely hinted at the difficulties to come while making teasing reference to the most novel addition to the landing plan he had been working on for the past ten days:

> I climbed up into the fore-top, a more dangerous proceeding than I thought when I suggested going there; up a sort of steel rope-ladder from the ship's side, ratlines I believe is the term, then up some extraordinarily inconveniently placed iron rods fastened into the mast and then up perpendicularly through a small steel trap-door in the floor of the top, through which I had great difficulty in squeezing with a haversack on one side and field-glasses on the other. What happens to anyone who gets fat in the Navy, I can't think; they probably leave him up on the top without food till he gets thin enough to drop through the hole. Very interesting seeing the whole ship from above the height of the top of the funnels; the men were all standing by the guns, in case any land batteries opened on us, and in the distance we saw two battleships and three destroyers shelling some forts on shore and being shelled in return; the land shooting was very wild; the ships hit the land all right, but as we couldn't see what they were firing at I don't know whether they hit it. Then we went into the same area, and we were all hauled down into the casemates in deadly fear that they were going to fire their colossal guns; luckily they didn't. The Turks fired a few shots from field-guns and one lot of three shell[s] from sort of howitzer. I saw one shell fall about a thousand yards away and I don't think anything else was much nearer. One felt pretty safe, as we were loaded up with generals and admirals, and they wouldn't risk the Turks making a bag like that.
>
> Well, we are off in a day or two, if the weather stays fine; just like the Greek fleet going to Troy, people collected from all over the known world; we have even got our wooden horse which I will explain later on. As far as the intelligence reports tell us, however, there seems to be no Helen at the other end, and I hope we shan't be ten years over the business.[54]

The cryptic, almost jocular, reference to the *River Clyde* represented a dramatic change of plan, not least for the 2,000 troops of the Covering Force who found themselves suddenly reprieved from the grim prospect of assaulting the strongest of all the enemy beaches in open boats. Expert though some of them had become in descending swinging rope ladders and squeezing into unsteady cutters, there were few who were not relieved to discover, even at this late juncture, that all their training had been for nothing.

The men of the 1st Royal Munster Fusiliers, together with a company of the 1st Royal Dublin Fusiliers, the headquarters and two companies of the 2nd Hampshire Regiment and an assortment of support units that included medics and bearers from 89th Field Ambulance, sappers from 1/1st (West Riding) Field Company and a platoon from the Royal Naval Division's Anson Battalion were, for the most part, only too happy to find themselves pioneers in an experimental new landing scheme only recently endorsed by the joint naval and military staffs.

On 16 April, with the earmarked invasion just a week away, the men destined to ride ashore in the expeditionary force's new-found 'wooden horse' were ordered to stand by for their formal introduction to their novel new mode of transport. That same day the twenty-four-year-old commander of the small Royal Naval Division contingent snatched a few moments to reflect on the latest and most curious twist in a circuitous journey he whimsically likened to a 'Cook's Tour'.[55] Since leaving England at the end of February, Sub-Lieutenant Arthur Walderne St Clair Tisdall had travelled seemingly aimlessly around the Mediterranean, stopping off at Lemnos, before moving on to Egypt and then returning to Lemnos. A distinguished Cambridge scholar and a gifted poet, 'Pog' Tisdall, as he was known to his family and friends, was a veteran of the division's disastrous baptism of fire in Belgium. The misery of retreat and defeat while Antwerp burned was a painful experience that marked him. 'The sight of the poor women and children driven from their homes makes one's blood boil,' he wrote. 'It's horrid to feel so useless.'[56] The struggle against Turkey seemed a heaven-sent opportunity to at last do something worthwhile. Like others in the expeditionary force, he romanticised the coming campaign as a latter-day crusade, writing,

> to turn the Turks out of Constantinople, etc, would … give me a feeling I had really done one satisfactory piece of work. Here one really feels that we are fighting on the side of civilisation.[57]

Promised a 'fairly exciting'[58] six-week or two-month campaign, the Navy's 'amateur' soldiers, described by Hamilton as 'living monuments … to Winston Churchill's contempt for convention',[59] bridled with frustration at the lack of action. Even worse was the news that reached

'Pog' and his fellow officers in Egypt that the Anson Battalion was to be temporarily detached from the division for the impending invasion and employed not in a combat role but as 'navvies' in support of the 29th Division. The thought of supplying beach parties and carrying out 'routine fatigue duties' induced 'nothing but disappointment'[60] among men desperate for the fray. The discovery that No 13 Platoon, D Company, would be embarking on one of the boldest of all military operations aboard a man o' war like no other was, therefore, a considerable consolation to its young commander. Informing a friend back home of the latest surprising turn of events, 'Pog' Tisdall wrote with renewed excitement:

> Tomorrow at 7am I go to another ship with my men, a collier. War is an amusing game – lots of changes – isn't it.[61]

The next day, as the troops briefly set foot on the *River Clyde* for the first time, a naval memorandum setting out orders for the movements of ships and transports involved in the landings confirmed the humble collier's elevation to leading role in the Sedd-el-Bahr operation.

Things were now moving fast. So fast that, as *River Clyde*'s captain commented, 'it was impossible to rehearse the whole thing properly'.[62] Along with the commanding officer of the 1st Royal Munster Fusiliers, Lieutenant Colonel Henry Tizard, he 'went into the question of stowing the men on board'.[63] However, with the work on the suspended gangways still incomplete, a practical demonstration of the landing plan was out of the question. All he could do in the limited time available was to practice bringing them on board and show them the positions they would take up before sallying forth from the holes cut in the sides and across a bridge of boats to the shore. Hence the exercise that took place on 17 April. For the troops involved it would be their only experience of the ship prior to the actual operation. Nevertheless, Unwin considered it 'very useful', adding: 'They weren't quite so strange [to it] as they would otherwise have been.'[64]

For Davidson, the thrill of anticipation was followed swiftly by a fretful few hours of anxiety. Shortly after returning from the *River Clyde*, he noted: 'There is now a rumour that 89th Ambulance may not have the honour of participating in this dash.'[65] Upset at the possibility of missing out on such an extraordinary operation, he hoped 'to goodness' it was 'nothing but a mistake'.[66] The uncertainty lasted into 19 April when, to his great relief, he learned 'we are not to lose our post of honour after all'.[67]

A day later, two other officers, both senior members of Hamilton's staff aboard *Arcadian*, received their orders too: they were to take their place in the *River Clyde* as representatives of GHQ for what would prove a portentous assignment – and, for one of them, the crowning glory of an already remarkable career.

Chapter 7

'An Extremely Dangerous Job'

To Unwin, there was an air of mystery about the appointment of two red-tabbed lieutenant colonels from Hamilton's staff to the *River Clyde* operation. He regarded Weir de Lancey Williams and Charles Hotham Montagu Doughty-Wylie as 'sightseers'[1] who had 'wriggled on board'[2] for the sheer hell of it. 'I never discovered why,' he later wrote, 'but there they were.'[3]

There was no such uncertainty so far as the military planners were concerned. The orders issued for the allotment of officers from GHQ on 20 April made clear the distribution and roles during the first day of operations. The bulk of the staff was to either accompany Hamilton and Braithwaite on the *Queen Elizabeth* or to remain aboard *Arcadian*. Only eight officers were assigned to the landing beaches, six of whom were to go ashore at Cape Helles. They were: Brigadier General Alexander Roper, the Principal Military Landing Officer; Captain Frank Dunlop, who was acting as his staff officer; Lieutenant Colonel Williams and Captain Charles Bolton, representing GHQ; and Lieutenant Colonel Doughty-Wylie and Lieutenant Hoyland, who were to carry out intelligence duties. Of the six, four – Roper, Dunlop, Bolton and Hoyland – were to land via fleet sweepers, while Williams and Doughty-Wylie were instructed to join the *River Clyde* 'before noon, two days before the first day of operations'.[4]

A subsequent entry in the GHQ War Diary appears to indicate that the composition of this party may have changed late on, with two Special Service officers, Captains George Lloyd and Ian 'Jan' Smith, the latter of whom had been working closely with Doughty-Wylie since 18 March, being attached as additional intelligence officers. The same note clarifies Williams' task as GHQ representative. It states that he and Captain Bolton were to carry out 'staff duties on the beaches after landing'.[5]

Far from being mere 'sightseers', Williams and Doughty-Wylie were key to the successful execution of a landing plan that was reliant on speedily overcoming the inevitable chaos of the initial landing. As well as keeping GHQ appraised of progress, they were responsible for establishing order as soon as the beach was secured and for maintaining the momentum of the push inland. As Doughty-Wylie observed:

> If I can get ashore, I can help a good deal in the difficult job of landing enough troops to storm the trenches on the beach – and see the most dashing military exploit which has been performed for a very long time.[6]

Doughty-Wylie was a late recruit to the *River Clyde* operation. Originally, he had planned to go ashore with Birdwood's Anzacs in the diversionary landing further up the coast at Gaba Tepe. It was Williams who persuaded him to join the main assault, though, as Williams later wrote, 'he did not want much inducing'.[7] The sheer audacity of the scheme with its allusions to the most famous of all military deceptions appealed to the romantic adventurer in him. Doughty-Wylie considered the "wreck ship', or wooden horse of Troy' an 'ingenious arrangement',[8] but he was realistic enough to recognise the hazards of what he called 'an extremely dangerous job':[9]

> This is a very interesting show from every point of view – but it runs a great many chances however one looks at it. It may be a really startling success, and is certainly bold enough an idea.[10]

Although the two men had known each other for only a short time, they had much in common. Williams regarded Doughty-Wylie as 'a very splendid soldier of the very best type'.[11] He knew a little of his past from his brother who had served in the same regiment. 'He had been hit on more than one occasion,' observed Williams, 'and knew no fear.'[12] Much the same could have been said for him. Their records read like a roll-call of imperial wars straddling the end of the nineteenth and the beginning of the twentieth centuries. From fierce struggles in the forests of West Africa and the rugged hills of the North West Frontier to testing times in the desert of the Sudan and on the rolling veldt of South Africa, they had seen fighting aplenty and had the medals and the scars to prove it. Their combined careers added up to almost half a century of devoted service to three monarchs.

At forty-three, Weir de Lancey Williams was the junior of the two in age, but the senior in rank. Popularly known as 'Hampshire' on account of his proud regimental affiliations, he was a Guernsey-born general's son with a Distinguished Service Order earned on 'special extra-regimental service' during expeditions into the remote heart of Nigeria. After being severely wounded in South Africa, he had held a series of staff appointments in India that included spells as a brigade major and deputy assistant adjutant general prior to a posting in 1913 to the Welsh Division as a general staff officer, second grade (GSO II). At the outbreak of war, Williams was promoted a grade, to GSO I of the 1/1st Welsh Division, part of the Home Defence's Central Force, under the overall command of Sir Ian Hamilton. He was still serving in this role in March 1915 when he received a telegram appointing him as one of only two first grade staff officers to the newly formed Mediterranean Expeditionary Force. 'I had just two hours' notice to leave London,' he later recalled, 'and did so as I stood.'[13] Much to his delight, he discovered that the 2nd Battalion of his old county regiment was part of the force.

To Williams' considerable gift for administration and organisation, 'Dick' Doughty-Wylie, as he was more familiarly known, added an almost unrivalled knowledge of Turkey and the Turkish psyche. The son of a retired naval officer and nephew of the celebrated Arabian explorer Charles Doughty, he proved himself to be both Doughty by name and by nature. A veteran of at least eight conflicts and one civil war, he had been wounded three times and narrowly escaped death twice. On one occasion, his life had been saved only by the bravery of an Australian medical officer who, by a strange coincidence, was now on a troopship bound for Gaba Tepe.[14]

What had thus far been a conspicuously gallant but otherwise conventional career with the Royal Welch Fusiliers ended with his marriage to wealthy widow, Lilian Oimara Adams Wylie in 1904. A few months later, Captain Doughty became, by deed poll, Captain Doughty-Wylie and the following year the newly-weds indulged their fascination for the Near East with a prolonged leave that took them, via Baghdad, the archaeological sites of ancient Babylon and Constantinople, to England, where he sought a transfer to the political service. His wish granted, he was posted in September 1906 to the Turkish Asia Minor province of Konia as British military vice-consul, thus beginning an extraordinary association that would see him feted by his countrymen and his future enemies.

Promoted major shortly after his appointment, he had just added Cilicia to his area of jurisdiction when an outbreak of fratricidal violence threatened an all-out civil war. As attacks on the Armenian Christian community by Turkish Moslems in Adana turned into a full-scale

Above left: Edward Unwin, the man behind the *River Clyde* landing operation. When the scheme foundered, he played a heroic role in trying to rescue the plan from disaster. Above right: George Drewry, the midshipman in charge of the steam hopper *Argyle* which went off course with tragic consequences for the landing. He was wounded during brave efforts to establish a link from the collier to the beach.

Below left: Arthur 'Pog' Tisdall, the Cambridge scholar and Royal Naval Division officer who joined the rescue effort from the *River Clyde*. Below right: 'Geordie' Samson displaying his Victoria Cross earned for multiple acts of heroism before being wounded on the second day of the landing.

Above: 'Geordie' Samson being given a hero's reception in his home town of Carnoustie in August 1915.

Below: Boat drills being rehearsed in Mudros harbour before the landings. Prior to Unwin's intervention, all of the troops were to go ashore at V Beach from open lifeboats.

Above left: William Williams. The Welsh reservist volunteered for the *River Clyde* and died in his captain's arms. Unwin later called him 'the bravest sailor I ever knew'. Above right: Guy Nightingale, the Munster Fusilier officer who bore a charmed life at the landing. Later awarded the Military Cross, there were some who felt he merited the highest honour.

Below left: Josiah Wedgwood MP, sometimes known as Josiah Wedgwood IV. The commander of No 3 Squadron, Royal Naval Armoured Car Division, he lobbied for a role in the landings and later wrote a vivid account of the *River Clyde* operation for his friend Winston Churchill. Below right: Geoffrey Rumming. One of the naval machine-gunners aboard the *River Clyde*, he risked his life saving wounded men but never fully recovered from a serious head injury sustained in the only armoured car attack of the Gallipoli campaign.

Above left: Jim Parkinson was 'a loveable rogue' who lied about his age to enlist and became one of the greatest heroes of the landing from the *River Clyde*. (Courtesy of Roger K. Bingham). Above right: 'Dick' Doughty-Wylie, the soldier-diplomat who was a late addition to the *River Clyde* party. The GHQ staff officer took charge of the advance through Sedd-el-Bahr on 26 April and was killed at the moment of victory on Hill 141.

Below left: Garth Walford, an artillery staff officer who died leading an infantry attack out of the ruined fortress and into the streets of Sedd-el-Bahr. Below right: William Medhurst, leader of one of the boat parties from *Cornwallis* who was killed rowing the Dublins ashore on 25 April.

Above left: Cecil Grimshaw, the senior surviving officer of the Dublins who played a prominent part in the attack on 26 April until he 'simply threw away his life'. Above right: Desmond O'Hara, the 22-year-old who rose from subaltern to commanding officer of the Dublins within a couple of days of stepping ashore from the *River Clyde*.

Below left: William Cosgrove, the 'Irish giant' and shy hero of the V Beach landing who carried fragments of metal in his body till the end of his life. Below right: 'River Clyde' Drewry, his head swathed in bandages, is pictured on the beach shortly after the landing. The figure on the right is thought to be the ship's Irish surgeon, Peter Burrowes Kelly.

Above: 'Place in the stalls'. Lieutenant the Hon Arthur Coke, far left, with Petty Officer David Fyffe, second left, and a party of naval armoured car machine-gunners beside one of the steel-plated Maxim gun emplacements on the *River Clyde* shortly before the landing. (Courtesy of Stephen Chambers)

Below: Hero in waiting, John Hepburn Russell, second from the left, with a group of chief petty officers from Wedgwood's machine-gun detachment aboard the *River Clyde*. (Courtesy of Stephen Chambers)

Above: The deck of the *River Clyde* under-going its conversion to a Heath Robinson-like landing craft. The steel-plated 'forts' which housed the naval armoured car machine-gun parties are clear, as are the decked lighters on the ship's port side.

Below: The 'Wooden Horse' of Gallipoli. The collier SS *River Clyde* displaying her starboard side 'sally ports' and gangway from which Z Company, 1st Royal Munster Fusiliers, under Captain Eric Henderson, led the rush for the shore.

Above: Doughty-Wylie, right, in conversation with Sir Ian Hamilton on board the *Arcadian* headquarters ship in Mudros harbour shortly before the landings.

Right: Doughty-Wylie, with his wife Lily, pictured in Konia, Turkey, where he was serving as a military vice-consul before the war.

massacre, with the local authorities either powerless or unwilling to intervene, Doughty-Wylie took matters into his own hands. Wearing British Army uniform, he rode out with a force of fifty Turkish gendarmes to confront the mob. During one foray, he was shot in the arm by an Armenian who mistook him for a Turk, but, undeterred, he returned after having his wound bandaged, and succeeded in restoring order. More than 2,000 people had been killed, but that figure would undoubtedly have been far higher but for Doughty-Wylie. His brave intervention was acclaimed around the world and was recognised by his own government, who appointed him a Companion of the Most Distinguished Order of St Michael and St George (CMG).

Four years later, it was the turn of the Sultan to honour him. Together with his wife, who was a trained nurse, he took charge of the Red Cross services operating in Turkey during the Balkan Wars. His efforts in helping to alleviate the suffering of Turkish wounded were rewarded with the Imperial Ottoman Order of the Medjidieh, 2nd Class, to add to the 4th Class award granted him for his work as a brigade-major attached to the Egyptian Army during the reconquest of the Sudan almost fifteen years earlier. His diplomatic career also continued to prosper. Promoted to consul-general, he was made British representative and then chairman of the International Boundary Commission set up to approve newly recognised Albania's borders with Greece.

Appointed a Companion of the Order of the Bath (CB Civil Division) for his services, he was in Addis Ababa, where he had been engaged in treaty negotiations with the Ethiopian Government, when war broke out in Europe in the summer of 1914. With the permission of the British ambassador, Doughty-Wylie made his way to Cairo where General Sir John Maxwell, the Commander-in-Chief, attempted to add the forty-six-year-old soldier diplomat to his staff. However, his efforts were forestalled by orders from London instructing Doughty-Wylie to proceed to Lemnos. There, he was to join Hamilton's staff as a lieutenant colonel, GSO II, as the second-most senior officer responsible for intelligence gathering in the still-forming MEF.

Doughty-Wylie arrived in Mudros, accompanied by Captains Smith and Wyndham Deedes, in the early morning of 18 March, the same day that Williams reached Lemnos aboard the Phaeton.[15] For much of the following month, they worked independently of one another. While Williams remained at GHQ, initially at Mudros and later in Egypt, where he met with fellow Hampshire officers from the 2nd Battalion, Doughty-Wylie, with Captain Smith in tow, departed for Athens on 24 March. Between then and his return to Lemnos on 11 April, he was kept busy monitoring reports and gathering intelligence to assist GHQ in its preparations for the impending operations in Gallipoli. His sources were myriad and not always entirely reliable. They ranged from specially recruited agents sent to spy out the land to chancers and misfits. Among them were a Greek naval attaché recently returned from Constantinople, an Armenian contractor based in the Dardanelles, a 'Greek of good position' and a handful of deserters from the Turkish Army.

It was Doughty-Wylie's job to interpret and disseminate the welter of reports and rumours that found their way on to his desk, many of them based on gossip and hearsay. Some of the intelligence touched on political and military developments in the, as yet, still neutral Balkan states of Bulgaria and Rumania, but Doughty-Wylie's main focus was on events in Turkey with the highest priority given over to information relating to the Dardanelles.

Reports concerning enemy morale, troop movements, the flow of munitions and the ongoing Turkish efforts to improve defences on land and at sea were carefully entered into a diary he kept while based in Athens and which sheds light on his little-known clandestine role during the build-up to the landings. The following selection of raw intelligence relating to the campaign in which he was to play a prominent if unexpected role is typical of the material he gathered during his temporary detachment from GHQ:

> March 27: Two sources report considerable number of troops moved from Constantinople to Gallipoli between March 9th and March 13th; believed to be 6th Division. 10,000 Mustafiz reported between Kavak and Zunguldak. 71st Regiment reported at Ada Bazar, 41st, 42nd, 43rd Regiments Ismidt and Kartal, all under Yaver Pasha. Ships not allowed to proceed down Sea of Marmora beyond Silivri. Reported that sheds for 40,000 men are being made at Chataldja.

> March 28: My wire stating: 'Amongst other munitions of war said to have arrived at Constantinople via Roumania [sic] were ... large shells of which twelve were sent Dardanelles in Austrian motors.' For shells I suspect howitzers to be meant, Greek words not being dissimilar; am inquiring.

> March: Report of hitherto untried agent:

> En route to Constantinople I observed that at Lule Burgas there were three large warehouses, two contained flour and provisions, the third war material and ammunition brought from Bulgaria. My

delay of nine hours here due to lateness of … train which was held up owing to 65 wagons of war material arriving in Lule Burgas before it. Afterwards train stopped at every station to allow military trains to pass on mainline going to Constantinople. These trains full of troops, mostly artillery, coming from Adrianople … At Constantinople … I went on board Greek steamer and verified fact that she had loaded a number of guns, ammunition and war material. Ship left for Dardanelles, on its return my friend told me officer had informed him these guns were to be placed at Nagara. General opinion in Constantinople is that Nagara is the hardest fort to destroy and the big guns there can do great damage. Germans say once Nagara falls Allied Fleet have won half the battle … On March 9th 15,000 Infantry arrived in Panderma. Impossible to discover numbers of regiments nor whence they came. Men had green ribbon on their headgear. Good appearance, well clothed and armed: they were under orders to leave for unknown destination …

Gallipoli: Between seventy and eighty thousand troops in Gallipoli Peninsula, many of whom have been brought from Adrianople and Rodosto. Many guns also sent from Adrianople to Gallipoli. Troops seem to be continually drafted to Gallipoli, mostly embarked at Constantinople during the night. These men are mostly drafts from depots where recruits have been hurriedly trained and formed into extra-service regiments, or are sent to supplement existing companies. Impossible to find out their real division or regiment. There are no numbers on uniforms, the only sign is sometimes blue, green, yellow or red ribbon on their head gear. It is continually rumoured that 8th Army Corps is to arrive, but there are no signs of it in Constantinople or anywhere on shores of Marmora. 150 German officers arrived on 11th March, half sent to Dardanelles … I saw Goltz Pasha in Constantinople …

March 29: With reference to my telegram of March 28 reporting part of IIIrd Army Corps at Lampsaki, I learn from another source that band of 9th Division (which normally accompanies divisional headquarters) was at Chanak, March 9th: it seems probable that 9th Division is on Asiatic side of Dardanelles.

March 31: Turk named Hakki went to Mudros a few days ago as a spy. Aged 35 to 40, height medium, moustache chestnut, mark on left side of neck, talks Greek like a Greek, was formerly spy at Chanak and Constantinople.

March 31: I learn from reliable source that by 12th March, 14 guns of 35cm and others, mostly 6-in, and 1700 mines and torpedoes had reached Constantinople from Germany. Informant states this information is from best possible source in Constantinople ...

April 2: Person from Constantinople ... believes that 40 trucks ammunition arrived from Germany recently ... and some fifteen inch guns about 15th March ...

April 6: Summary of report from reliable agent who arrived Tenedos 3/ 4/ 15.
Landed Tacakli [sic] 14/ 3/ 15. Headquarter camp is at Ilidja. There were 3,000 gunners at Erenkeuy on 18th March. Two dummy guns on the white cutting below Erenkeuy. There are six real heavy guns below and on either side of them, but invisible from sea. At Chemenlik and Hamidieh false trenches have been made above the real ones. A friend of mine estimated troops in Gallipoli town at 30,000. Covered trenches lead from below Yeni-Shehr past Orkanieh to Kum Kale. There are about 32,000 reserve troops near these places. At Sed-ul-Bahr [sic] troops are Kurds, Lazes and Gypsies. My friend thinks there are 40,000. On 18 March I saw 5 Pashas arrive by motor car... with the American Ambassador and a Swedish officer. 2nd April heard Koniah Regt was arriving near Tabakly. No traffic between Maidos and Chanak owing to mine-fields. Floating mines start from valley below Dardanos where there is a mine store.
　There are twelve guns among the pine trees above factory south of the white cliffs, between factory and Quarantine Pier there is a torpedo battery. Search lights are portable. On European side there are five torpedo batteries of four tubes each between Hovousieh and Yeni Mejidieh. In valley a quarter of an hour East of Yildiz Tabieh four small ammunition depots, well hidden. Good road from Maidos to Krithia, three and a half hours. Good water supply at Krithia, pipes bring it from 2 hours distance. Good road from Maidos to Seraphimchiftlik, one and a half hours, and abundant water at both places. North of Krithia there is a big force in the hills ...[16]

And so it went on in a seemingly endless flow, each snippet of information like a fragment in a giant jigsaw puzzle that, pieced together, told only of growing Turkish strength and mounting preparations. Reports reaching Doughty-Wylie during the first week of April spoke of reservists up to the age of fifty-five being prepared for call-up and villagers being armed as makeshift auxiliaries. One spy who had spent almost a month inside enemy territory made his way out to Tenedos with news that the number of enemy troops in the Dardanelles had risen to somewhere in the region of 100,000 men. The identity and quality of the units was not certain, but the morale among at least some of them, according to Doughty-Wylie's report, was thought to be 'sullen'.[17]

His own mood during this time is more difficult to discern, complicated as it was by events in his tangled personal life. Outwardly, he appeared the model of convention and propriety. But this man of secrets masked a secret of his own, one that would come back to haunt him in the days leading up to his embarkation on the *River Clyde*. For almost two years he had been engaged in an extra-marital love affair with the celebrated traveller and writer Gertrude Bell. Their relationship, born of a mutual respect and a shared fascination with the Middle East reaching back to their first meeting in Turkey in 1907, had, by 1913, developed into something beyond mere friendship. To a man 'serious in mind and grave in demeanour',[18] she brought laughter and unpredictability. She, in turn, found him 'spiritual and unflinching',[19] qualities she adored. Admiration quickly grew into mutual attraction. Theirs was a union of hearts and minds reflected in a torrent of secret correspondence that followed them on their disparate journeys. To a friend, she would remark that 'there were never love letters like these between other couples'.[20] No one had aroused such passions in her before, nor would anyone ever do so again. Though Doughty-Wylie could not bring himself to sacrifice his marriage, they remained entwined in what she called 'an irretrievable misfortune'.[21] In one letter, written after she had escaped into 'wild travel' with a journey deep into the heart of Arabia, he told her:

> I cannot tell you how it moves me ... to see it – written by you – that you might have married me, have borne my children, have been my wife as well as my heart ... I shall never be your lover, my dear, never ... But what we can have, we will keep and cherish. Yes, we will be wise and gentle as you said. I love you, but I shall never have you – only always in the real world be your lover, your obedient servant, your loyal friend ... And I will try to be more like your lover might be ... but it will be sometimes hard, because I am an ordinary man – and follower of delights.[22]

The war, far from putting an end to the affair, served only to heighten emotions. Though they met only once more, Gertrude remained in his thrall and utterly bereft at his parting. Another letter reached him as he prepared to join the Mediterranean Expeditionary Force:

> Dearest, dearest, I give this year of mine to you and all the years that shall come after it … You fill my cup, this shallow cup that has grown so deep to hold your love and mine … I have filled all the hollow places of the world with my desire for you.[23]

Her last letters to him in the spring of 1915 were from a soul in torment. Fearful of the hazards facing him, she wrote of taking her own life. The thought horrified him. Not long before, he had written telling her of his wife Lily's threat to commit suicide should he die. Now, as he received his orders to join the *River Clyde*, he appeared 'caught between a distraught wife and a lover bent on following him into the afterlife'.[24] That same day, he posted two letters, one to his wife's mother and the other to Gertrude. In the first, he wrote:

> I am going to embark tomorrow on … the wreck ship of which you will see in the papers. If the thing went wrong, Lily would feel intolerably lonely and hopeless after her long hours of work, which tell sorely on anybody's spirits and vitality. She talks about overdoses of morphia and such things. I think that in reality she is too brave and strong minded for such things but still the saying weighs on my spirits. If you hear I'm killed go over at once to France … Don't take her away from the work, for it will be best for her to work, but manage to stay somewhere near and see her through. Tell her what is perfectly true that the work cannot go on without her. I haven't told her yet of this wreck ship because I don't want her to know till it's over …[25]

To Gertrude, he wrote pleadingly:

> My dear, don't (this is what weighs me down) don't do what you talked of – it's horrible to me to think of – that's why I told you about my wife – how much more for you – don't do anything so unworthy of so free and so brave a spirit. One must walk along the road to the long end of it. When I asked for this ship, my joy in it was half strangled by that thing you said, I can't even name it or talk about it. As we go steaming in under the port guns in our rotten old collier, shall I still think of it. I am afraid I shall – don't tie this thing to drown me – you to die for whom the world holds so much! For whom there is always the pure delight of capability and power well used. Don't do it … Time is nothing, we [will] join up again, but to hurry the pace is unworthy of us all …[26]

As he prepared to accompany Williams aboard the *River Clyde*, his words betrayed a confusion of emotions:

> On the eve of any adventure my spirits have always risen. But at the moment, hangs about my neck, so many memories my dear queen, of you and your splendid love and your kisses and your courage and the wonderful letters you wrote to me, from your heart to mine – the letters, some of which I have packed up, like drops of blood … [27]

It was almost as though he were glimpsing his own journey's end.

Chapter 8

'Blowing Big Guns'

By 21 April preparations for the landing were all but complete. The first moves were scheduled for later the same day in readiness for the attack to be launched on St George's Day, 23 April. Apt or not, it was not to be. The bad weather that had been so disruptive to 'Rosy' Wemyss' efforts a few weeks' earlier had returned to haunt the planners. 'Blowing big guns,' observed Hamilton. 'The event with which old mother time is in labour is so big that her pains are prodigious and prolonged out of all nature. So near are we now to our opening that the storm means a twenty four hours' delay.'[1]

The strong northerly winds that forced the operation's postponement had been battering Mudros since 19 April. Sheltered anchorage though it was, the storm made even the shortest of boat journey a potentially perilous enterprise. Guy Geddes was caught out when he took a party of Munsters ashore on 20 April. The return trip, with a 'heavy sea running', was 'absolutely wicked'.[2]

He was not alone in feeling the blast of what he referred to in his diary as that 'awful bundebust'[3] [sic]. The day before, Captain Clement Milward had been charged with distributing copies of the landing orders to all the units of the Covering Force in transports spread across the harbour. In normal circumstances, the trip would have been a long but not unduly arduous one, but with gusting winds it turned into a nightmare, as Hunter-Weston testified in a letter home:

> While going round from ship to ship ... the steamboat (launch) shipped an extra big sea which put the fire out and she drifted helpless. Fortunately she drifted on to one of my transports. The officer and crew spent the night on the transport, tying up the steamboat to the ship. During the night the painter holding the

steamboat pulled out the bows of the boat and she drifted away. She was chased and recovered by another boat. The officer started in her again in the morning after getting the engine and the bows put right. But again the boat was swamped and she drifted with the officer and crew in a dangerous position. They were rescued by a battleship's launch and the officer, crew and boat returned safely this morning after an adventurous night.[4]

Two days after Milward set out on his ill-fated errand, the storm showed little sign of abating. To Sub-Lieutenant Douglas Illingworth, in charge of three of Wedgwood's Maxim guns aboard the *River Clyde*, the pounding of wind and rain was 'fiercely vile'.[5] Hampshires officer Reginald Gillett on board the transport *Aragon* was of a similar opinion. He had been ordered to parade his platoon at 8 am to transfer to the *Alaunia*. The first stage in an operation that would see them taking their places in the holds of the *River Clyde*, it should have been completed the previous day but the sea was too rough. More than three hours later, with the sea bashing against the ship's side, they were still waiting to move. They eventually departed at midday, though Gillett thought it hardly worth the effort. The *Alaunia* was bigger than *Aragon*, but she was not nearly 'so nicely fitted up'.[6] 'The cabins are small and four people in each,' Gillett noted, 'but still I don't suppose that we shall be kept waiting about much longer now.'[7]

Indeed, they would not.

While he was preparing for the rough crossing, General Hunter-Weston was gathering his senior commanders – 'my COs, Brigadiers and Staffs'[8] – together for the last time to explain his plan for carrying out Hamilton's bidding. At the end of his 'big meeting', he wrote a letter to his wife:

> I think I have 'enthused' them all, and that the Division will do well in the big enterprise that lies before it. Long before this reaches you, you will know all about it, and another leaf in the Book of Fate will have been turned and that which is written on it, now unknown to us, will be known to all. The common herd, being wise after the event, will say either: 'How easy, why think twice about so obviously correct an operation', or will say: 'Criminal idiots to attempt the impossible'.
>
> Personally, I should not have undertaken this operation, the chances of success being so small and the consequences of defeat so disastrous. I expressed that view to the C-in-C but he decided

otherwise. That being so, I am wholeheartedly for carrying the plan to a successful issue and I intend to pull off the outside chance and make a success of it. I tell the Division that we shall succeed. I believe we shall succeed and I think I have made the Division full of confidence of success after hard fighting, which latter they are all on for. They are out for blood and will take a lot of stopping ...[9]

Before leaving, the officers were given copies of a 'Personal Note' Hunter-Weston had had specially printed for distribution to 'each man of the 29th Division on the occasion of their first going into action together'.[10] Intended as an eve of battle rallying cry, it mixed realism with echoes of martial glory past and present:

The Major-General Commanding congratulates the Division on being selected for an enterprise the success of which will have a decisive effect on the War.

The eyes of the World are upon us and your deeds will live in history. To us now is given an opportunity of avenging our friends and relatives who have fallen in France and Flanders. Our comrades there willingly gave their lives in thousands and tens of thousands for our King and Country, and by their glorious courage and dogged tenacity they defeated the invaders and broke the German offensive.

We also must be prepared to suffer hardships, privations, thirst, and heavy losses, by bullets, by shells, by mines, by drowning. But if each man feels, as is true, that on him individually, however small or however great his task, rests the success or failure of the Expedition, and therefore the honour of the Empire and welfare of his own folk at home, we are certain to win through to a glorious victory. In Nelson's time it was England, now it is the whole British Empire, which expects that each man of us will do his duty.[11]

They were sentiments shared by Hunter-Weston's 'special Admiral'.[12] Writing to his wife, 'Rosy' Wemyss commented:

Dearest, we are entering onto an enormous business. By the time you receive this I suppose the whole world will know the result. Be they victory or otherwise I feel sure that nothing has been left undone here that could have been done. The difficulties of organisation have been immense, and the Admiralty as usual expect everything and don't help. However, I trust I might be alive to write you a full description of all the doings later on. We have a tough job in front of us but I think we shall crack it alright [*sic*]. If we do, the fruits should be enormous. I humbly pray that I may do my duty ...[13]

As naval commander of the Cape Helles' landings, with 'entire responsibility in organising the transport and disembarkation arrangements for the Army',[14] Wemyss spent 21 April finalising his preparations. A flurry of personally signed orders went out to beachmasters, the captains of transports and 'attendant' warships responsible for covering the assault. Among the instructions was a chart marking out the main landing zone, now officially styled V Beach. Stretching eastwards from the lighthouse above Cape Helles as far as the ruined castle of Sedd-el-Bahr, it was divided into six sectors (V1-V6) with a landing force allocated to each one. The half-dozen tows that would carry the first wave of Royal Dublin Fusiliers in to the shore was to comprise six steam boats each pulling four boats made up from six cutters provided by the battleships *Cornwallis*, *Agamemnon* and *Lord Nelson*, seventeen lifeboats and one pinnace from *Lord Nelson*. A second steam pinnace from *Cornwallis* was assigned to work off the beach with another from *Vengeance* held in reserve. The procedure for landing was set out in detail:

> Each attendant ship to be responsible for safe conduct of one flotilla, each flotilla consisting of two fleet sweepers and 2 trawlers: each attendant ship to tow two complete tows and each sweeper and trawler a tow each. Ships to arrive at their disembarking positions at 4.30 am on day of landing, then get boats alongside. The men are to be embarked, the tows formed and clear of the ship by 5.30 am.
>
> The bombardment will commence at 5.15 am, and the boats should reach the shore at 6 am. They are to advance in line abreast, and when the Steamboats cast off their tow, the pulling boats are to come up on the Port hand of their next ahead, giving way as hard as they can. The oars are to be out, and kept clear ready for giving way from the time the boats leave the ship.
>
> Immediately the men are out of the boats, the boats are to return to their steamboats who will take them back to the Fleet Sweepers from which they will fill up for a second flight.
>
> One Surgeon and 2 Sick Berth ratings are to be held in readiness to proceed to the beach at any time they may be required after 2 pm to attend and embark any wounded in the launches. The launches will, if possible, be taken to an empty Transport which will be called up for the purpose or to a Hospital Ship, if ordered. Attendant ships will have to provide the towage.[15]

Of particular relevance to the Cape Helles operation were Wemyss' instructions for the smaller, subsidiary landing in Morto Bay, known as S Beach. A late addition to the military plan, the assault to be carried out below the De Totts' battery was part diversionary and part intended to outflank the Turkish positions by Sedd-el-Bahr. The landing force was to be put ashore from four trawlers covered by the guns of two destroyers and the battleship *Cornwallis*, which was also assigned as the main 'attendant' ship for the V Beach landings. The question of where *Cornwallis'* priorities lay, however, was not in doubt. Once the trawlers had started on their run-in to the shore, Wemyss' orders made clear she was 'not to delay her return to V Beach'.[16]

Nevertheless, it was a dual role that would have unfortunate consequences for the Cape Helles operation and would leave a legacy of bitter recrimination that was destined to embroil Admiral De Robeck's chief of staff and the man in charge of delivering the largest single force on to the main beach. All of that, however, lay in the future. For now, Edward Unwin, specially promoted acting captain for the operation, was focused on his job. Specific orders issued by Wemyss on 21 April pinpointed precisely where the *River Clyde* was to be beached and left no room for doubt as to her importance to the landing:

> The RIVER CLYDE is to weigh at [time not given] pm and regulate her speed so as to arrive off the ALBION by 6am.
>
> The desired direction of the RIVER CLYDE's keel when fast aground is NE and SW. At 6am the first flight of boats should have reached V Beach, and if time is well calculated, the RIVER CLYDE should be able to go straight in. Care should be taken to avoid running down any boat, but it must be clearly understood that the successful beaching of this ship is of far higher importance than the safety of one boat. I desire to impress my wish that the fear of any accident is not to deter the Captain of the RIVER CLYDE from grounding in the desired position.
>
> The RIVER CLYDE should take her ground just AFTER the boats of the first flight on V Beach have landed.[17]

For the troops who were to embark in her, there were similarly detailed instructions. Issued by Brigadier General Hare, commanding the Covering Force, they devolved responsibility for carrying them out to the scheme's senior infantry officer: Lieutenant Colonel Herbert Carington Smith. Army protocol dictated that Smith, 'a real good man and a first class soldier',[18] was given command of the military part of the landing operation despite the fact he was neither commander of the largest unit in *River Clyde* nor a member of Hare's own brigade. Together with his headquarters and two companies of 2nd Hampshires, he had been detached from 88th Brigade, with the remainder of his split battalion forming part of the second wave of tows. Quite how he would gather his scattered unit amid the inevitable confusion of an opposed landing for the advance inland was unclear, but so far as the 'wreck ship' part of the plan was concerned his orders from Hare were explicit:

> As regards the landing at 'V' from the collier RIVER CLYDE the OC Hants will arrange that troops are disembarked in the following order:
>
> 1st Royal Munster Fusiliers
> One Company, 1st Royal Dublin Fusiliers
> 2nd Hampshire Regiment (less 2 Coys)
> 1 Platoon, Anson Battalion
>
> GHQ Signals Section
> West Riding Field Company, RE
> 3 Bearer Sub Divisions.[19]

Daunting though the prospect was, the landing and the capture of the beachhead at Sedd-el-Bahr was only a part of 29th Division's ambitious first-day objectives. Revised from the original plan drawn up on 13 April and distributed among Hunter-Weston's scattered command with some difficulty by Captain Milward on 20 April, Operation Order No 1 made clear that the expedition's overall objective was 'to assist the Fleet to force the DARDANELLES by capturing the KILID BAHR plateau and dominating the forts of the NARROWS'.[20] It listed the various operations to be carried out simultaneously – a feint by the Royal Naval Division, the landing of the Australian and New Zealand Army Corps between Gaba Tepe and Nibrunesi Point, a demonstration by the French around Kum Kale on the Asiatic shore and the landing of the 29th Division on the 'Southern extremity of the Peninsula'. The orders for the latter stated:

> The task of the 29th Division is the attack of the KILID BAHR Plateau from the South.
>
> The general plan to carry out this task is to land under cover of the bombardment of the fleet –
> (a) A force on the coast West of KRITHIA [Y Beach]

85

(b) A force near ESKI HISSARLIK [S Beach]
(c) The remainder on three beaches on the south end of the Peninsula
[X, W and V Beaches].

The lines to be gained successively are –

(a) the hills 141, 138 and 114.
(b) a line running from the hills at the E[ast] of OLD CASTLE to join
hands on the left with the force landing at 'Y' beach.
(c) a line from ESKI HISSARLIK – about ½ a mile east of KRITHIA
– hill 472 – to the sea.
(d) the capture of ACHI BABA and the spur running south from it.
(e) the occupation and fortification of a line running east from ACHI
BABA to the sea about level 300, and west from ACHI BABA via hill
472 to the sea.[21]

Described by one historian as 'bold, intelligent and ambitious',[22]
Hamilton's plan, which flew in the face of conventional wisdom by
failing to concentrate his limited forces, was founded on the premise
that the Turkish defence, once pierced, would crumble as it had thus far
done in Mesopotamia and on the banks of the Suez Canal. The whole
focus was on landing the Army and breaking through the outer crust.
As Hamilton later admitted:

> In my mind the crux was to get my army ashore … Once ashore, I
> could hardly think Great Britain and France would not in the long
> run defeat Turkey … the problem as it presented itself to us was how
> to get ashore![23]

As well as fatally under-estimating Turkish resolve and skill, his plan
also dangerously over-estimated the effectiveness of naval support.
Instructions to air crews assigned gunnery 'spotting' duties for the
landing revealed just how reliant the military operation was on naval
gunfire which, to this point, had enjoyed only limited success against
shore defences, stressing:

> It is of vital importance that the covering force of the 29th Division
> should advance as far as, and capture, the Achi Baba Heights before
> dark on the day the landing takes place. This can only be affected if
> the naval gunfire is sufficiently well directed to pulverise the
> enemy's defensive efforts and clear the front …[24]

Given that only two aircraft were readied for observation work during the landings and that one of these was to operate over the Asiatic shore, the destruction of enemy positions stretching from Sedd-el-Bahr to Achi Baba by ships' gun crews firing mostly blind was never a realistic proposition.[25] And still there was the problem of dealing with the beach defences identified during earlier reconnaissances.

The battleships *Albion*, *Lord Nelson*, *Dublin* and *Cornwallis* were to support the main landings at V Beach and the subsequent advance as far as the ridge running east from the peak of Achi Baba. Each ship had its own clearly delineated fire zones, with instructions for 'artillery co-operation' between the Navy and 29th Division stating:

> The first action of the ships will be the bombardment of the area in which troops are to land and the engaging of any batteries located previously or at that time, the guns from which can reach the anchorage or beaches. During the bombardment all trenches, wire entanglements and works, as well as buildings and localities near the beach which may conceal machine guns, must be demolished. Any batteries which open fire will be engaged by the ships in whose area they are, at a steady rate of fire until they are silenced, when an occasional round should be fired at them to prevent them reopening fire. Heavy guns will fire sparingly at any definite works or buildings known to contain enemy troops and on the batteries round Achi Baba.
>
> As soon as the first tows leave the ships, a most careful watch must be kept for any batteries opening fire which have not previously disclosed themselves. While the tows are proceeding to the shore the rate of fire must be increased on all batteries which can reach the beach.
>
> When troops land the fire of ships will be shifted to the reverse slopes of the areas in which they land, and a careful look-out kept for hostile counter attacks.
>
> As the forward movement progresses the fire of ships will be brought to bear more and more to the North on the artillery and infantry opposing the advance of our troops. When the ridge running South from Krithia to Eski Hissarlik point has been gained by the troops a ship will be moved NE to the mouth of the Domuz Dere.[26]

In this way, it was intended that the bombardment, which was scheduled to begin a little more than an hour before the landings, would ensure that 'all the ground may be watched and every objective engaged by at least one ship'.[27] This applied even to those objectives that were 'invisible' to the bombarding ships lying offshore. However, there were limits. Contrary to the impression given in some of the instructions, a shortage of shells meant there could be no prolonged pulverising bombardment. Orders to ships' captains stated:

> As the proportion of lyddite in ships is small, it should, after the preliminary bombardment, be reserved for such objectives as may be reported by the troops to be doing most damage at the time, and for any batteries that have been accurately located and are keeping up their fire, and then only when angle of impact will ensure their detonation.[28]

At the same time, shrapnel was only to be employed, in short bursts of rapid fire, 'against enemy troops visible in the open or against entrenchments which it is known that our troops are about to assault'.[29]

Such niceties were unknown to the majority of rank and file preparing to take their leave of Lemnos for their fatal rendezvous with Gallipoli aboard the *River Clyde*. Perhaps it was just as well. The orders that George Davidson noted in his diary were thought-provoking enough. With the attack postponed and, as Guy Geddes put it, 'nothing doing'[30] for at least twenty-four hours, there was plenty of time to contemplate the thicket of barbed wire rumoured to be 25ft deep and 6ft tall that they would have to somehow breach if they were to reach even the first line of Turkish trenches let alone the summit of Achi Baba.

As a haze settled over a wet and windswept harbour, the worrisome wait went on for what Guy Nightingale called the 'big show'[31] to begin.

Chapter 9

'Tis a Grand Adventure'

All eyes were on the sea and sky as a new day dawned bleak and wild on 22 April. 'Wind worse than ever,' noted Hamilton, 'but weather brighter.'[1] Welcome though it was, the lightening sky did nothing to reduce the swell. It was not good news. With calm waters essential for the landings another postponement of twenty-four hours was inevitable. Ever the optimist, Roger Keyes, De Robeck's ebullient chief of staff, wrote to his wife: 'It is only a question of waiting for the weather to settle – that is everything. We want 3 fine days and then I am sure we will achieve an overwhelming success.'[2]

Not all, however, could retain such confidence amid the days of enforced idleness. Hamilton was well aware of the potential damage to morale from a prolonged hold-up. 'Delay,' he observed,' is the worst nerve-cracker.'[3]

For now, though, there was nothing for it but to wait and pray for the weather to break, while aboard wind-blown troopships, men did their level best to fill their time usefully.

In *Ausonia*, George Davidson and his fellow officers in 89th Field Ambulance doled out iodine ampules together with copies of General Hunter-Weston's address in which he congratulated the brigade on having the 'honour' of taking the 'chief post of danger in the coming attack'. Though the harbour was a hive of 'great activity' with torpedo boats in particular flitting to and fro, there was no movement so far as the transports were concerned.

In his diary, Davidson noted:

> No boats have been allowed to leave our ship for two days, the order being that this can only be done if to save life. Water, which we were much in need of, was brought on board last night, and we are ready to start off – and have been since yesterday at 4pm, the appointed

hour. But it would be contrary to all my experience if we got away at the fixed time.[4]

Some men took advantage of the delay to write letters to loved ones. Old Etonian Lieutenant Caryl Boxall was among the parties of 2nd Hampshires that had transferred to the *Alaunia* the day before. To his family in England, he wrote excitedly:

> I am writing this eve of great happenings … If you hear anything of the doings of the *River Clyde* you will know that I participated in them. We are undoubtedly engaged in a dangerous enterprise, but one which if successful will greatly assist the general trend of the operations … Personally I feel an extraordinary indifference for what may be in store for me, chiefly I think because the situation is so without precedent, the possibilities are so numerous, that the powers of ordinary imagination are completely eclipsed, and give up the problem as being beyond their scope. In addition to this one realises very forcibly that man alone is a very insignificant object and that one's destinies must rest with a higher being, and it is a great relief to be able to put one's trust in Him. Our men are simply splendid … Those of us who get through will have memories which time will never efface …[5]

On the *River Clyde*, Josiah Wedgwood dispensed with any attempt at subterfuge or secrecy. With the landings likely any day, he felt certain his revelations would be old news by the time his correspondence reached home. To his younger son, also called Josiah, he wrote:

> My dear son,
>
> I am writing from my wreck ship – the latest addition to the Navy whose sole existence as such will last but a week. Soon we push off for Tenedos. There we embark 2500 men [*sic*] of the 29th Division Munster and Dublin Fusiliers and Hampshires. Then on Saturday night we move off to within 1½ miles of the shore. At dawn we pile ourselves up on the beach, while the whole fleet shoot over our heads to keep down the Turkish fire.
>
> Once well aground a lighter is fixed at our bows and a steam hopper ahead of that. Then men rush out of big ports in the ship's sides and along balconies on to the lighter and hopper and over a

brow, dry shod on the shore. Thereafter our good ship (of what is left of her), forms a landing jetty for the guns and stores.

I have got 18 of my motor cycles and, with them and the guns, I mean to carry on till I can land my cars in a country where they can move.

My guns are now all in armoured and sandbagged casemates along the decks of the ship ...

The whole thing is the idea of Commander Unwin, who captains this ship, and calls it the second Wooden Horse of Troy.

You will know long before you get this if I have got through all right. Remember that in the worst case I expect you to look after your three youngest sisters and to get into the House of Commons as soon as possible ...[6]

In a second letter, written to his mother, he wrote enthusiastically of their mission. 'It is just exactly the job I would have liked to get,' he said. But as he contemplated the charge ashore aboard a ship 'like a collier gone wrong' and imagined men springing out from her hull 'in thousands armed to the teeth', he could not help but ponder his own fate:

There is always of course the chance that I may be killed. If I am, I should like you to know that I think you the best mother in the world, and that I am infinitely grateful to you for all the unselfish loving kindness that you have lavished on me and mine. I have had, on the whole, a very happy life, and I owe it all to you. My children will carry on our good name and traditions. You and Frank and others will look after them, and I have no fear of their coming to harm. Josiah, I hope, will go into Parliament, and with all the good friends he will have, he will become Prime Minister.

I am at perfect peace with God and man.[7]

So, too, was the man whose enthusiastic backing for the 'wreck ship' scheme had made it all possible. 'Rosy' Wemyss was relieved at being able to take temporary leave of his civil duties and relished the prospect of, at last, turning all his hard work into action as naval force commander for the southernmost landings.

The storm had finally relented to produce a gorgeous day of bright spring sunshine. St George's Day might no longer be the day of attack, but the conditions – still, hot and clear – were all that was required for de Robeck to signal the beginning of operations. Having bade farewell to Hamilton, Wemyss went aboard *Euryalus*, which would serve as his headquarters' ship, to join the procession of warships, transports, liners and colliers heading out of Mudros. Somewhere between Lemnos and the invasion fleet's rendezvous at Tenedos, the man responsible for so much of the planning and who would now oversee the main assault, found time to write to his wife:

My own dear Love,

I begin this letter in peace and quiet … I wonder what I shall have to tell you before I end it. Well, all these weeks I have been preparing and organising for landing the Army on the Gallipoli Peninsula, and now here I am on my way … and tomorrow night we leave Tenedos to attack on Sunday morning.

The scheme is audaciously bold and I think we have done all we can to help to make it a success. But the authorities at home! They seem to think it is a picnic party for all the assistance they have given us. Of course the initial mistake was bombarding before we had an army to land. Had we had troops to pour in after the first bombardments the whole thing would have been finished and done in a very short time. But we hadn't. The ignorance of the Admiralty is nothing less than criminal. Then this hastily devised plan of sending troops out to Lemnos without any organisation or Staff to do it. The whole of the troops [transports] had to be unpacked and repacked again, and this had to be done at Alexandria. Then the whole thing had to be reorganised by me out here, and I had no Staff!! By beseeching and telegraphing we got 12 officers out from England, and we should have had 50 – and everything else in the same proportion. You can imagine now why my letters have been so short and scrappy.

However, that part of it is all finished, and now we are all going to utilise what we have created. But alas! We have given the Turks, or rather the Germans, time to prepare, and the landing will be a very different thing now to what it would have been a month ago. We have 18,000 regular troops – splendid – our 30,000 Australians [sic], splendid material, but their worth has to be proved, 18–20,000 French troops, and about 15,000 of 'Winston's Army' [Royal Naval Division]. In all about 80–85,000 men.

Never in the history of the world has such an expedition sailed. Never has a big campaign been so hastily organised and put together, and never has such an undertaking had so little consideration given it from home.

> I believe we shall succeed, simply because everybody is determined that it must. There is no alternative. Certainly the Generals are full of dash and determination and everybody Naval and Military is full of the right sort of spirit. Sunday will be a wonderful day but we must have fine weather. Tonight I feel a great load off my shoulders. The hard thinking work is over and finished, and tomorrow morning I shall be as fit as a lark …[8]

For a few moments he allowed himself the luxury of dreaming beyond the landing and the destruction of the forts, which he considered a foregone conclusion once the Army was ashore. If all went according to plan, the fleet would be surging through the Dardanelles three days after the first blow was struck. 'And then for Constantinople,' he wrote, 'of which I propose to be the first Christian Governor since the 15th Century … We want just a little bit of luck and we shall make history.'[9]

On a day awash with great hope and tantalising possibility it was a forgivable conceit. The whole force seemed infected by a carnival-like atmosphere. Hamilton described the closing scenes in Mudros as 'the most brilliant and yet touching of pageants'.[10] To the sound of bands and a raucous chorus several thousand strong, ship after ship raised steam before jinking across 'the wonderful blue of the bay'[11] towards the open sea.

After all the 'trying delays',[12] the expeditionary force's commander-in-chief was simply relieved, at last, to have 'an opportunity to strike a blow':[13]

> All the troops are as keen as mustard [he wrote to Kitchener], and I am sure it will not be their fault if anything goes wrong. Birdwood is absolutely confident … Hunter-Weston is more inclined to see the barbed wire and machine guns, but I know he is one of those men who will be daring and venturesome to a fault when once the flag drops …[14]

In fact, contrary to Hamilton's impression, Hunter-Weston was now full of confidence and raring to go. In the *Alaunia* bound for Tenedos, where he was to join Wemyss aboard his flagship, the 29th Division's commanding officer wrote to his wife:

> Tis a Grand Adventure and though I should not have counselled it myself, I believe that we shall pull it off and be successful. Anyway, we'll have a great try … I start at the top of my form, very fit and

well, happy and equable in mind. Without any worries, without any anxiety …[15]

Among the first to depart, between noon and 1pm, was the *River Clyde*, her dowdy shape rendered distinctive by 'her extra gangways tacked on to her side and her sand-bagged upper structure'.[16] Strung out along her sides were what Unwin called 'my weird collection'[17] of craft: two specially decked lighters, a hopper and steam pinnace on the port beam and a third lighter to starboard. The 'wreck ship' was travelling light on the first leg of her epic mission: just her crew of twenty-four, Wedgwood's fifty-odd machine gunners, Lieutenant Colonels Williams and Doughty-Wylie and a couple of donkeys.

Weaving her way past a mighty fleet of British, French and Russian warships and a host of transports, she was treated to an unforgettable farewell from sailors and soldiers lining the decks. *River Clyde*'s surgeon, Peter Burrowes Kelly wrote:

> The send-off was tremendous; bands playing, cheering, singing and messages from all the ships, wishing us success and a safe return. As we passed the flagship, *Euryalus*, Admiral Wemyss signalled us himself from the quarter deck using his left arm and telescope.[18]

It was a moment to stir the soul. 'Can you imagine how proud I felt as we steamed down the line, I on the forecastle head,'[19] wrote George Drewry, *River Clyde*'s 'Adonis-like beauty'[20] and second in command. Safely through the boom, Unwin lengthened the tows before handing control to his young deputy. For the rest of the journey to Tenedos, they would alternate watches. Between spells on the bridge, Drewry busied himself with final preparations 'for there were,' as he noted, 'many things to be done'.[21]

Behind them came the troop-carrying transports, one after another, throughout the afternoon. The *Caledonia*, carrying the 1st Royal Munster Fusiliers, left at 5.30 pm at the start of what Guy Geddes called 'the great adventure'.[22] It was, he wrote, 'a perfect evening as we steamed stealthily out … an incident memorable for its solemnity and one might say grandeur'.[23] They passed men-of-war, transports and ships 'of every sort'. Those with bands struck up martial airs and music hall favourites, those without relied on their crews to cheer themselves heartily hoarse. It was answered by an unnatural silence, as Geddes recalled:

> What struck me most forcibly was the demeanour of our own men from whom not a sound, and this from the light-hearted, devil-may-

care men from the South of Ireland. Even they were filled with a sense of something impending which was quite beyond their ken.[24]

It was an almost sepulchral silence, 'as if they were but too familiar with that which was to happen shortly'.[25] Such feelings were hardly surprising. In a letter written shortly before leaving Mudros, Guy Nightingale noted: 'Our ship is being turned into a Hospital ship, as they expect 2000 casualties in the first 48 hours!'[26]

Aboard the *Ausonia*, whose troops included the 1st Royal Dublin Fusiliers who were to go in the first wave, the air of foreboding was even more marked. George Davidson sensed the mood before departing:

> A different atmosphere pervades our ship today, a feeling of strain and anxiety is more or less on every mind, not that it would be apparent to an outsider except in a case or two.[27]

He put it down to 'bad news' emanating from the latest aerial and naval reconnaissance reports. They spoke of a peninsula swarming with 'well-armed Turks, wire entanglements of great breadth and height everywhere, and, of course, trenches'.[28] Though they had been given plans with the enemy positions marked, he felt these could only be 'roughly correct'.[29] Added to this uncertainty was the alarming discovery, reported only the day before, that the number of gun positions had been greatly increased. In his diary he wrote:

> We may be outnumbered ten or twelve to one, and our having to face their well-defended positions in open boats is not altogether comforting, and naturally all feel a bit anxious. General Hare … spoke to me on the '*Caledonia*' and I thought he looked worried, and is thinner than when I saw him last at Coventry. Colonel Rooth of the Dublins does not look over happy. He came down to lunch, had a look at the table, and went up to deck with a cigarette, and at the present moment he stands near where I am writing with both hands in his pockets, peering straight down the side of the ship into the waters.
>
> Those of us with less responsibility are certainly less troubled; all are prepared for great sacrifices, and everyone is ready to play his part in what will certainly be a great tragedy.[30]

Watching from the deck of the *Arcadian*, Orlo Williams, the expeditionary force's chief cipher officer, found the proud procession of transports overwhelming. His thoughts were of his colleague

Doughty-Wylie and the 'gallant company' who were departing, 'a great many of them for ever'.[31] His emotions got the better of him. 'Tears rolled down my cheeks,' he wrote, 'as those men went so gaily to their desperate enterprise.'[32]

The *Ausonia* led *Caledonia* out of Mudros shortly before 5 pm She was the third of the A-class converted liners to leave, though the first two anchored just beyond the boom leaving the way clear for her appointment at Tenedos. Progress across the still waters of the Aegean was slow, hampered by the drag of three large lighters. Wandering up on deck after dinner, Davidson spotted the dark bulk of three warships which he took to be, *Swiftsure, Dublin* and *Euryalus*. None was showing any lights. With his cabin port-holes covered with cardboard and steel shutters, he pondered escaping the close atmosphere below by sleeping on deck. A watery looking moon was ringed with a big halo. The sea was still calm, the evening warm, but the ship's officers 'prophesised'[33] wind.

Their forecast proved correct. In transports dotted about the bay of Tenedos, thousands of troops woke on 24 April to pitching seas and a stiff breeze blowing in from the north-west. 'Rough this morning,' noted Reginald Gillett in the *Alaunia*, 'doubtful whether we shall attempt landing or not …'[34] On the *Caledonia*, Geddes felt the same way:

> The wind had got up, and in consequence, the sea. Wild rumours were prevalent that the elements might force a postponement.[35]

No doubt based on his recent misadventures at Mudros, Clement Milward thought a further delay 'probable'.[36] The weather did little to relax already strained nerves. Milward observed:

> General Hunter-Weston, again, in his highly-strung way, going through the arrangements for the landing, the naval artillery support of the ships and his over-sanguine four phases of the advance to beyond Achi Baba on the very first day. We none of us said what we thought.
>
> I was busy, too, with marking maps from the latest Intelligence Aerial Reports, putting in the enemy's guns and trenches north of Achi Baba.
>
> Just before lunch the General and Wolley-Dod went over to the '*Euryalus*' in a pinnace. We watched them with amusement as they narrowly escaped falling in the water while getting into the dancing boats; they got an awful tossing going across. It looked no landing tomorrow.[37]

Hunter-Weston had every right to be concerned. Following his 'uncomfortable'[38] and somewhat undignified transfer, he was only too aware that the operation was hanging in the balance yet again. From *Euryalus*, he wrote to his wife:

> Smooth weather is an essential for our enterprise. Rough seas would play the Devil with our landing. So we will hope the weather will be favourable to us. That like so much, so very much, in this Adventure is on the lap of the Gods.[39]

The heavy seas had already caused enough damage. The *Ausonia*, her lighters almost swamped by the dashing waves, eventually reached the rendezvous at 9.30 am, more than five hours later than expected. She took her place among a cluster of transports, torpedo boats, destroyers, minesweepers, tugs and 'other small fry' in a bay protected by eight battleships 'drawn up in line facing the open sea'.[40] Lying nearby, Davidson could see the *River Clyde* and he admitted:

> The thought of spending the coming night on her lowest deck is not attractive. She is painted khaki on one side I see, but only in patches, the idea evidently is to make her resemble a sandstone rock – all very ingenious no doubt, but she will make a good target in spite of her paint.[41]

The *River Clyde* had reached Tenedos around dusk the previous evening after an uneventful passage. Following a dinner of pheasant, a gift from the captain of the *Soudan*, Unwin and his crew 'worked till midnight getting things ready'[42] for the arrival of the troops the following day. However, the unsettled weather, 'blowing fresh'[43] as Unwin put it, threatened to undo all their efforts. 'Things looked bad,'[44] wrote Drewry. The young midshipman was 'afraid our show would not come off'.[45] And there were other concerns too, as he explained:

> About 6am a signal came to us telling us we were in someone's berth, so we had to weigh [anchor] and for an hour we wandered among the ships with our long tail just scrapping [sic] along ships' sides and across their bows. We were nobody's dog, nobody loved us.[46]

It wasn't a case of finding any spare berth. Even at this late stage, there was still vital work to be done to make *River Clyde* ready for the landing. 'As we couldn't rig the foremost stages with the anchor down,' wrote Unwin, 'I had to find a ship to lie to.'[47] The best option seemed to be the

Fauvette, but reaching her across the crowded anchorage with a tow of lighters and steam boats trailing behind was no easy matter. It was made even harder by the weather. 'The trouble was, with the wind abeam, trying to cross a ship's bow time after time we just got our tail clear and only just,'[48] observed Unwin. After no little drama, they eventually managed to tie up to *Fauvette*'s stern. And there, wrote Drewry, 'we put the last touches to the staging on the bow'.[49]

Their struggles were not in vain. 'After lunch,' noted Milward, 'the wind suddenly dropped and the sea became calm.'[50] Without delay orders were passed to the transports for the troops to prepare to transfer to *River Clyde*. Suddenly, it was, in George Davidson's words, 'all hurry and bustle'.[51] As his men dashed off for a last meal, he was left guarding a pile of coats and an assortment of equipment while contemplating the prospect of the next day's 'murderous work'.[52] Within an hour of the message's receipt, the first shipment of troops was on its way. Their arrival was watched admiringly by Petty Officer David Fyffe. The twenty-four-year-old member of Wedgwood's armoured car machine gun party wrote in his diary:

> About six o'clock at night, a big tug drew up alongside and the first of the two thousand troops began to come on board. They were the Irish Brigade [*sic*], the 1st Dublin and Munster Fusiliers, splendid fellows and some of the best of our crack regular regiments ... These are the first I have seen of our first line regular troops, as fit as fiddles, trained to the inch and splendidly equipped. If the landing can be effected, these men will do it. I have never seen such a collection of splendid manhood, and the very sight of them gives one confidence in our success. These famous regiments have been splendidly chosen for this, the most difficult and hazardous enterprise of the war ...[53]

Arthur Coke, Fyffe's section officer aboard the *River Clyde*, had spent most of the previous night with Peter Burrowes Kelly. In the cabin they shared, the English aristocrat and Irish surgeon smoked and swapped stories 'about all kinds of things, from Holkham to Ireland, and the reception the Turks had in store for us'.[54] Kelly later recalled:

> We both decided to believe in Commander Unwin and as he had said it would mean death for hundreds, so we believed him. It struck me that night that Arthur had a presentiment that he was not coming back, as his luck had been too great in France for him to get through this time.[55]

Now, as fleet sweepers began delivering troops to the *River Clyde*, Coke rushed off a last letter home:

> This is just a line on the eve of the great landing. We run ashore on this ship at 5.30 tomorrow morning. I only pray everything will go satisfactorily and no shell will strike this ship as we have two whole regiments on board, so it would mean a terrible loss.
>
> They are coming on board now off the transport, and are being packed like sardines in the holds. It is all fearfully exciting and I think tomorrow will be the greatest day of my life, as I have got 3 Maxims on the focsle [*sic*] and am practically responsible for keeping off any attack while the troops are landing.[56]

From late afternoon until well into the evening the flow of fleet sweepers packed with men and equipment was almost continuous. Among those clambering aboard the *River Clyde* were men of the 2nd Hampshires. Major Arthur Beckwith's Z Company and Captain Alfred Addison's Y Company, together with Headquarters' Company filed into No 3 hold, abaft the funnel, where, as one officer noted, they were 'in a grand position to receive it, if it fell'.[57] They came burdened with gear that included 200 rounds of ammunition, a full pack and haversack, a waterproof sheet, some firewood, three days' iron rations which might have to last five days and a full water bottle which was not to be drunk from without permission as it was thought possible the Turks had poisoned the wells on the peninsula. All told, every man carried 80lb of kit, all of which had to be crammed into the cramped holds. 'There was hardly even sitting room,' wrote one of the Hampshires, 'and sleep was out of the question.'[58] Fyffe did not envy them their night in 'the stuffy, uncomfortable holds':[59]

> The lower ones must be a pretty fair reproduction of the Black Hole of Calcutta, and we have been doing our best to keep them going by making enormous cauldrons of coffee in the galley and handing it round.[60]

The situation was not helped by changes to the original complement of units. According to Henry Tizard, who as commander of the only complete battalion on board had organised stowage arrangements with Unwin, 'the detail of troops was altered twice, and was altered yet a third time just before we left at the last moment so that others were put in who had never been on board before'.[61] Though he didn't specify who the late additions were, he may have been referring to the six officers and 162 men of the 1/1st West Riding Field Company. Despite being listed in the *River Clyde* 'Order of Battle' issued on 21 April, they had apparently been omitted from the exercise arranged by Tizard and Unwin four days earlier.[62]

One of the Yorkshire sappers, George Smith, a grocer's son from Sheffield, later maintained that neither he nor his chums knew anything about the landing plan. Prior to boarding at Tenedos on the eve of his twenty-first birthday, he had not set foot on the *River Clyde* let alone taken part in any rehearsals. As far as he could recall, their only preparation for the landing was 'a bit of training going down ladders on to little boats'.[63] According to Smith, it was only when they were safely aboard that they learned of the part they were to play next day and the equipment and stores they were to carry.

Together with the Scottish territorials who made up three bearer sections of 89th Field Ambulance, they struggled with all their equipment into No 4 Hold, which they shared with 'Pog' Tisdall's Anson platoon and the GHQ signals party. What Tizard called 'the place of honour',[64] the fore-end Nos 1 and 2 Holds, were occupied by the Munsters who were distributed as follows: X Company (Captain Guy Geddes), Z Company (Captain Eric Henderson), Headquarters and the battalion machine gun section in the forward upper deck hold and Y Company (Major Charles Jarrett) and W Company (Major William Hutchinson) in the lower deck hold.[65]

The location of the 1st Royal Dublin Fusiliers' W Company (Captain Herbert Crozier) is unclear. Tizard has them in one of the fore-holds, as indeed does an anonymous source from the Hampshires, while Geddes places them in No 3 Hold. Either way, they, together with all the other troops on the *River Clyde*, had little room and even less comfort.

The constrained space was not the only cause of complaint. Geddes was disappointed to find the promise of a hot meal did not materialise. 'The men's fare was bad and similarly that of the officers,' he noted. 'Bully beef and biscuits with hot tea at a premium.'[66] For all the grouses, many aboard the collier were favourably struck by the manner in which most of the troops adapted to their grim surroundings. Fyffe reflected:

> They are big, rough fellows these, but kindly and generous to a degree and it is a pleasure to be among them. Of a truth the British Tommy has a heart of gold under his rough and rather unattractive exterior, and it gave one a queer, choking feeling when one watched these big, light-hearted schoolboys, and thought of what might be awaiting them within twelve short hours.[67]

Unwin, too, was impressed. He found the troops to be 'in capital spirits'[68] and later wrote:

> We had plenty of stores on board, so I had a dinner party in my so-called ward-room of all my crowd plus as many of the regimental officers as we could seat, for many of whom it was their last dinner.[69]

George Davidson was one of those who partook of Unwin's rudimentary dining arrangements. Around 10.30 pm, he noted in his diary:

> Arrived on 'coal boat' at 6.30. Place in stern fitted up for officers' supper; two lime barrels and a few rough boards form table: whisky; tinned meat; biscuits; 2200[70] of us on board; all happy and fit. We start in two hours …[71]

In fact, *River Clyde* was ready earlier. At 11.30 am Unwin told Drewry to 'snatch some sleep'[72] in readiness for the off. His orders were, as he later remarked, 'simplicity itself'.[73] He merely had to ensure the collier was standing off V Beach at 5.30 am ready to follow the first 'tow' in. Free to set off whenever he liked, he decided to give himself plenty of time by steaming out at midnight:

> It was a perfectly calm night and we could see the Chanak searchlight the whole [way] and most useful it proved to me as, owing to the amount of iron I had put round the bridge, my compass hadn't much idea where the North Pole was.[74]

A big silver moon 'made fretted silver of the glassy, ink-black waters'[75] as the *River Clyde*, with an ungainly collection of craft dragging along her sides, 'glided slowly between the jutting headland and the island which formed the outer gateway to the Dardanelles'.[76] Lost in the 'intense excitement'[77] of it all, David Fyffe found himself drifting back through the tides of time:

> Now we were fairly embarked on our perilous enterprise and one thought with a thrill that dawn would bring our baptism of fire. One felt somehow as if one were clasping hands across the centuries with the great adventurers of ancient times. Was it on such a night as this that the Roman fleet put out from the Gallic shore toward the unknown cliffs of Britain. Did Norman William gaze at that same

silvery moon when his flotilla set out on their great enterprise? And the old crusaders: were their warlike spirits watching eagerly the start of this new crusade against the ancient foe? We felt, that night, on the old *River Clyde*, that we were living history over again as we forged ahead toward the Turkish coast.[78]

Up on the bridge the focus was more prosaic than poetic. Around 2 am, cocoa was 'whacked out'[79] to all hands and Unwin handed over to his twenty-year-old second in command. Drewry later wrote:

> I found myself on the bridge very sleepy with only the helmsman, steering towards the Turkish searchlights ... just making headway against the current, shadowy forms of destroyers and battleships slipping past me.
>
> Visions of mines and submarines rose before me as I thought of the 2½ thousand men in the holds and I felt very young.[80]

Below deck tension of a different sort was knotting stomachs and keeping men awake. 'Our nerves were now fully strung,'[81] Davidson confided in his diary. Having finished his supper, the medical officer remained with a group of officers in the dim-lit ward-room Unwin had created in the stern deck house:

> Some sleeping or pretending; others smoking; I doing latter and sitting on board after trying to snooze with head on a big box and less high one in small of back; but too uncomfortable for anything, so whipped out my 'bookie' and scribbled; light bad, only an oily lamp with glass smoked black, and nearly 20 feet distant. Queer scene altogether.[82]

Unable to settle, Reginald Gillett also sought a better berth:

> The night was bitterly cold ... Some of the officers went up onto the deck. I tried to get some sleep but the cold and hard iron decks were not congenial to sleep. I did find a warm sheltered spot near the engines, but as I was dozing off a heavy sea boot was planted firmly on my face. I had overlooked the fact that I was lying across the doorway to the engine room.[83]

Guy Geddes couldn't sleep either, on account of there being 'too much noise',[84] but was grateful for a comforting cup of hot chocolate and a massage from Josiah Wedgwood, *River Clyde*'s MP turned protector, whose cabin he shared for the night. There was little else to do but wait and get what rest he could:

> The orders regarding the landing had been given us … and we all knew our job and what was expected of us, but, we felt we should have liked to have viewed in reality the scene of our landing beforehand. The maps issued were indifferent, and painted but a poor picture of the topographical features as we found out later.[85]

As for his own feelings, he was under no illusions about what lay ahead:

> I felt we were for it. That the enterprise was unique and would demand all I was possible of giving, and more. That it was no picnic but a desperate venture. I just longed to get on with it and be done with it.[86]

The torment of waiting was almost at an end.

Chapter 10

'Dad, it Was Glorious'

The progress of the invasion armada was slow against the current in the early hours of 25 April. As well as the warships, transports and fleet sweepers crowded with troops, more than 100 small boats – naval cutters, lifeboats, lighters and steam pinnaces – had to be towed to their appointed positions off the southern landing beaches. For all the detailed planning and organisation that had gone into the operation, little allowance appeared to have been made for the strength of the current rushing out from the Dardanelles. Hampered by tows and tide, most ships barely exceeded five knots, making the short journey fraught with worry.

From the specially fortified bridge of the *River Clyde*, Unwin peered anxiously into the darkness, his gaze fixed on the searchlight sweeping the waters ahead of him. 'I was terribly afraid that I was adrift,' he later wrote, 'but if I was others were worse.'[1] Some of the ships and tows were as much as an hour behind schedule, while he needed 'every minute'[2] of the 4½ hours he had allowed himself to reach his rendezvous.

Aware that he would be unable to sleep even if he had the opportunity to do so, Unwin had spent most of the night standing watch on the bridge. Drewry took an occasional turn between snatches of sleep before being called, together with Seaman George Samson and a party of six Greek volunteers, to go aboard the steam hopper *Argyle*. As they climbed over the side and made their way across the lighters to reach the hopper, day was breaking to reveal a tranquil sea flecked with shipping and a distant shore wreathed in early morning mist. 'Dad, it was glorious!' Drewry would later exclaim in a letter home. 'Dozens of ships; Battleships, cruisers, destroyers and transports.'[3]

A 'pearly-grey light' had chased the night away and red flashes could be seen through the murk. David Fyffe had been busy filling machine gun belts with ammunition below decks when the distant thunder of gunfire brought him up on deck:

> Now as we clustered on deck watching the dim flashes that came and went at frequent intervals on both our bows and straight ahead, and listening to the dull thudding and rumbling of the bombardment, there loomed up suddenly out of the grey obscurity the long black shape of a battleship, silent and motionless. Hardly had we passed it when a long low destroyer, her knife-like bows slicing the water into two great foaming rolls that surged along her sides, slid alongside and a hoarse megaphone bawled orders from the dim bridge. Almost at once the *Clyde* began to speed up and soon we were forging ahead toward the booming guns ...[4]

Approaching from the west, the escorting ships of the 3rd Squadron had arrived some 1,500 yards off Tekke Burnu more or less as planned at around 4.30 am. It was, in the circumstances, a splendid feat of navigation. One of the officers responsible, Lieutenant John Godfrey, was aboard Wemyss' headquarters' ship. He later wrote:

> The problem ... was to lead the tows of boats and small craft in the right direction during the night, and deliver them accurately off W, X and V beaches an hour before dawn ... I became conscious of the loom of the land ahead about 3am. As we were approaching a Cape (Cape Tekke) I was soon able to get a rough fix by bearings of the right and left extremities of the land at Sedd-el-Bahr and the cliffs to the west of Achi Baba ...[5]

Immediately behind W Beach, a dip in the hills, which Godfrey had identified during a reconnaissance ten days earlier, was visible well before dawn, though it would shortly be obscured by the 'blinding sun'[6] that rose just half an hour later.

On board *Euryalus* the troops forming the first wave for the assault on W Beach began descending rope ladders to reach the cutters and lifeboats that were to carry them ashore. 'There was no noise, no confusion,' Wemyss reported, 'and the operation was carried out as if many days drill had been given to it.'[7] True though this was, the impression of an operation progressing with clockwork-like precision is misleading. From an early stage, it was clear that the main landings were not going according to plan. The force on its way to S Beach in Morto Bay was already late and, as would soon become apparent, the tows bound for V Beach were falling behind schedule. Whether Wemyss cared to admit it or not, the plan of attack, which called for a co-ordinated naval bombardment at 5 am followed by near simultaneous landings at five beaches half an hour later, was unravelling even as the fleet collected off Tekke Burnu.

None of this, however, was apparent to the men aboard *River Clyde*. Those who ventured on deck in the grey light of dawn were struck not only by the size of the force but by the thunderous roar of a bombardment the like of which few of them had ever witnessed. One of the Hampshires' officers wrote:

> It was a wonderful sight. Destroyers hurtled across our bows, rushing to the Straits to cover the ships; pinnaces each with six ship's boats in tow [sic] were making for the respective beaches. The flashes and thunder of the ships' guns, the rush of the big shells over our heads towards the land, and their terrific explosion on impact, together with the mild excitement caused by the enemy's shells pitching near us, and the surmise as to what would happen when the ship struck, whether she would go over to one side, whether the funnel would fall, or the boilers burst, and finally whether we should come under a tremendous fire on landing, everything combined to make an ineffaceable impression on one's mind.[8]

To Sapper George Smith it heralded an unforgettable 21st birthday. He later recalled 'salvo after salvo' raining on the peninsula:

> As we drew near we could see the shells dropping right into the trenches, throwing up showers of earth, and occasionally one would land on the fort or among the houses of the village, and immediately there would rise amid the red flash, a great mass of stones and other debris.[9]

Peter Burrowes Kelly thought the bombardment 'awful in its grandeur'.[10] Army medic George Davidson went further, describing it as 'a grand roar such as the world had never heard'.[11] Within minutes of the first salvo, shortly after 5 am, it seemed as if every ship had joined the deafening chorus. In an allusion to his Scottish roots, Davidson recorded:

> The peninsula was quickly one dense cloud of poisonous-looking yellow-black smoke, through which flashes of bursting shells were to be seen everywhere. It was truly a magnificent sight and the roar of the guns stirred one's blood like some martial skirl from the bagpipes.[12]

He was not alone in being awed by the show of naval might. From his post on the still-attached steam hopper, George Drewry was transfixed by the sight of a shoreline transformed into a quivering 'mass of fire and smoke'. 'The noise was awful,' he wrote, 'and the air full of powder.'[13] Two midshipmen were more distant observers. From the decks of HMS *Agamemnon*, patrolling the entrance to the Straits, Fraser MacLiesh called the bombardment 'the the most awe-inspiring affair I have ever witnessed'. Later in his diary, he noted:

> 20 ships in all were engaged and they went at it hammer and tongs as fast as they could load for ½ an hour. The noise was terrific as the air quivered and vibrated with the boom of the guns and the whistle and rumble of the exploding shells. After a time the coast was almost entirely enveloped in the smoke of bursting shells and it seemed inconceivable that man or beast could still be alive …[14]

The 'roar and screech' of so many guns and bursting shells was such that Herbert Williams could not distinguish which ship was firing what shell:

> It was like hundreds of Maxims. The whole of Sedd-el-Bahr and the surrounding country was shelled and in the half-light the bursting shells and the glare of the burning houses spread a reddish glow over everything. It seemed impossible that anything could live in such an inferno: wire entanglements, parts of houses, clods of earth and everything else being blown sky high. It was an extraordinary sight. Above all this away inland a glorious red sun rose and I was quite appalled to see the terrific destruction. The town wasn't there. I've seen ruined towns before but there wasn't a wall standing.[15]

Appearances, however, were deceptive. For all its fury, the bombardment achieved relatively little. A few shells landed on enemy positions, but most of the earthwork defences together with the rows of barbed wire straddling V Beach escaped destruction. Hunkered in their trenches on Hill 141 (Harabkale to the Turks), the men from 3rd Battalion, 26th Regiment, stuck doggedly to their posts while the earth erupted around them. Their grim resolve in the face of a deluge of fire that smothered their positions in a smog of 'blueish-black and greenish smoke'[16] earned high praise from their commanding officer, Major Mahmut Sabri:

> The area was altogether small compared to the weight of fire being put down by the fleet. Many shells were falling side by side and

many shrapnel shells were exploding one after the other. The fire was coming crosswise from south and west, later on it also started coming from the north-west. At this time two of our 37.5 mm guns were destroyed … and many rifle and communication trenches were flattened out. Some of the rifle trenches which had been dug to protect the soldiers' lives, instead became their graves. At the same time, wounded who were able to walk began coming into the first aid posts. As the men had been taught in their training … on arrival at the first aid post they … asked, 'I have been wounded and cannot continue my duty. I have given my ammunition to my comrades in the section. Here is my rifle, who should I hand it over to?' And then they waited their turn to have their wounds bandaged.

The shrapnel bullets which the enemy fired from time to time … were of a type not previously seen … Some of them were as big as eggs.[17]

The discipline of the troops undergoing the bombardment was, indeed, remarkable. Major Sabri wrote with pride of the 'intrepid demeanour' of his reserve force, kneeling and waiting, rifles at the ready, to occupy the front-line trenches and confront the invaders:

> Giving not the least heed to the enemy's superior forces nor to his ammunition and equipment, these warriors, although they had seen some of their comrades buried in the ground beside them or their arms and legs flying in the air, impatiently awaited the moment when they would be able to use their weapons.[18]

As the *River Clyde* steamed on, smoke obscuring the Helles shore, the men cramped in the holds had no idea that the fire-plan on which they depended was already falling apart, its myriad failings masked by the very pall many mistook as a mark of success. In reality, the bombardment in support of the main landings was ill-directed and wholly inadequate as the Covering Force would soon discover to its cost. What naval officers variously referred to as a 'heavy'[19] and 'thoroughly searching'[20] bombardment initially targeting the landing beaches, their approaches and the positions of 'known batteries'[21] was anything but, being severely hampered by an overly cautious decision not to close the shore and a desire to conserve the fleet's limited supply of ammunition in readiness for the charge through the Dardanelles which, it was anticipated, would follow shortly after the landings. Another difficulty, one which could and should have been foreseen, was noted by many of the attendant ships' captains and summed up succinctly by Captain Cecil Maxwell-Lefroy of the *Swiftsure*:

> The light was extremely bad, everything being in complete shadow with the glare of the approaching sunrise behind. It was therefore impossible to select definite points of aim on the beach and vicinity.[22]

At V Beach, the plan was even more flawed. In what seems an astonishing oversight, initial naval support for what was considered the most important landing was confined to a solitary ancient pre-dreadnought boasting only four 'woefully inaccurate'[23] heavy guns. HMS *Albion*'s orders were to take up position 1,300 yards from the Cape Helles lighthouse and keep 'watch' over V Beach, from Hill 138 in the west via the western and southern slopes of Hill 141 in the centre as far as the village of Sedd-el-Bahr in the east. Described by one historian as 'a sorry farce',[24] *Albion*'s pitiful contribution to the assault was not helped by the absence on board of its military artillery adviser.

Major Alan Thomson, commanding 368th Battery, 29th Division, had taken part in a preliminary reconnaissance, observing the enemy defences from *Swiftsure*'s foretop in order to help pinpoint targets during the landing operation. But plans for him to join *Albion* at Tenedos the day before the landing were scuppered when he arrived to find the ship 'on duty at the entrance to the Dardanelles'.[25] The blunder would leave *Albion* without a military adviser until late in the evening of 25 April. It was a mishap typical of a confused action detailed in the report compiled by *Albion*'s acting captain, Commander Hector Watts-Jones:

> In accordance with orders, *Albion* anchored S.10.E true, 1300 yards from Cape Helles on the morning of 25th. At 5am there was a slight mist especially between Seddul Bahr [*sic*] and No 1 Fort, and hardly light enough to distinguish objects. *Albion* opened fire at 5.[0]4[am], and from then onwards fired deliberately into all objects overlooking V Beach that seemed to be of military importance.
>
> At 5.25 as the smoke over Area A [the navy's designation for the eastern tip of the peninsula around V Beach] was very thick, and no boats were approaching, checked fire. Expenditure of ammunition up to this time being, 6-in: 121 rounds, 12 pr: 54 rounds, 12-in: 2 rounds, both latter having been fired into SW Tower of Seddul Bahr [*sic*] Castle.
>
> At 5.33 opened fire again, and continued as before. At 5.50 observed boats from *Euryalus* passing *Swiftsure*. *River Clyde* and Fleet

Sweepers approaching; increased rate of fire whenever boats seemed to be coming, decreased again when they proved not to be for V Beach.

At 6.[0]5 *River Clyde* passed to Starboard, but later dropped back. Observed boats on W Beach were under heavy fire.

At 6.25 *Sapphire* signalled that our shot was falling on her landing party (Y Beach). *Albion* had fired at a trench on crest of hill close to Fort No 1. Checked fire accordingly.

At 6.33 observed *Cornwallis* approaching with boats, and opened heavy fire, but checked again at 6.35 on observing the boats were not loaded …[26]

The stop-start nature of the covering bombardment was mirrored by the landing force's less than smooth approach. 29th Division's General Staff war diary describes an assault in disarray:

5.30am: *Cornwallis'* tows for Beach V unable to make headway against tide and it was evident that landing would be delayed at least half an hour.

5.45pm: *River Clyde* ordered to run in simultaneously with tows from *Euryalus* for W Beach. She went ahead but was stopped by HMS *Albion* owing to misunderstanding.

6am: Still delayed by tows for V Beach and collier [*River Clyde*]. But troops were landed at Y Beach and tows from *Euryalus* and *Implacable* [at X] were ordered in. Troops at Y Beach reported to be all ashore.

French Squadron, with transports astern, came up and shelled Asiatic shore about Kum Kale and commenced to disembark troops in that neighbourhood.

6.30am: Troops intended for Beach S were very late owing to strength of the tide, and as their role of cutting the enemy's communications could not now be carried out, they were diverted to the V Beach by RA [Rear Admiral Wemyss] Commanding, but the signal apparently did not get through, as they landed at Beach S successfully about 7.30am.

Lancashire Fusiliers from *Euryalus* pulled in under a heavy fire of rifles and machine guns into W Beach which was lined with wire …[27]

The view from the bridge of *River Clyde* was hardly less confusing. Having rendezvoused off Tekke Burnu, Unwin scoured the sea in vain for any sign of the tows that he was to follow in to V Beach. All he could see and hear was the roaring bombardment. Steaming past W Beach he glimpsed the Lancashire Fusiliers 'getting a dusting'.[28] In what he called 'a foresight of what we were in for', he saw them splashing ashore from their open boats and 'being bowled over fairly often'.[29] But of the tows carrying the Royal Dublin Fusiliers that were to spearhead his landing there was not a trace.

Uncertain what to do, Unwin slowed as he continued making for his objective. It was around 6am and alongside him on the upper bridge were Lieutenant Colonels Carington Smith, the military commander, and Tizard, commanding 1st Royal Munster Fusiliers. Tizard later wrote:

> The sun was right in our faces and it was very difficult to make out things on shore on account of the smoke from the bursting shells; there being no wind to clear it away … At the time we could not make out whether the boats' tows had gone in ahead of us or not. As we passed close to a battleship Captain Unwin [sic] called out to ask if the boats' tows had gone in, and the reply he got was 'Don't know, but go on in.'[30]

The battleship was the *Euryalus* and the order came direct from Wemyss. Accounts of what followed vary. According to Tizard, *River Clyde* 'steamed on'[31] to within a few hundred yards of the shore when Unwin 'thought better of it and turned about'[32] at which point 'we then saw the tows coming towards us'.[33] Unwin, however, remembered it differently. He stated that the change of course came about only following the intervention of Carington-Smith, who was adamant they should adhere to the original plan. To do otherwise would, he claimed, 'upset the whole arrangements'.[34] With both of GHQ's senior staff officers, Lieutenant Colonels Williams and Doughty-Wylie, siding with Carington-Smith, Unwin felt he had no option but to ignore Wemyss' instructions.

This then, was the cause of the strange manoeuvre that *River Clyde* now undertook and which staff officers of the 29th Division aboard *Euryalus* erroneously put down to a 'misunderstanding'.

Unwin knew straightaway that it would be 'impossible'[35] to bring *River Clyde* to a stop. The sea around him was 'thick with shipping'[36] and to try to halt while trailing an assortment of craft was to risk either a collision or a fouled propeller or possibly both. His solution was to 'take a turn out of the ship',[37] in other words to coax the collier in a full circle round the crowded 'sea lane'. It was a course fraught with danger, for we were already pointed for the beach, and ships were firing on all sides of me, and the French were making over to Kum Kale. I couldn't cross their bows and I didn't want to get between our ships and their targets; I jammed the helm hard-a-port and just managed to clear the stern of the *Agamemnon* [in actual fact, it was *Albion*] but saw that I could not clear two destroyers lying on her starboard side with a sweep out between them, so I did the only possible thing [and] went between them knowing that they had plenty of time to slack down the wire and let us run over it. If I had attempted anything else certain disaster would have been the result, probably a fouled propeller and 2300 [*sic*] men waiting to be landed whilst I tried to clear my propeller.

Well we got her round and still no tow was in sight, but I said to myself 'now or never' and, full speed, in we went.[38]

According to some accounts, *River Clyde* had to circle twice to give sufficient time for the six tows carrying the Dublins 'to come up'.[39] Unwin, however, mentioned going round just once before starting his dash for the shore. They had about half a mile to go and the time, according to the war diaries for the 29th Division and the Royal Munster Fusiliers, was somewhere around 6am, some 30 minutes after the first wave should have landed.

It was about then, or shortly before, that the *River Clyde* first came under direct fire from Turkish gun positions on the other side of the Straits. Petty Officer Fyffe reckoned they were opposite Sedd-el-Bahr, 'steering slowly up the channel through the lines of ships, when he suddenly saw 'a big splash in the water a few yards astern':[40]

A friend and I, by virtue of our position as 'bargees', were now on the poop along with two sailors, standing by the hawsers that were towing the barges alongside and we had scarcely time to mark the spreading rings that circled in the water close to our stern, when on a sudden there were two more 'plops' in the water a few yards short of the ship, and we were now fully conscious that shells were being fired at the *Clyde* from somewhere or other… We ducked hastily behind the flag house on the arrival of two more visitors that shrieked close overhead and splashed into the water on the far side of the ship …[41]

According to his account, it was just after the first shells bracketed the ship that Unwin made his manoeuvre. Quite how many shots were directed at her and with what degree of accuracy is not clear. Fyffe reckoned they fell 'uncomfortably close'[42] and Drewry, who was particularly vulnerable aboard the steam hopper, described them as splashing 'round us thick'.[43] But an officer of the Hampshires, who reckoned the fire was a reaction to the *River Clyde*'s turning movement, considered the shooting 'very poor'.[44]

Up on the bridge, Unwin was oblivious to it all. As the *River Clyde* completed its final turn he was concentrated on one thing only: finding the right landing point. Through the cascades of water he strained for a glimpse of any landmarks. He later admitted:

> It was very difficult to locate the beach owing to the smoke and dust, but I had luckily taken a trip up the week before, and had taken a transit of a sort of gravestone on the beach in line with a conspicuous tree on the hill. I got these in line and made for them.[45]

By then, his engine room team had worked up 'a good head of steam'[46] and, aware that it was 'now or never',[47] he decided to go 'hell for leather'[48] for the beach. 'We steamed full speed,' wrote one of the Royal Naval Armoured Car squadron machine gunners, 'all wondering what would happen when we struck the beach …'[49] Fyffe observed:

> Never had the old ship attained such a speed, and with her whole hull quivering under the straining engines, and the smoke pouring in oily black clouds from her funnel, she dashed towards the little bay. Nearer and nearer she grew, and as she approached the land the ships ceased firing and an uncanny silence reigned.[50]

Commander Watts-Jones on the *Albion* had spotted boats 'close to [the] beach'[51] and, in accordance with his instructions to take the 'greatest care … to avoid firing on our own troops',[52] had ordered his guns' crews to hold their fire. The *River Clyde* was barely 200 yards from the shore when George Davidson ran below to tell his men 'to lie down in case we struck rock'.[53] As the collier ploughed on, more than 2,000 men braced themselves for the impact. Shortly after, noted an officer of the Hampshires,

> the [ship's] hooter was sounded (a final warning of the impending bump), and then a few moments later a voice came from the bridge, 'All right, she's aground'. It was hardly credible. There had not been the slightest vestige of a tremor through her, and she was perfectly upright … some 40 yards or so from the beach …[54]

All around the ship there was astonishment at the seeming anticlimax of it all. 'The impact was so slight,' wrote Reginald Gillett, 'we hardly felt it.'[55] Where Fyffe noticed 'a soft jar that quivered from end to end of the ship',[56] Guy Geddes felt nothing at all. Further back, George Smith remembered only 'a grinding sort of noise' followed by 'a gentle slowing down'[57] as *River Clyde* gradually lost way and settled down. There was a momentary 'bustle'[58] and then calm. 'For a short space,' added Gillett, 'there was dead silence.'[59]

Ever the professional, Unwin took swift mental note of their position. 'As I feared,' he wrote, 'it was a little too far to the Eastward. We were on the extreme edge of the reef. Still, we weren't far off.'[60] Standing nearby, Lieutenant Colonel Williams could scarcely believe his eyes. 'There was not a sign of a Turk,' he wrote. Turning to Doughty-Wylie, he said: 'I believe we are to land unopposed.'[61]

Even as he spoke, he saw the first trip of tows with more than 700 Dublin Fusiliers aboard pulling in towards the shore.

Chapter 11

'Slaughtered Like Rats in a Trap'

Dazed and weary-eyed, the defenders of Sedd-el-Bahr steeled themselves to meet the assault they had anticipated for so long. Few had slept in more than thirty hours. But now, at last, the waiting was over. The nightly harassment of British destroyers trying to disrupt their efforts to strengthen the shore defences had given way to the real thing. After more than an hour of heavy but intermittent bombardment, during which they could do little but pray and wait for the storm to abate, they emerged from their shelters amid the rubble of the ruined fort and in trenches cut along the shell-pocked rise to see a strange armada approaching.

Strung out in an uneven line across the bay were small steamboats pulling a straggle of lifeboats filled with soldiers. More bizarre and puzzling, however, was the presence of a large cargo vessel, its bows pointed straight towards the beach. Unlike all the other ships, it showed no sign of stopping as it steamed steadily on, its progress across the glassy sea undisturbed by a shower of shells coming from the Asiatic shore. Gradually it dawned on them that she was being deliberately run aground, though to what purpose was not immediately clear. Whatever she was and whatever she meant to do she was, in any case, too far out to open fire just yet. So, too, were the smaller boats.

The orders issued the day before by Major Mahmut Sabri were clear and unambiguous:

> When the enemy attempted their disembarkation, there was to be no hurry and concentrated fire was to be opened after the boats and sloops were within 2-300 metres of the shore. When the alarm was sounded the reserve companies were to assemble from the west and the south at the eastern slope of the covered ridge [Hill 141 or Harabkale].[1]

115

Displaying a discipline to match their fortitude, the survivors of the three platoons defending V Beach [Ertugrul Cove to the Turks] continued to bide their time. Hidden from view in positions inside the ruined fort, close to the jetty at Sedd-el-Bahr and by a mill north of the village as well as the wire-screened strongpoint on Hill 141, they watched and waited as the invaders drew ever nearer. But while the Turkish plan was holding firm, the British one was already unravelling.

Lieutenant Colonel Rooth, the man with the unenviable job of leading the boat landing, was well aware of the hazards facing his men. He had seen and heard enough about the beach defences at Sedd-el-Bahr to know the scale of the task confronting his three companies of Dublin Fusiliers. Before leaving Mudros he had worked out a plan which he thought offered them their best chance of success. It involved one company hitting the beach head-on with the other two companies landing on the right, with one party directed towards The Camber, to the south-east of Sedd-el-Bahr. Once ashore it was hoped that the Dublins would forge quickly inland in a pincer-like movement that would meet on the high ground above the village. All being well, they would have half and hour's start on the second wave coming in on the *River Clyde*, long enough, so it was thought, to be in a position to support their landing.

As Lieutenant Colonel Tizard, the Munsters' CO, wrote:

> In consultation with Lieut Colonel Rooth … I had arranged that he should endeavour to enfilade a trench we had seen on the hill above the village when we got through as it would greatly assist my attack on the 141 hill.[2]

In accordance with the landing plan, Rooth had divided his force at Tenedos. While W Company went aboard the *River Clyde*, X, Y and Z Companies transferred to the former Great Eastern Railway Packets turned fleet sweepers *Clacton* and *Newmarket*, where they were joined by a beach party composed of fifty men from the 4th Platoon of the Anson Battalion under Lieutenant John Denholm, RNVR, and a party of midshipmen. Among the latter were five 'snotties' from the battleship *Cornwallis* of whom we shall hear more: Arthur Hardiman, Maurice Lloyd, Wilfrid Malleson, William Monier-Williams and Howard Weblin.

The journey across from Tenedos was cramped and uncomfortable for sailors and soldiers alike. Lloyd recalled a 'very crowded' *Clacton* and an unsettling night spent 'sleeping on the hard deck' with 'packs for pillows'.[3] It was even worse for the bluejackets from *Albion*, *Cornwallis* and *Lord Nelson* assigned to act as coxswains, bowmen and oarsmen for the boats ferrying the troops ashore. Able Seaman Ernest 'Dick' Rickus, a thirty-five-year-old reservist, wrote:

> When we went and had our supper – the last meal I had in *Cornwallis* – at 8.30 [pm] we got into our boats, which were tied up astern, and she [*Cornwallis*] towed us all night. About half an hour before daybreak our steamboats took us in tow and we went and got our troops at daybreak.[4]

The transfer of Rooth's force of around 750 men into the small boats took longer than expected. By the time the pinnace-led tows set off, they were already thirty minutes behind schedule. More time was lost when the trawlers carrying troops to S Beach blundered across their path. That and the struggle against the current meant that the Dublins were almost an hour late when Unwin finally spotted them in their 'crocodiles' of boats, making slowly for V Beach.

Captain David French, second in command of Y Company and reputedly the biggest man in the battalion, recalled:

> As we approached the shore shrapnel began to burst over the boats but caused no damage ... As soon the 'tows' got into shallow water the picquet boats ... cast off & the bluejackets commenced to row. You can imagine how slowly we progressed – 6 men pulling a heavy boat with about 30 soldiers – each carrying over 60lbs kit & ammunition on his body –!![5]

In those last moments, as the *Albion* ceased firing and a strange stillness settled over the invasion armada, there was nothing the Dublins could do but sit and hope that the bombardment had done its work. Unwin's impromptu manoeuvre allowed the tows to draw briefly ahead. But as the *River Clyde* started its run-in it appeared to those on shore as if ship and tows were advancing side by side in a rough line astern formation spread across the bay.

The question of who landed first remains unresolved. From his sandbagged position on the wing of the *River Clyde*'s bridge, Josiah Wedgwood thought the first and second waves landed 'simultaneously'.[6]

Tizard and Williams, however, reckoned the tows were a little behind when the collier grounded. Unwin was too distracted to be sure either way. But he was certain of one thing: their arrival on V Beach was the signal for the Turks to open fire with every available weapon. From 'front, right and left'[7], they were assailed by 'shell, pompom, maxims and rapid rifle fire'.[8] To David Fyffe, in the foremost casemate, it seemed as if the 'whole slope leapt into a roar of firing'.[9] It felt, wrote Surgeon Kelly, as though 'we [had] entered a perfect hell'.[10]

The hapless Dublins bore the brunt of the onslaught. Stuck in their boats, barely able to move, they were sitting ducks. It was the realisation of Richard Rooth's worst nightmare. Trapped in the open, with nowhere to hide and no chance of fighting back, they never stood a chance. 'The Turks were waiting for us,' wrote Private Fox. 'They mowed our regiment down in dozens.'[11] Rooth was one of the first to fall, killed at the water's edge. Many others did not make it as far. Lance Sergeant A Morrison reckoned 'half the regiment were 'knocked out' before we reached land'. 'By God,' he wrote, 'we did not half go through it. It was like going through Hell itself.'[12]

Lieutenant Cuthbert Maffett, a platoon commander in Major Edward Molesworth's X Company, was in a boat that came in on the *River Clyde*'s port side:

> The Turks let us get very close, and then they opened a terrible fire on us with machine guns and pom-poms, the shells of which contained an incendiary mixture. They began to hit the boat I was in very frequently, and killed many of my men as we were rowing ashore. We were also unlucky enough to lose several of the blue-jackets who were rowing us in, and the men had to take over their oars, and as they did not know much about rowing the result was that we often got broadside on to the shore and presented a better target to the enemy. Just before we grounded the boat got hit once or twice with incendiary shells, and commenced to go on fire. She was also half full of water from the many holes in her by this time. Several of the men who had been wounded fell to the bottom of the boat, and were either drowned there or suffocated by other men falling on top of them; many, to add to their death agonies, were burnt as well.
>
> We then grounded, and I jumped out of the bows of the boat and got hit in the head by a machine gun bullet, others going into a pack that I was carrying on my shoulders. I went under water and came up again, and tried to encourage the men to get to the shore and under cover as fast as they could as it was their only chance. I then went under again. Someone caught hold of me and began pulling me ashore, and as I got to dry land a blue-jacket joined him … Two men got ashore beside me, and then two more that were wounded. We took cover under a low sort of bank that was about ten yards from the water's edge, and bound each other up as best we could. Looking

out to sea I saw the remnants of my platoon trying to get to the shore, but they were shot down one after another, and their bodies drifted out to sea or lay immersed a few feet from the shore ...[13]

The first time Captain French knew his boat – the last in the tow – was under direct attack was when one of the men sitting close to him 'fell back – shot':[14]

I realised immediately that having practically wiped out the other three boats ahead they were now concentrating their fire on us. I jumped out at once in the sea (up to my chest) yelling to the men to make a rush for it & to follow me. But the poor devils – packed like sardines in a tin & carrying this damnable weight on their backs – could scarcely clamber over the sides of the boat and only two reached the shore un-hit while the boat just ahead of mine suffered as much – the same number escaping from that. The only other officer in my boat never even got ashore, being hit by five bullets. A picquet boat most heroically came right in close & towed the boat back to the battleship '*Albion*' which was now anchored about 800 yds [*sic*] from the beach.

I had to run about 100-150 yds in the water and being the first away from the cutter escaped the fire a bit to start with. But as soon as a few followed me the water around seemed to be alive – the bullets striking the sea all round us. Heaven alone knows how I got thro' – a perfect hail of bullets. The beach sloped very gradually – fortunately. When I was about 50 yds from the water's edge I felt one bullet go through the pack on my back & then thought I had got through safely when they put one through my left arm. The fellows in the regt had told me I was getting too fat to run but those who saw me go through that bit of water changed their opinions later – I ran like h-ll!!!!!![15]

Private Robert Martin of X Company was one of only three men out of twenty-five in his boat to survive the storm of fire. He later recalled:

It was sad to hear our poor chums moaning, and to see others dead in the boat. It was a terrible sight to see the poor boys dead in the water; others on the beach roaring for help. But we could do nothing for them ... I must have had someone's good prayer for I do not know how I escaped. Those who were lying wounded on the shore, in the evening the tide came in and they were all drowned, and I was left by myself on the beach. I had to remain in the water for about three hours, as they would fire on me as soon as they saw me make a move. I thought my life was up every minute.[16]

'It was awful,'[17] wrote Corporal James McColgan. He was among half a dozen men from a boatload of thirty-two to reach the beach alive and they included one man – Private Arthur O'Hanlon – who had a hand 'blown off'.[18] In a letter home, McColgan, who was wounded in three places, wrote:

He and I were trying to save one another when he got hit again in his foot and fell back into the boat. Two bullets went through my pack, and I dived into the sea. Then came the job to swim with the pack, and one leg useless. So I managed to pull out the knife and cut the straps and swim to the shore, about half a mile. All the time bullets were ripping around me. My God I'll never forget what we went through …[19]

The naval parties fared no better than the Dublins. Thirty-one year-old Assistant Beachmaster Commander Neston Diggle, who was in charge of taking the first six tows into V Beach, wrote:

They started on us with shell and shrapnell [sic] at 3000 to 4000 yards and at 2000 with rifles, maxims etc: it was a 'mauvais quart a'heure' [a brief unpleasant experience], and about 70 or 80 were hit before landing. The Turks were very strongly placed in big barbed-wire trenches and the village and Fort were full of them. They did not seem to pay any 'respect' to the heavy bombardment, but I think they were so dug-in and also hidden in the cellars of the Fort and village, that our shells had very little effect on them. The bravery of our men was beyond description: unless I had seen it with my own eyes I could never have believed they could have faced and overcome what they did, but they were all Irishmen with their blood well up, which I suppose may be taken as the definition of the word 'Irresistible'!![20]

One of the boats crewed by men from the Cornwallis was peppered as it neared the shore. The bullets were flying 'like a storm of hailstones':[21]

Directly she touched the beach the bowman, [Able Seaman] Taylor, jumped out with the painter, and he was instantly shot, dying later in Malta Hospital. The few untouched soldiers jumped into the water, and of the thirty-two originally in the boat only three got ashore, a Major, Captain, and Lieutenant being killed or wounded with their men.

By this time there were only two left at the oars – Skitmore, AB, and Boy [J T] Darling, with Leading Seaman [T C] Ford at the tiller. Cragie, AB, and Boy Runacres were in the bottom of the boat dressing the wounded. [W G] Lyne, AB, had been hit in the leg by a bullet which had first passed through the boat's side, and though he could not move he dressed the wounded who were within his reach. Boy Darling was shot next, and Ford left the tiller and took his oar.

'Cheer up, my son; it will soon be over,' he said; and almost immediately a bullet found a billet in his shoulder. He continued to row with one hand, and he and Skitmore between them backed the boat out.[22]

No less brave but rather less fortunate was Petty Officer 1st Class William Medhurst's crew of six tasked with ferrying sixty Dublins into V Beach aboard *Cornwallis'* sailing pinnace. Having slipped their tow near the *River Clyde*, they pulled hard through a galling fire that ripped into the boat. Within minutes,

> every sailor at the oars, with the exception of Ward, AB, was shot down; and on seeing this, Petty Officer Medhurst … sang out, 'Jump out, lads, and pull her in!' There was only himself and Ward to answer the call, and out the two of them got, one on the port side and the other on the starboard.
>
> Only three soldiers are believed to have got ashore – all the others were killed in the boat or in the water as they landed. Two of them saved their lives by remaining alongside Ward in the water under the lee of the gunwhale from 7am to 5pm. Medhurst was at first safe, but when the stern of the pinnace swung to the tide, he was exposed to the enemy's fire, and he was not seen again until we recovered his body from the water on the following day.[23]

The pinnace, itself, was later found drifting in the blood-coated surf. It was riddled with holes and filled with dead bodies.

To 'Dick' Rickus it felt as though they had entered 'the gates of hell'.[24] His own survival during two trips in to V Beach that morning was nothing short of miraculous. On the first pull in, he had seen the Dublins in his boat 'fall like leaves in the autumn'[25] as they struggled to get ashore. Then, having managed to draw away, they returned to pick up another boatload and prepared to face the same ordeal all over again:

It was then I got hit in the Right shoulder and, of course, down I went. Anyway, we got the boat ashore and the soldiers – those that could – got out. By this time all my boat's crew were either killed or wounded, so we had to stop there under a hail of bullets from Maxims and Rifle fire.[26]

The valour displayed by the boat crews in the face of almost certain death all but beggared belief. Wemyss considered their gallantry and determination 'beyond praise'.[27] It was a service from which 'few returned'.[28] In his report of the landings, De Robeck singled out the actions of Able Seaman Lewis Jacobs, a twenty-three-year-old Londoner who was a member of one of *Lord Nelson*'s boat parties. With the rest of his crew and all the soldiers in his cutter dead or wounded, he doggedly pressed on, unaided, towards the bullet-swept beach. 'When last seen,' noted De Robeck, 'Jacobs was standing up and endeavouring to pole the cutter to the beach.'[29] Of the six men specially cited by the admiral, four were killed and the other two wounded.

From their positions on the *River Clyde*, officers and men watched with a mixture of dismay and disbelief as the disaster unfolded before their very eyes. 'As each boat got near the shore,' wrote Guy Nightingale, 'you could see men dropping everywhere.'[30] Guy Geddes saw two companies that came in on the port side 'practically annihilated' by the 'ghastly'[31] fusillade. 'They were literally slaughtered like rats in a trap,'[32] he wrote. 'In ten minutes,' observed Josiah Wedgwood, 'there were some 400 dead and wounded on the beach and in the water. Not more than 10 per cent got safe to shore.'[33] As the Turks continued to pour a 'perfect hurricane of lead'[34] across the decks of the *River Clyde* and into the cutters below, De Lancey Williams spotted a cutter 'drifting helplessly'[35] on the tide. 'Every man in it had been killed.'[36]

Peering out from one of the sally ports, medical officer George Davidson could scarcely comprehend what he was witnessing:

It was an extraordinary sight to watch our men go off, boat after boat, push off for a few yards, spring from the seats to dash into the water which was now less than waist deep. It was just at this point that the enemy fire was concentrated. Those who got into the water, rifle in hand and heavy pack on back, generally made a dive forward, riddled through and through, if there was still life in them, to drown in a few seconds. Many were being hit before they had time to spring from the boats, their hands were thrown in the air, or else they heaved helplessly over, stone dead ... Along the water's edge there was now a mass of dead men [and] on the sand a mixture of dead and weltering wounded …[37]

From their 'seats in the stalls' the machine gunners in Arthur Coke's steel-plated casemate were helpless spectators to the massacre. David Fyffe was transfixed:

> Out of six boats that formed one tow, only one reached the shore and beached side-on, and out from among the crowded benches only about a dozen men leapt into the water and rushed for the sand. Their comrades still crouched upright in the boats but they were strangely still, shot dead where they sat. The other four [sic] boats never reached the shore. One by one the oars fell from the dead hands of their occupants and drifted slowly away, and the big white boats lay rocking idly on the shot-torn water many yards from the shore, with not a movement amid the huddle of khaki figures that filled them to the gunwales. As we watched in wordless horror, one of the boats floated slowly past us, bumping along our side, and we could look straight down into her motionless cargo. It was a floating shambles. A mass of corpses huddled together in the bottom of the boat and lying heaped above one another across the crimson benches. Here an arm and hand hung over the gunwale, swaying helplessly as the boat rocked on the waves. There a rifle stuck upright into the sunlight out of a mass of shapeless khaki figures. And everywhere crimson mingling with the brown, and here and there a waxen-white face with draggled hair staring up into the smiling heavens. Slowly the ghastly boat scraped along our sides and slowly drifted out to sea leaving us frozen with a nameless horror and an overpowering dread. Such was our introduction to the glories of war, and when one big fellow turned his drawn white face to us with a slow 'Good God!' as we stared at the vanishing boat, we could only look at him in a queer tight-throated silence and wonder what in Heaven's name it all meant.[38]

And still the boats came in. An officer of the Hampshires saw one tow led by a pinnace making for the centre of the bay:

> When about 150 yards from the shore she cast off, and the boats began to row in. When about 50 yards from the beach a heavy fire was opened on them, and in a few moments every boat had many men in it hit. Still they went on except, I think, for two boats, in which the rowers and every man appeared to be hit, and the oars

123

lost. But from the others, which got close enough in to enable the men to jump out about knee-deep, only about 16 got ashore, about half of whom were wounded.

Most gallant efforts were made by the pinnace commander to tow the boats again and to rescue wounded, who had taken shelter in the water under the seaward side of two of the boats by the shore. Three times the pinnace stood in, each time effecting something, but it was impossible to get some of the boats out again, which was a serious loss as boats were none too plentiful ...

Meanwhile one boat had drifted away to the west side of the bay, where it remained under the cliff out of fire, so that an officer and two wounded men were able to get out of her on to the rocks. Another two were lying on the left centre of the beach, broadside on to the enemy, with a lot of wounded men sheltering in the water under the boats' sides with an arm passed through the lifelines ...[39]

Standing on the *River Clyde*'s bridge, Henry Tizard counted four or five such boats at intervals along the shore. A cluster of men clung to their sterns in a desperate effort to escape the torrent of fire:

Some were holding on to the gunwales and others were hanging on with their arms through the ropes which are looped round the boats so as to prevent themselves sinking in the water which was up to their waists. After a time I noticed these men, sank from exhaustion and loss of blood and were drowned. The water by this time all along the shore and especially around the boats was red with blood.[40]

Tizard reckoned fewer than fifty unwounded men made it ashore. Many of the casualties were hit more than once. A number could be seen crawling across the sand to slump, numb with shock, behind a bank a few yards from the water's edge. Most of those who made it that far sought only to burrow themselves deeper into the beach. But a few brave souls continued to defy the Turkish fire with dire results. Tizard wrote:

I saw many cases ... where men who had jumped out of the boats ... got hit and fell face downwards in the water. A chum, who had got ashore, seeing this, would [then] come back and pull him out of the water so that he should not be drowned. In nearly every case the men who did this were killed.[41]

Prominent among them was Father William Finn. The Dublins' Roman Catholic chaplain, 'a thick set little man with a determined face and piercing eyes',[42] had insisted on accompanying the first wave despite his colonel's entreaties to go aboard the *River Clyde*. Having spent the night before distributing religious tokens to his flock, he had joined one of the leading tows into V Beach. According to some accounts, he was wounded during the run-in but made it on to the beach as far as the sheltering bank. He did not remain there long. Seeing the wounded and dying struggling in the surf, he called out, 'I'm going to those fellows',[43] and ran back into the curtain of fire. Eyewitness reports collected by Finn's friend and fellow chaplain Henry Foster told an extraordinary story of self-sacrifice:

> Under heavy fire, and in great pain, he crawled about administering extreme unction, until a shrapnel shell burst over the beach. He was again severely wounded – in the head this time – and yet, fearless and brave, he continued his work of mercy until he lay down to die from sheer exhaustion and loss of blood.[44]

Moved by the padre's selfless bravery, another soldier, thought to have been his orderly, risked his life to drag him under cover. Finn was fading fast. Before slipping into fatal unconsciousness, he whispered: 'Are our fellows winning?'[45]

It scarcely seemed so. From *River Clyde*'s open sally-ports the scene was one of total devastation. 'You never saw such a shambles,'[46] wrote Lieutenant Desmond O'Hara. According to fellow Dublin officer Captain Alexander Molony, 'the beach was a harrowing sight; bodies were lying all over it, in some places in little clumps, in others half in and half out of the water. Wounded men were all over the place, and it was impossible to bring them aid.'[47] Barely a quarter of an hour into the assault, the men clinging desperately to the shoreline looked more like bedraggled and bewildered survivors of some terrible shipwreck than the spearhead of an invading army.

It appeared much the same to the Turks. Reports reached the commander of 3/26th Regiment that five boatloads of men approaching the 'pier' [*sic*] at Sedd-el-Bahr had been 'completely sunk'[48] and the sea stained 'with the blood from the bodies of the enemy'[49] Having endured the agonies of the naval bombardment, Major Mahmut Sabri's men showed no pity. He recorded:

> Shells and machine gun bullets fell ceaselessly at the points where rifle fire was observed, but in spite of this enemy fire, heavy fire was opened from all our rifle trenches. In a vain attempt to save their lives, the enemy threw themselves from the boats into the sea.

However much the enemy boats, on receipt of flag signals from their commanders, strove to open out and pass behind the headland, they were still unable to save themselves. In spite of the terrific enemy artillery and machine gun fire directed at our trenches, our fire was very effective and was knocking the enemy into the sea. The shore at Ertugrul cove became full of enemy corpses, like a shoal of fish.[50]

The only bright spot on a morning of almost unrelieved suffering was at the Camber, or boat harbour, to the east of the *River Clyde*. There, on the Straits' side of the bay where a rough track led up towards Sedd-el-Bahr, the right-hand No 1 tow had landed virtually unopposed. The four boats, led by a picket boat commanded by Midshipman Denis Last and with Commander Diggle on board, carried half of the Dublins' Z Company under Captain John Mood and Lieutenant Raymond de Lusignan. Crewing the leading boat was a party from *Cornwallis* comprising seventeen-year-old Midshipman Haydon Forbes, Leading Seaman Baldwin (coxswain), Able Seamen Foam, Grose, Harper, Sawyer and Smith (oarsmen). Their run-in had been eventful. Since leaving the *Clacton*, they had been bracketed fore and aft by shells fired from the Asiatic shore. Forbes later reported:

> In front of us more shells, though only small, were raining down. We passed astern of the *River Clyde*, and being the right flank tow, went in on her starboard side.
>
> About fifty or a hundred yards from the shore the steamboats slowed down, the pulling boats were slipped, and the orders 'Oars down!' 'Give way together!' were given, and we were pulling like mad for the beach.
>
> Whiz! A shrapnel burst overhead; everybody ducked. Next second I looked round. Nobody was touched. But going in yet closer we were peppered with the stuff, and a lot of balls fell into the boat.
>
> We were soon alongside the Camber, which was directly under the wall of the fort, and all the soldiers ... jumped ashore and took cover under a wall with no casualties. My boat was the first to beach, likewise the first to get away, and as we went out we received a few more words of cheer in the form of shrapnel.[51]

Sadly, their efforts were to little avail. Despite penetrating as far as the windmills and the houses on the eastern fringes of Sedd-el-Bahr, the two platoons were too few. Held up by 'a crowd of snipers',[52] they were almost overwhelmed and forced to beat a hasty retreat during the afternoon. In the scramble to get back to the Camber, the Dublins lost eighty-six men. Among the dead was Lieutenant de Lusignan, who was reportedly killed by a shell while attempting to set up a 'screen' indicating the position's capture.[53] John Mood was one of only twenty-five men from the half company who survived to be rescued later in the day by boats taken in by Lieutenant Francis Sandford and Midshipman Geoffrey Norman:

> On the way off to the *Queen Elizabeth* [wrote Norman] I received a good deal of back-chat from one of the soldiers in the stern of our boat, who merely sat tight with a pipe in his mouth. I was a bit curt with him as he would give orders and make no effort to move. When we got to the ship we helped out all the others, and at last he said, 'Come on, give us a hand,' and for the first time I saw that one of his legs was almost completely shot away. That night I went to the sick bay to find out how he was getting on and was told that he had insisted on the others being dealt with before him. His first words on getting over his anaesthetic were to ask for his pipe, the stem of which he had already practically chewed away.[54]

Grievous though his injuries were, he was one of the lucky ones. In what Alexander Molony called 'a terrible affair', Rooth's magnificent battalion was 'decimated' in a matter of 'a few minutes'.[55] Among several hundred casualties were a high proportion of the battalion's leaders. As well as the commanding officer, the Dublins lost their forty-nine-year-old second in command, Major Edwyn Featherstonhaugh, mortally wounded in his boat, the adjutant, Captains William Higginson and Denis Anderson, who were killed on the beach, and both of their machine gun officers, Captain George Dunlop and Lieutenant Reginald Corbet.

The senior surviving officer was Z Company commander, Cecil Thomas Wrigley Grimshaw. The forty-year-old Dubliner's mood can only be imagined. A married man with two young sons, he had devoted almost half his life to the regiment, first as a militia man and then as a regular. As a young officer, he had shared a Boer prison camp with a war correspondent by the name of Winston Churchill and had gained a DSO for his brave leadership. And as a more mature officer, he had helped put his stamp on the unit. During a five-year spell as adjutant, which ended only with his promotion to major *en route* to the Dardanelles, he was credited with being instrumental not only in ensuring the battalion's splendid peacetime reputation but in making certain that it was 'so well prepared for service'.[56] And now the unit that was his pride and joy lay shattered and scattered on an alien shore, the remaining officers and non-commissioned officers spread about the bullet-whipped beach with small bodies of men clustered round them in various states of stupor.

From the extreme left, where Lieutenant Maffett, his bloodied head crudely bandaged, sought to rally the few survivors around him, to the far right, where the wounded figure of Captain French had taken charge, it appeared as though the Dublins were already more or less a spent force. Anticipating a Turkish counter-attack, Maffett put all the men around him 'on the alert for a rush from the enemy'.[57] It was more in the way of a diversion than anything else. As he later acknowledged, they were too few and in no fit state to 'have done any good'.[58] French had similarly abandoned as impossible any hope of attaining their objectives. Crawling painfully along the beach, he managed to collect about thirty or forty 'intact'[59] men from a mixture of companies and immediately set them to work, digging in beneath the low cliff that represented their best chance of salvation. 'Why the Turks with their vast preparations did not level this bank of earth down I cannot imagine,' wrote French. 'Had they done so not one of us would have escaped.'[60]

The focus for those ashore was no longer about securing the beach and still less about seizing the heights of Achi Baba. It was about staying alive. If the deadlock was to be broken, it would have to be done by others. All eyes were now fixed on the *River Clyde* and the men marooned inside her bullet-pelted holds.

Chapter 12

'The Hardest Haul'

In theory, Edward Unwin's 'Wooden Horse' plan was a simple one. At the precise moment *River Clyde* bumped ashore, the steam hopper *Argyle* was to move ahead on the port side, pulling 'decked' lighters to form a bridge that connected the ship to the beach via the *Argyle*'s drawbridge-like brow. One imponderable was how far out *River Clyde* would actually run aground. All being well, two lighters would be sufficient to span the gap, but if they were not enough Unwin had taken the precaution of adding an extra lighter to his assortment of tows.

Another imponderable was how the six Greek civilian crewmen who accompanied George Drewry and 'Geordie' Samson aboard the *Argyle* would behave in the likely event of fierce Turkish resistance. To this key element of the scheme, Unwin appeared to have devoted little thought. It was an oversight that was to have immediate and grave consequences.

Unwin barely had time to register *River Clyde*'s grounding and the 'awful'[1] struggles of the men in the first tows before he realised that the plan on which he had laboured so hard and upon which so much was expected had miscarried. He later recalled:

> Directly we took the beach I rushed to the side of the bridge to see how the hopper was getting on and was horrified to see Drewry hacking at the tow rope with an axe. I had told him only to put the eye over the bollard as, of course, when we struck, the tow would slacken and all he had to do was to lift it off the bollard. When he did get free, she [the *Argyle*] sheared off to port and was of no further use, except as a death trap to a lot of men who were trying to land in boats ...[2]

What seemed an inexplicable calamity was, actually, a valiant attempt to regain control of the wayward vessel. For what Unwin did not know,

129

but probably should have foreseen, was that the torrent of fire coming from the Turkish positions had sparked an instant panic among the *Argyle*'s Greek crew. Only moments before it had seemed to 'Geordie' Samson that, contrary to expectations, the landing might be unopposed:

> Not a shot was fired at us as we neared the beach. We thought we were going to have a picnic when, all at once, out buzzed the rattle of rifle and machine gun fire.[3]

It was at that vital moment, just as *River Clyde* ran ashore, that everything went wrong:

> Hardly had the hopper's bow appeared beyond her huge consort [wrote machine gunner David Fyffe] than the whole slope leapt into a roar of firing, and a tempest of lead poured down upon the devoted craft and her gallant crew. Disaster overwhelmed her in an instant. Nothing could live in such a torrent of lead and in a moment the middy at the wheel and every sailor on the deck of the little ship was shot down …[4]

Or at least that was the way it seemed from the transport's forward casemate. The reality was rather different. Rather than pulling ahead as intended, the *Argyle* had actually gone into reverse before suddenly lurching to port at right angles to the *River Clyde*. Either by accident or design, the Greek crew had effectively sabotaged the hopper's mission. Then, with bullets falling like hail, they had, in Samson's words, 'bolted down into the engine-room'.[5]

Chasing after them, Samson cajoled them back on deck only for another burst of firing to send them scurrying back. It was a performance repeated several times before Samson gave up. In truth, the damage had already been done and, in spite of the best efforts of Drewry and Samson, was beyond repair.

> Devoid of guidance [wrote Fyffe], the hopper went astray and beached side-on while the barges all went out of line, the connecting ropes broke under the strain, and they came to rest in a hopeless muddle with the farthest barge lying helplessly in deep water about 20 yards from the shore. The bridge of boats had failed …[6]

Terrible blow though it was to Unwin, the disaster came as little surprise to at least one man in *River Clyde*. Despite volunteering for the enterprise, Douglas Illingworth, one of Wedgwood's subalterns, had been sceptical of the plan from the outset. In a letter written a few days later, he told his brother:

> The idea was bad and the scheme a failure and but for extraordinary good luck there would not have been a single survivor to tell the tale. One gun and a few shells and we were finished. However, fortune favoured us. The Turks had no guns to speak of and what they had were very bad – bad range on bad shells … We ran ashore all right but the barges we towed alongside did everything but what was intended – of course. No sane man would ever expect otherwise …[7]

By then, 'the fun',[8] as Drewry put it, had well and truly begun. Either side of *Argyle*, where the water shoaled, lifeboats carrying the first wave of Dublins were being pulled to shore through a welter of fire. Drewry looked on helplessly as the soldiers and boats' crews were shot down in droves, 'almost all of them wiped out'[9] before reaching the beach. With their own craft stranded, surrounded by scenes and sounds of bloody slaughter, Drewry and Samson strove to salvage at least something from the wreckage of their failed mission:

> We had a line from the stern of the hopper to the lighters [wrote Drewry] and this we tried to haul in, the hardest haul I've ever tried.[10]

It was then, with bullets beating against the sides of the stricken hopper, that Drewry noticed Unwin standing fully exposed on one of the misplaced lighters. He was bawling at the crew of a steam pinnace, instructing them to gather together the lighters. With Unwin and Drewry looking on, the small boat 'plucked them in until she could go no closer'.[11] Thus began an extraordinary effort to rescue the landing operation.

Maddened by the failure of the hopper, on which he had 'pinned' his faith, Unwin had decided to take matters into his own hands. 'Something had to be done,' he wrote, 'and quickly'[12]:

> Seeing what an awful fiasco had occurred I dashed over the side and got hold of the lighters which I had been towing astern, and which had shot ahead by their impetus when we took the beach, [and] these I got under the bow …[13]

It was no easy task, but, as he discovered to his surprise, he was not alone for long. Braving the fire alongside him was Leading Seaman William Williams, the Welsh reservist who had offered to 'chuck his hook' in order to join the band of volunteers from *Hussar* aboard the *River Clyde*. The night before, while issuing final orders to 'all hands', Unwin had told Williams to stay close to him as his 'personal attendant'[14]. It was an instruction he took literally, irrespective of his captain's seemingly suicidal tendencies. Unwin wrote:

> He dashed over the side with me and helped me get the lighters into position, [although] how we managed to do this has always, on thinking it over, astonished me.[15]

Drewry was hardly less astounded by what he saw. Instead of joining the lighters to the now defunct hopper, Unwin, with Williams' heroic assistance, had decided to 'make the connection with a spit of rock on the other [starboard] bow'.[16] Following their example, Drewry and Samson put themselves in harm's way a second time. Letting go their rope to the lighters, they made their way through heavy fire to the bow where they attempted to lower the brow. But it was all to no avail. Without the assistance of their Greek crewmates, who had 'run below'[17] again, they could not manage it and after struggling for a few minutes they were forced to admit defeat. Telling Samson 'to get out of the 'rain',[18] Drewry leapt over the bow and waded ashore through a hail of bullets to join Unwin:

> Meeting a soldier in the water, we (I and another soldier from a boat) tried to carry him ashore but he was again shot in our arms, his neck in two pieces nearly, so we left him and I ran along the beach towards the spit. I threw away my revolver, coat and hat and waded out to the Captain.[19]

The pinnace having towed the lighters in as close to the shore as possible, Unwin and Williams were toiling to finish the job they had set themselves. Waist-deep in the blood-stained surf and seemingly oblivious to the enemy fire, they were forced to resort to manpower to push and tow the lighters the last few yards towards the finger of rocks. They were joined there by Drewry who, having helped haul the lighters into place, then clambered up on to one of them and succeeded in lowering the brows. Their problems, however, were far from over. Unwin explained:

> We got them connected to the bows [of *River Clyde*] and then proceeded to connect to the beach, but we had nothing to secure to, so we had to hold on to the rope ourselves.[20]

What followed was a truly Herculean feat. With nothing but their courage to sustain them, Unwin and Williams coiled the rope around their exposed bodies and took a firm grip, grappling against the current and a torrent of fire to hold the makeshift bridge steady. Bullets lashed the water all around. It seemed to Unwin that the Turks were now focusing their fire on the lighters rather than the *River Clyde*. But there was nothing for it but to cling on. As the last link in a precarious chain tying the ship to the shore, they were all that stood between the slimmest chance of success and abject failure.

After what seemed an eternity but was in reality only a few minutes, Unwin reckoned they had done all that was humanly possible to drag the lighters close in to the rocks. The moment had arrived to put their valiant effort to the test and for the 'Wooden Horse' of Gallipoli to reveal her secrets. Gripping the painter of the lighter nearest the beach, Unwin looked up towards *River Clyde*'s gaping sally-ports and 'yelled to the troops to come out'.[21]

Chapter 13

'No Finer Episode'

Guy Geddes felt like a man standing on the edge of the abyss. He always suspected the landing was going to be a 'desperate venture'.[1] Now he knew it. The massacre of boatloads of Dublins before his very eyes had removed the last shred of doubt. As he hovered by the opening cut into the *River Clyde*'s port bow, bullets and shrapnel were clanging and clattering against her hull. He felt his whole body tighten, his nerves 'tense and strung up'.[2] He was moments away from exiting the ship and, for all he knew it, this world. In what seemed an act of suicidal folly, he was about to lead his company out in single file on a 100-yard sprint across a narrow gangway and a 'bridge of boats' in full view of an alerted enemy in broad daylight. It was the stuff of Boys' Own heroes; a death or glory charge into the 'cannon's mouth'. Only Geddes didn't feel much like a hero, lacking, as he put it, 'the pluck of a louse'.[3] Yet for all his own self-doubt, he never for a moment questioned the courage of the men lined up behind him, still less their ability to 'win through'. As he later wrote, 'I knew the splendid fellows at my back, highly trained, strictly disciplined and they would follow me anywhere'.[4] Never was such faith to be more sorely tested.

Waiting in the dim-lit forward hold, the men of X Company, 1st Royal Munster Fusiliers had seen little of the execution wrought among the Dublins. But what they heard was enough to convince them of the strength of Turkish resistance. The murderous noise was deafening as a hail of lead beat against the hull and churned the water around them. According to Geddes, the wait, an eternity of a few minutes, lasted until 0645 when an instruction was passed to him telling him it was time to go. There was a momentary delay caused by a jammed gangway and then they were off, 'cheering wildly'[5] as he led them out of the gloom and into the glare of an Aegean morning brutalised by war. For many of those dashing along the narrow gangway their first glimpse of the enemy shore would also be their last.

> We got it like anything [wrote Geddes], man after man behind me was shot down but they never wavered. [Second] Lieut [John] Watts who was wounded in five places and lying on the gangway cheered the men on with cries of 'Follow the Captain'.
> Captain French of the Dublins told me afterwards that he counted the first 48 [in his letter Captain French gives the figure as 42] men to follow me and they all fell. I think no finer episode could be found of the men's bravery and discipline than this – of leaving the safety of the *River Clyde* to go to what was practically certain death.[6]

According to French, who was lying on the beach barely 50 yards from where the collier grounded, not a man faltered as platoon after platoon was 'mown down'.[7] Awed and appalled in equal measure, he later wrote:

> It was an awful sight but they were a real brave lot. After a few minutes it became even harder for them to get ashore. After passing down the gangways & across the lighters under a heavy fire they had to run along about 25 yds of jagged rocks – each side of the ridge now being covered with bodies.[8]

From his forward casemate, David Fyffe heard 'splash after splash as the gallant fellows fell dead from the gangway'.[9] By some miracle, a few men evaded the scything fire. Reaching the nearest barge, Fyffe watched then as they 'raced across her open deck and crouched for shelter in the adjacent open boat'[10]:

> One after another the devoted fellows made the dash down the deadly gangways until a considerable number gathered in the bottoms of the open boats or were lying prostrate on the deck of the barge. Then the order was given up and up they leaped and rushed for the rocks while a hail of rifle and machine gun fire beat upon them. Wildly they leaped [*sic*] from boat to boat in that gallant rush while we on the ship cheered wildly at the sight, until they reached the last boat when they leaped down into the water and started wading towards the rocks that were their goal, holding up their rifles high above their heads. But to our horror we saw them suddenly begin to flounder and fall in the water, disappearing from view and then struggling to the surface again with uniform and pack

streaming, only to go down again never to reappear as the hailing bullets flicked the life out of the struggling men … We almost wept with impotent rage. Nonetheless some fifty or more survivors had reached the edge of the rocky point and were crouching up to their necks in the water behind this slight shelter waiting for a chance to rush over the rocks to the beach.[11]

Of Captain Eric Henderson's Z Company that charged out of 'Number 1 exit' on the starboard bow 'not more than about one Platoon reached the beach'.[12] Owing to the brief hold-up on the port-side gangway, they had been first away from the ship and suffered accordingly. 'They were simply shot to pieces,'[13] wrote Lieutenant Norman Dewhurst, one of the battalion's machine gun officers. Many of the casualties occurred in the first few yards as they ran out along the gangway. In a report dictated to the battalion's adjutant, Captain Harry Wilson, Henderson added:

> The remainder were either drowned jumping off the barge, shot in shallow water or remained on the barge after it drifted into deep water. Most of the latter were hit by snipers.[14]

In no time at all, the gangways and makeshift pier that Unwin and Williams had so bravely constructed had become 'an absolute causeway of death'.[15] One of the few who made it safely across was Henderson's second in command, Captain Raymond Lane, who was at the tail-end of the first platoon leaving the *River Clyde*. He later recorded:

> One by one they popped out and then my turn. All the way down the side of the ship bullets crashed against the sides, but beyond a few splinters I was not hit. On reaching the first barge, I found some of the men had collected and were firing. I mistrusted the second barge and the track to the shore so I led them over the side, the water nearly up to our shoulders. However, none of us were hit and we gained the bank. There I found Henderson badly hit and heaps of wounded.[16]

Against all the odds, Henderson, a thirty-three-year-old Indian Army doctor's son and veteran of the Boer war, had made it as far as the sandy ledge unscathed. His luck did not last much longer. Barely ten minutes after splashing ashore a sniper's bullet fired from somewhere west of the ruined fort hit him in the elbow, shattering his arm. He struggled on in charge of the few men from his company until a second bullet struck him in the side, effectively putting him out of action. With the survivors taking cover behind the bank, command devolved on Lane:

> Any man who put his head up for an instant was shot dead, and we were rather mixed up with the Dublins. Nearly all the NCOs were hit. Then on came [Second Lieutenant Francis] Lee with his platoon and formed up on the left of mine. The bank we were under had a small nulla[h] running up towards the barbed wire. I worked my way up under the right-hand wall, and then tried to cross it running as fast as I could. A sniper at the top let fly at me and got me beautifully right in the middle of the nulla[h]. The bullet went through my right ankle and carried on sideways smashing my left leg to bits. One of my platoon then came out very pluckily and pulled me into safety. I had only been on the beach five minutes and never saw a Turk.[17]

By then, five officers from Z Company had been killed or wounded, leaving Guy Geddes the senior surviving officer among a straggle of Munsters scattered about V Beach.

As with Henderson, the X Company commander's arrival unharmed on the shore had been little short of miraculous. In a letter home written five days later, he told of being on one of the barges when it broke adrift, carrying him and those others still on board broadside towards the shore. 'We were shot down like flies,' he wrote. 'It was *'hukum hai'* and – we had to do it!'[18] Forced to swim the last 20 or so yards, he somehow contrived to reach the shore without being hit. 'How – I simply can't tell you,' he added. 'I was completely exhausted and lay on the beach until I was able to crawl up to the slender cover the Dublins were holding – 10 yards from the water's edge.'[19]

Later, he gave a fuller account of the episode:

> Leaving the *Clyde* I dashed down the gangway and already found the Lighters holding the dead and wounded from the leading platoons of Z Company, including 2nd Lieut [Timothy] Sullivan, an ex CSM [and] a fine fellow. I stepped on the second lighter and looked round to find myself alone, and yelled to the men following out of the *Clyde* to come on, but it was difficult going across the Lighters. I then jumped into the sea and had to swim some dozen strokes to get ashore. There is no doubt that men were drowned owing chiefly, I think, to the great weight they were carrying – a full pack, 200 rounds of ammunition and 3 days' rations – I know I felt it. All the Officers were dressed and equipped like the men.

> There was a small rocky spit jutting out into the sea which was absolutely taped down by the Turks and few, if any, survived who attempted to land there.[20]

Among the few who came through the ordeal with him was his orderly, Private William Flynn. Years later, he recalled the scramble across the lighters, with 'bodies piling up … like a barricade',[21] and his desperate struggle to reach the shore in his company commander's wake:

> I had a big periscope that I was carrying for him. We had double ammunition, double rations, double everything I think, but he had the sense to tell us to throw our coats off before we made to land.
>
> I followed Captain Geddes down the gangway, along the gunwale of the lighter, lay down in about just enough cover … and he looked back and called for the … remainder to come. They couldn't. They must have stopped it. So he said, 'Well, come on, over we go. We're going to fall into the sea.' Of course, I lost him! I came up once or twice for fresh air and I drifted to my right and came up by this strip of rock. It was piled high with dead. Some of the other company … instead of running across the gangway which they saw was useless, they must have jumped into the water and managed to get to this rock but eventually got killed – the majority of them. I managed to just crawl onto the rock. I was exhausted. I thought that my knees had bullet holes in 'em all over where they'd been on the bottom … They were still pumping lead into all the bodies … Anyway [we] managed to scramble on to the shore. We had about 8 or 9 feet to go and we got behind a bank about 5 foot high and we were quite safe there.[22]

Geddes was there too, among a bedraggled confusion of Dublins and Munsters squatting beneath the sheltering ledge of sand. 'Here,' he wrote, 'we shook ourselves out and tried to appreciate the situation …'[23] It was, he conceded, 'rather a sorry one'.[24]

The original plan had envisaged Z Company attacking the enemy positions on the right and X Company on the left from the village of Sedd-el-Bahr across the heights above the beach as far as Fort Number 1. But a little more than a quarter of an hour into the assault, and with both companies all but annihilated, it was already clear to Geddes that the capture of the 'tier of trenches'[25] running just under the crest of the hill was beyond his shattered force. The three rows of barbed wire entanglements that had so bothered Hamilton and Hunter-Weston stood untouched by the naval bombardment. In front of the nearest row, scarcely 25 yards in front of the ledge behind which he was sheltering, Geddes could see the bodies of those men 'told off on wire cutting ... their dash incompleted [sic]'.[26] They were victims of the galling cross-fire from the fort and village on the right and the trenches and defence works on the left that had turned the slopes between into a killing zone. Even had they succeeded in reaching the wire, it was doubtful they would have achieved anything. Strung between spiked iron stanchions set deep in the ground, the wire with two-inch barbs spaced every three inches was, according to Geddes, 'so thick that no wire cutters as supplied could make any impression'.[27]

The only option, as far as Geddes could see, was to hold on to their slender toe-hold along the foreshore. But even that appeared a daunting task:

> Seeing that Sedd-el-Bahr and the beach to our right was unoccupied, and fearing the Turks might come down, I called for volunteers to make a dash for it and make good the right of the beach. The men responded gallantly. Picking Sergt [Patrick Joseph] Ryan and 6 men we had a go for it.[28]

Of the six, three were killed and two others, including Geddes, wounded. In a letter home, he wrote of having a button shot off before being 'plugged'[29] through the shoulder. 'Didn't feel it till sometime after,' he added, 'though it knocked me over.'[30] The bullet passed clean through, exiting via his back. 'Another fraction of an inch and my career would have been ended,'[31] he remarked. Once again, he had enjoyed 'the luck of the Devil'.[32] Despite his wound, Geddes made it across to the right-hand side of the beach where he later joined forces with fourteen stragglers, remnants of the Dublins' Z Company which had landed at the camber.

> This little party attempted to get a lodgement inside the Fort [wrote Geddes] but we couldn't do it so we dug ourselves in as well as we could with our intrenching [sic] tools.[33]

It was a little after 0715 and Geddes had done all he could to secure the right flank. Contrary to his own expectations, he had risen magnificently to the challenge. When it mattered most and when the chips were down, he had displayed leadership and heroism of the highest order. More than that, to his considerable relief and evident surprise, he had felt 'no fear or doubt'.[34] From the moment, he burst into the sunlight and began running along the gangway 'it [had] all seemed quite ordinary'.[35]

Geddes joined a long list of heroes that day, men who conquered fear and adversity in the most ghastly of circumstances. As a result of the exceptionally heavy casualties, many acts of bravery went unrecognised, but a few were witnessed by comrades who lived long enough to tell of their heroism during those first terrible minutes on V Beach.

Prominent among them was Z Company's Sergeant Patrick Ryan who earned the admiration of both Geddes and Henderson. As well as playing a leading role in helping Geddes shore up the exposed right flank, Ryan, a Limerick-born regular in his mid-twenties, proved a constant source of inspiration. According to Henderson, he set 'a splendid example of coolness and personal valour'[36] which served as an encouragement to men who were mentally and physically exhausted by their ordeal. Later in the day, he led a small party on a 'daring reconnaissance'[37] beyond the beach, returning to report the positions of snipers in Sedd-el-Bahr and the unwelcome news that the far side of the fort was 'well held'[38] by enemy troops.

Another who shunned the shelter of the sand cliff was Private John Bowater. Like Ryan a member of Z Company, he risked his life on several occasions, braving heavy fire from snipers and machine guns, to find safer positions out of sight of the Turkish marksmen who were taking a terrible toll of those who made it on to the beach. Darting along the bullet-swept foreshore, he discovered, in Henderson's words, 'that by moving more to the right it was possible to obtain cover from the snipers on both flanks'.[39]

Others who distinguished themselves did so in full view of officers on board the *River Clyde*. They included Lance Corporal H Quinault of Z Company and Privates Flannery, Slattery and T Hennessey of X Company together with another unnamed soldier who did not survive the landing. All five displayed 'conspicuous bravery'[40] on the barges that were filled with dead and wounded. Hennessey was spotted picking up and carrying three wounded men, 'one after the other',[41] back to the safety of the ship. Quinault brought in two more despite fire so heavy that it seemed no man could move without being hit. Not content with their efforts, they then sallied out again along the gangways and on to the lighters where, together with Privates Flannery and Slattery and another unidentified private from the Munsters, they were seen 'crawling' through a hail of bullets in an effort to 'make them fast'.[42] It was while they were 'endeavouring to throw planks across to connect them with the shore'[43] that they were wounded and the unnamed soldier killed.

Whether or not this took place while Unwin and Williams were battling to hold the lighters in position or after the barge nearest the beach had drifted away is unclear. But there is no doubt that the naval party, which by then included Midshipman Drewry, was in need of assistance. By Unwin's reckoning they managed to keep the 'bridge' in place for around an hour in the face of a furious fire. Allowing for exaggeration, and Geddes' account of the drifting barge would suggest a somewhat shorter duration, their achievement was as incredible as their survival. 'We were literally standing in blood,'[44] observed Unwin. Surrounded by scenes of carnage, they stuck steadfastly to their self-imposed task. Bullets and shrapnel whipped the water around them. Unwin's mind, however, was elsewhere. 'I had no time to think of myself,' he wrote, 'as I was so sick at the failure, as I considered it, of my scheme.'[45] He added:

> Men were falling very fast but still they never hesitated, and soon they were crawling ashore over the dead bodies of their pals.
>
> After about half an hour of this I thought I would try and make a better connection by getting one of the light brows ashore. I knew there was one on the lighter but I couldn't make the troops understand what I wanted, so I asked Williams if he could hang on to the lighters [by] himself whilst I got out of the water and placed the brow, but he said he was too cold and couldn't hang on alone. So, there was nothing for it but to sit it out. A shell from Asia came and cheered us up by dropping within a yard of us …[46]

It proved to be a 'dud' which was later salvaged to find a place as a garden ornament in Unwin's Derbyshire home. But, like their strength, their luck was all but exhausted. No sooner had Williams exclaimed, 'Whatever is that?' than he let out a strangled gasp. Hearing what sounded like 'a thud', Unwin looked round. Williams said weakly, 'a shell has hit me'.[47] Seeing that he was slipping into unconsciousness, Unwin let go the rope and grabbed him lest he fall and drown. 'I tried to get him on to the lighter,'[48] added Unwin. His efforts were all in vain. Before he could reach the barge Williams died in his arms.

That was the last the captain of the *River Clyde* remembered for a little while. Frozen from his immersion and exhausted by his exertion, Unwin's body gave out. 'For some reason or other,' he wrote, 'I collapsed at the same time and somebody got me on board.'[49] That 'somebody' was George Drewry. Unwin's faithful second-in-command had been dodging bullets in his frantic efforts to assist his captain ever since the *Argyle* had blundered off course. Joining Unwin and Williams at first in the water, he helped them pull some of the lighters towards the spit before climbing aboard one of them and lowering the brows ready for landing. Drewry later wrote:

> The Capt[ain], still in the water, sang out for more rope, so I went aboard [*River Clyde*] and brought a rope down with the help of a man called Ellard [a seaman volunteer from *Hussar*]. As we reached the end of the lighters the Capt was wading towards us carrying Williams. We pulled him onto the lighter and Ellard carried him onboard the ship on his shoulders, but he spoilt the act by not coming down again ...
>
> I got a rope from the lighter to the spit and then, with difficulty, I hauled the Capt onto the lighter. He was nearly done and I was alone.
>
> He went inboard and the Doctor [Burrowes Kelly] had rather a job with him ...[50]

By the time Unwin recovered, with the help of 'a little rubbing and a lot of brandy',[51] the landing that he, Williams and Drewry had risked their lives to make possible had been temporarily halted.

To the Munsters' commanding officer it had been clear from an early stage that all hope of carrying out Brigadier General Hare's plan of attack had been rendered 'impossible'[52] by the deadly cross-fire that had decimated the Dublins and two companies from his own battalion. So heavy was the fire that Henry Tizard considered 'nothing could live on the ground about the beach'.[53] By his reckoning more than half of the men who charged out of the *River Clyde* were already either dead or wounded. From the ship's bridge, Tizard could see a possible way up to the village via a path running to the left of the fort. But no attempt was made to exploit it on the mistaken grounds that 'as it was not protected or closed by wire in any way ... it appeared to be an obvious trap'.[54] Not till the following day would they discover their error. With the *River Clyde*'s exit ports and gangways effectively taped by the Turks and the lighters and foreshore strewn with the bodies of his shattered companies, Tizard thought enough was enough for the time being:

> Seeing that the task set us would mean a fearful waste of life under the conditions then existing and that if we continued to send the men out that our force would be weakened to such an extent that we should not be able to tackle the enemy, I went back to Lieut Colonel Carrington Smith, who was on the upper bridge watching

the fight, and told him that I considered that we should hold on and wait till dark when I thought we should stand a better chance of getting the men out without such heavy casualties. He agreed with me that he thought it would.[55]

To Major Mahmut Sabri news that the British had been 'compelled to hold up his disembarkation'[56] was vindication of his dispositions and further evidence of his men's staunchness. Two attempts to rush the beach from open boats and a makeshift landing craft had foundered in the face of his soldiers' devastatingly accurate fire. Even with the slopes above Cape Helles enveloped in smoke and his men increasingly pressed from Tekekoyu, where the 1st Lancashire Fusiliers had bloodily bludgeoned their way ashore, he could not resist indulging in a degree of hyperbole as he exulted in his men's heroic defence of Sedd-el-Bahr:

> The enemy troops were so frightened that they refused to disembark from the large transport which entered Ertugrul cove. Their commanders and officers had drawn their swords and were sending the men down the ladders but they were observed and could not escape the Turkish bullets. Not one of our soldiers' bullets was fired in vain. In fact in many cases one bullet accounted for several of the enemy. The enemy understood how much his landing cost him and how high was the bravery and courage of the Turkish Army. In short, this battalion dealt the enemy as severe a blow as his action deserved.[57]

Yet, bloody setback though it was, it merely marked the end of the beginning in what would prove the bloodiest struggle of all the landings on the peninsula that morning. As what remained of the V Beach invasion force took shelter along the foreshore and inside the *River Clyde*, the focus shifted to the shallows and the jumble of boats and barges where a gallant band of boy midshipmen were about to take centre stage.

Chapter 14

'Have You Secured the Hawser?'

The scale of the crisis at V Beach was slow to dawn on Hunter-Weston and his staff aboard *Euryalus*. Stationed off Cape Tekke, their focus fixed on the progress of the 1st Lancashire Fusiliers and their efforts to secure W Beach and the hills either side, they could see nothing of the main landing. The entire expanse of V Beach, from the cliffs at Cape Helles to the old fort at Sedd-el-Bahr was out of sight if not out of mind.

They were aware of a hold-up in getting ashore, having observed with a measure of bewilderment *River Clyde*'s mystifying manoeuvres during her run-in to the shore. At 0640, with the second line of tows approaching W Beach and the first line struggling to get back, Major Oscar Striedinger in *Euryalus* reported seeing the collier 'still abreast of us', 10 minutes after she 'should have been ashore'[1] and drew the erroneous conclusion that she was 'unable to stem the current'.[2] But apart from the delay there was evidently no immediate hint in the scanty reports reaching *Euryalus* of the disaster unfolding a little more than a thousand yards away. For more than an hour after the first wave of Lancashire Fusiliers splashed ashore at Tekke Burnu, the fantasy of a smooth operation taking place at Cape Helles persisted, as indicated by the entries in the 29th Division's War Diary:

> 7am: *River Clyde*, under light shell fire, grounded some way out from Beach V, and lighters forming pier to the shore were pushed out. The tows with Dublin Fusiliers pulled in at the same time. Lancashire Fusiliers reached cliffs each side of Beach W.

> 7.30am: Troops at Beach S (Eski Hissarlik) landed from four trawlers, the first three practically without casualties, and reached Hill 236.
>
> Bde Major, 86th Brigade, reports Lancashire Fusiliers making progress towards Hill 114. They separated into two parties, the

smaller on the South side of the beach, working towards the lighthouse on Cape Helles. The larger portion, on the North side of the beach advanced most gallantly against the trenches covering the beach, which were shelled by the ships (*Euryalus* and *Swiftsure*), and reached the lower ones, but could not make good the top of the ridge.

86th Brigade reported that Lancashire Fusiliers are making progress against Hill 114, Royal Fusiliers had landed (Beach X) and that General Hare [who landed on W Beach] was wounded. Troops from collier appeared to be getting ashore well. Some shrapnel fire.

7.50am: *Lord Nelson* reports that our troops are now in Seddel Bahr [*sic*] village.[3]

The reality, of course, could hardly have been more different. Yet, blind as Hunter-Weston and his staff were to the plight of more than two-thirds of the Covering Force, the delusion of an easy landing was not shared by all those watching events from offshore. From the bridge of V Beach's attendant ship, *Albion*, the calamitous turn of events was plain to even the most junior members of its crew. Leslie Berridge, a fifteen-year-old midshipman, had been witness to *River Clyde*'s dash for the shore and the horrors that followed the almost simultaneous arrival of the first tows. In a letter home, he wrote:

> The slaughter was awful and you could see them falling on the beach and in the water (they had to wade some way) ... All the time they landed there was an infernal noise going on. The rattle of maxims and pom-poms and the pinging of rifles going on almost ceaselessly. How the Turks stood our fire I don't know. I don't mind admitting I'd have hopped it full speed ...[4]

Having ceased firing as the *River Clyde* and first wave of tows neared the beach, *Albion* renewed its bombardment with what Commander Watts-Jones called 'a continuous deliberate fire over head of [the] boats'.[5] It had little effect. According to his chronology, which differed slightly from that of the troops aboard *River Clyde*, the first soldiers to hit the beach at 0653 were clearly seen to suffer 'heavy loss, only a few men succeeding in crossing the beach and reaching the shelter afforded by the fore shore'.[6] The carnage wrought by the Turks was painfully apparent. Watts-Jones reported:

> Many boats were drifting helplessly, some broadside on to the beach with men in the water sheltering behind them. V Beach, and

especially a rocky spit off the starboard bow of *River Clyde* being strewn with dead and wounded. The lighters were ahead of *River Clyde* mostly on her port bow.[7]

Despite the heavy cross-fire, Watts-Jones observed from as early as 0705 a few of the boats from the first tow struggling back. Some, with dead and wounded sprawled about them, came alongside *Albion*. Others made for the fleet sweeper *Clacton*.

In keeping with its original instructions, the former Great Eastern Railway Packet had closed V Beach as soon as *River Clyde* ran in to the shore. Her orders were clear: to await the return of the boats of the first flight and then to 'discharge her troops with all despatch'.[8] Once her job was done, she was to retire to one of the transports in the 'outer anchorage' and embark more infantry to reinforce those already ashore. Under no circumstances was she to 'hamper the movements of the *River Clyde*'.[9]

On board *Clacton* that morning were a mixture of Army and naval parties, including some men of the Dublins and the Royal Naval Division together with an assortment of blue-jackets representative of the various ships making up the East Mediterranean Squadron. The latter formed part of the Beach Party assigned to the main landing under the command of Beachmaster Captain Robert Lambert and composing a lieutenant and midshipman from *Cornwallis* and *Implacable* and petty officers, leading seamen, seamen and signallers drawn from *Agamemnon*, *Cornwallis*, *Fauvette*, *Lord Nelson* and *Swiftsure* with an additional pair of carpenter ratings from Unwin's *Hussar*. Kitted out in 'white working rig dyed khaki',[10] they carried with them rolled up blankets, haversacks filled with a supply of tinned beef and hard tack biscuits, water bottles and fifty rounds of rifle ammunition.

Among those stoically waiting their turn to be ferried ashore was the group of five 'snotties' from *Cornwallis* who had spent such an uncomfortable night on *Clacton*'s open decks with their haversacks for pillows. Arthur Hardiman, Maurice Lloyd, Wilfrid Malleson, William Monier-Williams and Howard Weblin were little more than boys. Naïve and keen in almost equal measure, their unshaven faces in stark contrast to the matelots and soldiers in their charge, they were desperate to impress. But, like lambs being led to slaughter, they had little understanding of the ordeal awaiting them and still less experience to help them through it.

The earliest inkling they had that all was not well was watching the first tow go in. 'It really did not cheer us over much,' observed seventeen-year-old Lloyd, 'to see the reception they got'.[11] It was a rude awakening and the sight of the splintered, blood-streaked boats returning from V Beach served only to confirm their worst fears. As part of the third tow, they had expected to arrive on a beach that was already captured and secured to begin the task of clearing it in readiness for a rapid advance inland. Instead, their first task was 'the unpleasant job of helping the dead and wounded out of the boats as they came back from the 1st and second tows'.[12]

Their grisly work complete and with no suggestion that the original plan should be in any way amended, the young 'snotties' took their places in the boats for the tow ashore. Weblin was in the first boat, together with his shipmate Maurice Lloyd, Sub Lieutenant Denholm, of the Anson Battalion, six seamen, some 'Tommies', as he called them, and a few members of Lambert's Beach Party. All told, there were about 28 men and three 'barricoes', or casks of fresh water, squeezed aboard the whaler. Behind them was a boat carrying Midshipmen Hardiman and Malleson and Acting Bosun M Spillane with more of the Beach Party. Lambert and his Military Landing Officer, Captain George Stoney, were in the third boat and the tow was led off by a steam picket captained by seventeen-year-old Midshipman Vivian Voelcker and carrying Lieutenant Tony Morse, senior officer of the *Cornwallis* beach detachment.

The first part of the passage to shore was uneventful if a little fretful. Lloyd later wrote:

> We followed the usual routine of boats, being towed in … cast off, and pulling ourselves to the shore. After leaving the picket boat, we had got half-way to the shore, when we met Forbes in his boat, who shouted to us to go to the starboard side of the hopper.[13]

Midshipman Forbes, who we last encountered delivering a boatload of Dublins to the eastern fringe of V Beach, was just emerging from his own private hell. Since leaving the Camber, he had taken his empty boat back to another sweeper where he filled up with a party from the Anson Battalion before heading in again. This time he made for the port side of *River Clyde*, slipping his tow in line with the beached collier's stern:

> As soon as we got fairly close to the shore, we received a warm reception from six maxims or more and four pom-poms, while snipers and troops in the trenches fired incessantly. One of my bowmen had the top of his head shot off, and the other was wounded in both feet. The other four sailors pulled the boat on to the beach, and the instant she touched the soldiers [sic] jumped

147

ashore. Many were killed and wounded in doing so, and we had to leave the latter, unfortunately, as there was no time to be lost if the boat was to be got off safely. I made the men sit in the bottom of the boat on stretchers and [rowed] back for all they were worth, whilst I sat on the bottom of the boat in the stern-sheets and steered. Several bullets passed over my body, and one grazed my right arm. Of the seamen left, one was now hit in the thigh and another in the arm, so the coxswain took an oar. At last, after what seemed an eternity, we began to glide off the beach, and Harper, who was hit in the arm, now took an oar again, and helped matters greatly; and after being nearly run down by a life-boat, we backed out to where the picket-boat was.[14]

The 'life-boat' in question was most probably the whaler carrying Lloyd and Weblin. Up to then, they had not suffered any casualties, but all of that changed as they 'pulled straight for the beach, between the *River Clyde* and the hopper'.[15] That was when, as Lloyd put it, 'the fun began'.[16] Like Forbes before them, they were entering the killing zone, a bullet-churned stretch of water delineated by its blood-red colouring. Within seconds, man after man in the boat was struck. 'When we were 30 yards from the beach [and within 15 yards of the hopper] there was only myself, Weblin and the RND officer [Denholm] untouched,'[17] wrote Lloyd.

One of the rowers was a fleet reservist renowned for his scruffiness and his reputation for being a bit of a joker. Able Seaman J. A. Leach was badly wounded early on in the foot and through both thighs. But despite the pain of his injuries, this man, who often had the appearance more of a rat-catcher than a sailor in His Majesty's Navy, managed to retain his oar as well as his sense of humour. He 'pulled perfectly the whole time', wrote Lloyd, 'and cheered everybody up ... and altogether behaved splendidly'.[18] Such defiance, however, had its limits. In spite of his best efforts to gee everybody up and to encourage those unwounded soldiers to take an oar, it was not long before he was the only man in the boat still pulling. To Weblin, it seemed as if the moment had arrived to take drastic action:

> Seeing that we could not reach the beach, I suggested to the Sub [Denholm] that we should pull to the hopper, but on finding ourselves in the condition already described, we found that quite impossible, and so the Sub shouted to us all to jump over board and swim for it. He ran forward and jumped in and struck out for the beach, Lloyd and I following his example.[19]

Unfortunately, while Denholm had the forethought to discard his back-pack before taking the plunge, Lloyd and Weblin, in their haste to escape the slaughter, jumped overboard in 'full marching order' with the result, as Weblin noted, 'we soon started to sink'.[20] With some difficulty, they succeeded in swimming back to the whaler, where they found Leach clinging to the gunwale amidships, his foot and legs oozing blood and his face disfigured by a fresh wound. Grabbing hold of life-lines, they weighed up what to do next while bullets spattered around them. It did not take long to decide their best course of action was to draw the boat towards the hopper. Almost immediately they seemed to be targeted, but somehow and 'with great difficulty'[21] they managed to tow the boat through the maelstrom to the starboard side of the hopper.

Once there, they edged themselves round to the opposite side of the boat, furthest away from the shore, where they imagined it was safer. But it soon proved a vain hope. 'Unfortunately,' wrote Lloyd, 'they were firing at us from both sides and the bullets were coming through the boat about 90 to the dozen. And so we decided we couldn't be much worse off in the boat than we were out of it.'[22]

The problem was climbing aboard. Both of them were, by Lloyd's admission, 'absolutely exhausted' and the whaler seemed 'so high out of the water'.[23] But there was no alternative, for, as Weblin observed, the boat afforded them 'the only method of scaling the hopper's side'.[24] After a wearying struggle Lloyd eventually managed to lift one foot on to the gunwale and, with Weblin shoving him 'by the seat of his trousers',[25] he finally succeeded in climbing inside. Weblin then looked round for Leach, who by then was clinging to the rudder of the hopper. 'We couldn't persuade him [to] move and no one could haul him out as he was under the counter,'[26] he wrote. However, the drama was not yet over.

> In the process of Lloyd's embarkation the boat drifted away from the hopper [wrote Weblin] and Lloyd disappeared to get an oar out to pull her back, but seeing it was such a short distance I could do it better from the water. When this operation was over, Lloyd hauled me out ...[27]

Their survival thus far had been nothing less than remarkable, but they had not escaped entirely unscathed. While holding on to the life-lines, Lloyd had been hit by a bullet that tore through his vest and across his shoulders, scraping some flesh from his shoulder blade. More fortuitously, another bullet had removed his cap without touching his head. Lloyd later recalled:

> All this time a very heavy fire was being kept up. Bullets were flying everywhere, some coming on one side and some the other. The boat was riddled, full of bullet holes, and half full of water.
>
> We knew it was hopeless to stay where we were, so we sat at the bottom of the boat in the water, and rowed towards the hopper, pulling with our arms above our heads. We got there all right, jumped out, and secured our boat. Here I got another bullet across the back of the hand.
>
> By this time we were rather exhausted, so we sat down under what we thought was cover. But we soon found we were being sniped, so I moved round the corner.[28]

It was at this point, with the hopper being pelted by Turkish fire, that Lloyd spotted Lieutenant Morse standing on one of *River Clyde*'s lighters as it bumped alongside the *Argyle*. How he came to be there was a mystery to Lloyd but there was no time for questions as Morse called across to him to secure the lighter to the hopper. Ignoring the bullets that were skipping along the deck, he did as he was told. And as he ran forward, Weblin saw another officer, his head roughly bandaged, emerge from down below. It was George Drewry.

When we last encountered the *River Clyde*'s youthful second in command, he had just assisted Unwin back aboard the ship having tied one of the lighters to the spit of rocks. Since then, he had done his level best to follow his captain's heroic example. He later wrote:

> I stayed on the lighters and tried to keep the men going ashore but it was murder and soon the first lighter was covered with dead and wounded and the spit was awful, the sea round it for some yards was red. When they [the Munsters] got ashore they were little better off for they were picked off many of them before they could dig themselves in. They stopped coming and I ran onboard into No 1 [Hold] and saw an awful sight. Dead and dying lay around the ports where their curiosity had led them. I went up to the saloon and saw the Capt being rubbed down. He murmured something about the third lighter [the reserve lighter towed by *River Clyde* on her starboard side], so I went down again and in a few minutes a picket boat came along the starboard side and gave the reserve lighter a push ...[29]

This was the boat commanded by Midshipman Voelcker with Tony Morse on board. The arrival of the senior officer of *Cornwallis'* beach party at around 0800[30] was fortuitous. Having let go his tow and seen one of his boats narrowly miss being 'smashed up by *RC's* propellers',[31] Morse had become separated from the Beachmaster.

Approaching the *River Clyde*, Lambert's boat had pulled along the ship's port side. The air was thick with bullets and the carnage all too obvious. George Stoney, who was in the boat with him, observed:

> The firing was so hot that the Beachmaster ... decided that there was no object in our going ashore and we came aboard the steamer ... I nipped up the ladder pretty quickly as we were under the fire of a maxim from the shore. One could hear the bullets hitting the ship's side all round one.[32]

While Lambert took shelter in the *River Clyde*, Morse's picket boat together with the cutter carrying Midshipmen Hardiman and Malleson travelled along the collier's starboard side. There, they were quickly catapulted into the maelstrom of the Navy's frantic effort to rescue the landing. As Voelcker nudged his boat forward, Morse leapt on to the reserve lighter, where he found Drewry struggling to make good his captain's failed plan. By the time they came together, the link to shore, which had been courageously if precariously established by Unwin and Williams, was broken and the two lighters had 'drifted away from the spit'.[33] Morse now took charge. He worked out a scheme whereby he would use the picket boat to shunt the reserve lighter round the bows of the *River Clyde* to connect with the steam hopper as a first step towards reconstructing the landing 'bridge'. What followed was observed from one of the errant lighters by eighteen-year-old Midshipman Wilfrid Malleson.

Thus far, Malleson's focus had been on self-preservation. Having sustained some casualties on the way in, it was clear that an attempt to land on the beach would risk heavier losses. So, instead, they made for one of the lighters lying under the *River Clyde's* bows. Under fire from the shore, Malleson scrambled unscathed out of the boat and on to the lighter, but his fellow 'snotty' was not so lucky. As he clambered out of the boat, Arthur Hardiman was fatally wounded, barely 2ft from where Malleson was standing. Of all his myriad miraculous escapes that day it was the nearest Malleson came to death. But there was too much happening to worry about it. A few more followed him on to the lighter, where they were 'immediately and violently abjured by those lying on the lighter's deck still alive to lie down and stay there',[34] but the rest remained in the boat. Malleson wrote:

> Sub-Lieut Waller and Mr Spillane with the crew ... took her round to the stern of the *River Clyde*. We then lost sight of them. Our remnant of the Beach Party was now on its face in the lighter. Nothing very much was possible as bullets were whistling over our heads and the lighters were all isolated and swaying backwards and forwards on account of the current. After about an hour of inaction, during which time, [the] occupants of the lighter sustained about 1 casualty every 10 minutes, I observed a lighter on the starboard side, manned by Lieut Morse and Mid Drewry, being pushed from behind by our 2nd Picket Boat.[35]

Even from his decidedly uncomfortable position on the bullet-spattered lighter, he could not help but admire Voelcker's expert boat handling. Given the 'numerous shoals, constant rifle fire and general unwieldiness of the lighter', he thought it 'a very skilful performance'.[36] The approach to the *Argyle* was not, however, without human cost. 'Just as we hit the hopper,' wrote Drewry, 'a piece of shrapnel hit me on the head, knocking me down for a second or two and covering me with blood.'[37] He was not the only casualty. As he went below to have his wound dressed, Maurice Lloyd took over, answering Morse's call to lend a hand by making the lighter fast to the hopper. Together with Morse, he hauled the lighter astern,

> giving the stern a kick out so as to meet the other lighters. We both [then] jumped into the lighter; but as she was moving, Morse said: 'Have you secured the hawser?' My reply was: 'No, sir, I thought you had.' So again I jumped out on to the hopper, before the lighter swung out, and secured the hawser round a bollard. Just in time, as I got another bullet through my lung.[38]

What felt like 'a red hot steam hammer' hitting him in the back, spun him round and, he added, 'as was only natural, I collapsed'.[39]

Just as Lloyd's active role in the landing was ending, Drewry's part in it all took a hazardous new turn. Emerging from the hopper's engine-room, with his scarf as a bandage round his bloodied scalp, he noticed Weblin. The young 'snotty' was in a state of shock, lying in 'a somewhat dangerous place' with cramped legs and 'feeling somewhat the worse for wear'.[40] Drewry, who was a few years senior in years if not rank, urged him to take shelter below deck. Then, ignoring his own advice, he headed back into the storm of fire. With the reserve lighter secured to the hopper, his next mission was to gather up the other lighters drifting beneath the bows of the *River Clyde*. His method was as simple as it was extraordinary. 'I took a rope,' he wrote matter-of-factly, 'and swam towards the other lighters but the rope was not long enough and I was stuck in the middle.'[41]

As luck would have it, he was seen by Malleson, who was still lying marooned on one of the lighters. Realising he was in 'difficulties',[42] struggling against the current with a rope that was too short, he decided to act. With no other rope available but that which had originally been used to hold the lighters near to the spit of rocks, he began hauling it in. It was a job fraught with danger that entailed him having to stand up in full view of the enemy while he reeled in almost half a coil. His own modest account gives little clue as to the risks he ran or the courage he displayed, dismissing the entire episode in a few bland sentences:

> I … got together some rope and, getting a soldier (Munster, name not known) to pay it out, managed to get it across. I was a bit done, so Lieut. Morse made it fast.[43]

Getting it across, as he put, it was a remarkable feat made necessary by Drewry's losing battle with the current. By the time Malleson had finished hauling in the rope, the *River Clyde*'s second in command had drifted out of sight, leaving Malleson to complete the job in the face of a galling fire. Even then, tired though he was by his exertions, he was not quite finished:

> The new lighter [the reserve one that had been pushed into position by Voelcker] had by now drifted to seaward of the hopper. I, therefore, swam to the hopper and managed to get a rope from it and started to tow one end back. However, [the] rope was too short, and, feeling exhausted, I scrambled aboard the lighter again …[44]

What seemed a vain effort was saved, according to Morse, by a gust of wind which 'swung'[45] the lighter near enough to the hopper for a line to be passed between the two. The successful link-up marked the end of Malleson's valiant contribution to the landing. Ordered by Morse to get a 'dry change'[46] of clothing, the youngster crawled across the lighters and into the *River Clyde*. There, he found an exhausted Drewry who had only just made it 'home'[47] after being forced to abandon his extraordinary effort. Drewry later admitted:

> I … had a job climbing up the lighters for I was rather played out. When I got onboard the Doctor dressed my head and rubbed me down. I was awfully cold. He would not let me get up and I had to lay down and listen to the din.[48]

Outside, the struggle was unrelenting. With his fellow 'snotties' engaged in an all-out effort to salve the landing, Midshipman Forbes was involved in his own desperate battle for survival in a boat pocked with bullets and with a crew that was shrinking by the minute. Backing away from the beach, they narrowly missed being run down by a lifeboat before they heard Commander Diggle shouting above the din. He was telling them to make fast to the stern of his picket boat. It was an instruction Forbes chose to ignore. He later explained:

> Had I done this the cutter would certainly have been sunk, as shots from a maxim were continually playing astern of her; so I stayed where I was, out of the line of fire, and the other boats as they got off made fast astern of us.[49]

Further proof of the young midshipman's wisdom came moments later when Diggle was struck by a bullet that tore through his left knee. Unusually on that morning of random execution, Diggle reckoned to have glimpsed his actual assailant. 'I saw the fellow who fired it,' he later wrote from hospital, 'a Turk on top of a house about 350 yards off!'[50] Midshipman Last then took the picket boat alongside Forbes' makeshift tow and pulled them straight to the *Aragon*, which had been converted to a hospital ship.

Forbes later recalled:

> I took a comprehensive look round. There were two or three soldiers in the boat, one nearly dead and the others wounded, and with one was a little brown dog, who sat beside his master. Three of my boat's crew were wounded badly and a fourth slightly. Grose was the most severely injured, and he only lived an hour after being hit. Smith was shot in both legs, and I bandaged him up, and did the same for Sawyer, after which I turned my attention to the soldiers. The boat was in a sad state, being about 18 inches deep in blood and water, with bullet holes in her bows and the same number aft. When we at last got to the *Aragon*, I hunted all over the ship for a doctor, but

could not find one for three-quarters of an hour, and it was two hours before my wounded were all in-board.

Midshipman Monier-Williams was astern of me in his boat. He had been hit in both thighs, and was severely wounded. That night they gave him up as hopeless, but he pulled through ...[51]

Commander Diggle counted himself fortunate, too, once the 'aggravating' frustration of being 'hit so early in the proceedings'[52] wore off and the realisation of the heavy losses sank in. 'I should be thankful to have got off alive,' he wrote, 'which is more than 50 per cent of my party did!'[53]

Diggle was not the only one to return with evidence of the shambles at V Beach. About 0810 a boat drew alongside *Albion* carrying a Royal Naval Division officer belonging to one of the Anson beach parties. He was followed by Diggle's senior officer, Robert Lambert. The beachmaster risked the 1,400-yard journey from the *River Clyde* to provide an accurate picture of what was going on. The depressing story both men related merely added details to the disaster *Albion*'s captain had already observed: 'that the *River Clyde* and *Argyle* were 50 ft apart, and that troops could not disembark, and that our troops were nowhere more than 100 yards from [the] shore'.[54]

Commander Watts-Jones was still digesting the information at around 0815 when he was joined off Sedd-el-Bahr by the *Queen Elizabeth*. The flagship, with Hamilton, De Robeck and their respective staffs on board, had already witnessed the successful landing of 4,000 men of the Australian and New Zealand Army Corps at Gaba Tepe before steaming slowly south to Cape Helles. On the way, Hamilton had noted that the landings at X and Y Beaches 'appeared to be going quite well'[55] and that 'another lodgement had been effected'[56] at W Beach albeit after 'very desperate and bloody'[57] fighting.

Three out of six beaches appeared to be secured. Even the weather – 'the one thing that even optimists feared'[58] – seemed to be smiling on their extraordinary accomplishment. From his lofty position on *Queen Elizabeth*'s searchlight bridge, Jack Churchill picked out the ruin of the Helles lighthouse, which was clearly occupied by British troops. The Covering Force here had evidently 'made good considerable ground'.[59] He saw infantry 'lying down all along the top of the cliff', their progress barred by 'a mass of wire entanglements'.[60] All the ships around about were firing rapidly. It sounded like 'a continuous royal salute from the whole fleet at Spithead'.[61] But as the *Queen Elizabeth* rounded Cape Helles he observed between the western headland and the castle at Sedd-el-Bahr an altogether more dispiriting spectacle.

In a letter written to his brother, Winston, two days later, he wrote:

> In the little bay between these two points we could see the 'Wooden
> Horse', otherwise the '*River Clyde*'. It soon became clear that all was
> not well here. The boat had done well and was piled up on the shore.
> The lighters formed a pier from her bows to the beach, but she was
> still full of men. Under a little ridge, where the sand joined the
> mainland, crouched a couple of hundred men. Evidently they had
> landed and could not make any progress. As I watched 2 or 3 men
> tried to get back into the ship. At once the beach and water all round
> them sprang into the air, and the rat, tat, tat, of a couple of maxims
> broke out. Inland 20 yards beyond the men more wire could be seen.
> The situation was clear. It was an amphitheatre. The 'Wooden Horse'
> and her advanced party were in the centre of the stage. The semi-
> circular 'house' was 'full'. Any man who moved on the stage
> received the 'applause' of everyone from the stalls, 20 yards in front
> of that beastly wire, from the 'stage boxes' which contained maxims
> on each flank, and from the 'dress circle and gallery', who occupied
> various trenches all up the steep slope ...[62]

As the *Queen Elizabeth* drew nearer it was plain to Churchill that
'something had to be done to help the poor 'Wooden Horse''. 'She had
promised to give us a star turn,' he added, 'and was in a bad way.'[63]
Such feelings were shared by others. Roger Keyes, De Robeck's chief-of-
staff, was aghast at what he called the 'storm centre'[64] of the landings:

> The foreshore was strewn with dead bodies and wreckage of
> stranded boats. The sea was whipped up by bullets. Between the
> *River Clyde* and the shore we could see men struggling up to their
> shoulders in the sea; others lying under the shelter of a ridge in the
> sand, to move from which meant certain death from machine guns,
> which could not be located from the covering ships.[65]

The 'ghastly sight',[66] made infinitely worse by being viewed 'from a
position of absolute safety',[67] was, as he confided to Hamilton, almost
too much to bear. It was 'a hateful feeling'[68] shared by the commander
of the Mediterranean Expeditionary Force who, for all his years spent at
war's sharp end, had never experienced a sensation quite like it. Years
later, he was moved to comment:

> Often a Commander may have to watch tragedies from a post of
> safety. That is all right. I have had my share of the hair's breadth

156

business and now it becomes the turn of the youngsters. But, from the battleship, you are outside the frame of the picture. The thing becomes monstrous; too cold-blooded; like looking on at gladiators from the dress circle. The moment we became satisfied that none of our men had made their way further than a few feet above sea level, the *Queen* opened a heavy fire ... upon the Castle, the village and the high steep ground ringing round the beach in a semi-circle.[69]

It was 0820 and the shuddering force of the ship's big guns caught Churchill unawares:

My cap went one way and my note book another. My pipe fell to the floor and after a gulp or two, I looked at the village in front. About 150 yards of houses seemed to suddenly rise in the air in a great cloud of smoke and dust. It was two or three minutes before the debris settled. A shrapnel burst near our bows and we fired again. We closed in near the shore and must have been well within rifle shot, but I saw no sign of any bullets directed at us. We were now well into the straits. What a situation! In front of me the great 15-inch shells were blowing the last village in Europe to hell ...[70]

The thunderous roar continued to little effect. As Hamilton observed:

The enemy lay very low somewhere underground. At times the *River Clyde* signalled that the worst fire came from the old Fort and Sedd-el-Bahr; at times that these bullets were pouring out from about the second highest rung of seats on the West of that amphitheatre in which we were striving to take our places. Ashore the machine guns and rifles never ceased – *tic tac, tic tac, b r r r r - tic tac, tic tac, b r r r r r r* ... Drowned every few seconds by our tremendous salvoes, this more nervous noise crept back insistently into our ears in the interval ...[71]

In the midst of it all, a signal arrived from *Albion* seeking permission to send a launch and sailing pinnace loaded with 'casks lashed under thwarts'[72] and manned by volunteers to help fill the gap between the *River Clyde* and the shore. Request granted, preparations for the perilous mission were still being made when another explosion of fire erupted from the beach. It sounded like rather more than just 'nervous noise'.

Chapter 15

'Red With Blood'

Wind whistled through the wires of the elderly biplane as it swooped low across Helles, its initial sortie of the day at an end. The last few hours had been intensely frustrating ones for Charles Samson and his observer Edward Osmond. Their best efforts to direct the fire of the attendant warships standing off W Beach had been a failure with signals apparently disregarded and the majority of the shells falling too far inland to be of any use. Even their own attempts at bombing had been wide of the mark.

In the course of their 'spotting' duties, they had observed 'the sea literally whipped into foam'[1] by a hail of bullets and small shells that disrupted but could not stop the charge ashore. By the time Samson left, the small cove was covered in dead but secured with naval beach parties clearly visible, toiling 'regardless of the fire'.[2] What had seemed 'Hell let loose',[3] however, was as little compared with the sights that awaited them as they passed over the ruins of Sedd-el-Bahr:

> The *River Clyde* was fast ashore but the lighters ahead of her were not in the right position ... and gaps occurred. These lighters were full of corpses; the beach and water close to the shore were strewn with bodies. It was an appalling sight for us to look at from our safe position in the air, and made one think that we were not doing our bit. I could see, however, that some of our men were holding out behind a ridge about 30 yards [*sic*] or so inland. The Turks were keeping up a hot fire on the *River Clyde*, and it seemed impossible for anyone to get ashore from her. Some shells were arriving from the Asiatic side; but undoubtedly the most serious obstacle was the rifle fire from Sedd-el-Bahr village ... The sea for a distance of about 50 yards from the beach was absolutely red with blood, a horrible sight to see.[4]

At 0905 a signal reached Hamilton aboard the *Queen Elizabeth*. It stated: 'Aeroplane reported gap of 50 feet between *River Clyde* and lighters and that troops cannot disembark.'[5] Whether it was sent by Osmond or his relief is not clear, but the sudden explosion of firing from V Beach was deafening proof that it had already been overtaken by events.

There had been no movement from *River Clyde* for more than an hour following Carington Smith's order to temporarily halt the landing. Throughout most of that time, despite the renewed bombardment by the *Albion* and *Queen Elizabeth* and the relentless shooting of Wedgwood's machine guns, the Turkish fire had remained, in Tizard's words, 'heavy and well directed'.[6] The impasse lasted until around 0900, by which time the Munsters' commanding officer felt that the enemy fire had 'died down somewhat'.[7] He immediately decided to take advantage of the 'lull' by trying to get some of Y Company across to reinforce the remnants of X and Z Companies pinned down on the foreshore. Tizard later insisted that 'the men were all as keen to get off the boat as anyone as by this time the upper deck of No 1 Hold was getting filled up with wounded and a few had been killed in the Hold'.[8]

Casualties on *River Clyde* were, indeed, mounting, especially around the exposed sally-ports and particularly among officers. Captain Wilson, the Munsters' adjutant, had been shot through the elbow at around 0700, since when Major Roger Monck Mason, the unit's senior major, had been wounded in the chest and Lieutenant Gerald Pollard killed by a bullet through the head while standing waiting in No 1 Hold.[9] 'The scene was indescribable,'[10] wrote Lieutenant Norman Dewhurst. The Munsters' machine gun officer reckoned there were 'fifty or so seriously wounded men lying around me',[11] some of whom were survivors of the first rush who had dragged themselves back inside.

However, dangerous as it was, it was a good deal safer than running the gauntlet of the Turkish fire. And having witnessed the slaughter of two of his companies, Tizard was understandably wary of giving the Turks more shooting practice. In an attempt to avoid a repetition of the earlier bloodbath, he, therefore, tempered his original landing plan with caution. This time there would be no helter-skelter rush by an entire company strung out along the gangways. Instead, he would try to outwit the Turks by sending Y Company over in short rushes, 'a few … at a time'.[12]

Leading the way was Major Charles Jarrett, an imposing forty-year-old veteran of colonial wars fought on the South African veldt and the peaks of the North West Frontier. That Jarrett should have insisted on going out first after witnessing the fate of X and Z Companies was little surprise. Universally admired, he was widely regarded as 'the finest officer in the regiment'.[13] A 'true, brave officer and gentleman'[14] was how Guy Nightingale remembered his friend and company commander.

Like Geddes and Henderson before him, Jarrett did not hesitate when his moment came. Running at the head of the leading party, he made it safely on to the first barge. The men following were not so lucky. What Tizard mistook for weakening resistance was merely a display of fire discipline by well-drilled troops trained not to waste ammunition. As soon as they saw what was happening, they opened up again with a steady and lethal stream of accurate fire that sent men tumbling off the gangway and into the sea. 'Jarrett got about one platoon over, but a lot were hit,'[15] Tizard bleakly noted. Few of those who made it across the gangway ventured beyond the barges, where they took cover, adding to the crush of bodies, living and dead, lying trapped between the beach and the *River Clyde*.

Nightingale followed Jarrett out of the collier and in a letter home he later wrote:

> I can't tell you how many were killed and drowned, but the place was a regular death trap. I ran down to the lighters but was sent back by Jarrett, as there was no room on them. Then the wounded began crawling back, the Turks sniping at them the whole time. The men who managed to reach the shore were all crouching under a bank about 10 feet high, among them Jarrett.[16]

According to the Munsters' wounded adjutant, Harry Wilson, Y Company, caught by a barrage of shrapnel, machine gun and rifle fire, 'suffered heavily':[17]

> The spit of sand and half-submerged rocks over which the men had to pass proving a veritable death trap, the enemy having the range to the inch.[18]

Tizard, under the illusion that 'men were still being got across gradually to the shore',[19] persisted a while longer with the landing. And it was only Nightingale's sudden appearance at the port exit of No 1 Hold that made him think again. Nightingale's return was something extraordinary. To have survived one dash was incredible enough, but to have come back the same way unscathed was little short of miraculous. By then, the gangways and barges were 'choked'[20] and the spit of rock 'thickly covered'[21] with dead and wounded men. The news Nightingale brought with him was no more encouraging. Jarrett's message urged that 'no more men ... be sent ashore for the present'[22] and Tizard responded with another cessation of the landing. Giving orders to those of his men still on the *Clyde* to 'hold on and wait',[23] he decided to bide his time:

> Those that had got ashore by this time were taking cover under the bank, and I saw that it was useless to crowd too many men together there. The men were digging themselves in under the bank and the wounded were being made as comfortable as possible under the circumstances.[24]

Around this time, amid all the confusion of the failed landings, Tizard learned that Brigadier General Hare had been wounded at W Beach and, as a result, Lieutenant Colonel Carington Smith had succeeded him in command of 86th Brigade. Not that it made any practical difference. As senior military officer on the *River Clyde*, the Hampshires' commanding officer could scarcely exercise control over his own operation let alone another one a mile or so away. An acting brigadier without a brigade to lead, Carington Smith would remain a more or less helpless spectator, marooned on the *Clyde*'s bridge while others around him sought to seize any opportunity, no matter how small or hazardous, to break the deadlock. In his narrative of the landing, Tizard recalled:

> About 0930 a Staff Officer came to me and said that he thought there were a good many men in the barges who were not hit and could be got ashore so I went down to the nearest barge to see if this was so and found that there were a few taking cover amongst the dead – about 7 or 8. I happened to see a Lance Corporal in the nearest barge, and called to him through my megaphone and told him to get the men on shore who were not hit. After crawling about amongst them, he started them off singly. They crawled from one barge to the other, and then jumped into the water on the far side of the ship's cutter and waded towards the spit of rock, but directly they got on this they were fired at and about three of this party lived to get to the cover of the bank.[25]

Another pause followed before a message from Hunter-Weston, 'saying that the men must be pushed over',[26] propelled Carington Smith into further futile action. Turning to his own battalion, he ordered Y Company to make another attempt to break through to the men stranded ashore. Once again, it appeared to Tizard that 'the fire had died down somewhat'.[27] And once again his optimism proved misplaced. As soon as the Hampshires emerged from the sally-ports cut in No 2 Hold the Turkish positions burst into life with the same devastating results as before. Around twenty men of Captain Boxall's No 9 Platoon were killed or wounded within the first few seconds. Among those hit was the Old Etonian officer who had written of his 'extraordinary indifference' to his fate just days before.[28]

With their leader down, the men soon lost heart. 'After a few had gone down the gangway,' wrote Tizard, 'I noticed that some were coming back into the Hold, so I asked what was the matter and was told that there was too much of a crowd on the barge.'[29] Not long after, Carington Smith ordered the rest of Y Company to remain in the *Clyde* to avoid further 'useless sacrifice'.[30] But even as the landing stuttered to a standstill a further attempt was under way to save the operation from disaster.

At around 0950 *Albion*'s launch and sailing pinnace despatched by Captain Watts-Jones bumped alongside *River Clyde*. Their volunteer crews, many of them reservists, were set on what seemed a suicidal course to try to establish a more secure 'bridge' between ship and shore. As soon as they left the shelter of the collier the tiny craft entered a vortex of fire. Able Seaman Frank Dawe, coxswain of the sail boat, was one of the first hit. But no sooner had he fallen than his place was taken by Able Seaman Samuel Forsey. Together with Petty Officer 2nd Class Frederick Gibson aboard *Albion*'s launch, Forsey made repeated efforts to manoeuvre his small bullet-riddled craft between the hopper and the beach. But it was all to no avail. Every time they closed the shore they were forced away again by a hail of fire until, eventually, they were compelled to seek refuge behind the sheltering bulk of the *River Clyde*.

Watching the ghastly spectacle unfolding from *Queen Elizabeth*'s armoured conning tower, Hamilton was overwhelmed by a sense of helplessness. 'As men fixed in the grip of nightmare,' he later wrote, 'we were powerless – unable to do anything but wait.'[31] Not so Roger Keyes. Dismayed by the military commanders' apparent paralysis, de Robeck's chief of staff was already actively seeking an alternative to pouring more troops into the maelstrom of V Beach's stalled landing. With the transports carrying the follow-up force already in position having been ordered forward by Hunter-Weston's staff at 0830, Keyes proposed they be diverted to Y Beach where troops were reported to be ashore unopposed. By thus helping turn the defenders' flank and threatening their line of retreat, he contended that they would offer far more effective support to the men trapped on V Beach. However, though Hamilton was sympathetic to the idea, others on his staff were not. The GOC later wrote:

Braithwaite was rather dubious from the orthodox General Staff point of view as to whether it was sound for GHQ to barge into Hunter-Weston's plans, seeing he was executive Commander of the whole of this southern invasion. But to me the idea seemed simple common sense. If it did not suit Hunter-Weston's book, he had only to say so. Certainly Hunter-Weston was in closer touch with all these landings than we were; it was not for me to force his hands: there was no question of that: so at 9.15 [the MEF General Staff (GHQ) War Diary has it six minutes later] I wirelessed as follows:

GOC in C to GOC *Euryalus*. Would you like to get some more men ashore on Y Beach? If so, trawlers are available.

Three-quarters of an hour passed; the state of affairs at Sedd-el-Bahr was no better, and in an attack if you don't get better you get worse; the supports were not being landed; no answer had come to hand. So [I] repeated my signal to Hunter-Weston, making it this time personal from me to him and ordering him to acknowledge receipt:

General Hamilton to General Hunter-Weston, *Euryalus*. Do you want any more men landed at Y? There are trawlers available. Acknowledge the signal.[32]

So what was happening on *Euryalus*? As we have already seen, for almost an hour following *River Clyde*'s landfall, Hunter-Weston was unaware of the true severity of the struggle on V Beach. But by a little after 0900 the original misplaced optimism based on erroneous or exaggerated reports of troops 'getting ashore well' and being 'in Sedd-el-Bahr village', had been thrown into doubt, if not entirely blown out of the water. For the first time, troops advancing from the hard-won beachhead at W had been able to see across towards Sedd-el-Bahr and what they saw did not look good.

From a position near the Cape Helles lighthouse, not far from the Turkish redoubts that were blocking the Lancashire Fusiliers' eastward advance, it seemed clear to Captain Mynors Farmar, 86th Brigade Staff Captain, that while 'some of the Munster and Dublin Fusiliers were ashore', the 'majority were still in the Collier'.[33] Farmar's bleakly accurate report was noted as having been received by Hunter-Weston's headquarters at 0920, roughly the same time that Hamilton sent the first of his two signals. What came of the GOC's message is a mystery. The 29th Division's General Staff War Diary makes no mention of it, referring only to Hamilton's second signal at 1030. What is certain is that in the intervening period between the two messages, when the news from V Beach grew ever more depressing, Hunter-Weston did nothing to alter his original plan in order to try and prevent an even greater catastrophe.

Quite why he failed to act remains a matter for conjecture. Perhaps, he believed that reinforcements would swing the tide in favour of the men scattered along the foreshore or marooned inside *River Clyde*. Perhaps, he was fearful of throwing all his plans for the capture of Achi Baba into even further disarray. Perhaps, he had allowed himself to be too distracted by events on and around W Beach which, unlike those at V Beach, he could see for himself.

Quite possibly it was combination of all these things, but the truth is we do not know because Hunter-Weston never felt moved to offer an explanation. Neither his diary nor his letters give any clue as to his thinking at this critical juncture. A brief chronology he wrote of the landings on the southern beaches has a yawning gap of more than five hours between 0730 when troops were reported ashore at S Beach 'with few casualties' and 1300 when the landings at V Beach were 'hung up still'.[34]

There was, however, at least one man on *Euryalus* who was in no doubt about what had gone wrong. Lieutenant John Godfrey, whose responsibilities for the landings had included producing a plan showing where the *River Clyde* should be run aground, blamed command failures on the flawed decision to base Hunter-Weston and his headquarters with Wemyss on an 'attendant' ship, reasoning:

> The duties of an attendant ship are administrative. She has to look after the beach parties, transport crews, boats and boats' crews, [the] evacuation of the wounded, repairs to boats and lighters, buoyage and so on. She is, therefore, somewhat immobile.
>
> The Admiral and their operations staff had five landings to control ... in fact, the whole conduct of the battle at the tip of the peninsular [*sic*]. They should have been together in a sloop, destroyer or small cruiser so that they could move rapidly from one beach to another, go close in shore if necessary and see what was going on.
>
> To tie them to one ship, the *Euryalus*, drawing 28 feet, unable to leave the vicinity of W beach or to go close in due to her draft, was a mistake.
>
> Had Hunter-Weston and Admiral Wemyss appreciated the strength of the opposition at V beach and the complete lack of resistance at Y beach (which they did not) the whole course of the Dardanelles campaign might have been different ...[35]

Godfrey argued that the error was compounded by a rigidity of thinking. From the outset, he had been unimpressed by the Army's 'Achi Baba tonight'[36] approach and his pessimism was reinforced by the performance of Hunter-Weston and his staff, whose grip on events appeared to him to be 'fragile and, at times, almost impalpable'.[37] Like his colleague and friend, Keyes, on the *Queen Elizabeth*, Godfrey found the workings of the military mind incomprehensible. From his position, alongside Hunter-Weston's staff, it seemed obvious that

> something was going radically wrong just round the corner ... We couldn't see what was happening. My instinct, following the naval tradition, would have been to go and look, either in the *Euryalus* or, better still, in some small craft and, if necessary, intervene. But this would have been contrary to military ethics and so we continued to pour troops into V beach where the resistance was strongest and failed to exploit the soft spots at Y and S ...[38]

Godfrey's conclusion was as simple as it was uncompromising. 'General Hunter-Weston,' he wrote,' lost control of the battle through lack of mobility and adherence to the military doctrine of non-intervention.'[39] However, the commander of 29th Division did at least respond to Hamilton's second message, albeit after another delay of thirty minutes:

> From General Hunter-Weston to GOC, *Queen Elizabeth*
> Admiral Wemyss and Principal Naval Transport Officer [Captain Dent] state that to interfere with present arrangements and to try to land men at Y Beach would delay disembarkation.[40]

Indeed, it was Dent, rather than Hunter-Weston, who had argued against the switch. According to Wemyss, Dent 'pointed out how such a change would involve considerable alteration in the original plans for landing guns, stores, etc, and after consulting with me the General came to the conclusion that the delay inevitably arising from such a change would be greater than he could afford ...'[41] The matter, however, did not end there. In ruling out Y Beach as a viable alternative, Hunter-Weston, in Wemyss' words, decided instead to land the main force on W Beach on the grounds that its 'proximity to their original destination would not create any such dislocation of arrangements'.[42]

The belated decision to divert boats from V to W Beach, relayed to Watts-Jones in *Albion* at 1130 but enacted a while earlier, would be in time to spare the bulk of the 88th Brigade but not its unfortunate commander.

Chapter 16

'I'll Have a Damned Good Try!'

The troops crowded on the decks of the *Aragon* and *Dongola* had been following the course of the battle from first light. They watched the 'flash and thunder of the great guns of the warships'[1] and saw, 'dark against the rising light',[2] the low irregular shape of the land shrouded by smoke from bursting shells. As they drew nearer, the outline of cliffs grew clearer until it was possible to distinguish the beaches where the men of the Covering Force were already struggling to fight their way ashore.

By 0830, in accordance with Hunter-Weston's original instructions, the troops making up the 88th Brigade were ready to begin their journey into V Beach. As the sweeper *Newmarket* nudged alongside *Aragon* half an hour later, boatloads of wounded men were drawing towards the transport, but their approach was not allowed to interfere with the disembarkation of the Main Force. The priority was to reinforce the men ashore and within minutes the sweeper began to fill with troops from W Company, the 4th Worcestershire Regiment, commanded by Major Harry Carr, and W and X Companies of the 2nd Hampshires under Major Edward Leigh. Aged forty-two and forty-seven respectively, Carr and Leigh were already veterans with more than half a century of accumulated service between them. They were joined on the *Newmarket* by the commanding officer of 88th Brigade, Brigadier-General Henry Napier, and his complete headquarters staff headed by Brigade Major, John Costeker.

Like the two company commanders, Napier and Costeker had both enjoyed long and distinguished careers. Formerly of the Cheshire Regiment and Royal Irish Rifles, Napier was a Suffolk-born fifty-three-year-old veteran of the South African War. Married with three children back home in Chester, he was popular with his fellow officers, one of whom described him as 'a most kindly and courteous man' and 'a thoroughly sound commander'.[3] Though junior to the others in age and length of service, Costeker, at thirty-six, was the more experienced in modern warfare. As well as a fine record as a fighting soldier against the Boers, which had earned him a Distinguished Service Order and two mentions in despatches, he had more recently served as a brigade major on the Western Front. Wounded at Ypres in November, his work with 9th Infantry Brigade was recognised by a third 'mention' just two days before he joined Napier's staff in February.

With men and equipment crammed aboard, *Newmarket* slipped *Aragon* and headed slowly towards the shore. A mile or two off V Beach, the little vessel stood-to and waited. Shells roared overhead, with a few dropping uncomfortably close. A private in the Hampshires noted:

> The land batteries got our range, or nearly so, had they not been firing high, and we were obliged to move backward and forward to put them off; however, they dropped one low enough to clip off the fingers of one of our chaps who was grasping the taffrail.[4]

The crowded troops watched 'for some time the spectacle of the flagship, *Queen Elizabeth*, firing her great 15-inch guns at the Turkish defences'.[5] What they saw was hardly inviting. 'V Beach was an inferno of bursting shells. The sea before it was flecked and torn by falling shot.'[6] The *River Clyde* was clearly visible and so, too, were the ghastly consequences of the enemy's 'fierce and deadly'[7] fire. According to Hunter-Weston's ambitious plan, Napier's brigade was to land on a secured beach, its defenders vanquished or in retreat, and push on rapidly towards the heights of Achi Baba. It was plain to all, however, that the operation was in serious trouble when, at around 1000, a steam launch towing four boats from HMS *Albion* drew alongside.

Their appearance was hardly designed to raise spirits. 'These boats had already landed some of [the] 102nd [the Royal Dublin Fusiliers were originally the 102nd Foot], had been much knocked about [and had] blood and water in the bottom,'[8] wrote Carr. Undeterred by what he saw and determined to lead from the front, General Napier insisted on taking his place in the first boat, where he was joined by some of his staff, together with Major Carr and fourteen Worcesters. Behind them, in the remaining boats, came more of W Company, including a platoon commanded by Lieutenant Walter Bush. Their ride into V Beach would be a grisly one, with blood-stained seawater slopping over their boots in a grim augury of things to come.

As they drew away, their progress was followed from the *Newmarket* by troops waiting their turn. One of them, Private Ben Ward of the Worcesters later recalled:

> We watched the little boats till they were about one hundred yards
> from land – and about fifty yards from the *River Clyde* ... Then we
> saw a hail of bullets dropping around the little boats ...[9]

From his seat in the lead cutter, Napier could see a makeshift 'floating
bridge' forking out from the bows of the *River Clyde* that included a
couple of lighters and, nearest to the shore, *Albion*'s steam boat. Bullets
were showering the water around them and as the boats drew nearer
Carr realised that the lighter was 'covered with men, many [of them]
dead and wounded'.[10] The launch led on down the collier's starboard
side until a voice was heard calling above the din: 'For God's sake go
round the other side!'[11] It was Colonel Carington Smith.

Private George Keen of the Worcesters later recalled:

> Had it not been for the Colonel of the Hampshires we would have
> all been drowned and never have the chance of getting on land ...
> You see, the Turks were waiting for the boats just there – and
> blowing them to pieces.[12]

Carington Smith directed them round to the port bow where, amid a
heavy fire, the steam launch and boats drew alongside the nearest lighter
and made fast. What followed is far from clear. According to Captain
Wilson, the Munsters' wounded adjutant, Napier and his staff came on
board the *River Clyde* 'and orders were issued for more men to be sent
ashore'.[13] This tallies with both Tizard's and Nightingale's recollections
as well as an account written by an officer of the Hampshires who placed
Napier on the collier 'somewhere about 11am'.[14]

In Wilson's version, 'two companies of the Hampshire Regiment
were ordered to make the attempt, but after about fifteen men had gone
down the gangway the barge again drifted into deep water and only
one or two got ashore'.[15]

According to one of the Hampshires' officers, Napier and Costeker
paused only to speak with Doughty-Wylie and Williams before they
'made a rush by the port gangway on to the lighters'.[16] There was
another burst of fire and both were shot as they reached the barge
nearest the shore, which then 'swung off with the tide and thus
prevented further transit by that side'.[17] In a letter home, Nightingale,
who claimed to have seen it all, gave a fuller account:

> Gen Napier ... was hit in the stomach on the barge between our ship
> and the beach. He lay for ½ an hour on the barge, and then tried to
> get some water to drink but the moment he moved, the Turks began

Above: A grainy shot of the *River Clyde* approaching V Beach on the morning of 25 April, 1915. The steam hopper *Argyle* is clearly visible with a lighter sandwiched between her and the collier's port side. (Courtesy of Stephen Chambers)

Below: This view from the deck of the *River Clyde* on 25 April, 1915, shows a line of men sheltering beneath a sand bank on shore with a larger group bunched together above the spit of rocks. The slopes leading up to the battered fortress and village of Sedd-el-Bahr are straddled with barbed wire entanglements.

Above: An artist's fanciful interpretation of the landing from the *River Clyde*. The reality was altogether less orderly.

Below: An artist's impression of Unwin and Williams hauling the lighters into position in the face of a storm of fire in the early morning of 25 April.

Above: With his head bandaged, Midshipman George Drewry is portrayed helping carry a wounded soldier onto a bullet-swept V Beach.

Below left: An artist's impression of Midshipman Malleson's brave efforts to restore the bridge of lighters on the morning of 25 April. Below right: Sub-Lieutenant Tisdall is portrayed helping wounded into a lifeboat while the invasion continues around him. In reality the landings had been suspended when he embarked on his rescue effort.

Above: A shell hole through one of the troop decks on the *River Clyde*. The collier suffered repeated hits both during and after the landing operation. (Courtesy of Stephen Chambers)

Below: The 'Wooden Horse' becomes the work horse of the invasion as V Beach is converted into a base camp for the advance inland.

Above: A transformed V Beach as seen from the deck of the *River Clyde*, its redundant machine-gun emplacements still visible, in the weeks after the landing. Note the breakwater 'pier' which curves round to the right and which was used to help evacuate men and equipment the following January.

Below: The postern gate where Garth Walford was killed leading the charge into the village. The photograph was sent to Walford's widow with the comment that the Turks had met them with bombs thrown from near the bush in the right foreground. (The Liddle Collection)

Above: Portrayed with a cane in his right hand, 'Dick' Doughty-Wylie leads the charge through the narrow streets of Sedd-el-Bahr in this contemporary artist's impression of his Victoria Cross-winning action.

Below: A French officer pays his respects at 'Dick' Doughty-Wylie's lone grave on the summit of Hill 141.

Above: Edward Unwin, left, is congratulated on the award of his Victoria Cross which was announced while he was serving as beach master at Suvla Bay. (Imperial War Museum)

Below: A ceremony in Rotherham honours home-town hero James Malia, one of the Anson platoon party that helped rescue wounded from the spit of rocks.

Above: The *River Clyde*, its sally ports blocked up, in Malta in 1919 after the successful salvage operation. (Courtesy of Stephen Chambers)

Above: The *River Clyde* in her third incarnation as the *Maruja Y Aurora*, sailing under the Spanish flag. The First World War veteran survived the Spanish Civil War and the Second World War before being broken up in the mid-1960s.

firing at him again and whether he was hit again or not I don't know, but he died very soon afterwards ...[18]

The first Tizard saw of Napier was as Captain Boxall's faltering attempt to land was fizzling out. Heading up on to the bridge 'to see what was going on', he spotted the brigadier and his brigade major 'on the nearest barge':[19]

> I don't quite know what happened just then, but I fancy that the furthest barge had broken loose again, and the men who had gone down found there was no way over and got crowded. General Napier, seeing this, apparently ran down, and as the enemy now opened a very heavy fire on the barges, many were hit, both the General and his Brigade Major being killed.[20]

Others, however, told a different story. Captain George Reid, the Hampshires' adjutant, put the general's arrival almost an hour earlier, at 'about 10am'[21] and a 'little after we were hung up'[22] following the slaughter of Boxall's platoon. In a letter written to his wife five days' later, he made no mention of any contact between Napier and officers on the *River Clyde*. He merely stated that:

> the General and Costeker came along in a boat and got on to a lighter alongside us to try and land. They were both hit, and the fire was so heavy we could not get to them ...[23]

His brief record fits with Tony Morse's later recollection. Morse, who was still engaged in trying to construct a temporary 'bridge' between the collier and the shore, was 'almost certain'[24] that Napier was shot 'onboard the Hopper ... immediately he left the gig'.[25] He added: 'As far as I know Napier did not get onboard *RC* until after he was wounded.'[26] The Official History concurs. It states that the commander of the 88th Brigade made a fatal error as his boat drew alongside the collier's port side. Seeing the lighters nearby choked with men, he made straight for them with the intention of leading them ashore, 'not realising that they were dead'.[27] Someone on *River Clyde* tried in vain to stop him, calling out: 'You can't possibly land!' But Napier's mind was made up. 'I'll have a damned good try!' he shouted back.[28] Private Cecil Jeffries of the Worcesters was in Napier's boat. He recalled:

> I gave the General a leg-up on to the lighter [more likely the hopper], then his Brigade-Major. Then I was pushed up and the deck ... was covered with dead men.[29]

Napier and his staff officers were closely followed by Carr's fourteen Worcesters:

> There was no time to be lost, for bullets were striking all around. Major Carr and his Company-Sergeant-Major hurried along the floating bridge to gain the shore; but on reaching the last boat of the chain the Major found that the current had swung the floating bridge from its position, and that a gap of deep water now lay between the boats and the beach … The gap … which widened every moment as the boats swung with the current, was an impossible obstacle for troops in heavy equipment. As he realised that fact Major Carr turned and found that save for his Company-Sergeant-Major he was alone.
>
> Going back along the floating bridge Major Carr found that most of his men had already been struck down. The survivors were taking such cover as they could find behind the bulwarks …[30]

Carr had gone as far as the *Albion*'s steam launch before he could go no further. Along the way he had encountered Napier trying to direct operations. With the air thick with bullets, he had reported the hopelessness of their situation and left him to gather those of his men who were still alive. A little later he heard that the general had been fatally hit. Quite where or when Napier died remains a matter of further conjecture. Most accounts have him succumbing on either the lighter or the hopper.

According to Reid, an effort was made later to rescue both Napier and Costeker. 'At last,' he wrote, 'I managed to get over to them with three men, but unfortunately found them both dead. The General looked quite peaceful, as if he had not suffered; Costeker had been dead some time, and he, too, looked as if he had not felt it.'[31] This tallies with Tizard's account, which states that 'their bodies were recovered during the afternoon'.[32] Morse, however, insisted that Napier was still alive when he was carried aboard the collier. He stated: 'I took him from *River Clyde* in my boat and he died either just before or just after he reached a Hospital Ship.'[33]

Either way, any chance of fathoming what he was seeking to accomplish died with him. But whether he was a victim of blind obedience to orders he ought to have countermanded or of his own desperate courage was immaterial: the result was the same. Henry Napier's impetuous charge across the lighters not only cost him his life, together with that of his brigade major, it robbed 88th Brigade of its leader even before it had landed and contributed nothing to the operation beyond further useless sacrifice.

Edward Unwin had no time for such pointless heroics. He regarded the bodged landing by Napier and Costeker more as an act of reckless folly than a bold attempt to revive a stalled invasion. Forthright as ever, he insisted that 'their lives were absolutely thrown away', adding: 'They had no business [being] on the hopper at all.'[34] The same charge might have been levelled at him. Discharging himself from Surgeon Kelly's tender care, the *River Clyde*'s indefatigable captain ventured out again. While recovering from his earlier exertions, he had been brought up to date by Midshipman Drewry, who had returned to have his head wound dressed. The youngster informed him that the 'bridge' of lighters had been completed and so Unwin decided to go 'to see if I could do any good'.[35] He made straight for the *Argyle* and found the hopper 'a shambles'.[36]

The deck was crowded with troops. 'Most of them were wounded and many were dead.'[37] Among those he recognised were Napier and Costeker, who at that stage were still breathing. Few, he noted, had come from the *River Clyde*, the majority having landed with Napier and been 'turned back … by warning shouts from those lying under the ridge'[38] along the foreshore. He 'messed about'[39] on the hopper for some time. With the help of 'an old merchant seaman',[40] who looked to him to be at least seventy years of age, and 'a boy',[41] who was presumably one of the midshipmen from the beach or boat parties, he succeeded in getting another line out to hold the lighters in place. Splendid feat though it was, he frankly doubted whether it served any useful purpose. 'I don't think it was ever used,'[42] he later admitted. Not long after attaching the rope, he heard a shout from somewhere amid the heap of bodies. It was Napier's brigade major. Unwin recalled:

> Costeker yelled at me to lie down as he said I was drawing the fire. This I did for a bit. Then he gave a yell and said, 'They've got me'. I believe he was shot through the stomach. A bullet then hit a stanchion alongside me and spluttered over my face and neck, and, as I was doing no good there and I couldn't see a live man, I ran up the inclined staging [and went] in through the foremost port …[43]

Bullets pursued him all the way into the *River Clyde*, but once again his luck held. Not so for the man who reached out to help him aboard. He was shot through the lungs, though Unwin did not realise it at the time. And not so for Costeker either. His wound proved fatal. Before dying, he was said to have raised himself up on one knee to urge his men to 'Carry on'.

It was a gallant if futile gesture. The rush across the lighters and on to the *Argyle* served only to draw more fire on to the hopper, where survivors of the earlier failed landings had congregated. Among them was Maurice Lloyd, the teenage midshipman injured in the prolonged struggle to link the *River Clyde* to the shore. He had been lying on the hopper's exposed deck, his wound untreated, for half an hour when he became aware of a sudden commotion close by:

> I saw a lot of men just getting ready to charge and so I thought I had better get out of it and so I crawled to the lee-side of the so-called superstructure, but unfortunately I left my ankle sticking out and, of course, that got knocked.[44]

Wracked with pain, he lay helpless as around twenty soldiers, presumably Worcesters from Harry Carr's company, swept across the hopper. They didn't get far. As Lloyd looked on 'the Turks turned a machine gun on to them and killed the lot'.[45] It was the last thing he remembered before being picked up and spirited away. His rescuer was none other than 'Geordie' Samson. Drewry's brave-hearted assistant had long since given up trying to induce the *Argyle*'s reluctant Greek crew to further effort and instead sought alternative ways to make himself useful.

According to his own account that meant helping to link the 'bridge' of lighters to the shore as well as fetching wounded from the beach and ferrying them first to the hopper and then on to the *River Clyde*. For much of the time he was under a galling fire, but carried on any way, drawing courage and inspiration from the example of his officers and shipmates, Captain Unwin and Midshipman Drewry:

> Every moment they were risking their lives, and really it was nothing short of a miracle that they were not hit. As long as I live I shall treasure memories of the bravery of these men; they hurried hither and thither, giving a hand when needed, just as if they were aboard the *Hussar* in peace-time. As for myself I cannot say that I felt quite as cool as I may have looked. I am not a very excitable sort when there is serious trouble about. It takes a good deal to disturb me, but I can say without hesitation that this was the 'goods' for excitement. During these first hours … I had many narrow escapes just the same, of course, as my companions … Bullets were whizzing about our heads every few minutes, and we were soon aware of the

fact that machine guns were in operation … Men were falling down like ninepins quite near us, and perhaps it was only the thought that we must give them a helping hand that made us forget our own danger …[46]

Terrible though the destruction was on the hopper and lighters, it may have contributed to one of the day's rare successes: a largely bloodless landing in the midst of the carnage that was V Beach.

It was effected by around fifty men from the Hampshires in two boats that formed part of the second tow to leave the *Newmarket*. Each boat carried twenty-five men apiece from W and X Companies under Captains Hubert Wymer and Richard Spencer-Smith and their part in the landing, overshadowed as it was by the tragic events that overtook their brigade commander, has been largely ignored until now.

Following much the same course as Napier's tow, they, too, reached the *River Clyde* more or less without loss. But whereas the general's party were led to the port side, the two boatloads of Hampshires found themselves being waved along the starboard side. Here, they were spared the worst of the fire by a combination of the alignment of the ship's hull and the fact that Turkish attention was mostly focused on the 'bridge' of lighters and Napier's ill-advised attempt to land. In a letter home, Captain Spencer-Smith described the Hampshires' final approach to the shore:

As soon as we got opposite her bows they opened fire on us. I saw the Colonel on the ship watching us, and he gave a shout of encouragement. One hardly realised at first that we were being fired at, until I saw splashes in the water all round.

When we were about 40 or 50 yards from the shore I looked down and saw there was only three or four feet of water, so jumped in and ordered the men to do the same. I made at once to the shore as fast as I could, where there were a lot of men of another regiment shouting to us which way to go. We got some protection from a line of rocks, but could not go very fast owing to the rocks under foot and also the weight of one's clothes and equipment being submerged. I eventually reached the shore untouched and got cover under a steep bank, and I think I was one of the first of the regiment to set foot on the land …[47]

The time was a little after 1040. Spencer-Smith knew that with some certainty as it was precisely at that moment his watch stopped after being submerged during his wade ashore. Astonishingly, two-thirds of the men in the two boat parties succeeded in splashing and crawling ashore unharmed. Theirs was the last and most fortuitous boat landing on V Beach that day. However, they were too few to tip the balance against a redoubtable Turkish force that, in the face of continued bombardment, mounting pressure from W Beach and rising casualties, had succeeded in defeating another attempt to secure a beachhead in front of Sedd-el-Bahr. From the reports reaching Major Sabri's command post a kilometre or so inland, it was clear the British assault had once more ground to a halt. As the Turkish commander observed:

> Those of the enemy who succeeded in landing and who were not casualties hid themselves under cover behind the ruins on the shore and remained silent and motionless behind the walls.[48]

Yet for all the prodigious heroism displayed by Sabri's embattled force there was no disguising the difficulties confronting them. Squeezed on two sides by a numerically superior enemy supported by machine guns and the heavy guns of the British fleet ranged offshore, the five platoons of the 3/26th Regiment were short of everything but courage. At Sedd-el-Bahr, where less than a platoon of men lay among the ruins of the village in desperate need of reinforcement, Sabri, nevertheless, had 'every confidence'[49] that their bravery and training would see them through. 'Although our forces were small,' he wrote, 'it was certain that the enemy would not destroy them without further forces.'[50]

For now, those reinforcements earmarked for V Beach had, as a direct result of his men's epic defence, been deflected westwards. The troops, including Lieutenant Colonel Douglas Cayley's 4th Worcestershires less Major Carr's two platoons, half of the 2nd Hampshires and a portion of the Anson Battalion, were headed past the roaring guns of *Swiftsure* and *Euryalus* to the relative safety of W Beach.

Henry Foster was among them. Climbing into the first of seven lifeboats in what was supposed to have been the fifth tow into V Beach at around 1130, the Ansons' chaplain could hardly fail to notice that the boat was 'running with blood'.[51] 'There was blood on the oars,' he wrote, 'blood on the seats, blood all over, and bits of skin here and there.'[52] A seaman standing in the bows, nonchalantly smoking a clay pipe, helped him take his place. 'She 'as two bullet 'oles in 'er bottom now sir,' he said disconcertingly, 'but I 'ope she'll last out.'[53]

They were in the process of drawing away from the *Newmarket* when a boat came alongside and a naval commander with a megaphone shouted across: 'Admiral's orders. No more men to be landed on V Beach; you have to go to W Beach.'[54]

The baleful sound of gunfire carried across the wine dark water. They were fewer than two miles from the disaster-strewn shore when they turned away from Cape Helles and made towards Cape Tekke. To a man of Foster's faith the change of course was a clear case of 'Divine' intervention. He was quite certain in his own mind that they were spared the tragedy that was engulfing their comrades around the 'Wooden Horse' 'only by a merciful Providence':[55]

> Had we landed on 'V', as was originally intended, we should have suffered exactly in the same way as the Dublin Fusiliers.[56]

Chapter 17

'Some Fuss About the Cornwallis'

As the originator of the 'Wooden Horse' scheme, Edward Unwin surveyed the wreckage of his plan with dismay. The lighters he had so valiantly hauled into place were covered with the bodies of the dead, the dying and those men desperately clinging to life. Most of those with a breath inside them remained as still as the lifeless corpses around them. To move was to invite a Turkish bullet. 'They were simply picking us off as they pleased,'[1] observed Unwin. It was time to call an end to the useless slaughter and 'knock off the landing'.[2]

Having returned to the shelter of the ship, his face bearing evidence of his latest narrow escape, he made straight for Carington Smith and bluntly told him that 'it was no good trying to land any more men as it was certain death'.[3] The colonel of the Hampshires had already reached the same conclusion. He told Unwin that he had issued instructions to stop sending men out. It was the last order he would give.

Shortly afterwards, the pair of them spotted a party of British troops over to the west. According to Unwin, they were 'coming along from W Beach to try and outflank the Turks'.[4] Carington Smith gave a cheer and so did the troops around him. As Unwin climbed a ladder towards the upper bridge, with its quarter of an inch thick layers reinforced steel, Carington Smith started to follow him. But he never made it. Pausing on the unprotected lower bridge, he raised his binoculars to scan the beach again. Fearful of the danger, Unwin called to him 'to come up on the upper bridge'. 'Oh, I'm all right here,' he replied. In that same instant Unwin heard the crack of a bullet. 'I saw him fall, shot through the mouth,' he wrote. 'His servant was close at hand, but we could do nothing. He must have died instantly.'[5]

First Rooth, then Napier and now Carington Smith. Two out of three battalion commanders from the Covering Force and the general commanding the break-out brigade had been killed in the first four hours or so of the invasion. With Brigadier-General Hare also wounded and out of action, local command of the faltering V Beach landing devolved on the shoulders of Henry Tizard.

The Munsters' CO learned of his sudden promotion as he was trying to bring some order to the chaos left by Napier's failed intervention. He headed to the lower bridge, where he found Carington Smith lying dead, his binoculars close by, and some staff officers who he did not recognise but assumed had come on board during the course of the most recent boat landing attempt. His first order was for Major Hutchinson, his second-in-command, to take charge of the battalion, while he took stock:

> I had now on board, as far as I can remember, the following troops:
>
> No 1 Hold, Upper and Lower Decks – One platoon of Y Coy, R M[unster] Fus[iliers]; W Coy, The Headquarters and four Machine Guns, R M Fus; Two platoons the Hampshire Regt; and One Coy, R Dublin Fus.
>
> No 2 Hold – One Coy, Hampshire Regt; One platoon, Worcester Regt.
>
> Distributed in 3 and 4 Holds – The West Riding Coy, Field Engrs; One platoon of Anson Battn, RN Div; and 3 Sub Divns, Ambulance Corps.[6]

Like Unwin and Carington Smith, Tizard saw no merit in persisting with a landing scheme that had so obviously come unstuck. Instead, he proposed to play a waiting game, while leaving his options open to take advantage of any opportunities that might present themselves:

> I still considered that our best plan was to hold on till the light failed when the enemy's fire would not be as accurate. However, if I saw a chance when the fire died down I intended to try and get the men over gradually [and] with this idea the men of the Hampshire Regiment, then in No 1 Hold, were still trying to get over, but they sustained many casualties.[7]

For the time being, however, his priority was to try to reduce the amount of incoming fire that was making life on board the *River Clyde*, the lighters jumbled around her and along the foreshore a misery.

Leaving his battalion medical officer, Lieutenant Harold Atlee, and his team of stretcher-bearers attending to the increasing number of wounded in No 1 Hold, Tizard visited the casemated machine gun stations manned by Wedgwood's armoured car detachment in an attempt to locate the enemy positions. He wrote:

> It was very difficult to get any definite target. The furthest trenches of the enemy were between four and six hundred yards distant ... Captain Lambert, RN, also assisted me in this and he also directed the gun fire from the supporting ships on to various points of the village and ground commanding the beach.[8]

The immediate focus was less on capturing Sedd-el-Bahr and the heights above V Beach and more about dissuading the Turks from attempting a counter-attack, which the men scattered about the foreshore were in little state to resist. To that end, Wedgwood's machine gun teams were instructed to maintain a furious fire in the general direction of the Turkish positions while shooting up any specific target that presented itself. Sub-Lieutenant Illingworth, who was in charge of three guns sited on the port side of the *River Clyde*, later wrote:

> The hillsides leading up from the little bay were covered with trenches, which were comparatively little damaged. So we had to keep on firing hard to protect our handful of men on shore from being rushed and then land the rest under cover of darkness.[9]

Through the slits of their sand-bagged casemates they had witnessed all the horror and the heroism of the terrible struggle. 'It was horrible,' wrote Wedgwood in a letter to Churchill, 'and all within 200 yards of our guns trying to find and shoot the shooters.'[10] In a later account, he added:

> One moment it had been early morning in a peaceful country, with thoughts or smells of cows and hay and milk; and the next while the boats were just twenty yards from the shore, the blue sea round each boat was turning red. Is there anything more horrible than to see men wading through water waist-high under a heavy fire? You see where each bullet hits the water, which, like a nightmare, holds back the man for the next shot which will not miss ...[11]

Even more terrible had been the wretched spectacle of the rushes from 'the Wooden Horse'. He saw them all, first the Munsters, with sprigs of shamrock decorating their caps, then the Hampshires and the Worcesters led by Napier and Costeker, until the lighters and the spit of rocks were strewn with 'dead and dying'. From his post on the bridge, he was also an awed spectator to the astonishing feats of bravery performed by Midshipmen Drewry. He watched him swim across to one of the lighters that had broken loose, 'with a line in his mouth and a wound in his head'.[12] It all but beggared belief, as he wrote:

> All these things I saw as in a dream as I moved from casemate to casemate, watching to see Turks, wearing an 'Election smile', and trying to pretend in an even voice to men who had never seen death that this was the best of all possible worlds. Columns of smoke rose from the castle and town of Sedd el Bahr as the great shells from the fleet passed over our heads and burst ...[13]

During one of the lulls, Arthur Coke, commanding the guns in the forecastle, left his sandbag shelter to see how his friend Surgeon Kelly was faring. His presence proved a real tonic. According to Kelly, he was utterly fearless and 'very cool about everything':[14]

> The saloon was full of wounded officers and some dead ones and he cheered us all up and put his hand on my shoulder and said, 'Will I kill a Turk for you?' and then went off smiling ... He very nearly lost his life as he went out of the saloon as a bullet missed his head by inches and entered the pantry from the port side, wounding the captain's servant.[15]

Coke carried on, seemingly unflustered. If it was an act, or an affectation like Wedgwood's, it was a convincing one. To Kelly, it seemed that his friend, along with his fellow machine gun officer, Sub-Lieutenant Parkes, were having 'the time of their lives'.[16]

The noise was deafening. One of Wedgwood's machine gunners wrote:

> All the while shot was being poured on us from everywhere you could see within a mile of the sea, and we were shooting back at them with our guns, while our fleet were bombarding the village and hills and creating the biggest din you could ever think of, firing hundreds of shells as hard as they could.[17]

With the landings suspended, the supporting ships, led by the *Queen Elizabeth*, redoubled their efforts, pounding the slopes and the village ahead of them before turning their attention to the ruined castle. Petty Officer Fyffe wrote:

> There, in a chamber in the walls a Maxim gun was spluttering busily through a small window, and not all our painstaking efforts could get at that gun. It was situated opposite my gun position on the forecastle and Lieutenant Coke was devoting all his energies to putting the nuisance out of action. But although the bullets from his gun were knocking little spurts of dust off the walls all around the look-hole, the aperture was too small and the belts rattled through the breach all in vain. Then suddenly one of the 'Lizzie's' six-inch presents blew the top off the wall just above the hated window and with a fervid 'At last' , Coke crawled out of his steel cubby-hatch and crouched behind the rail, glasses glued on the spot. Again the 'Lizzie' fired and again the battlemented parapet dissolved as if by magic above the window. 'Too high, you blighters, too high!' came in muttered accents from the officer, now flat on his face on the deck, for the air was full of whining bullets. Again came the crash behind us, again the shell groaned over our heads and this time the whole face of the wall disappeared in a cloud of fallen masonry and dust and yellow fumes. For a second nobody spoke, and then suddenly 'Got him! Got him clean! Beautiful oh beautiful!' came in cries of ecstasy from behind the rail, and our worthy lieutenant danced upon the deck as the dust blew away and we saw that a huge hole gaped in the wall where before the window had been.[18]

It was a small victory but hardly offset the fire concentrated on the *River Clyde*. One of the Hampshires wrote:

> In spite of every effort on the part of the officers, not a single place could be definitely located from which the fire was coming, and though our four Maxims in the foc'sle head and about four others of the Naval Division used to fire on likely places to try and keep down the enemy's fire, but little effect was apparent. Messages were being continually sent to our covering ship to fire on certain places, and this had the effect of lessening the fire from that locality temporarily, but never permanently.[19]

To Petty Officer Fyffe it seemed as though there was 'nothing the fleet could do ... to daunt the defenders'. He wrote:

> The village with its huddle of partially ruined houses was a very nest of snipers and from behind the tree-clad garden walls and the

corners of the narrow streets came a never-ceasing hail of deadly fire ... Such of us as were not engaged working the guns, would crouch with ready rifle waiting to catch a snap-shot from behind the bulwarks at the dim figures that flitted from house to house as the shells smashed and wrecked the buildings. And that was all we saw of the enemy that day ...[20]

Throughout the morning, the *River Clyde* remained a tempting target for enemy positions around V Beach and on the other side of the Dardanelles. Sub-Lieutenant Illingworth noted:

Our old boat was riddled with bullets and hit a good many times by shells from the Asiatic side. It is a ghastly thing to be in a ship stranded and unprotected in any way. Both bullets and shells went right through. I had a gun on the bridge and had put up plates which kept the bullets out, but several officers were killed beside me who would persist in standing up too much.[21]

The long-range shelling of the *River Clyde* began almost as soon as the ship grounded, though accounts of those on board vary as to its accuracy and duration. The number of direct hits recorded ranges from three to five during a bombardment that most agree lasted until late morning but according to one witness persisted all day. What is certain is that the shooting from a gun, or guns – again, accounts vary – situated on the Asiatic shore, either in or close to Kum Kale Fort, placed an additional strain on men whose nerves were already stretched taut by the fear of the unknown. Imprisoned for their own safety in sweaty and crowded holds, they could do nothing but wait and listen to the terrible din of battle exploding all around them, not knowing when or where the next shell would fall.

According to Lieutenant Colonel Williams, 'the good ship *Clyde*'[22] was a sitting target for 'two 4.7 guns from the Asiatic shore, four pom-poms from 700 yards on the left, and maxim guns from both sides'.[23] As far as, he could tell, the men inside the ship's holds were largely safe from what he took to be machine gun and pom-pom fire. The shells, however, were a different matter. 'Her good old iron sides,' he wrote, 'were proof against all these, excepting the 4.7s which fortunately only hit her five times that day.'[24]

Even so, it was, in the words of the Hampshires' adjutant, 'a most uncomfortable time'[25] during which the men confined aboard the stranded collier were at the mercy of 'a brute of a gun'.[26] A fellow officer, whose men were spread mostly about No 3 Hold, wrote of the Turkish bombardment becoming 'most persistent' from a gun or guns on the other side of the Dardanelles, with 'shells ... dropping first short and then over with an ever-decreasing bracket'.[27] To Reginald Gillett, who was in the same part of the ship, it felt as if 'shells were falling all round us'.[28] Eventually, the Turks found their range. Gillett recorded three direct hits, while another officer counted four, all of which passed through the ship without exploding:

> One was dug out of the coal bunkers; it was about a 4.7 calibre, and the shell was curiously silent in its approach. This particular one missed our Sergeant-Major by about 3ft, as it passed across the engine-room alley-way where he was standing ...[29]

Among those who enjoyed miraculous escapes was the *River Clyde*'s surgeon. Moments before one of the shells struck, Peter Kelly had gone to assist Commander Unwin, who had collapsed from exhaustion after trying to save Seaman Williams from drowning. But before he could reach him, he was hit by a bullet that struck him a glancing blow on his right shin. It was 'stinging like the very devil'[30] when, barely a yard further on, he was hit again, a bullet tearing into his left foot and leaving him flat on his face, where he was found by Lieutenant Colonel Williams and helped into cover:

> Just then a large shell entered the top of the boiler casing at the root of the ship's funnel and the result was awful, fearful fumes which were choking myself and several others close by. I tried to get away but fell down a hatchway as we could not see and then I remember no more until I was roused.[31]

Others were not so fortunate. Two shells ripped through No 4 Hold where the Yorkshire sappers of 1/1st West Riding Field Company were situated, together with stretcher bearers from 89th Field Ambulance and the Anson beach party. According to one of the medical officers, Lieutenant Davidson, the first shell penetrated the hold at an angle of 45 degrees, 'coming through the deck over our heads and going out at the junction of the floor and side wall':[32]

> In its course it struck a man on the head, this being splashed all through the hold. Another man squatting on the floor was hit about the middle of both thighs, one leg being completed severed, while the other hung by a tiny shred of skin only. He fell back with a howl with both stumps in the air. In five minutes, a second shell entered

our hold, wounding two or three where we were, mostly by the buckling of the floor plates, then passing down below to the lowest hold where many men were sheltering under the water line. Here six or seven were laid out.[33]

The impact on such a confined space was terrible. Sapper George Smith recalled:

That was the first time most of us had ever seen anybody killed. It was a horrible moment and we did not know when another shell might come along with worse results.[34]

Petty Officer William Perring, of the Ansons, was within a couple of yards of two of the most seriously injured sappers. He wrote:

The hold was packed with troops as thickly as ever you could stow men together, and the terrible sights and the cries of the wounded will never be forgotten by those who are alive to tell the tale ... I now went down to my men, who were in No 4 lower hold, and I addressed them, and told them to keep cool, to try and keep their heads ... While I was talking to the platoon another shell came in and killed three of them. This was the second shell I had seen explode within a few minutes; it was rather bad, especially for young lads like these, but I knew I was there to show them an example and take care of them.[35]

The number of casualties caused by the long-range shelling is not clear. The war diary of the 1/1st West Riding Field Company lists two men killed and five wounded as a result of 'shell fire from the Asiatic coast and rifle fire from the forts'.[36] However, Lieutenant J. A. Morris, commanding the 89th Field Ambulance contingent aboard *River Clyde*, reported three men killed from the engineers and Anson platoon and several more severely injured. Morris was impressed by his men's reaction to their first test. In circumstances that might have shaken the most battle-hardened troops, he reckoned 'they behaved with remarkable coolness'.[37] As soon as the first shell struck they set about attending to the wounded 'in spite of [the] risk from bullets entering the wide ports at either side of the ship'.[38]

However, despite their best efforts, they were not able to save the most grievously injured. George Smith recalled the vain attempts to staunch the flow of blood from one of his comrades whose leg had been severed. He was probably one of the two sappers Perring saw succumb to their agonising wounds within twenty minutes of the first shell plunging through the deck and into the hold.

As hard as such losses were to bear among men new to battle who had yet to set foot on the peninsula, they were as little compared to the slaughter outside or the slaughter many feared could have been inflicted inside had the Turks brought more guns to bear on them. Referring to the artillery piece on the Asiatic shore that appeared to do most of the damage, Perring later commented: 'I have often wondered since what would have happened had that gun not been put out of action when it was. They had the correct range.'[39] Given the damage wrought from such distance, Wedgwood could not help but ponder how perilously close to disaster they came. 'One gun on the ridge,' he wrote, 'and we should be smashed to pieces.'[40] As it was, the greatest threat to life and limb aboard *River Clyde*, were not, in Wedgwood's estimation, the 'great shells' that hit the 'shivering ship' but the relentless fire from Turkish positions dotting Sedd-el-Bahr and the slopes above V Beach that forced everyone to keep their heads 'below the bulwarks and boiler-plate'.[41]

Whereas the heavy shelling appeared to fade away by mid-morning, what Reginald Gillett described as the 'concentrated fire' directed against *River Clyde* 'continued for a considerable time', slowly dying down only to be resumed 'each time fresh troops tried to reach the shore'.[42]

Time after time, or so it seemed to the men trapped aboard the collier, the fire from their machine guns or from the heavy guns of the supporting battleships appeared to silence enemy positions only for them to burst into destructive life the moment any further movement was attempted. One such post in a house to the west of the *River Clyde* proved particularly troublesome. An officer of the Hampshires wrote:

> It was only about midday, when a sudden burst of fire opened …
> that some of the enemy were definitely located … but though the
> ships were at once communicated with and landed a good many
> shells near the spot, it is doubtful, in view of the excellent cover
> afterwards found to exist here of a permanent nature, if they did any
> damage. Certainly the fire was re-opened from there at intervals,
> though our Maxims generally subdued it immediately. The whole
> place was such a rabbit warren of little holes and tunnels, some of
> them in the cliff itself, and absolutely invisible from 100 yards off or
> less, that the enemy were able to fire at will with impunity.[43]

As has already been seen, the supporting fire from the *River Clyde*'s attendant ship *Albion* supported, from 0820, by the *Queen Elizabeth*, was rendered largely ineffective by their positions too far out, not to mention the inadequacies of their gunnery guidance systems and weaknesses in aerial target 'spotting'. Still in its infancy, air observation was rudimentary and its failings came as little surprise, least of all to the aviators themselves.

A veteran of the campaign in Belgium, Lieutenant Bernard Isaac, No 3 Squadron's acting intelligence officer, spent a frustrating day disseminating reports from aircraft flying 6,000ft above the 'gruesome debris' littering the beach at Sedd-el-Bahr before signalling the results to Wemyss and the various attendant ships. It was, as he noted in his diary,

> a task made more difficult by the sudden swelling of the heads of pilots except Collet, Marix and Osmond ... I quarrel with everyone. Vice-Admiral signals that our spotting is of very little value as we don't know tables. A natural result of employing pilots who know all about oil and flying machines, but nothing of wireless telegraphy.[44]

Such shortcomings were not helped by the lack of a military artillery adviser aboard *Albion*. Major Alan Thomson had been left 'high and dry' by the battleship's assignment to the mouth of the Dardanelles on the eve of the landings. In later years, he maintained that the Navy's failure to provide effective covering fire at V Beach was, in large measure, due to a strict adherence to Wemyss' instruction to take up gunnery stations at least 1,300 yards, and sometimes further, from the shore. Only at X Beach, where, as Thomson put it, the attendant ship 'steamed straight for the beach until the anchor slung from her bows grounded',[45] was the landing '100 per cent successful' thanks to its short-range 'intensive covering fire'.[46] He wrote:

> I am convinced that had the *Euryalus* and *Swiftsure* at W Beach and the *Albion* at V Beach acted on the 25th April as did the *Implacable* at X Beach, the casualties would have been infinitely less than they actually were; the troops would, in all probability, have been able to advance inland on the first day and join up with the successful landings at de Tott's [S Beach] and at Y Beach and that the whole story of the subsequent campaign might have read differently ... I definitely put down the failure – or set-back, call it what you will – on 25 April to the entire lack of covering fire from the supporting ships at V and W Beaches during the critical period when the ships' tows were going in ...

Two officers – a Major and a Captain – who landed from the *River Clyde* on the 25th have told me that the *Albion* was far too far out to be of any use. They and everyone else on shore knew exactly where the machine guns and occupied trenches were situated but although messages were semaphored to the *River Clyde* and duly passed on, it was obviously impossible to direct the fire of the *Albion* on to precise spots from such a distance apart from the question of the danger to our own troops. In actual fact, attempts to do so failed completely.[47]

Albion's feeble support aside, there was another failing, more contentious and controversial, which contrived to impair the troops' chances of a successful landing at V Beach. At its heart was the dual role of the battleship *Cornwallis* and the impetuous behaviour of its commander, Captain Alexander Davidson.

As already outlined, *Cornwallis* had been tasked with convoying and then covering the easternmost landing on the peninsula below the De Totts' battery, before hurrying back to her main station off Sedd-el-Bahr to join *Albion* in supporting the V Beach operation. Having instructed Davidson 'not to delay'[48] returning to the scene of 29th Division's main thrust, Wemyss had signalled him again on the eve of the landing:

When you take trawlers up to Morto Bay, instead of returning immediately you are to remain to support them until the troops are landed, then returning to your anchorage … Report if you thoroughly understand.[49]

Intended by Wemyss as a reiteration of his earlier order, the strangely ambiguous signal was interpreted by Davidson as offering him 'generous latitude'[50] to use his own initiative. His brief reply simply read: 'Thoroughly understood.'[51] In fact, as subsequent events proved, nothing could have been further from the truth. There had been no hint of the trouble to come when *Cornwallis*, with 800 men of the 2nd South Wales Borderers and a detachment of the 2nd London Field Company, Royal Engineers, on board, anchored off the entrance to the Dardanelles at 0300. An hour and a half later, according to plan, the troops were transferred to four trawlers and *Cornwallis* began escorting them in towards S Beach. As the small convoy passed Sedd-el-Bahr, Davidson observed *River Clyde* 'taking the ground'.[52] Their progress was delayed, just as Unwin's had been, by trawlers astern of the battleship *Agamemnon* blocking their path. Carrying on, Davidson gave orders to his gun crews to engage the 'Asiatic Batteries which were ranging on

River Clyde and [his] ship's attendant trawlers'[53] as well as Turkish positions on the northern side of Morto Bay as far as Essarlik Point and on Hill 238. Finally, having dropped anchor in Morto Bay at 0630, he directed twenty-four lifeboats and cutters under the command of Lieutenant Commander Ralph Janvrin to begin ferrying the troops in to Point Essarlik.

So far, so straightforward. It was at this point, to the consternation of Wemyss and Keyes, that Davidson deviated from the original plan. Not only did he chose to reinforce the military landing force with a contingent of twenty-five Bluejackets and twenty-five Marines under the command of his gunnery lieutenant, he made the extraordinary decision as captain of an attendant battleship to accompany them ashore. What the commanding officer of the South Wales Borderers, Lieutenant Colonel Hugh Casson, considered 'far more personal assistance than I had any right to expect'[54] Keyes felt showed 'a complete lack of judgment'[55] that would have profound and prolonged repercussions for the men at V Beach.

Under the covering fire of *Cornwallis'* guns, the troops, supported by Davidson's naval party who had the unique distinction that day of carrying out a bayonet charge on a Turkish-held trench, swarmed ashore against weak opposition. By 0830 the entire enemy position was securely in British hands at only minimal cost. It was a remarkable success that Casson believed owed much to the Navy's close support. Wemyss was frankly astonished that a beach he regarded 'as presenting the most difficulty'[56] had been 'captured the most easily'.[57] He was even more astonished to learn that the rapid victory at S Beach did not result in *Cornwallis'* equally rapid move to V Beach where her supporting fire was so desperately needed. A flurry of increasingly angry signals followed. One of Wemyss' staff officers aboard *Euryalus*, Lieutenant Godfrey, later wrote:

> Although the *Lord Nelson* had signalled from Morto Bay that the South Wales Borderers were already on the top of Eski Hissarlik [*sic*], above de Tott's battery, the *Cornwallis* had not come away (to take up her allotted position to provide covering fire at V Beach); *Queen Elizabeth* signalled to her to take up her new station. Still (unknown then to Admiral de Robeck or Admiral Wemyss) Captain Davidson was too busy getting off the wounded, to obey at once. Again and again the signal was repeated with increasing emphasis – but it was not until 10.00am when the Asiatic guns ceased to be troublesome and the troops seemed firmly established that he began to withdraw his landing party.

> I can well remember the exasperation on the bridge of *Euryalus* caused by *Cornwallis'* failure to do what she was told, and Wemyss' anger when it was subsequently discovered that her Captain was ashore taking personal command of a platoon of sailors.[58]

Wemyss was not alone in his displeasure. On board *Queen Elizabeth*, Keyes was incensed over Davidson's failure to comply with his instructions. What Hamilton later understatedly referred to in his diary as 'some fuss about the *Cornwallis'*[59] was, in fact, the beginning of a furious exchange that would rumble on long after the campaign was over.

In a report on the landings and subsequent operations written on 29 May, Davidson delivered a robust defence of his actions. He stated that he had

> landed personally to assume naval direction of [the] landing as, owing to [an] unavoidable lack of steam boats towing boats up to the beach, and the very strong current after [the] previous North Easterly Gale, I had reason to apprehend [the] failure of boats arriving, and I considered their best chance of success was to enable the Borderers to carry out their role as a military unit on landing without the additional responsibility of looking after the boats... Further, as the subsequent orders for *Cornwallis* were mainly as attendant ship and to look out for boats, I knew no alternative of carrying out the spirit of Rear-Admiral Wemyss' orders, viz. to support the Borderers till landed, than by anchoring and rendering naval support till the position of the Borderers was made good which, I had been informed by General Hunter-Weston, was an extremely important one.
>
> The subsequent apparent slowness of *Cornwallis* to return to her position as attendant ship was due to the fact that I felt bound in humanity to bring off wounded men from the beach who were in an exposed position. Further, I could not turn the ship round and come up to [the] anchorage without [interrupting the] fire of ships and fouling transports who were then coming up to their appointed stations.[60]

By Davidson's own reckoning it was not until well after 1000, by which time the 'Asiatic batteries had been temporarily silenced'[61] and the Borderers were in a commanding position with only 'desultory firing and sniping going on',[62] that he felt compelled to respond to the 'repeated recalls ... for the ship to go to her station off V Beach'.[63] Even then, his 'imperative duty'[64] to withdraw his small naval party and evacuate the wounded entailed further 'unavoidable delay'[65] so that it was only shortly before midday that *Cornwallis* eventually reached V Beach. She immediately began, in Davidson's words, to 'plaster the … slopes between Sedd-el-Bahr and Helles Light House',

> without however making any tangible result, though at the time of arrival all landing appeared to have ceased, and the only troops alive observed were those sheltering on the beach behind a sand ridge.
>
> The firing appeared to be concentrated on *River Clyde*, which however gradually slackened … *Cornwallis* kept up intermittent fire on [the] slopes of Sedd-el-Bahr, and on [the] Asiatic Batteries till silenced …[66]

Of his unorthodox and unsanctioned role at S Beach, Davidson remained unrepentant, insisting:

> It was a very great relief to the General in command that his right flank was secure, especially in view of the failure of the centre, at V Beach, to make good a landing; and though it will always be a matter of judgment whether the order to support the Borderers was not carried out in too wide a sense, the alternative of a half-hearted support – viz, to let the Borderers run their own show without assistance from the *Cornwallis* in boats and men – would have been, in my opinion, absolutely fatal.[67]

However, neither his actions nor his argument were enough to sway Keyes. Adamant that the delays were, as Davidson himself conceded, 'from the naval point of view … inexcusable',[68] Admiral de Robeck's chief of staff accused Davidson of having 'no sense of proportion'.[69] More than that, he maintained that the consequences were very nearly disastrous for the main landing:

> V Beach was left for some hours with *Albion* only in attendance. But for the arrival of the *Queen Elizabeth* the Military might well have had good reason to complain at the failure of the Navy to carry out the covering and landing operations as arranged …
>
> *Cornwallis'* primary duty immediately after the landing was completed at de Totts was to proceed to V where she was attendant ship charged with the duty of regulating the landing. Admiral Wemyss' signal … in no way qualified this. You will remember several tows went in to suffer severe loss which should have been

diverted or held up – Fleet sweepers full of men hung about waiting for orders – in fact the landing at V Beach was not regulated! The landing of Marines at de Totts was absolutely unauthorised and an improper proceeding having regard to their value in a ship required for naval operations …

Captain Davidson is so gallant and so anxious to do all in his power to assist the operations I feel rather a brute to 'crab' him like this but there is no end to the trouble caused by his foolish and ill-considered acts.[70]

Unwin went further. Though Davidson insisted that 'no artillery support could have adequately secured' the 'landing at V Beach',[71] the captain of the *River Clyde* was adamant that his behaviour was chiefly responsible for the troops' failure to make headway on 25 April. Writing twenty years' later to Captain Hughes Lockyer, who had commanded the *Implacable* to great effect as attendant ship at X Beach, Unwin declared:

V Beach would have been easier for me had Davidson in *Cornwallis* carried out his orders and, after sending in his party, come round to V Beach, right in like you did at X, he could have saved 100's [*sic*] of lives, but he chose to leave his ship and go for a joy ride on the Beach, where 25 Turks were awaiting his Battalion. He ought to have been court-martialled.[72]

Such thoughts belonged to a future reckoning. On the day itself, Unwin had more important things to think about than the misconduct of a single maverick officer. As a frantic morning full of despair and desperate courage faded into an afternoon of frustrated stand-off, V Beach's most industrious combatant turned his attention towards the hundreds of wounded men lying untreated and exposed to enemy fire on the lighters and along the foreshore of what had become the peninsula's bloodiest no-man's-land.

Chapter 18

'Calls for Help from all Around'

Standing alongside Colonels Williams and Doughty-Wylie on *River Clyde*'s bullet-pecked upper bridge, Edward Unwin despaired at his impotency. 'I could think of nothing more to do but wait till dark,' he wrote, 'so I remained … staring at the beach.'[1] Frustrated by the failure of his plan and infuriated by the lack of support and appalling slaughter, his mood grew blacker as he searched in vain for a suitable target on which to vent his anger.

It was hopeless. 'Not a Turk did I ever see,'[2] he wrote. On the one occasion he thought he saw an enemy soldier, he snatched up a rifle, took aim and fired only to see 'an old vulture'[3] flap its wings and fly out of a tree. Much of his time was spent trying to prevent Doughty-Wylie from suffering the same fate as Carington Smith. But his words fell on deaf ears. Nothing he said would keep him from 'unnecessarily exposing himself over the iron screen',[4] so in the end he simply 'gave it up'.[5]

By then the landing had stuttered to a standstill and for as far as he could see was a scene of devastation:

> The beach was strewn with dead. It was a sight we had before us. I saw a party of 6 men leave the beach and clamber over the ridge evidently with the intention of trying to cut the wire. They got 10 yards, 5 fell down shot instantly and one ran back and jumped over the heads of the men lying under the ridge. One of those shot turned imploringly round towards us and rolled about but eventually was still … I felt a brute in not going to his assistance.[6]

How long he remained an uncomfortable spectator is not clear. According to Wedgwood, it was around 1100 when he next glimpsed him from his machine gun position. He was in the water on the

191

starboard side of the collier, single-handedly, so far as he could tell, trying to manoeuvre a lifeboat towards the heaps of wounded sheltering on and around the ragged spit of rocks.

As bullets skipped across the water, it appeared to those looking on in awed disbelief another hopelessly brave enterprise that was almost certain to end badly. But Unwin, who put the time at nearer 1400, was not to be deflected. Only hours after being carried on board the *River Clyde* in what Surgeon Kelly had feared was 'a dying state',[7] he was pushing his body to the limit yet again. Only this time his mission was not to rescue his landing plan but to save lives. In his own account, Unwin stated:

> As the moanings [*sic*] of the wounded lying on the reef under our starboard bow were more than I could stand I got a boat under the starboard quarter as far from the enemy as I could get and, taking a spare coil of rope with me, I got some hands to pay out a rope fast to the stern of the pinnace I was in, and paddled and punted her into the beach, eventually grounding alongside the wounded. They were all soaking wet and very heavy but I cut off their accoutrements with their bayonets or knives and carried two or three into the pinnace. But as her side was rather high out of the water I'm afraid they were not too gingerly put on board, but still they were very grateful. I could not pick up any more so I got on my hands and knees and they got on to my back and I crawled along to the pinnace ...[8]

To the astonishment of those sheltering along the foreshore and those watching from the *River Clyde*, Unwin repeated his feat at least three more times during, which his dogged determination was matched only by his near-miraculous survival. Captain Richard Neave, who had been lying out on the same lighter as Brigadier Napier and Major Costeker, had already seen the *Clyde*'s captain dash past him on his way to one of the boats between the ship and the shore. Now, having managed to get aboard the collier, the 88th Brigade staff officer saw him 'standing in the water with a wounded man on his shoulders, lifting him out of the water, into a boat'.[9] Another officer watched transfixed as he repeated the feat at least half a dozen times before pushing the boat 'back under cover of the starboard side'.[10]

Crouching beneath the sandy ledge on V Beach, Guy Geddes had a perfect view of it all. 'Though wounded and under fire,' he wrote, Unwin, in his white shirt and flannels, could be clearly seen 'picking up wounded men, putting them in a boat and bringing them back to the *River Clyde*.[11] It is not known precisely how many trips Unwin made. Geddes personally saw him going out three or four times and, according to Captain Angus Sinclair Thomson, brigade major of the 86th Brigade, each journey was completed in the full knowledge that 'it was almost certain death to cross the area between the *River Clyde* and the Beach'.[12] Wedgwood fairly marvelled at his charmed existence. 'I looked at the Commander on the spit of rock trying to lift in the wounded,' he wrote, 'and every splash by his side meant a bullet.'[13]

Having completed four trips back and forth, Unwin was crawling along the rocks with another wounded soldier on his back when he was suddenly aware of the presence of someone else alongside him. Wearing only a pair of trousers, John Hepburn Russell had swum out from the *River Clyde* to lend a hand.

A petty officer in Wedgwood's armoured car detachment, Russell was a twenty-six-year-old banker's son from Glasgow who had abandoned his university studies to enlist. Having seen Unwin struggling to help the wounded, he left his machine gun post and, in the words of his commanding officer, 'dived in, without leave'.[14] Splashing out for the spit, he scrambled up on to the rocks to reach Unwin. Together, they managed to lower one man into the pinnace before Russell collapsed with a bullet in the stomach. Tearing off his own shirt, Unwin used it as a bandage to staunch the flow of blood. Then, with the wound roughly bound and with bullets splashing around them, they 'lay in the water as though dead for a while'.[15] Eventually, during a brief lull in the shooting, Unwin helped Russell into the boat with the other wounded.

By then, exhaustion was setting in. 'I was again beginning to feel a bit dicky,'[16] wrote Unwin. With what little strength he had left, he clambered into the pinnace and then shouted to some men on the *River Clyde* to haul them across by the rope he had prudently attached. On the way over, Unwin noticed somebody wading out to join him. He 'wanted to know why I was going back,'[17] recalled Unwin. Momentarily taken aback, he replied with equal candour. 'Because I could do no more,' he said, 'and I really couldn't.'[18] Not until much later did Unwin discover the identity of the man in the water. It was all he could do to climb back aboard the *River Clyde*. Mentally drained and physically exhausted, Unwin had finally reached the limits of even his extraordinary endurance. In truth, it was a marvel he had lasted so long. As he headed for his cabin and a few hours of precious sleep, the rescue effort he had so heroically initiated was left to others to carry on, most notably by the young officer he had passed going the other way.

'Pog' Tisdall had been an awed witness of Unwin's solo act of mercy. According to Able Seaman Arthur Illingworth, Tisdall had gone up on deck after learning that the disembarkation of troops was being discontinued owing to the heavy casualties. While there, he had seen Unwin ferrying injured men to the starboard sally-port that led into No 4 Hold where his platoon of Ansons were sheltering. It was a remarkable achievement, but for all his efforts 'the wounded', wrote Wedgwood, 'were still crying and drowning on that awful spit'.[19] At some point, Tisdall, like John Russell before him, felt moved to help. Turning to Wedgwood, he said: 'I can't stand it; I'm going over' and 'dived off the gangway into the sea'.[20]

Moments later, Tisdall encountered Unwin returning to the *River Clyde*, his own mission of mercy nearly at an end. Not put off by Unwin's inability to continue, he made his way back to the collier in search of other assistance. He followed the line established by Unwin to No 4 Hold, where his platoon was oblivious of what he had been doing. Able Seaman Illingworth recalled:

> He had been away a short time and when he came back his clothes were wet as if he had been in the water. He called for Leading Seaman Malia to come and help him to bring back some wounded …[21]

James Malia remembered it slightly differently. A pre-war miner from Rotherham in south Yorkshire, Malia was married with four children. Along with many of his friends, he had answered Kitchener's call for volunteers in September 1914. However, having served barely a week in his local unit, the York & Lancaster Regiment, he found himself transferred to the Royal Naval Volunteer Reserve and the newly formed Anson Battalion. Malia claimed he had volunteered rather than been ordered to go, having responded to his officer's request for help made to Petty Officer Perring. Either way, he quickly followed his platoon officer into the water, pushing and pulling a boat towards the spit. He later wrote:

> Men were moaning on every side and calling for me to fetch them in. After fetching in two or three boats full of wounded the officer gave the shout for more assistance. While going out for another boat of wounded, the oar was broken between my hands with a bullet and [I] had to jump into the water for shelter from the exceedingly heavy fire to which I was exposed.[22]

Malia was 'completely exhausted'.[23] With difficulty, he made it safely back to *River Clyde*, where his place was taken by two more men from No 13

Platoon, Leading Seaman Fred Curtiss and Able Seaman James Parkinson, with assistance from Petty Officer Perring. As they left the sally-port, Able Seaman Illingworth headed up on deck to watch their progress. There was a call for blankets to cover the wounded, and then he saw Tisdall, Curtiss and Parkinson heading back towards the starboard side of the *River Clyde* in a 'cutter' filled with wounded. He wrote:

> Their clothes were wet as if they had been in the water and Able Seaman Parkinson had a bullet through his cap comforter. I saw them make three trips to and from the shore in the cutter and pick up wounded men on the beach and bring them back to the *River Clyde*.[24]

Jim Parkinson's escape was remarkable. So, too, was his bravery. A stonemason by trade, he was a much-travelled Lancastrian who had lied about his age when he volunteered the previous September in Sheffield. After two days with the Northumberland Fusiliers, he, too, enlisted in the RNVR, giving his age as thirty-four. In reality, the man remembered by his family as 'a loveable rogue'[25] was actually forty-four when he shipped aboard the *River Clyde*. Parkinson had spent the previous night and most of the morning with his pals in the lower No 4 Hold, surviving unharmed the shell that burst in the hold above them. He had seen nothing of his officer's first foray with Malia. 'The first I knew of this was when they arrived back to the *River Clyde* with a few wounded,' he later recounted. 'I helped to unload this boat and then went into the boat along with LS Curtis [*sic*], Sub Lt Tisdall and a RNAS man.'[26]

The addition to the party was another of Wedgwood's machine gun detachment, Petty Officer Mechanic Geoffrey Rumming. Wedgwood recalled:

> One of my men came to me: 'May I go over and help get in those wounded?' 'Why?' I said, and I remembered the story of Stephen Crane's of the man who went across the shell-swept field to get a drink because he was 'dared to' by his companions. 'I can't stand hearing them crying.'[27]

From Purton in Wiltshire, Rumming was twenty-six and unmarried. A spare driver and Maxim gun hand in Francis McLaren's armoured car, he had volunteered at the outbreak of war, abandoning his job as a mill worker at Holbeach in Lincolnshire. When he joined Tisdall's party, he had no idea who any of them were, other than that one of them was 'a black bearded 1st class Petty Officer and the other a seaman with no badges or stripes on his sleeves'.[28] Together, he said, they made two runs ashore, collecting seven or eight wounded men and variously walking and swimming the boat back. He later recalled:

> Beyond getting a few bullet holes in the boat above the waterline, the first trip was quite successful. On the 2nd trip Sub-Lieut Tisdall and myself clambered over a spit of rock, to get the men lying higher up. We both got shot at and lay down for a time. As we were lifting the last wounded man into the boat he got hit again in the back. We had taken the boat a little further ashore, and when we went to push off again, we found her grounded. When we did eventually succeed in getting her off, Lt Tisdall and myself were unable to climb into the boat and so we hung on to the side and the two men, keeping as low as possible, rowed us back to the *River Clyde*. Unfortunately on the way back Lt Tisdall got some wooden splinters off the boat driven into his wrist by a bullet, and the black bearded PO got hit just between the fingers.[29]

The return journey on that second trip was a precarious one. Parkinson wrote:

> By this time the boat was leaking very badly and one of the last three [wounded] was drowned in the boat bottom. We were then called back by one of the Ship's Officers who stated that it was sheer madness to go on, and if we did not return on board and under cover, anything we did would not be recognised. And if we did carry on we would probably be dead men because the Turks had by now got a machine gun trained on us. We had no other alternative than to obey orders ...[30]

According to one account, the tow-line was severed by enemy fire and the last part of the journey was completed only after Rumming took hold of the rope and manually 'manoeuvred'[31] the boat with its wounded back to the ship. Among the many who watched its painful progress was Wedgwood, who was struck by one incident in particular. As the boat was dragged nearer, he saw 'one of the wounded stretch out his hand and stroke Rumming's as he hung on to the side'.[32] It was, he told Churchill, 'the most pathetic thing I have ever seen'.[33] By the time, they reached the side of the *River Clyde*, the bullet-ruptured boat, swilling with blood-stained water, was barely afloat. All but worn out, they had just enough strength to haul themselves out of the water. 'We were able to grasp the holes in the side of the *River Clyde*,' wrote Parkinson, 'and pull ourselves inboard.'[34]

The rescue operation mounted from the 'Wooden Horse' was over. Quite how many lives had been saved, first by Unwin and Russell and then Tisdall and his party, is unclear. No one was keeping an accurate tally, though it probably amounted to around twenty men. A subsequent report credited Tisdall with making four or five trips to and fro the shore, with Curtiss, Malia, Parkinson, Perring and Rumming variously accompanying him on two or three occasions. Theirs had been a truly heroic endeavour carried out at great personal risk. But perilous though their work had been, they may have owed their survival to Turkish charity as much as good fortune.

According to Wedgwood:

> The Turks could easily have killed all those who went to the wounded. They did not fire on them sometimes for ten minutes and then a burst of fire would come. Then and afterwards I found them extraordinarily merciful as compared with Germans in Flanders …[35]

One of the Hampshires aboard the *River Clyde* agreed. Referring to Unwin's selfless efforts, he observed:

> Though at first under considerable fire, his task was later only interrupted seriously by the enemy when they saw that men were trying to get ashore.[36]

None of this in any way belittles their actions. When they embarked on their self-ordained rescue mission there was no way of knowing how the Turks would react. That they did come under fire, whether it was intentionally directed at them or not, is incontrovertible, as testified by the injuries to Russell, Tisdall and Perring. What is certain is that they had risked their lives to save others – and, brave though they were, they were not alone. Some of those feats of life-saving went unnoticed and recognised but one outstanding case proved impossible to ignore. 'Geordie' Samson's serial heroism were destined to become a part of the legend of V Beach and the 'Wooden Horse' of Gallipoli.

We last encountered the Scot on the scuppered hopper *Argyle*, carrying the wounded Maurice Lloyd to safety amid a torrent of fire. By then, he had already ventured ashore at least once to help Drewry and Unwin with the lighters before carrying a wounded Irish soldier back to the *Argyle*. As he scrambled back on board, the Turks began another furious fusillade. He later recalled:

197

I lay flat on the deck of the hopper. This time I began to think that any moment would be my last. Indeed, it became so hot that I finally decided to make a bold bid for safety. I began to roll over towards the side of the little vessel. There was no rail, and that fact was very much in my favour, for I was able to keep low down all the time. Bullets were flying about the deck; once again I seemed to bear a charmed life … 'Keep down, Samson, or you'll be getting a souvenir.' I could not help smiling when I heard these words. From whom they came I do not know to this very day. They came from the hatchway of the hopper. I suppose they were the words of some optimistic friend of mine. Anyway, I took my unknown friend's advice, and when I reached the side of the hopper I gave myself a big lurch, and fell into the sea.

My ultimate object was to get back to the *River Clyde*. For some time, I had not seen my officers, and I thought that from all points of view it would be better to get back to the ship, as there might be fresh developments … The sea, when I took my plunge, was extremely choppy, but thanks to my youthful days at Carnoustie I was a good swimmer, and I did not find the slightest difficulty in getting back to the ship …[37]

He did not remain there long. Late morning found him back on the hopper in the midst of a scene of pure carnage. 'It was not fighting,' he later said, 'it was murder.'[38] With 'calls for help from all around',[39] he, like Unwin, Tisdall and the small band of volunteers from the *River Clyde*, joined the rescue effort. By his own reckoning, he variously swam, waded and scrambled ashore thirty times, often under fire, during the course of which he managed to bring away fifteen wounded men. Some of these were brought off in a boat, others were carried in his arms or on his back. Either way, they were found shelter on the *Argyle*, some of them on deck, but most of them below where, in the cramped confines of an engine room turned makeshift hospital, Midshipman Weblin took charge. Not surprisingly, given the paucity of medical supplies, the treatment administered by the young 'snotty' was rudimentary:

Men were brought down every few minutes until we had about a dozen, 2 [of them] very bad cases. There was no one there who knew anything worth calling first aid and so I busied myself with field dressings and iodine. I put iodine into all the wounds and then a pad and bandage and in some cases an improvised tourniquet. My brandy flask also came in very useful and we collected what water

bottles we could find and got some tea from the Greeks and made a
bowl of hot tea, which seemed welcome though scarce.[40]

With the Turks firmly in control of the beach and the landing at a
standstill, there was nothing more Weblin or Samson could do but sit
and wait. 'We tried in vain to get medical assistance from the *Clyde*,'[41]
noted Weblin. The reluctance to help was, in the circumstances,
understandable. Although, observed Weblin, 'things were fairly quiet',[42]
the risk of provoking another burst of Turkish fire was enough to induce
paralysis among those still alive on the *Argyle* and the nearby clutter of
lighters. 'Anyone who moved,' wrote Weblin, 'was at once noticed and
picked off.'[43] Risk of death or injury aside, there was another simple
reason for the lack of assistance reaching the hopper: the medics on
board the *River Clyde* were already stretched to the limit trying to cope
with their own flood of wounded.

Even before Unwin had launched his own rescue effort, the injured
had begun to drift back towards the collier where the ship's surgeon,
Peter Kelly, was working miracles in spite of having been wounded
himself early on. According to Unwin, he simply 'bound himself up'[44]
and went straight back to work treating the wounded. Using the ship's
saloon as a surgery, Kelly, who 'could only just get about in great pain',[45]
performed countless operations in the most adverse of circumstances.
A report would later credit him with personally attending to 750
casualties on the *Clyde* between 25 April and 27 even though he was
unable to walk for the last twenty-four hours. 'He was simply
splendid,'[46] wrote Unwin.

No less magnificent, according to the commanding officer of 89th
Field Ambulance, was the contribution made by the two officers, three
non-commissioned officers and 108 bearers from the Scottish territorial
unit who formed part of the *River Clyde* landing force. Intended to
follow the infantry ashore, they found themselves instead dealing with
an incoming tide of injured men in the ship's holds. George Davidson,
who was in charge of the bearers of B Section, wrote of bullet-riddled
boats drifting back to 'our starboard hole'[47] and of the wounded being
lifted up and attended to:

Repeatedly the whole of our floor was covered with wounded and
dead men; a pinnace would arrive from a ship and relieve us of our
wounded, but we filled up again almost at once.[48]

In a brief report contained in the unit war diary, Davidson described
'stretcher cases being laid out in rows along the sides'.[49] There they

remained until they could be evacuated to hospital ships via small boats that puttered their way in 'as frequently as occasion offered'.[50] For many it was a miserable wait spent in terrible agony. Beyond cleaning and binding their wounds, there was little the medics could do to ease the suffering. Their only comforts were brews of beef tea and a supply of blankets collected from 'Pog' Tisdall's Anson beach party.

And as the day wore on the number of wounded continued to grow as more men took advantage of the impasse to creep back to the relative safety of the *River Clyde*. By mid-afternoon, according to Lieutenant Colonel Tizard, many of the wounded recovered from the lighters and the spit of rocks were spread throughout the ship. Parts of every hold were given over as dressing stations, and the Munsters' Roman Catholic chaplain, Father Thomas Harker, who had helped in the rescue work, went between them, comforting the living and helping dispose of the dead.

The stalemate appeared absolute. 'Till about 4pm,' wrote Tizard, 'things were practically at a standstill except for the fire from the Maxim guns and the supporting ships.'[51] However, the man in charge of the troops holed up on the 'Wooden Horse' had not yet given up hope entirely of a resumption of efforts to secure V Beach. Now, after hours of relentless bombardment, Tizard felt the moment had come to put Turkish resolve to the test once more.

Chapter 19

'A Good Deal of Wire'

Henry Tizard was a man labouring under the most intense pressure. In an unexceptional career spanning a quarter of a century of largely undistinguished service he had commanded nothing bigger in action than a double company of troops. That was seven years earlier on the North West Frontier of India where his opponents were lightly armed tribesmen engaged in what amounted to guerrilla warfare. Now in the space of a few hours, he had gone from leading a battalion into battle for the first time to taking charge of a badly mauled brigade in the midst of one of the most daunting military operations of the war faced by an enemy that was well-armed, well-disciplined and thoroughly well led.

A more challenging initiation to senior combat command is hard to imagine. In what must have seemed like the blink of an eye, all the plans he had helped prepare had been shot to pieces, his splendid unit decimated and the 'Wooden Horse' reduced from innovatory invasion springboard to iron-clad sanctuary and makeshift hospital. With the landings at V Beach spiralling out of control amid so much carnage and confusion, the *River Clyde*'s newly elevated military commander was effectively caught between a rock and a hard place; torn between the need to secure the beach as rapidly as possible in pursuance of the expeditionary force's strategic objective and a duty to those under his command to spare them further useless slaughter.

To the fuming frustration of Hunter-Weston, impatient, implacable and out of touch on the *Euryalus*, Tizard had erred too much on the side of caution. His first reaction to the costly attempts to storm ashore had been to urge Carington Smith to desist until nightfall. However, having assumed command, he changed his mind. Perhaps out of a desire to appease his superiors or those more forceful colleagues alongside him on the *River Clyde*, he decided to try and push more men ashore. Though

201

even then, he was reluctant to repeat past mistakes. Rather than sticking bull-headedly to the original failed plan of company-scale rushes along the exposed gangways, he sought to trickle men on to the beach whenever an opportunity presented itself. It was a pragmatic response to the crisis confronting him, but hardly one that was guaranteed to endear him to Hunter-Weston any more than his behaviour did to inspire confidence among his fellow officers.

Some of his subordinates had misgivings about his ability as a commanding officer even before the landing. Though none said so publicly, they feared he was not up to the task and would soon be found wanting. They found him erratic and excitable, weaknesses of character that were most cruelly exposed by the disaster that threatened to overwhelm him at V Beach.[1] And they were not alone in their concerns. While in broad agreement with his 'wait and see' approach to the landing, Edward Unwin was scathing in his assessment of Tizard's performance as military commander following the death of Carington Smith. In a withering commentary, he later informed Admiral Wemyss:

> I soon saw he was not the man for the awful position he found himself in. It does not inspire men who don't know what is going to happen to see a little man running about with a *papier maché* megaphone in his hands all day doing nothing ...[2]

Frank though it was, Unwin's verdict was hardly fair. While clearly not a leader cast in his own larger-than-life mould nor an officer possessed of the galvanic powers of a 'Dick' Doughty-Wylie or a Weir de Lancey Williams, Tizard was 'essentially a sensible man'[3] who recognised that his 'real responsibility'[4] was to try to bring some semblance of order to the chaos that they found themselves in. Whatever his style of command, he was certainly not 'doing nothing'. In balancing the strategic imperative with preserving as many of his men from certain annihilation, his overriding concern was to find some way of breaking the deadlock that had paralysed the landing across the length and breadth of V Beach.

From early on, he was convinced that their best hope lay not with his shaken troops scattered beneath the sandbank near the water's edge, nor the men sheltering inside the 'Wooden Horse', but rather with the units of the 86th and 88th Brigades, which were advancing from the by now secured W Beach. The first glimpse of British troops moving along the high ground in the direction of Cape Helles served only to reinforce that belief. As he later reported:

During the afternoon I saw men on the cliffs to the left of the bay. These were some of the Worcester Regt who had landed at W Beach [part of Napier's force that had been diverted from V Beach]. I had sent a message early in the day to the 29th Divn asking if an attack could be pushed up from W Beach towards my left, because I saw if this could be done the enemy's trenches on that side could be taken in reverse, and this would enable me to push my attack up by the left of the village on to the hill [141].[5]

Even as he was looking on, much the same plan was taking shape in the minds of others whose attention was increasingly drawn towards the developing situation between W and V Beaches.

Among those anxiously watching the scrambling advance were Hunter-Weston and his staff aboard *Euryalus*. After a morning of high drama, the impression that was gradually emerging from a myriad of messages and reports reaching 29th Division's floating headquarters was largely positive.

All of the landings at S, W, X and Y Beaches had apparently been successfully accomplished with junctures made between X and W where reinforcements were already going ashore. The only blemish on an otherwise encouraging outlook was at V Beach from where the news continued grim. Reports spoke of 'staggering'[6] casualties, of senior officers being killed and of formidable Turkish resistance turning the landing 'bridge' between the *River Clyde* and the shore into 'an absolute causeway of death'.[7] Entries in the 29th Division war diary paint a bleak picture. One, timed at 12.30, read: 'Troops landed … cannot get forward … connection between Collier and beach is very bad and casualties heavy if men try to get ashore.'[8] Another, half an hour later, stated: 'Troops at V still held up by barbed wire in front of beach and fire from trenches all round from Seddel Bahr [*sic*] by Old Fort to Hill 138.'[9]

Not even a crushing bombardment from *Queen Elizabeth*'s heavy guns seemed to make the slightest difference. As the shoreline disappeared beneath another pall of dust, 29th Division staff officer Clement Milward observed:

It seemed a wonder that the village and Fort remained standing, but still the old Turk stuck it out. The village was burning merrily, but still no progress could be made by us and things seemed thoroughly unsatisfactory there.[10]

To the litany of bad tidings came even gloomier news delivered first-hand by one of the heroes of the failed landing operation. Having done all he could to establish a makeshift 'bridge' between the *River Clyde* and the shore, Tony Morse had volunteered to brave the enemy fire again, plying messages and wounded back to the command ships and then returning with ammunition for Wedgwood's machine guns. Keyes, for one, was 'much struck'[11] by Morse's 'bearing' when he came aboard *Queen Elizabeth* around noon. However, the story he related was a wretched one, 'of the desperate nature of the fighting round the *River Clyde* and the severity of the losses'.[12]

When he left, the 'inferno'[13] engulfing the collier was such that Keyes 'never expected to see him again'.[14] But Morse continued to confound expectations and to defy the death-dealing fire. Shortly after 0230 he chugged alongside *Euryalus* with a message for Hunter-Weston. Once again, 'his tale was not inspiriting'.[15] Till then, the commander of 29th Division was either in ignorance or denial about the true situation at V Beach. Seemingly blind to the impossibility of 'any further movement'[16] on that exposed shore, he 'continued to urge the capture of the western defences of the beach, in order to assist the troops from W Beach in their advance on Hill 138'.[17] However, the message that Morse so gallantly delivered finally removed any lingering doubts about the plight of the men marooned on and around the *River Clyde*. It stated:

> Your first two proposals I have already considered, but each attempt to disembark troops has ended in many casualties. Enemy's position round Beach V very strong, and tremendous lot of wire. Every attempt to reconnoitre ground has so far failed. My casualties are very heavy, including General Napier and his brigade-major, both killed. Unless in the meantime the high ground to the NW of me is taken by other troops, I intend to wait till dark and then attack position 141. To carry this out, can you send me a barrel pier, as I am very short of boats and our pontoon pier [bridge of lighters] does not reach the shore. I have a great number of wounded on the beach. I have 900 infantry still on ship. Of the half company Dublins landed at Camber only 25 remain. OC Munsters roughly estimates his casualties at 200. Mark VI ammunition for RNAS machine guns is required.[18]

The news was not well received. As Clement Milward glumly observed:

> So great was the depression that we had great difficulty in dissuading General Hunter-Weston from going himself to V Beach to lead the men to the attack.[19]

It was with some relief, tinged with more than a little apprehension, that 29th Division's staff switched their focus to the western flank. In his diary, Milward stated:

> We pointed out [to Hunter-Weston] that with the large number of troops now landed at W Beach we could afford almost to ignore Seddul Bahr by attacking their position there from the West and taking them in flank. From the first, landing parties of the Lancashire Fusiliers had worked their way to the right under the cliffs and had established a signalling station at Helles Lighthouse. Half a Company from there had advanced as far as the barbed wire of Hill 138 and had been seen lying there ever since, unable to go forward or come back …[20]

However, now those same troops were being reinforced by men from Napier's brigade who had been diverted, mid-landing, from V Beach to the relative safety of W Beach.

Like Hunter-Weston aboard *Euryalus* and Tizard in the *River Clyde*, Sir Ian Hamilton was 'cheered'[21] by the sight of 'our brave fellows'[22] pushing steadily eastwards. Watching them advance 'by rushes'[23] towards Sedd-el-Bahr, he 'prayed God very fervently they might be able to press on so as to strike the right rear of the enemy troops encircling V Beach'.[24]

His appeal to a higher power was an indication of the deepening crisis at Cape Helles. The Turkish defenders had not merely inflicted heavy casualties on the Covering Force, they had thoroughly dislocated the southern landing operation and, with it, the planned push inland. With the main assault in disarray, the fate of the whole expedition appeared to rest with the forces approaching from the western flank. Viewed from the bridge of the *Queen Elizabeth*, they seemed tantalisingly close to effecting a junction with the huddle of Dublins and Munsters scattered across the length of V Beach. But what appeared a short hop viewed from almost a mile away was rendered infinitely more difficult by the nature of the terrain as well as the resistance.

According to the maps issued prior to the landing, the high ground above Cape Helles rose to a single peak due north of the Helles lighthouse. Officially styled Hill 138 and later rechristened Hunter-Weston Hill, it was shown as being topped by a wire-screened redoubt that was thought to be the only serious obstacle separating the key landing beaches at W and V. But the maps were wrong. 'In reality,' observed the campaign's official historian, 'there was a second and somewhat higher crest 400 yards to the south-east of Hill 138.'[25] Worse than that, Guezji Baba, as it was known to the Turks, was crowned by another redoubt even larger than the position on Hill 138 that the troops advancing from Cape Tekke had regarded as their final objective.

Indeed, such was the surprise experienced by the first men to approach the 'unmarked' Turkish redoubt that they mistook it for Hill 141. Others, struggling to make sense of a landscape that bore no resemblance to the positions marked on their maps, imagined it to be the true Hill 138. The result was more muddle as conflicting reports confused one hill for another.

The earliest encounter with the Turks sited on Guezji Baba had actually taken place before 0900. A small number of Lancashire Fusiliers, bravely led by two staff officers, had skirted the first redoubt on their way to establishing a signal station by the Helles lighthouse. From there, they had an unrestricted view across the bay and could clearly see that the *River Clyde* 'was in difficulties'.[26] Gamely, they tried to push on, but their advance was soon halted by 'a maze of barbed wire'.[27] It barred their way along the top of the cliff and encircled an entrenched position on the ridge above them. One of the officers, Captain Mynors Farmar, staff captain of 86th Brigade, took cover in a slight dip while the other, Brigade Major Thomas Frankland, searched in vain for a way round. 'Fortunately, there was almost dead ground against the wire ... and in this most of the party lay,'[28] wrote Farmar. An attempt to cut the wire was met by 'an impossible fire to live in'.[29]

A dozen men led by a subaltern scrambled 50 yards further along the ridge that ran towards Sedd-el-Bahr before being stopped. Together with their comrades in the other party they remained pinned down throughout the morning and into the afternoon.

The only exception was Mynors Farmar. Being a little behind the leading group, he was able to creep away from the wire and made his way back to the lighthouse. From there, he was slipped over the edge of the cliff and climbed down to a position from where he could see the *River Clyde* wedged ashore beneath the walls of the Old Castle. 'There appeared to be a line of men holding a ridge across the beach, but who made no progress,' he wrote. It was a while before he realised that 'they were [all] dead', having been 'cut down by machine gun fire as they made a rush'.[30] Quitting his precarious vantage point, he scrambled on. He later wrote:

> By gingerly picking a way it was possible to reach a point above some men who had landed from the ex-collier and to shout to them. They could get no further, and the cliff was unclimbable.[31]

Farmar's hollered conversation with the troops below was as near as anyone came that day to effecting a link-up between W and V Beaches. However, communication of a kind was established between the *River Clyde* and the troops advancing from W Beach, with messages being flashed to the signal station near the lighthouse by engineers manning a heliograph on the collier. They confirmed what Farmar had seen with his own eyes: 'V Beach was impossible to live on, and almost impossible to land upon'.[32] His bleak report sent to *Euryalus* shortly after midday was the first indication of the scale of the bloody impasse at V Beach. It read:

> Two hundred men have landed on V Beach. These cannot get forward. Connection between *River Clyde* and shore is very bad and casualties occur as soon as men move from the ship … Landing is easy near lighthouse and cliff accessible. If redoubts 1 and 2 are taken it would facilitate capture of village.[33]

It reached 29th Division HQ at 1230. An hour or two earlier and it might have changed the course of the battle for V Beach. Instead of being diverted to W Beach, the Worcesters and half the Hampshires, originally bound for Sedd-el-Bahr, could have landed beneath the Helles lighthouse. Had they done so 'the situation at V must almost certainly have been relieved early in the afternoon'.[34] Or so, at least, the official historian surmised. As it was, a goodly portion of the 4th Worcestershires were already ashore by the time Farmar's report reached Hunter-Weston on *Euryalus*. Even then, the extent of the impasse at Sedd-el-Bahr was not fully appreciated. Colonel Owen Wolley-Dod, Hunter-Weston's chief staff officer who had landed at W Beach around 1230 to take charge from the wounded Hare, was far from clear about the difficulties facing the men stuck on V Beach.[35] However, he did at least realise, thanks to Farmar's report, that the Turks on Hill 138 and its previously undetected neighbour were still resisting and would have to be turned out before there was any hope of linking up with the troops at V Beach.

A hastily improvised plan of attack, making the most of the presence of Lieutenant Colonel Cayley's newly arrived 4th Worcestershires, was promptly set in motion.

It was this assault that had so excited Hamilton, Hunter-Weston and Tizard, raising expectations of a renewed advance into Sedd-el-Bahr. The attack was preceded by a twenty-minute naval bombardment notable for its accuracy and the unusual part played by one of the ship's captains – Cecil Maxwell-Lefroy of the *Swiftsure*. With the mixed force of Worcesters, Essex and Lancashire Fusiliers poised to storm the first redoubt, one of the ship's officers observed:

> It was a matter of considerable delicacy to fire over their heads at the trenches above them, and the difficulty was increased by the lack of knowledge of the position of our troops landed at S and V Beaches; it was thought that any 'overs' would fall into our own troops. In spite of these difficulties the 7.5-in guns fired with rapidity and regularity and extraordinary accuracy; the Captain himself laid and fired one of the 7.5-in guns at a particularly critical time when our troops were only about 50 yards from the trench under fire ...[36]

Out to sea, Hunter-Weston and his staff looked on as the infantry surged up 'the glacis-like slope'.[37] The tension among the spectators on *Euryalus* was palpable, as Clement Milward's diary entry makes clear:

> Eagerly did we now watch the advance ... and in suspense did we await again a sudden outburst of fire which would mow down these men and send the others reeling back down the hillside. Intent, with every muscle taut, the first man crept up to the Turkish trenches, looked over and jumped in. The wonderful shooting of HMS *Swiftsure*, dropping her 12-inch shells 10 yards [*sic*] over our men's heads, had been too much for the Turkish nerves and they had evacuated these trenches at the western end of the hill ...[38]

In the van of the assault was Captain Alexander Churchill of the Essex. He had been in the thick of the action since landing and had spent most of the morning dodging bullets on the slopes of Hill 138. He and his men were still hugging the ground when the 'tremendous'[39] bombardment crashed down on the enemy position just ahead of them. In a letter home, he wrote:

> As soon as they had apparently finished shelling it, we started off in about three lines ... and the whole of the line on our right pushed on too and we went up the hill without any resistance. Part of the battalion under the Colonel [Owen Godfrey-Faussett] went across behind us to the right and cut the barbed wire of the redoubt while I covered them ... I potted a Turk at 500 yds which rose [*sic*] my spirits somewhat and, as only his head and shoulders were showing, it was not bad work – was it?[40]

The Worcesters, with Y and Z Companies leading, found their way blocked by a thick belt of wire missed by the bombardment. With no option but to try to cut paths through it, Captains Archibald Ray and James Nelson led a party of volunteers forward:

> As they clipped away at the wire bullets from the redoubt struck all around them [wrote the Regimental historian]. Undeterred, the wire-cutters crawled under the fence and continued their work. Many turned on their backs and thus cut away at the wire above them. The fire was hot and one after another those brave men were killed or wounded. But lanes were gradually cut through the wire, and at about 2pm [most records, including Turkish accounts, give the time as being nearer 1500] the whole line, Essex and Worcestershire, advanced.[41]

For the heavily outnumbered Turks on Hill 138 the end was fast approaching. For more than six hours without support four sections of men had held off the better part of a battalion. Attempts to reinforce them had been defeated by the Navy's guns, with one detachment wiped out as it tried to run the gauntlet from V Beach. Now, with their shell-battered position almost surrounded, the survivors had no option but to withdraw or stand and die. Holding out as long as they dared, they pulled back at the last moment. Only the dead and a litter of 'broken and twisted rifles'[42] remained when the Worcesters and Essex dropped into the abandoned redoubt.

Hard though the struggle had been for the British, the loss of Hill 138 was a major setback for the Turks. Despite having inflicted heavy losses on the troops landing at W Beach, Major Sabri conceded that 'four times as many'[43] men had come ashore. The situation was now 'critical'.[44] For the first time, the Turkish defences around the shores of Cape Helles were under serious threat. Sabri wrote:

> The enemy began to fire at both our battle lines with machine guns which he had set up on Aytepe [Hill 138]. The officers began to ask what they should do. The answer was given that making use of the ground they should move from the trenches which were being shot at to others and that it was imperative that no-one should retreat a step from where they were.[45]

It was defiance spliced with desperation. With at least three battalions landed at Cape Tekke and more coming ashore, Sabri made no attempt

209

to disguise his concern when he signalled his superiors at 1515. Reporting the fall of Hill 138 and the British occupation 'in strength'[46] of the ridge girdling the western tip of the peninsula, he said enemy machine guns were now able to direct fire 'in every direction'[47] and warned that if help and ammunition were not quickly sent his forces 'would not be in a position to act effectively'.[48]

After so many delays, the British troops were anxious to exploit their success. As the Turks from Hill 138 fled northwards, the Worcesters pushed on to the next slope where their headlong rush ended in front of another belt of wire. Pausing to decide their next move, they came under a 'sharp fire'[49] from the second redoubt 'on another hillock, three hundred yards [sic] beyond'.[50]

This was the position that did not feature on the Worcesters' 'rough'[51] maps. It would prove a costly oversight. The wire around Guezji Baba was every bit as thick as that surrounding Hill 138 and the fire from its redoubt even more fearsome. But this time there would be no waiting for naval gunfire to subdue the defences. In a hurry to get on, the attack was spearheaded yet again by a brave group of wire-cutters led by the redoubtable Captain Ray. Dashing forward, he was barely 40 yards from the Turkish trenches when he was hit and fatally wounded. With his loss, the assault fizzled out.

An attempt was then made to bypass the position by sending the Worcesters' reserve company [X] along the cliffs as far as the lighthouse. From there, they were moved into dead ground, 200 yards west of Guezji Baba, near where some Lancashire Fusiliers had been sheltering most of the day. Just ahead of them, on a low, grass-tufted rise, stood another tall belt of wire. Once more there was no option but to send out wire-cutters. On *Euryalus*, Hunter-Weston's staff 'looked on in suspense'[52] as they crept up the slope. Milward wrote:

> We saw two brave men move forward and stand up on the sky-line cutting wire 'as though they were merely snipping grapes from a vine'.[53]

The wire-cutters were led by a private, Arthur Mountain.

> Crawling through long grass into the entanglement he crept beneath the wire [wrote the Regimental historian]. The watchers in rear saw his arm rise out of the grass and his wire cutters snap at the wire above him. Each time his hand went up, a shower of bullets struck round him and sprayed into the dead ground beyond. Presently he was hit; his hand fell. Other volunteers crawled forward to take his

place. At other points along the wire defences similar gallant efforts were made. At one point, out of a party of seven wire-cutters the last surviving soldier succeeded in severing the last row of wire before he also was hit. Officers and men alike hacked away, lying on their backs, sides or faces, while bullets struck around them.[54]

Bit by torturous bit, the work was carried on until a lane was cut. At that moment, Milward saw the rest of the Worcesters rise 'one by one'[55] and dash through the gap 'as hard as they could'[56] before throwing themselves down 'behind a bank beyond'.[57] Lieutenant Howard Field's platoon paused long enough to fix bayonets before rushing the nearest enemy trench. The defenders did not wait to meet them, bolting before they reached the parapet. Guezji Baba was in British hands and with it all the high ground that lay between the two main beaches at the southern end of the peninsula.

It was around 1600 and from the captured heights the victorious troops were able to see across an expanse of open country freckled with trees that rose in the north-east towards the summit of Achi Baba. Below them, a sharp fight was in progress over on V Beach where shells were throwing up clouds of dust above Hill 141.

Peering out from behind the iron screens shielding the *River Clyde*'s bridge, Henry Tizard had been a more than interested spectator to the struggle above the cliffs on the left. He had seen the Worcesters held up by 'a good deal of wire'[58] and he had kept in touch with their progress as best he could via the signal station established by the lighthouse. Though heavy enemy fire eventually forced his signallers under cover, he received a message from 29th Division HQ a little after 1600 telling him that Hill 138 had been captured. It was followed a little later by another, stating that the Worcesters had also seized Hill 141. He later wrote:

> This I knew was not correct as I could see that hill from the bridge of the vessel. I, therefore, thought it must mean Hill 114 which was on the other side of W Beach.[59]

In fact, as we have seen, the second position to fall was the unmarked redoubt on Guezji Baba that either the Worcesters or the staff officers on *Euryalus* had mistaken for Hill 141. Confusion aside, the news that the British grip on the western flank was secure was enough to spur Tizard on to make a further attempt to get men ashore. With a view to capitalising on the success, he told Lieutenant Nightingale to take the remaining Munsters of Y Company on to V Beach and to instruct Major

Jarrett 'to work one company along the shore to the left and get in touch with the Worcester Regt'.[60]

Having already made two journeys to and from the shore via the body-carpeted bridge of lighters, Nightingale can have been under no illusions about his chances of surviving a third trip. His second run back to the *Clyde* had been with the specific aim of stopping the landing before his company was wiped out. Now he would have to lead out those very same men whose lives he had been instrumental in saving. With or without opposition, it would be a daunting mission: the steam hopper's bow had swung round and 'there was no connection with the shore'.[61] But if he felt that he was tempting fate he gave no hint of it in his matter-of-fact account written to his mother. He merely stated:

> The Col[onel] told me to go down to the barge, collect as many men as I could and join the force on shore. We jumped into the sea and got ashore somehow with a rain of bullets all around us. I joined Jarrett and a lot of men, but very few [that were] not hit.[62]

On his way across the lighters Nightingale came across the body of Brigadier General Napier. 'I turned him over,' he wrote, 'and he was quite dead.'[63] Incredibly, his own luck held yet again, though those who followed him were less fortunate. 'Many of them were hit,'[64] wrote Tizard and the 'heavy fire'[65] that burst from positions all around the beach was enough to convince him that the Turks were too strong to persist. Major Hutchinson's W Company and the Munsters' machine gun detachment, who were waiting to follow Nightingale ashore, were ordered to stand down. Tizard reported the latest failure to 29th Division HQ:

> Still unable to advance. Casualties heavy. Gen Napier and Bde Major killed ... Cannot move until ground NW of line is taken.[66]

If no such action was possible he proposed waiting till dark before attempting an advance on Hill 141. Once again the onus was on the troops pushing out from W Beach to rescue the situation at V Beach.

Since occupying the second redoubt on Guezji Baba, the Worcesters had been busy. While two platoons stood guard against a possible counter-attack, a company toiled to reverse the defences in order to resist any threat coming from the opposite direction. Elsewhere along the ridge men sweated as they laboured to dig fresh trenches under heavy fire from the Turks on Hill 141.

Similarly engaged on Hill 138, the Essex were also attracting a lot of fire from the direction of V Beach. Taking cover in the former Turkish trenches and in sheltered ground just behind the redoubt, Captain Churchill's company lay low until orders reached them to 'help in an attack which was to be made on our right by some other battalion'.[67]

The 'other' battalion was the 4th Worcestershires. But details of the attempt to relieve the pressure on Tizard's beleaguered force are confused. According to entries in the 29th Division General Staff war diary, an 'advance East from [the] Lighthouse'[68] was first suggested to Colonel Wolley-Dod at 1615. At the same time, it was made clear to him 'that troops on Beach V are still unable to move owing to fire from Old Fort on Hill 141 and trenches on West side of beach'.[69] Yet just fifteen minutes later, 29th Division HQ received a puzzling question from Wolley-Dod, asking after the 'situation on V Beach, as he cannot get in touch with the troops there'.[70] More inexplicable delay followed and it was only after a briefing by Mynors Farmar an hour later that Colonels Cayley and Godfrey-Faussett were warned to prepare to resume the advance.

A signal informing 29th Division HQ of the planned attack was sent with a request for a supporting bombardment to help clear the way. Shortly afterwards, the guns of three battleships again began bombarding Sedd-el-Bahr, the old fort and the trenches on Hill 141. As shells rained down, 'the village broke into flames, and the whole amphitheatre was wrapped in a cloud of blinding dust and smoke'.[71] But it was not until 1830 that confirmation for the advance was received from *Euryalus*.

The instructions were 'to push on rapidly to take Hill 141'[72] and to take any further enemy trenches 'in reverse',[73] while leaving sufficient troops to consolidate the positions already gained. 'Action [was] taken'[74] immediately according to the entry in the 86th Brigade war diary with orders being issued for 4th Worcestershires to 'attack'[75] while 1st Essex continued consolidating Hill 138 and covered the advance.

By then it was already too late. Setting out in fading light, the Worcesters had not advanced far when they were stopped by a combination of enemy fire and more uncut wire. A few men from X Company managed to get on, pressing forward along the edge of the cliffs and down the slope that dropped away towards V Beach. They reached an abandoned gun battery with two disabled 9.2in guns inside and there, in the absence of any support, they halted. The sun was sinking fast, taking with it the day's last chance of relief for the men stranded on V Beach and inside the 'Wooden Horse'.

Chapter 20

'Treading on the Dead'

As evening approached on 25 April there was still considerable confusion as to the number and whereabouts of the men landed not to mention what they had actually accomplished.

So far as General Hunter-Weston was aware three companies of the South Wales Borderers were established, albeit isolated, around the De Totts Battery on the eastern flank near Eski Hissarlik. To the west, a bridgehead had been won that stretched from the Cape Helles lighthouse across Hills 138 and 114 as far as a point on the coast some two miles north of Tekke Burnu. Pushing out from W Beach, now the main landing point in the southern sector, the 4th Worcestershires, the remnants of 1st Lancashire Fusiliers, together with the 1st Essex, two companies of the 2nd Hampshires, another couple of companies of the 1/5th Royal Scots, the 2nd Royal Fusiliers and the 1st Border Regiment formed a thin but continuous line with only the 1st Royal Inniskilling Fusiliers in reserve.

As a result of the reports confusing Guezji Baba for Hill 141 Hunter-Weston was also under the false impression that the main Turkish redoubt above V Beach had fallen. At 1900 he communicated as much to Hamilton and further reported that the 'troops on V Beach [had been] ordered to push forward'.[1] His message, noted in the MEF General Staff war diary, ended with the promise: 'Shall advance against Achi Baba tomorrow.'[2]

The reality, of course, was very different. While units of the 29th Division occupied a 600-yard wedge from X Beach to Hill 138 and feverish efforts were being made to turn W Beach into a base camp, there was absolutely no doubt that the Turks were still very much in command of the high ground bordering Sedd-el-Bahr. Not only were the majority of the positions in and around the village still occupied, but the broad belts of wire entanglements, which had defeated the belated attempts to effect a link-up from the west, were still largely intact despite the pulverising power of the Navy's bombardment. It was a further tribute to their courage and discipline that they had thus far defeated a numerically superior enemy invasion force that continued to believe it was confronted by far more men than was actually case.

In fact, after a day of almost non-stop pressure, Major Sabri's scattered force probably amounted to no more than 450 men. But as night came on even their titanic powers of resistance were approaching breaking point. The fall of the redoubts separating W and V Beaches was a tactical disaster. Most damaging of all so far as the defence of Sedd-el-Bahr was concerned was the loss of Guezji Baba, or Ertugrul Fort to the Turks. Until then, the troops manning the key position on the western side of V Beach's amphitheatre had played a prominent role in wrecking each and every attempt to get ashore, whether by boats in the first instance or subsequently from the *River Clyde*. The prolonged resistance of this small force under the leadership of a non-commissioned officer would acquire legendary status in Turkish military annals.

The unlikely hero of the hour was a logistics sergeant called Yahya Cavus. A member of a supply detachment attached to 10 Company, 3/26th Regiment, he was catapulted into effective command of the garrison on Guezji Baba when his officer was hit early in the action. Undaunted, he wrought havoc among the British troops as they tried repeatedly to force their way ashore. Hailing his magnificent effort, Major Sabri wrote:

> Sgt Yahya, by his heroism and resolution, tenacity and devotion to duty with which he imbued those with him, held his position ... until evening against numerous and heavy bombardments, and was responsible for killing hundreds of enemy soldiers. It must have been late afternoon when the enemy at last realised that it was necessary to destroy the trenches of these four sections, who had been firing from the flank of Ertugrul cove, and part of the fleet opened fire on them and flattened out their trenches. The heroic Sgt Yahya with those of his men who were still alive, leapt from those trenches to a different position and continued to open fire to prevent the enemy's landing. However, word reached Sgt Yahya that the enemy forces who had landed at Takeout [W Beach], after taking Aytepe [Hill 138], had encircled Ertugrul Fort ... The heroic sergeant and the remains of the platoon under his command fixed bayonets and advanced on the enemy ...[3]

Miraculously, Yahya survived, fighting his way out to reach the redoubt on Hill 141. On a day in which both sides had displayed near-suicidal bravery his had been one of the most outstanding personal feats of all. For twelve hours and 'in spite of every kind of enemy fire',[4] he had inspired his dwindling force to carry out a duty that Sabri thought might have been expected of a battalion. The hill he had fought so hard to hold was only abandoned at the last gasp when the position was virtually surrounded and nigh untenable.

Its capture came as a relief not just to those men of the Dublins, Munsters and Hampshires who had spent much of the day crouching beneath the sandy bank near the water's edge, but to the scores of injured and uninjured men trapped on the lighters jutting out from the *River Clyde*. One who took advantage of the reduction in fire was Major Carr of the 4th Worcestershires, who had lain motionless on the *Albion*'s launch since the failure of Brigadier General Napier's ill-starred dash for the shore. As the firing 'died down'[5] around 1700, he crept back across the lighters, gathering together survivors along the way and leading them on to the *River Clyde*. Once aboard, he was reunited with Lieutenant Bush and more of his platoon. They were among the luckiest of all the men sent in to V Beach. Having been ordered straight from their boat into the collier they had mostly escaped the slaughter to be employed by Tizard as orderlies. While Carr and his men spent six hours exposed to torrents of fire, they had been spared the enemy's wrath by the protective bulk of the 'Wooden Horse'.

Of course, nowhere on V Beach, not even on the *River Clyde*, was entirely safe. Between 1700 and 1800, the ship was shaken by four direct hits from guns on the Asiatic shore. More shots went wide, but even these fell close enough to spread alarm. Of particular concern to Tizard was the possibility that the Turks might 'bring up guns and bombard the *River Clyde*'[6] from the heights above Sedd-el-Bahr:

> Fearing this development, I asked if the wounded could be got away from the boat as soon as possible and mine sweepers [*sic*] were sent for, for this purpose.[7]

His request for sufficient craft to evacuate 150 wounded 'before dark'[8] reached *Euryalus* via Admiral de Robeck aboard *Queen Elizabeth* at 1730 just as Wemyss was working out which ships were to remain offshore to provide cover for the landing zones during the night. Back on the *River Clyde*, Tizard was busy making plans of his own:

> I ... thought that the best plan to tackle the situation when the light failed would be for one Company R M Fus [Royal Munster Fusiliers]

to work to the left along the shore and get touch with the troops on the left, sending a party up the nulla [*sic*] which ran down to the shore from a road which went from the village across our front, whilst three Companies R M Fus, with details of the R Dublin Fus on the right worked round by the South East corner of the fort up through the village. Giving this attack time to get round and then force a way through the wire in our front with the two Companies of the Hampshires, one Company of the Dublins, the West Riding Company, RE, and a platoon of the Worcesters as a support pushing up by the left of the village, [and with] communication between the centre and the right to be got through the village ...[9]

Given the Turks' apparent strength and tenacity, it would have been a daunting enough proposition for the freshest and most highly motivated of troops. But the men who endured a wretched day dodging death on the beach were neither. Many were wounded and most of those who were not were either too exhausted or too numb with shock to contemplate moving. So far as organisation and unit cohesion were concerned, there was none.

The mixed up parties of Dublins, Munsters and Hampshires had little more on their minds than trying to stay alive. Even the bravest found their spirits flagging. Guy Geddes, who spent much of the day doubled up with pain and stiffness from his shoulder wound, could think of little beyond the fear of gangrene setting in. He estimated 70 per cent of his company and around 60 per cent of those Munsters who had charged off the *River Clyde* were casualties. 'The whole beach was strewn with dead,' wrote Lieutenant Maffett of the Dublins, 'and there were very few hale men amongst us.'[10]

Typical of them was a group about twenty-strong under Captain David French. We last encountered him in the first breathless moments of the landing. Wounded by a bullet that shattered his wristwatch, driving bits of it into his arm, he, like Geddes, spent a painful twelve hours lying on the beach. By the time Tizard was anticipating a renewal of the assault involving those same weary men confidence was low. With 'wounded groaning on all sides, and, surrounded by dead,' wrote French, 'I admit I thought it was all up'.[11] Well aware of the scale of losses already sustained, Tizard could only pray that the arrival of reinforcements from the *River Clyde* would act as a tonic, galvanising them to make another almighty effort.

At 1755, he signalled to headquarters his intention 'to move part of his force to Sedd-el-Bahr village after dark' and to work 'towards point

138 with another portion'.[12] The entry in the General Staff war diary also noted that he 'did not want any guns to fire over or searchlights to be used unless specially asked for'.[13]

With preparations already under way, Tizard was forced to make one alteration. Discovering that the Hampshires already ashore had worked their way towards the right, he decided to employ them as part of the force tasked with pushing on into Sedd-el-Bahr. The final plan was as follows:

> Left centre: Y Company Royal Munster Fusiliers under Major Jarrett to work to the left as before. One Company Hampshire Regiment and one platoon West Riding RE with wire cutters were to get through the wire and push on up by the left getting in touch with the right. Support – One Company Royal Dublin Fusiliers and three platoons West Riding RE.

> Right: W, X and Z Companies Royal Munster Fusiliers, one Company Hampshire Regiment and those of the Dublin Fusiliers who survived the landing from the boats to work round by South East corner of the Fort into the Village, and to get touch with the centre party.[14]

Quite apart from the difficulties of making a night attack across unknown country, with the prospect of street fighting thrown in, the plan represented something of a logistical nightmare. Two forces, one all but shattered and scattered across the length and breadth of the beach and the other yet to be disembarked, would have to be merged, briefed and reorganised on a darkened shore with little room for manoeuvre and all within a few yards of the nearest enemy positions. It was, to put it mildly, an ambitious plan and one over which its instigator would be able to exercise little control once set in motion. As military commander and sole survivor of the three battalion commanders on V Beach, Tizard decided to direct operations as best he could from the bridge of the *River Clyde* while giving Major Beckwith of the Hampshires the job of organising and leading the assault. His only method of communication with the men ashore would be by runner or via a solitary signaller located under the walls of the fort on the right.

With no information as regards casualties among officers ashore, Tizard 'left it', as he rather vaguely put it, 'to the seniors on the spot to carry out the idea'[15] of his plan. In other words, he effectively delegated responsibility for the conduct of the operation to the most senior infantry officers available, Majors Jarrett, assuming that he was still alive, and Beckwith.

Arthur Thackeray Beckwith was no stranger to adversity. Aged thirty-nine, married with a son and daughter, he had experienced one of the British Army's darkest days on the slopes of Spion Kop during the Boer War. In the space of a few hours some 1,500 men had been killed, wounded or taken prisoner. A regimental officer to the core, who had spent more than half of his life in the Army, most of it with the Hampshires, he was brave, resolute and unflappable. He was, in short, uncommonly well-suited to deal with the crisis in hand.

Like much else about those hectic and often chaotic hours at V Beach, the timing of Beckwith's foray ashore is not entirely clear. It was certainly before dusk and, most probably, during the late afternoon, although the orders placing him in charge of operations ashore may not have reached him till early evening. Either way, his first act on assuming command was to try to secure the beach in preparation for a disembarkation under cover of darkness. An earlier attempt by a few Munsters and Hampshires to force an entrance into the fort had melted away, leaving the survivors sheltering on the seaward side of its battered walls. So now he turned to Captain Spencer-Smith, together with the eighteen survivors of his original twenty-six-strong boat party and a mixture of Dublins and Munsters, in the hope that they could succeed where the others had failed. Their objective was a simple one: to capture and hold a gateway that led northwards out of the ruined fortress.

Crouching low, they hugged the sandy cliff for as long as they could before scrambling up and over. Then, having snipped their way through 'many strands of barbed wire',[16] they made a dash for the fort, the few Turks inside 'bolting before them'.[17] Spencer-Smith's party quickly secured a position on the northern face of the fort, where most of the medieval walls had withstood the Navy's bombardment. And there, as instructed, they halted and took stock. 'There was a good deal of firing not far off,'[18] wrote Spencer-Smith. It was not clear whether they were being deliberately targeted, but some of the shooting was uncomfortably close with 'pieces of stone ... being chipped off by bullets'.[19] For the rest of the night, he continued to occupy a fragment of the 'demolished fort',[20] thus enabling the disembarkation from the *River Clyde* to begin without the threat of a counter-attack from the right.

Further back, along the beach, not all was going as smoothly. Somewhere along the sandy cliff in the half light of dusk, Major Jarrett met with fellow Munster Guy Geddes. In charge of the left and central thrusts of Tizard's three-pronged assault, Jarrett had been busy mustering his disparate force. There were 'about 120 [men] in all',[21] comprising Lieutenant Nightingale, two other subalterns, remnants of the Munsters' X, Y and Z Companies and some Hampshires who had moved along the beach 'without molestation'.[22] The two senior officers chatted briefly, Geddes ignoring his painful wound to advise his friend about his next move. 'I suggested ... that the best thing was to establish oneself in the fort and try and get the village of Sedd-el-Bahr.'[23] He pointed out what dispositions he had made with the few men around and gave him all the information he could. Jarrett, who appeared 'as cool and collected as if nothing was happening',[24] then went off to make final preparations. Shortly after, Jarrett made an attempt to gain a foothold inside the fort. It was a brave effort by weary men, but was frustrated by machine gun and rifle fire from Turks holding out in the southern end of the fort. Pulling back, they took cover once again on the seaward face of the battlements. It was the last order Jarrett gave. Nightingale later wrote:

> We took up an outpost line and I had just put out my sentry groups and Jarrett came up to have a look, when he was shot through the throat by my side.[25]

Barely five minutes had gone by since his brief conversation with Geddes. Not long after, Geddes joined a long line of walking wounded awaiting evacuation. Before leaving, he met with de Lancey Williams and Beckwith who had appeared 'out of the dark'[26] at the head of around two companies of Hampshires. Geddes broke the news of Jarrett's death to them and told Williams 'all I knew'[27] about the dispositions on the beach. Geddes was relieved to be leaving and comforted by the thought that 'the situation was now in far better hands than mine'.[28]

By then, the disembarkation from the *River Clyde*, which began around 2000, was already under way. For the troops departing their steel-hulled sanctuary, the journey to shore had more than a touch of the macabre about it. Josiah Wedgwood, who abandoned his machine guns together with Geoffrey Rumming to assist in the operation, wrote of the wounded all around crying out 'for help and shelter':[29]

> For three hours I stood at the end of the rocks up to my waist in water, my legs jammed between dead men, and helped men from the last boat to the rocks. Every man who landed that night jumped on to the backs of dead men ...[30]

To Second Lieutenant Reginald Gillett, leading out No 13 Platoon, Z Company of the 2nd Hampshires, 'the sight that met our eyes was indescribable':

> The barges now linked together and more or less reaching the shore were piled high with mutilated bodies – and between the last barge and the shore was a pier formed by piles of dead men [almost certainly those heaped on the spit of rocks]. It was impossible to reach the shore without treading on the dead ...[31]

But this was not a time for squeamishness. Necessity not sentiment was the order of the day. In charge of one of the Munsters' machine gun teams, Second Lieutenant Norman Dewhurst had no qualms about 'using the dead bodies around us' to build an emplacement 'to give us some elevation to fire over the sandbank'.[32]

For almost four hours, during which there was a constant flow of men from *River Clyde*'s darkened holds, scarcely a shot was fired. The peace was an eerie one. David Fyffe put it down to the Turks being blinded by the searchlights which 'thrust their ... fingers through the gloom'.[33] Whether or not this was by accident or design is not clear. Tizard, who had originally been averse to using them, may have changed his mind, but if he did, he made no mention of it in his report. Whoever it was ensured a largely incident-free passage ashore for hundreds of men. For as Fyffe observed, while 'every stick and stone upon the terraced rise that bore the concealed enemy trenches stood out in fullest detail', the beach at the water's edge, the *River Clyde* and 'the awful barges' remained in 'pitch darkness' with only the glare from the burning village casting 'splashes of crimson on the inky water'.[34] He added:

> The enemy, dazzled by the searchlights, and unable to discern anything in the solid blackness that sheltered the *Clyde*, and the beach, were helpless to hinder the progress of the landing ...[35]

Nature also contrived to assist the disembarkation, as Fyffe's diary entry notes:

> The moon rise was late that night and even when the silvery orb did climb into the midnight sky, the shadows cast by the frowning walls of the castle were so long and dense that little could be seen of what was going on on the beach.[36]

It wasn't only the men disembarking from the *River Clyde* who had cause to be thankful for the shrouding darkness. For while the priority was to get men ashore, efforts were also being made to recover the wounded. Among those volunteer rescuers venturing on to the beach

were more men from Wedgwood's machine gun detachment. They
were led by Sub-Lieutenant Parkes and comprised Chief Petty Officer
Little and Petty Officers Barton, Cecil, Murray and Tailyour. Together
they scoured a mile of shoreline, searching abandoned cutters for
injured survivors. They recovered two from a boat that was barely afloat
and seven more aboard a boat filled with nine dead and a couple of
Maxim guns that they proceeded to row back to the *River Clyde*. 'The
Turks were not shooting,' wrote Wedgwood, 'but they passed them
within fifty yards like cats in the dark.'[37]

Another of those engaged in the rescue operation was 'Geordie'
Samson. Making the most of the lull, he slipped away from the hopper
and disappeared into the darkness to fetch a launch that he somehow
managed to man-handle back. With the help of Midshipman Weblin,
he then loaded it with all the wounded from the *Argyle*.

By then, the trawler requested by Tizard lay alongside the collier.
Weblin later wrote:

> We got everyone except one man who was too bad to move into the
> launch and went to the *Clyde*, which was by then of course joined to
> the hopper by lighters. I found Dr Kelly and asked him where to put
> them and he said he wanted them taken off to the trawler.
> [Midshipman] Drewry was told off to do this and Dr Kelly told me
> to lend him a hand with wounded ...[38]

Drewry, his own wounds hardly healed and his head still swathed in
bandages, led a party to recover the injured from the lighters. Many of
them had been lying out for the best part of fifteen hours. It was, he
later wrote, 'an awful job':[39]

> They had not been dressed at all and some of the poor devils were
> in an awful state. I never knew blood smelt so strong before.[40]

The stream of wounded flowing from shore to ship and ship to trawler
seemed endless and, with few men to spare to assist them, their
progress was slow and arduous. While Drewry's team trawled for the
living among the dead, the men of 89th Field Ambulance were doing
their best to cope with the wounded spread throughout every hold on
board the *River Clyde*. Such were the demands placed on them that
Tizard deliberately resisted sending them ashore. The only exception
was Lieutenant George Davidson.

At 2130, with the disembarkation in full swing, an officer dashed back
to the *Clyde*. He described 'the terrible condition and suffering of the

wounded'[41] and called for a medical officer to give assistance. Davidson immediately volunteered to go. He later wrote:

> I set off alone over the barges and splashed through the remaining few yards of water. Here, most of those still alive were wounded more or less severely, and I set to work on them, removing many useless and harmful tourniquets for one thing, and worked my way to the left towards the high rocks where the snipers still were. All the wounded on this side I attended to, an officer accompanying me all the time. I went to the other side, and after seeing to all in the sand my companion left me, and I next went to a long, low rock which projected into the water for about 20 yards a short way to the right of the *Clyde*. Here, the dead and wounded were heaped together two and three deep, and it was among these I had my hardest work. All had to be disentangled single-handed from their uncomfortable positions, some lying with head and shoulders in the tide-less water, with broken legs in some cases dangling on a higher level.
>
> At the very point of this rock, which had been a favourite spot for the boats to steer to, there was a solid mass of dead and wounded mixed up together. The whole of these I saw to, although by this time there was little I could do except lift and pull them into more comfortable positions, but I was able to do something for every one of them. My last piece of work was to look after six men who were groaning in a boat stranded close to the point of the rock. Three lay on each side with their legs inwards; a plank ran the whole length of the middle of the boat, and along this, as it rested on their legs, men had been running during the landing. Getting on this plank some of them howled in agony and beseeched me to get off. I then got into the water and, as I could do nothing more for them, my dressings being finished some time before, I gave each a dose of morphia by the mouth …[42]

The sheer volume of seriously injured men, many of them wounded in four or five places, presented a major difficulty not just to the medics, but to those struggling to organise the men coming ashore. According to one officer, 'the confusion', particularly during the early stages of disembarkation, was 'very great, owing to having to move badly wounded men away to prevent them being trodden on'.[43] And there were other obstacles to overcome. They included

> having to make a gangway of packs, etc, to the boat, owing to the rising tide … the necessity of getting a supply of ammunition and

tools ashore, and clearing ways through the mass of wire [in front of the battered fortress], added to the fact that there were still snipers concealed in the walls of the fort, in the ruins, galleries, and various places impossible to find any entrance to in the dark, especially at the corner nearest the ship. Moreover, frequent bursts of fire on both sides kept causing temporary cessation of movement from the ship.[44]

All of these snags combined to hold up the disembarkation and, as a consequence, Tizard's planned night assault.

Aside from Captain Spencer-Smith's party established on the northern face of the fort, only limited advances were possible. Two platoons of Hampshires under Captain William Penn-Gaskell had managed to creep forward with assistance from some sappers to penetrate wire defences to reach a line of low walls to the west of the fort. And a patrol made up of Munsters, mostly from W Company, scouted as far as an abandoned enemy earthwork at the beach's western extremity near a path that ran along the cliffs. But the rest of the Hampshires, composing of headquarters and three platoons, together with a roughly company-strength party of Munsters, were only finally assembled by Major Beckwith beneath the seaward face of the fort at around 0300.

As the disembarkation continued, an out-of-touch General Hunter-Weston boarded a launch bound for the *Queen Elizabeth*, still under the misapprehension that Hill 141 was in British hands. Together with members of his staff, the commander of 29th Division chugged across a moon-lit ocean, halfway to Tenedos to deliver his report personally to Sir Ian Hamilton. When he arrived at around 2100, the GOC was just finishing a hurried meal with de Robeck and their joint staffs. His interruption was timely.

Hamilton was still fretting about the 'hold-up'[45] at V Beach. 'The enveloping attacks on both enemy flanks have come off brilliantly,' he wrote, 'but have not cut the enemy's line of retreat, or so threatened it that they have to make haste to get back.'[46] A suggestion – though by whom is not clear – that they might have to evacuate the beach at night filled him with horror. 'It would never do,' he wrote. 'We must stick it until our advance from X and W opens that sally port from the sea.'[47] But gnawing away at the back of his mind was 'dread'[48] at the thought of enemy reinforcements reaching the defenders of V Beach 'before we have done with Sedd-el-Bahr'.[49]

In the face of so much soul-searching, Hunter-Weston's ebullience came as a much-needed shot-in-the-arm. Hamilton and the others listened 'with breathless interest'[50] as the commander of the 29th

Division 'breathlessly'[51] delivered his report. It was a bravura performance, albeit one based only loosely on the truth. Jack Churchill called it 'a glowing account'[52] even if it did refer to 'the capture of several points which we knew his men had not reached'.[53] For once, his bluff and bluster was welcome. Churchill declared his 'optimism ... an improvement on his former attitude',[54] while Hamilton, buoyed by his 'cheery' and 'stout-hearted' demeanour, described his presence as 'a good tonic'.[55]

They drank a glass of wine together and seemed 'much elated by the wonderful feat of arms'[56]. Not everyone, however, shared their confidence. Clement Milward, who had accompanied the general to the *Queen Elizabeth*, was one who felt disinclined to celebrate just yet. In his diary, he observed:

> One could not help wondering if all was well. We had gained a secure footing but had not gone far on our first day's programme to beyond Achi Baba. We had lost so much that it was doubtful if we had sufficient men now to advance immediately. And rapidity was all-essential. By that alone could we hope to cause the Turk to crack and to sue for peace. Give the Turks time to breathe and a long-drawn out struggle must ensue and many more troops will be required. From the start, the whole show was a toss-up ...[57]

Once back on *Euryalus*, Hunter-Weston, anxious for an update on progress at V Beach, immediately dispatched Milward to find out the latest. The signs were not good. As his pinnace neared the *River Clyde*, the midshipman at the wheel 'took shelter, [ducking] low down his armoured plated box':[58]

> They were busy collecting wounded off the beach and lowering them on stretchers and downwards into lighters some 10 ft below – a most painful process.
>
> I climbed on to the ship and found it full of wounded. I talked to all the officers on the deck and great depression was apparent. They had had a nerve-shattering experience. Colonel Carrington Smith [*sic*] was still lying dead on the Bridge and General Napier and Costeker [lay] on the lighters below.[59]

On board, he ran into Captain Garth Walford, Brigade Major and senior staff officer to Brigadier-General Richard Breeks, commanding the 29th Divisional Artillery. Walford, who had already impressed Hunter-Weston during the voyage overseas, had been sent over to the

River Clyde earlier in the day. 'He was anxious to return to his General,' noted Milward, 'so I took him off.'[60] As they backed away, the *Clyde* suddenly became the target for a heavy burst of rifle fire. With bullets ringing against the collier's hull, the pinnace drew out of range and the two staff officers headed back to *Euryalus* with their depressing news. 'We reported to the General,' wrote Milward, 'and Walford was sent back immediately to act as Staff Officer to the OC on V Beach.'[61] He carried with him orders for Tizard 'to push on at once and capture Hill 141'.[62]

Events, however, had changed since leaving the *River Clyde* a short while before. The firing that had broken out just as he departed in Milward's pinnace proved the precursor to an angry fusillade from the Turkish positions above V Beach. It began shortly before midnight, as Commander Unwin was helping to get men ashore. 'They gave us hell,'[63] he wrote. In a split-second the Turks' muted response to the disembarkation resumed its former wrathful fury. Once again, the clutter of lighters were spattered and sprayed with bullets. Not for the first time, George Drewry scurried to find cover. 'The Turks gave us an awful doing,' he wrote, 'shell, shrapnel and every other nasty thing, but everyone laid low and little harm was done.'[64]

He wasn't the only one forced to seek shelter. Weighed down with detonators, explosives, a shovel and rifle, Sapper George Smith was hurrying as best he could along the ship's 'rickety gangway'[65] when the firing erupted. Towering above him on one side was the *Clyde*'s rust-coated hull with a drop into open water on the other. Stumbling forward, he leapt down on to the first barge, landing 'with a crash',[66] and was suddenly aware of bullets 'spluttering all over the place':[67]

> I lay down flat on my tummy and looked around to get my bearings. And a terrible sight met me ... The barge was crowded with men who had died, and lots of wounded men whom we could not help as we had to push on owing to the other fellows coming on behind ... Eventually after crawling along three barges, I came to the place where I could push my face over the gunwale of the last barge, and make up my mind to jump into the sea – I managed it all right, and clutching my explosives – I had lost the shovel somewhere – I managed to get to a place where no bullets could reach me, and lay down under cover of a small strip of cliff ...[68]

Once more men of the Dublin Fusiliers found themselves directly in the firing line. Captain Herbert Crozier's W Company was leading his men out when bullets began zipping around them. Third in line was Sergeant Christopher McCann, commanding No 1 Platoon. So heavy was the fire, he was convinced they were being targeted by machine guns. The reaction was immediate and instinctive:

> We threw ourselves flat where we stood; two of my platoon were hit, and one of them fell headlong into the sea. After about ten minutes we moved on, but had only reached the two barges that formed the landing stage when we came under heavy rifle and machine gun fire again. We threw ourselves flat on the barges and lay still for some time; I was between two men of the Munster Fusiliers who were dead, but I did not realise this until I asked one of them to make more room, and as he did not move I pushed him off with my hand, and then found that his head was blown away. Captain Crozier now passed the word to get ashore; we moved off the barges over the small rowing boat [sic], scrambled ashore through the water, and lined up along the beach. All this time we were under a very heavy rifle and machine gun fire, several of the company being hit.[69]

Of the platoons that were following, one, commanded by twenty-one-year-old Lieutenant Lawrence Boustead, took shelter on the lighters, while another, led by Lieutenant Desmond O'Hara, was caught on the exposed gangway, with bullets 'simply whizzing up against the sides of the ship'.[70] In a letter home, O'Hara wrote:

> Crozier shouted to me to take my platoon back into the ship, which I did, though not before three men had been hit, including Redmond, my soldier servant, who was standing beside me; the bullet caught him under the ear and came out just behind the nose without doing him much damage.[71]

In the circumstances, they got off lightly, as, indeed, did the majority of those trapped on the launches and lighters clustered around the *River Clyde*. Most lay 'doggo' for as long as the firing persisted, but not everyone was as patient. Commander Unwin later wrote:

> We all lay down in whatever boat we happened to be in. Mine was a launch with pretty high sides, and somehow even a bit of wood seems a protection at such a time. So we lay whilst the bullets flew over our heads knocking the poor old *River Clyde* about but not

hurting us. I yelled at the machine gunners to give them 'gip', but I think they were afraid in the dark of hitting our men. The Turks were right on the beach. I wasn't going to spend the night like that so I ran the gauntlet for it and got safely on board ...[72]

As he later put it, 'I preferred to take my chance of a bullet to lying out all night in the boats'.[73] Few others were willing to take such a gamble.

George Davidson was standing waist-deep in water near the spit when seven or eight bullets fired from the direction of the fort 'spluttered'[74] around him. Thrashing out, he made for a small boat lying at the end of one of the gangways leading off the *River Clyde*. He hauled himself in just as five men leapt down from one of the lighters:

Here, none of us had any protection, and it was a miracle any one of us escaped, the fire from machine guns and rifles was so terrific. Each bullet as it struck the *Clyde* drove sparks, while the old ship was ringing like a great bell. Two of our six were hit, the man stretched alongside me fatally. A seventh man in the water hauled himself in beside us, and as he was getting over the gunwale shouted, 'Oh! I'm hit.' Hit or not hit, we could not pay the slightest attention to each other now. All we could do was to lie low.

All this time I was expecting a rush for the *Clyde* by the Turks, and the boat I was in would be the first part of the gangway they would reach ... I could not help wondering what it would be like to get a bayonet through my stomach, but the feeling that this would certainly happen was not half so terrible as I should have expected. I had my revolver in my hand all the time, and it was a comfort to think that I would almost certainly account for two or three Turks before I experienced this new sensation.

The fire was kept up for about four hours, mainly on the side of the ship. As soon as there was a lull an officer in my boat shouted out. 'This won't do. We must now land. Follow me.' He got up and splashed ashore, but the men, thinking he had been too hasty, preferred to wait a little longer after the Turks had ceased fire. But soon they began to move and dash singly for the land. I wished to get on the ship, and not half liking to get into an upright position either, I crept through and over those still on the barges, amidst much cursing from my paining the wounded, who must have been numerous ...

I must say I felt it a relief when I hopped through the nearest hole in the *Clyde*. It was now 4 o'clock, and I shivered with cold ...[75]

Out at sea, Guy Geddes was feeling the chill too. One of around 200 wounded transferred from the *River Clyde* on to the trawler requested by Tizard, he spent a thoroughly miserable few hours, 'without blankets, food or anything',[76] being 'tossed about the whole of a bitter cold night'.[77] A steady drizzle added to the discomfort of what he called a 'disgraceful show'.[78] Among those suffering with him was Maurice Lloyd, the young midshipman shot through the lung while securing a lighter to the hopper. After what must have seemed an eternity his brief but gallant involvement in the landing was finally over. Like many others that day he had never actually set foot ashore, but at least he was still alive. His last memory of V Beach was a grim one, listening to 'the most terrific fire' breaking out on the left of the bay and 'the Turks yelling as they charged'.[79]

What he heard was the first in a series of attacks launched against the eastern perimeter of the W Beach bridgehead around Hill 138. It prompted brief alarm. 'There were bad nerves and heavy firing,'[80] wrote Mynors Farmar. According to Clement Milward, 'a good many men'[81] drifted back to the beach amid a 'good deal of confusion'.[82] A senior naval officer aboard *Euryalus* was so 'afraid all was up'[83] he went as far as to prepare for an evacuation. However, as Milward noted, 'the fire was not sufficiently heavy to frighten Hunter-Weston'.[84] He had already turned in for the night when the fighting appeared to have reached its climax and it seemed to naval officers that the troops on W Beach were being pushed back. A messenger was sent to inform him of their growing concerns. According to John Godfrey,

> the General … listened for a moment but his trained ear told him that there had been no appreciable movement and he turned over and went to sleep.[85]

Edward Unwin, who had also retired to bed, slept soundly too, right through till 0500. But others found rest harder to come by. What sounded like thousands of bullets 'showering'[86] the sides of the *River Clyde* created a 'deafening din'[87] that was too much for those whose nerves were already frayed. 'Many had the wind up badly,'[88] observed George Davidson.

Henry Tizard was one of those in sore need of 'a bit of a rest'.[89] 'Having been running about all day directing fire and trying to spot targets in order to help the attack as much as possible',[90] he was all but done in. But as much as he needed it, he knew it was impossible. 'The noise and anxiety of the whole business,' he wrote, 'would not allow it.'[91]

Chapter 21

'An Awful Snag'

Reginald Gillett's first and last night on V Beach was an uncomfortable, unpleasant and, at times, unnerving experience. It was also unforgettable. Half a century on, he would vividly recall the shivering cold and the creeping fear as he threaded his men through the Turkish wire above the body-strewn foreshore.

Behind him lay a clutter of barges and launches snaking back towards the *River Clyde*, or the 'Horse of Troy' as he called it, which had been his sanctuary throughout a God-awful, gut-wrenching day. To the right, dark and menacing, rose the battered bulk of Sedd-el-Bahr's still defiant fortress. And somewhere in front of him, hidden from view, were an unknown number of Turks just waiting for him to make his move.

With his platoon, he had been manning his exposed position on the western face of the fort since dusk when Beckwith ordered him to push up through the wire to form a flank guard. Lying in the open, his men spread out 'in extended order',[1] he looked on nervously as, 'at intervals',[2] spears of light 'flashed hither and thither'[3] across the slopes. 'The Turks knew we were there,' he wrote, 'but not quite where.'[4] All through the night there were bursts of machine gun fire. It seemed to the young special reserve subaltern that they were 'searching for us'.[5] He later recalled:

> On one occasion they got our range and a bullet spat into the sand, nicely placed, one between each man. Once when I raised myself on my elbow a bullet struck the sand just beneath my chest. None of us had had much sleep since Friday night, and fearful that the men might fall asleep I kept a fairly continuous stream of messages passing up and down the line ...[6]

The majority of the troops collected by Beckwith lay closely gathered beneath the seaward face of the fort. There, they were protected from the heaviest of the Turkish fire that erupted around midnight, but not from the marksmen concealed within the ruins that loomed above them. 'We dug ourselves in,' wrote Guy Nightingale, 'the Turks sniping at us from every corner.'[7] He had 'never spent such a rotten night'[8] and his misery was made worse by the cold, drenching rain that fell. V Beach presented a grimly 'unforgettable scene',[9]

> with the thin line of tired troops still clinging to their precarious position, the sombre silhouette of ridge and fort still barring their advance, and the burning village reddening sea and sky.[10]

Tizard could not tell whether the fires raging in the middle of Sedd-el-Bahr were started by 'gun fire from the ships or intentionally by the enemy',[11] but either way the flames added to the growing unease. 'All through the night the village was burning and gave us too much light to be pleasant,'[12] wrote George Drewry. The tension was palpable. At times it seemed to Josiah Wedgwood as if 'everyone was firing at they knew not what'.[13] His own machine guns, so prominent throughout the day, were for once ineffective. As he later explained to Churchill, 'we could see nothing and [could] not help'.[14] However, what he failed to see, he could certainly hear. Mingling with the sounds of battle over to the left in the direction of W Beach, were the unmistakeable cries of 'Allah'[15] that heralded the Turkish bid to shatter 29th Division's slender hold on the southern tip of the peninsula.

The close-quarter fight that raged around the recently captured redoubts to the west of V Beach was a confused affair. It was delivered by a Turkish force bolstered by the arrival of three fresh battalions from the 25th Regiment. Of these, the largest contingent was deployed to push back the northernmost British landing at Y Beach. Another smaller force was sent to shore up the defences around S Beach, while a third party comprising two companies, a machine gun platoon and headquarters of 1/25th Regiment was despatched as reinforcements for Mahmut Sabri's sorely depleted 3/26th Regiment with orders to 'clean up the beaches'.[16]

Sabri had precious little time to plan and organise the attack. Barely 2½ hours separated the arrival of the advance party at his command post from the all-out assault. It was a task every bit as challenging as that facing Beckwith, though in Sabri's case he at least had the advantage of local knowledge. Exploiting this advantage, he fused the fresh units with remnants of his own companies who were better acquainted with the ground and the positions they were to attack. Sabri's intention was to contain the British on V Beach while focusing his efforts on recapturing Hill 138 and Guezji Baba. Sabri identified Hill 138 as the key to his overall objective of recovering all the lost ground west of Cape Helles, which would result in the invaders being 'hurled back into the sea'.[17] As he later explained, 'this hill took our right and left flanks in enfilade fire. If it could be retaken, the enemy's battle front would become exposed to the same danger'.[18]

His mind made up, the assault forces were guided to their assembly areas and 'a short attack order' issued. Two companies [numbered 3 and 4] of the 1/25th Regiment, together with survivors of 9 and 12 Companies, 3/26th Regiment, were assigned the task of retaking Hill 138 at the point of the bayonet. They would be supported by fire from two newly arrived machine guns. At the same time, the men of Sabri's 11 Company was to attack the redoubt on Guezji Baba. The remaining half company of the 1/25th Regiment were held back in reserve under their battalion commander in readiness for exploiting any success.

Despite all the difficulties, the attacks scheduled for 0330 were launched on time. They were met by a withering fire. Few made it as far as the redoubts as machine guns and grenades tore great holes in their ranks. Accurate naval gunfire added to the slaughter and, though some brave souls managed to fight their way into the British trenches they were too few to resist the inevitable counter-attack. The commitment of the small reserve made no difference. Within an hour it was all over and the assault everywhere repulsed. With dawn approaching, Sabri abandoned the attack:

> Reports coming from the southern front showed that the attack had been carried out but it was unsuccessful owing to the enemy's heavy machine gun fire both from Aytepe [Hill 138] and Gozcubaba [Guezji Baba].[19]

Audacious though the counter-attack was, the consequences of its bloody failure were inescapable. The British line on the western side of Cape Helles remained unbroken. And, despite the mostly indiscriminate fire that had been directed against V Beach in order to divert attention away from the main thrust and to prevent any further advance, it was clear that the landing of more troops had 'continued during the darkness'.[20] For all his defiance and determination it was apparent to Sabri that yet more powerful attacks by an enemy that had been greatly reinforced were inevitable. At about 0500, together with the commanding officer of the 1/25th Regiment, he filed a joint report. Its conclusion was bleak. It simply stated that 'it seemed most likely that the enemy would encircle them'.[21]

In reality, both sides were on the verge of nervous and physical exhaustion. Though it came too late to seriously disrupt the disembarkation of troops from *River Clyde*, the Turkish action had undoubtedly interfered with Beckwith's efforts to carry out Tizard's plan. For while most of the infantry were ashore by 0030 a number remained trapped on the lighters or, in the case of many of the West Riding sappers, on the *Clyde* itself until 0400. By then any hopes of mounting the night assault on Hill 141 envisaged by Hunter-Weston had long since vanished. In truth, it was probably never a realistic proposition. An earlier reconnaissance carried out by Lieutenant Colonels Williams and Doughty-Wylie, the GHQ liaison officers, had already concluded that an attack before daylight was 'out of the question'.[22] Their fellow staff officer, Cecil Aspinall, later wrote:

> The night was pitch dark, and most of the troops, other than those recently landed, were badly shaken by the events of the day. Major Beckwith had moreover explained to Colonel Doughty-Wylie that his preparations for an advance could not be completed before daybreak. He was organising the troops ashore into three parties for an early morning attack, and if the *Albion* could be asked to bombard the fort and village for half an hour at daybreak he would get his men into motion at 5.30 am. This plan was accordingly agreed to, and for the rest of the night the overwrought troops on the beach were left to get such rest as the Turks would allow them.[23]

It was a prudent decision. An unsupported attack made by exhausted men, many of whom had not slept for forty-eight hours, was liable to have been futile as well as costly. As it was, Beckwith needed until nearly 0300 to complete his arrangements and to ensure all those men landed were in position to advance. Williams agreed to take charge of the troops at the western end of the beach and a message was sent to Spencer-Smith, on the northern side of the fort, warning him to pull back before dawn in readiness for the renewed naval bombardment. Preparations complete, it seemed only a matter of nervously counting down the last couple of hours before the assault went in. But, unbeknown to Beckwith, his best-laid plans were about to be disrupted by an unexpected intervention by the man in titular command of the operation.

Henry Tizard had been struggling to maintain some kind of control over the landing during a night fraught with anxiety in which reliable information was sparse. He had thought about running a telephone wire under the cliff to link up with W Beach, but it was considered too risky. A signalling party did get ashore, but what messages did get through usually 'took a long time' [24] to do so.

Meanwhile, verbal requests to be kept informed of progress often went unanswered. He later complained: 'I asked the Officer in Command of the Hampshire Coy, whose task I had allotted to cut the wire and to let me know when this was done, but I never heard.'[25] Such breakdowns in communication, though inevitable given the state of affairs ashore, added to his frustration. Only vaguely aware of what was happening on the beach and all too aware that the few messages reaching him were liable to be out of date, he began to second guess what was going on rather than stick to his original plan to leave the decision-making to the men on the spot. He later reported:

> At about 2am I received a message from my right saying that they had got into the courtyard at the fort and were held up by snipers from all directions who were high up on the walls where they could not be got at.
>
> Asked for gunfire on the fort archway 1 hour after daybreak. This message I held up as I thought the situation would probably change before then … I heard that the left company had got touch with those on the cliff but where it came from I don't know. Otherwise I had heard nothing from my left. The turning movement on the right began to move across through the fort about dark, but the first party did not start till about 10pm …[26]

After a night full of apprehension and no little alarm, dawn brought with it only a little more clarity. Peering out from the sand-bagged machine gun 'turrets' on the bows of the *River Clyde*, David Fyffe searched for signs of progress. Straining to make sense of the scene confronting him, he wrote:

> The flat, flower-spangled stretch of ground between the crest of the bank of sand on the beach and the line of yellow earth that betokened the first enemy trench was dotted with khaki figures lying in curiously symmetrical lines like corn cut with a scythe, and all terribly still. Within the trench itself we could see khaki caps, hardly visible through the high grass, and we knew that the second step had been taken. At one place, where the trench ran more at an angle to the shore, close under the wall of the village, we saw that it was almost choked with figures of men, a huddle of khaki and blue-grey amidst which bayonet blades gleamed dully, but all dead still. And then we noticed that all the faces we could see there were

waxen coloured in contrast to the pink flesh tones that showed farther along the trench under the brown caps that moved sometimes; and then we understood. And after that, whenever we saw a khaki figure half hidden amidst the flowers and long grass, we tried to see the face, because only thus could we distinguish between the quick and the dead, a uniform stillness made necessary by the lynx-eyed snipers, making that the only method of recognition.[27]

From his more elevated position, Major Carr, whose small band of Worcesters were lining the upper and lower bridges in readiness to support the attack, noticed more encouraging signs on the high ground to the left. 'It could be seen,' he wrote, 'that [the] 'Lighthouse Hill' had been taken and our people there were on the flank of the Turks in front of us.'[28] Scanning the beach through binoculars, a fretful Tizard saw a small party of Munsters below the cliffs, apparently held up in a dry river bed. Directly ahead of him, he observed a body of men, which he estimated to be about a company in strength and almost indistinguishable from the piles of dead, crouching beneath the sandy cliff close to the water's edge. Beyond them, at a point above where the wire had evidently been cut, there were more men. Perhaps as many as half a company, they were sheltering behind a low wall, though their lack of movement suggested to Tizard that at least some of them were dead.

Over to the right, where the greater part of his force was situated beneath the castle walls, he could see some men 'moving over very slowly by the SE corner in single file'.[29] There was still a good deal of firing going on 'in all directions'[30] and, fearful that his men were too close to the area around the 'fort gate-way'[31] that Beckwith had requested be shelled, Tizard once more refrained from sending the message.

Quite what transpired thereafter so far as the order for the naval bombardment is concerned is open to speculation. But whoever eventually conveyed the instructions to *Albion* deliberately avoided all mention of the fort, asking only for the village to be shelled. The result was confusion.

Oblivious of Tizard's unfortunate if well-intentioned intervention, Beckwith withdrew his men from positions near to the fortress walls in accordance with his original plan. Final instructions were then passed round: as soon as the bombardment ceased, they were to charge *en masse*, Hampshires on the right, Munsters in the centre and Dublins on the left. With the Navy's big guns clearing the way, they were to seize the fort, root out any remaining snipers and then sweep on into the village. But it did not work out that way. To the consternation of Beckwith and the men sheltering around him, the Navy's shells thundered over the fort to land in the village beyond, leaving the sniper-riddled western and northern walls of the fort untouched. Bemused by what was happening and imagining it was only a matter of time before the ships shortened their range, Beckwith waited. But there was no change, no alteration in the direction of the bombardment. The only shells that fell anywhere near to the walls were from Turkish pom-poms sited behind Sedd-el-Bahr. One of the British officers waiting to attack later wrote:

> Apparently … there was some misunderstanding, as orders were sent from the *River Clyde* to advance, and when this was done another order came to fall back and let the ships shell. After two or three false starts in this way, orders were given to advance whatever happened …[32]

In a final irony, word was passed round warning men to look out for shells falling short. It drew wry smiles. 'Personally,' wrote Reginald Gillett, 'I wondered what exactly we were supposed to do if they did.'[33] By then, it was too late to care. 'We seemed somewhat fully occupied with other things,'[34] he added. Moments later, with a shout, they were off and running, a crowd of Hampshires, Munsters and Dublins, scrambling up and over rubble spewing out from myriad breaches.

By common consent, Cecil Grimshaw's Dublins led the race into fort. Tasked with keeping in touch with those Hampshires under Penn-Gaskell, who had crept up along the western side of the fort during the night, the remnants of the battalion that had suffered such crippling losses the day before poured forward. First into the bastion was Private Tom Cullen, a feat subsequently recognised by the award of a Distinguished Conduct Medal. Those following were flailed by fire from hidden marksmen and one particularly troublesome machine gun. Men went to ground and the attack momentarily stalled. But not for long. Ignoring the hail of fire, Lawrence Boustead, of W Company, ran straight towards the spitting gun. Incredibly, he reached the embrasure where it was sited unharmed, thrust his revolver inside and fired repeatedly until it fell silent. It was an astonishing single-handed act of daring and animated all around. According to one account, the men who watched his long charge with a mixture of disbelief and awe 'rushed forward and drove out the last of the Turks',[35] though not before the hero of the hour had been downed by a bullet through the cheek.

On the right it was a similar story of gallant leadership galvanising weary men, only there the inspiration came not from the wild courage of impetuous youth but from the heroic example of two officers of middle-aged maturity.

Thirty-five year-old Captain Alfred Addison, commanding Y Company, 2nd Hampshires, and Captain Garth Walford, Hunter-Weston's thirty-two-year-old personal emissary, were in the forefront of the assault from the start. Despatched to *River Clyde* to stiffen resolve and to assist in the execution of his chief's instructions to break the deadlock, Walford had chosen to interpret his orders literally. Having accepted that Hunter-Weston's call for an immediate attack was impossible, he had remained with Beckwith, helping him to organise the assault before taking his place in the front rank alongside Addison. From that moment on, the gunner turned staff officer was the life and soul of the attack; hustling men forward at every turn and always leading from the front. The fighting in the cramped confines of the fort was confused and savage, but both Walford and Addison appeared to bear charmed lives.

At around 0630, Tizard, looking on from the *River Clyde*, thought he saw Walford leading a small party of about six or seven men towards a path leading up towards the village between the fort and the last section of barbed wire:

> When about half way up this path and opposite to an abutment of the fort that had two windows in it, a machine gun opened on them from the nearest window. None of them were hit and they jumped over a low wall on their left and took cover ...[36]

Turning to Captain Lambert, the beachmaster who had come aboard *River Clyde* and was now pressed into service as a gunnery observation officer, Tizard pointed out the Turkish position and between them they were able to direct *Albion*'s guns on to it. Minutes later, shells demolished the walled-perch. 'The machine gun troubled us no more,'[37] noted Tizard. Searching again for Walford's party, he then saw them move forward and get behind some buildings on the left, where they were held up by snipers:

> A support of 8 men now went up to them from the men under the bank on the right and, after a bit, they got a little further into the village on the left side of it. About 7.30 am, or soon after, I saw this party coming back, taking cover under the compound walls and the houses and returning the fire of snipers who were in the houses. Another party now started off and reinforced them and after a bit of skirmishing behind walls, etc, they pushed on up into the village and I did not see them again.[38]

From time to time the men on the *River Clyde* caught glimpses of the splintered advance; of parties of men creeping through the long grass and moving cautiously, rifles at the ready, towards the village before disappearing 'round corners or through the huge holes that gaped in almost every wall'.[39] At first, wrote David Fyffe, Turkish opposition appeared slight,

> but a few minutes after the first parties had disappeared amid the tumbled ruins, rifles began to crack spasmodically in little gusts and outbreaks of sound, while at the entrance to the main street we saw a machine gun section, squatting low in the grass, firing briskly at some mark farther up the street which we could not see.[40]

What Fyffe and Tizard were witnessing were the opening moves in the struggle for Sedd-el-Bahr itself. Here, amid the rubble of houses laid waste by the Navy's bombardment, small parties of Turks and a few individual marksmen resisted with a desperation that seemed to the attackers to border on the fanatical. As one officer ruefully observed:

> They fought like rats in a trap, remaining in cellars or upper storeys and firing after our lines had passed, without a vestige of a chance of escape.[41]

One of the hardest fights took place around a postern gate that led into the village from the north-east corner of the fort. By the time the leading British troops reached it most of the fort had already fallen. The Dublins and Munsters had captured a cluster of sheds and barrack blocks on the left, but had been stopped near the northern wall by a combination of close-range and long-range fire. Some of it came from snipers concealed among rocks on top of the cliffs to the right and more from a line of trenches sited 700 yards away on a knoll above the village. But the heaviest fire was directed from the shell-battered houses directly opposite the gate, beyond a bush-covered rise, some 40 yards away. And it was in front of these positions, commanding the way out of the fort, the advance slowed and then stalled.

It was a critical moment. Making his way up to the gate, Walford could see that anyone charging through would be risking certain death. But there was little alternative. As Guy Nightingale later wrote: 'The only way into Sedd-el-Bahr village lay through the Castle, which had two main entrances for this purpose.'[42] Both consisted of a 'stone archway about 15 feet in breadth'[43] and each one was 'covered by a deadly fire from machine guns and marksmen hidden in the ruins of the village beyond'.[44]

Realising the importance of maintaining the momentum of the attack, Hunter-Weston's staff officer did not hesitate. Placing himself at the front of the Hampshires clustered around the opening, he leapt forward, calling on them to follow him as he ran through the gateway. A couple of machine guns and a party of riflemen under Captain Spencer-Smith who had gained entry into some houses on the right did their best to subdue the enemy fire, but they could not stop it entirely. The fight that followed was short and savage. Charging through a hail of bullets and a shower of hand-grenades, the Hampshires, led on by Walford and with Addison not far behind, stormed the houses in front of them.

It was the beginning of the painful efforts to clear Sedd-el-Bahr. For the next few hours the fighting was fierce, with no quarter given by either side as the British battled to eject the diehard remnants of Sabri's two platoons tasked with defending the village. Nightingale was among those caught up in the vicious street fighting. He later wrote:

> The village was an awful snag. Every house and corner was full of snipers and you only had to show yourself in the streets to have a bullet at your head. We spent from 9 am to 2.30 pm [sic] before we finally cleared them all out, [and] we lost a lot of men and officers in it. I got one swine of a Turk with my revolver when searching a house for snipers but he nearly had me first.[45]

Company Sergeant Major George Baker was among around twenty men from X and Y Companies of the Dublins under the command of Lieutenants Robert Bernard and William Andrews who found themselves pinned down behind a wall inside the village. He recalled:

> Andrews stood in a gap made by a shell, and was directing the fire when he was shot through the heart. Lieutenant Bernard called on the others to follow him, and saying 'Come on, boys', he dashed through the gap when he was shot.[46]

So it went on, bloodily and brutally. Room by room. House by house. And street by street. With the Turks disputing almost every single yard, the going was interminably slow. In an effort to hurry things along, Beckwith sent Second Lieutenants Gillett and Parker with their platoons on a precarious cliff-edge trek in an effort to bypass the nearest Turkish positions and take them in reverse. The prospects appeared initially unpromising. 'The rock cliff was high and almost perpendicular,' wrote Gillett. 'Below was the sea and on the rocks at the foot of the cliff more than one mangled body lay.'[47] Full packs, extra supplies of water and bandoliers filled with 200 extra rounds of ammunition slung round their necks made the climb 'even more difficult and perilous'.[48] Gillett observed:

> One was covered from direct rifle fire, but at one point a large boulder, evidently pushed over by the enemy, came bounding down the cliff straight for me. I thought I was about to be added to the mangled remains below, but the boulder bounced just above my head and again below my feet and I was still safe.[49]

Eventually, after inching their way along, they clambered up the cliff and made their way into the village, where the fighting was still going on amid the ruins either side of a 10ft wide street:

> Slowly we worked our way through … but with bullets whizzing down the street, crossing it was something of a hazard. However when necessary we did, one by one, somewhat after the fashion of children daring each other to be the last across the road in front of an on-coming car. On one occasion, one of my men had a nick taken out of his nose, poor man, but somehow I remember that we all thought this rather a joke.[50]

It was a rare moment of levity in an otherwise deadly serious struggle that proved both costly and time-consuming. Beckwith, as tireless and reckless as ever, was still driving the attack on, but two of his boldest leaders had fallen. Alfred Addison, who had spearheaded the Hampshires' charge into the fort, was killed by a grenade thrown at close quarters during the struggle for Sedd-el-Bahr. It was said that his revolver had 'failed him'[51] at the vital moment. And gone, too, was Garth Walford, though the circumstances of his death are far from clear. According to one account, he was killed by a bomb thrown by a Turk hiding in a clump of bushes as he continued to lead men through the postern gate. Another report claimed he had been 'shot dead from a house'[52] as he sought to inject fresh life into an attack in danger of running out of steam. Either way, he had, in the words of one of his fellow officers, 'proved possible the impossible'.[53]

Walford died with the battle for the village still undecided. His last message to the *River Clyde* for transmission to 29th Division HQ was recorded at 0845 and it had a plaintive air about it. 'Advance through Sedd-el-Bahr is very slow,' he reported. 'Am receiving no support on my left.'[54]

Chapter 22

'They Needed a Good Leader'

For the better part of twenty-four hours George Stoney had been a frustrated spectator to the grim events unfolding at V Beach. As Military Landing Officer he had expected to be fully engaged, working flat out to transform the beachhead into a springboard for the drive inland. Instead, he was left languishing on the *River Clyde* with 'nothing much to do'[1] but stand and watch as the landings he was supposed to help organise dissolved into near-disaster.

Since diverting on to the collier on the first morning his only contribution had been to venture out on to the barges during the night to assist with the disembarkation. His task, however, was an unenviable one: to stop the flow of wounded from the beach interfering with the movement of troops going ashore. Necessary though it was from a military point of view, it was, even to a thorough-going professional like Stoney, 'not a pleasant job with wounded men calling for help and groaning with agony'.[2]

A small, delicately featured man, bronzed by long service in the Near East, George Stoney was, like his father before him, a King's Own Scottish Borderer to the core. He was one of a number of officers attached to the Egyptian Army hurriedly recruited by the expeditionary force to fill a variety of logistical roles in the invasion. At heart, he remained an infantryman who wanted nothing more than to 'get back to the Regiment'.[3] But with that avenue temporarily denied him, he had sought and found 'a definite job'[4] as part of Beachmaster Robert Lambert's team. Unfortunately, with the beach he was charged with turning into a base still a battleground, that particular 'job' looked a distant prospect on the morning of 26 April.

A forlorn and seemingly redundant Stoney was, therefore, only too happy to accept the offer of employment better suited to his temperament and his training. It came to him, around 0900, from an officer whose instincts were not dissimilar to his own.

As a liaison officer with no clear role to play until the beach was secured, 'Dick' Doughty-Wylie had 'sat and suffered'[5] throughout the previous day's myriad agonies. Eventually, with all the men from *River Clyde* disembarked, he had accompanied Lieutenant Colonel Williams on a tour of the beach. What they saw was hardly inspiring. Most of those who had survived the storm of fire on the first morning were exhausted and dispirited. Williams later wrote:

> Next day we ought to have been able to seize the crest quite early but the men were sticky and lack of officers very apparent; they needed a good leader.[6]

Returning to the *River Clyde*, they talked the matter over. As a result of their discussion, they decided that Williams would go ashore 'and try to get the men together for [an] attack'[7] while Doughty-Wylie remained 'to watch progress and bring up the reserve of such stragglers as would be left behind'.[8] Having collected about 150 Dublins and Munsters, with 'practically no officers'[9] among them, Williams' plan was to lead his mixed force up the western slopes of V Beach in unison with Beckwith's eastern thrust into the fort and village beyond. But the operation did not fare well.

According to Williams' bleak commentary, the attack, or at least his part in it, simply 'withered away':[10]

> The Hampshires got a footing in the village but my party reduced itself to about a dozen, of the remainder the majority straggled, the rest were killed and wounded.[11]

Unable to do more and believing further advance at V Beach to be 'impossible',[12] Williams sent a message back to Doughty-Wylie informing him that he was going to try to reach W Beach to find out what conditions were like there.

Around this time, with desperate efforts being made to stave off defeat at Y Beach, 29th Division HQ aboard *Euryalus* received a flurry of messages. All of them underlined the critical nature of the fight around Cape Helles. Most alarming of all was the rapidly deteriorating situation at Y where HMS *Dublin* reported the troops landed the previous day were being attacked by 'overwhelming numbers'.[13] She was standing by to take off wounded, 'pending which troops will hold the ridge of the cliffs with rearguard'.[14]

Timed at 0830, the entry in the 29th Division war diary cited another report from Tizard that sounded a more optimistic note. He spoke of a link having been established between V and W Beaches by a company of Munsters and the Worcesters and of fierce fighting in Sedd-el-Bahr. His troops had 'forced their way into the village',[15] but their advance had been slowed 'owing to concealed machine guns'.[16] 'Sniping still continues,' he added, 'and casualties are heavy.'[17] A quarter of an hour later, 87th Brigade reported it could do nothing to assist the beleaguered troops at Y Beach until the ground in front of Hills 138 and 141 had been cleared. This news persuaded Hunter-Weston to accept Hamilton's offer of French reinforcements, which had first been muted an hour earlier. Consequently, Tizard was informed at 0900 that three French battalions were to be landed at W Beach and, from there, move via Hill 138 against the redoubt on Hill 141 overlooking V Beach. But such was the urgency, Tizard was instructed not to wait for them, but rather 'to try and get there first'.[18]

Whether or not Doughty-Wylie was aware of these developments is not clear. But he was certainly conscious of the need for decisive action. Sharing some coffee with Unwin aboard the *River Clyde*, he discussed the progress of the attack, or rather the lack of it. The collier's captain had watched several attempts to push on. All had ended in failure. During one he saw what looked like a platoon of men get into an orchard before fixing bayonets and dashing towards the village. 'They didn't get 20 yards and were all killed,'[19] he wrote. Doughty-Wylie had seen and heard enough. As the two went their separate ways, Doughty-Wylie turned to Unwin and said: 'I can't stick this any longer. I'm going to see what I can do on shore.'[20] Before leaving he met with Stoney and put a proposition to him:

> Col [onel] Doughty-Wylie asked me to come ashore with him as there was nothing doing on the boat and we might find something to do there. He walked about quite regardless of the snipers, but who as a matter of fact did not fire at us. After talking to lots of people lining fences he told me to go along the beach and whip up any effectives and advance up the front of the hill commanding the beach and get touch with a company of a Reg[imen]t that had worked up through a village on the right.[21]

It was in that direction that Doughty-Wylie headed. He was unarmed and carried with him nothing more threatening than a walking cane. For many who saw him that day, the sight of him striding out across the beach and into the ruined fortress with stick in hand would be an abiding memory. That and his *sang-froid*.

Guy Nightingale was near him when a bullet whistled through the same gateway where Walford had been killed, knocking his cap clean off his head. 'I ... remember being struck,' he later wrote, 'by the calm way in which he treated the incident.'[22] It was one of a number of narrow escapes during the dangerous hours that followed. Recalling his 'conspicuous contempt for danger'[23] throughout the fight for Sedd-el-Bahr, Nightingale, who found himself acting as Doughty-Wylie's aide, wrote:

> At that time there were countless small incidents happening all over the village which called for fearless leadership. These occurred whenever a house containing snipers had to be rushed, or a street corner, covered by a machine gun, passed ... I saw him on several occasions that morning walk into houses which might or might not contain a Turk ready to fire on the first person who came in as unconcernedly as if he were walking into a shop. Naturally this confidence of manner had a great effect on the men ...[24]

Doughty-Wylie's initial involvement was an anomalous one. He appears to have been acting under no one's direction but his own. Driven by a desire to 'do something', he advanced into the village not so much to take charge but to discover what the difficulties were and, where possible, to help inspire the troops to greater efforts. His intervention was as timely as it was fortuitous. As Nightingale commented: 'Senior officers were urgently required at the time, as nobody quite knew what was happening or what they were expected to do.'[25] But, outstanding though his contribution was, he was not the only one leading by example.

In a struggle that was characterised by almost medieval savagery, both Arthur Beckwith and Cecil Grimshaw were hardly less heroic. At one point during the fight for the village, Beckwith was seen wielding an axe he had used to cut a cable that was suspected of being linked to a land-mine. 'How Beckwith escaped, the gods know!'[26] exclaimed Williams on hearing of his exploits. 'He exposed himself recklessly, and led his men as one knew he would.'[27] Grimshaw's outstanding feats of gallantry evinced a similar mixture of praise and awe. Those who witnessed his 'deeds in the throes of close combat'[28] spoke of him in the manner of a latter-day Roland from the age of Charlemagne.

Yet, for all their bravery, the advance continued slowly in the face of dogged Turkish resistance. The pressure, however, was beginning to tell. By 1000 the men holding the positions around Hill 141 had lost their commander killed. British troops were bludgeoning their way remorselessly through the ruins of Sedd-el-Bahr. It was now no longer a case of whether they would secure a beachhead, but when. With the fight for the village continuing, a messenger arrived at Mahmut Sabri's command post on horseback. He brought with him orders to pull back to the Turkish second line, near Krithia.

Sabri was now faced with a dilemma: to carry out his instructions and risk having his men slaughtered trying to withdraw across ground covered by naval gunfire or to delay and risk seeing his men overrun in their trenches. Considering his limited options, he decided on a desperate compromise. He sent a message back saying he would try to hold out until evening in the hope of being able to retreat under the cover of darkness. Brave hope though it was, it was also a forlorn one. He later wrote:

> As time went on the enemy's strength gradually increased. Our strength on the other hand decreased and news was received from the officers that resistance could not be kept up much longer. However, our soldiers were still active and were pinning down the enemy. The enemy was advancing in rushes, [but] he was unable to assault. Many of those who rushed forward were being hit and there were many casualties. But there was no telling in what strength the landing had been made. Not an inch of ground remained which was not being shelled either by the shrapnel of the fleet or by the many machine guns of the infantry.[29]

The firepower ranged against the Turkish defenders was truly immense. And, compared with the previous day's shooting that, in Guy Geddes' opinion, 'did not material good',[30] it was far more accurate. As well as deluging the fort and village with shells, *Albion* and *Lord Nelson* were able to register hits on individual enemy posts that were holding up the advance. Such results, so gratifying to the troops struggling to make headway, were undoubtedly aided by the willingness of the ships' captains to disregard their instructions to remain 1,300 yards offshore that had hindered their efforts the day before.

Watching from *Euryalus*, Clement Milward noted with satisfaction the *Albion* 'going close in'[31] and giving the Turkish trenches above V Beach and Sedd-el-Bahr 'absolute hell with her whole broadside'.[32] An example of their effectiveness was given by one of the Army's shipboard artillery advisors, Major Alan Thomson, who had belatedly caught up with *Albion* the previous night after being inexplicably left at Tenedos:

Somewhere about 11am I saw 4 men suddenly climb the bank from the beach. As they straightened themselves out on the top all four were shot down. They fell like a pack of cards, never moved, and their bodies lay side by side on the top of the bank throughout the day. They had obviously been machine gunned. The *Albion* moved closer and yet closer in and I finally spotted through my field-glasses a couple of machine guns firing through an embrasure in the centre bastion of the south-western face of Sedd-el-Bahr fort. From the fore-top the officer in charge of the port 6-inch group was asked if he could see the machine guns and if he could lay a gun direct on to them. After a pause he announced excitedly that he could do both. The range was taken and reported to the fore-top as 600 yards. I gave the order to fire that gun myself. It was a real bullseye; a great bite was taken out of the bastion where the machine guns had been firing from and as the smoke cleared away a body of men rose up and advanced unharmed up the slope …[33]

By then, as observed by David Fyffe, British machine guns were also contributing to the storm of fire, the weapons having been lugged up through the fort and into the village. One of them, operated by Lance Corporal Stone of the Hampshires, gave splendid supporting fire from an exposed position in front of a house doorway. Blazing away, less than 200 yards from the nearest enemy trench, Stone helped counter the fire coming from Hill 141 and another position at the top of the village. He continued to do 'most excellent work' until his gun was hit and even then he refused to give in:

Lance Corporal Stone withdrew it into the doorway temporarily, while efforts were made to force a way through a back wall of a house 10 yards off, from which snipers were enfilading the advance of Z Company on the east side of the street.[34]

Most of Z Company's casualties were suffered during that final surge to the top of the village. Many of them were sustained at extreme close range, 'in some cases only five or ten yards'.[35] The last house had only just been secured a little before 1100 when Beckwith detailed Reginald Gillett to take two men and reconnoitre a small enemy redoubt still holding out on a knoll just above Sedd-el-Bahr. Gillett later wrote:

For the first time since the landing I felt completely at ease. It was, therefore, a very great shock when I received a sledge-hammer like blow on the back which sent me flying in the air. In fact, I thought I was never going to land. But I did … with a thump on my back, on top of a large heap of stone masonry and rubble. Later an officer approached me, bent down and said, 'What hit you?' My reply was, 'A damned shell, I should think'.[36]

With his back laid bare, Gillett was eventually helped back to the last ruined house in the village. There, Beckwith personally dressed his wound before leaving him to collect every available man for an attack on the Turkish position.

From just north of Sedd-el-Bahr, through the village and the fort, the ground on the right flank of V Beach had now been almost entirely cleared of defenders. But, despite having lost their commander, the remnants of Sabri's 10th Company manning positions on top of Hill 141 remained a thorn in the side of 29th Division's re-energised advance. During a morning of steady if unspectacular progress through Sedd-el-Bahr, the redoubt that overlooked the centre of the beach, though heavily shelled, was scarcely threatened by the troops pushing out from W Beach or those men gathered beneath the sandy cliff in front of the *River Clyde*. Williams' attempt to rush the western slopes had already come to nought, but what of the men sighted around the Helles lighthouse who had come so close to breaking the deadlock the night before?

Having only discovered around midnight that Hill 141 was not in British hands, Hunter-Weston had made a new plan. Accepting that a night attack was out of the question, he issued instructions for the troops holding the ridge around Guezji Baba to resume their advance at daybreak. The renewed push was to be carried out in conjunction with the attack from V Beach. But, unaccountably, the orders did not reach either the 1st Essex or the 4th Worcestershires. The only instruction given to Captain Churchill on Hill 138 was to assist the night attack that 'didn't come off'.[37] 'Bar that,' he wrote, 'we got no further orders except to j[oi]n up and dig in …'[38] Having been fully engaged helping repulse Sabri's counter-attack, they had no sleep and little appetite for the rations they ate before 'standing to' about an hour before daylight. Then, with no word of any renewed advance from V Beach, they simply stayed put in their trenches, 'firing a bit at snipers and being fired at'[39] while the troops from the 'Wooden Horse' fought and died amid the ruins of Sedd-el-Bahr. Their inertia was mirrored by the Worcesters. From his position in one of the captured Turkish redoubts, Lieutenant Colonel Cayley merely reported at 0833: 'Situation unchanged since this morning. Fairly hot fire maintained against my trenches from the direction of Sedd-el-Bahr.'[40] The rest of the morning was passed idly waiting for further instructions and being intermittently shelled with little loss.

The lack of action from W Beach in support of Tizard's force may, in part, be explained by the growing crisis further north. By the time the Dublins, Hampshires and Munsters were fighting their way into the village, Hunter-Weston's attention was fixed on Y Beach, where a full-scale evacuation was under way. His ebullience of the night before had evaporated. Fearing that the neighbouring beachhead at X might, in turn, be threatened, he warned Brigadier-General William Marshall at 0900 to 'establish his left strongly against an attack from the North'.[41]

Hunter-Weston's concern was further underlined a little over an hour later when, at 1010, he signalled commanders at both X and W Beaches, ordering them to consolidate and not to advance until the French reinforcements were landed.[42] Those orders remained in force in spite of a report, albeit a premature one, sent back to the *River Clyde* by Doughty-Wylie at 1035 in which he claimed Sedd-el-Bahr 'taken' and his force 'well posted for attack on 141'.[43] If this report reached Hunter-Weston, and it not clear that it did, it may have been enough to convince him that the advance was going well and did not require further help. Whatever the truth, nothing was done to assist, still less to exploit, the advance through the village until around midday when Tizard informed 29th Division HQ that he was 'reinforcing Colonel Wylie'[44] in readiness for a final push on Hill 141.

Until that moment Tizard's involvement in the direction of the attack had been minimal. Apart from passing messages back to Hunter-Weston and helping pinpoint targets for the supporting ships, he could do little to influence the course of the fighting. Having delegated responsibility for executing the breakout to Beckwith, Doughty-Wylie, Walford and Williams, he faced an uncomfortable wait for news aboard a *River Clyde* that had once more become a target for Turkish batteries on the other side of the Dardanelles. Resuming their long-range bombardment of the collier, the guns sited on the Asiatic shore 'secured two hits on the vessel, one of which cut the [ship's] steam pipe'.[45]

Stirred into action, he signalled *Albion*, calling for gun fire 'to be brought to bear on houses back from the shore, high up in the village'.[46] He then saw what he imagined was a party, about a section strong, of Worcesters on the cliffs to the left. 'Some had got through the barbed wire and had got as far as the hospital ruins,' he wrote, 'but they were driven out and went back to their original position.'[47] It was, therefore, with great relief that he received Doughty-Wylie's message telling him that his force was 'through'[48] Sedd-el-Bahr and poised to strike at Hill 141.

His response was swift. He resolved to support the planned attack by marshalling the men spread along the foreshore and mounting a direct assault up the terraced slopes, through the belts of barbed wire and into the redoubt. Sending word to Doughty-Wylie that he would 'push an attack up by the left of the village to co-operate with him at once',[49] he, at the same time, despatched a runner to Captain Stoney, outlining his plan and 'asking him to collect all men fit for work'.[50]

Stoney had spent most of the morning trying to do just that, but without much success. Those few officers he could find were mostly wounded and of 'very little help'.[51] And, after all they had been through, the men were reluctant to chance their luck again against Turkish defences that had repelled every previous attempt to get on. He was still trying to prod them into action when Tizard's message arrived telling him 'to take all I could find on the beach and advance with them'.[52] The time for shilly-shallying was over. 'That made it quite clear to me what I was to do,'[53] wrote Stoney.

Armed with his commander's written order, he began marshalling his troops. It proved a difficult task. 'They were distributed all along the bank,' observed Tizard, 'and care had to be taken as men were still getting hit directly they moved from under the bank.'[54] But move they did. Under Stoney's leadership, they were gradually brought together and positioned ready for the attack. Crouching beneath the bank, Stoney spoke to each small party in turn to make sure they understood what was expected of them. Then, pep talk over, he took his place among a group of Munsters and prepared to lead them forward. All was set, but the waiting was not quite over.

Further up the slopes, on the outskirts of Sedd-el-Bahr, 'Dick' Doughty-Wylie's had decided to call on the Navy for one more effort to further reduce the already battered defences on Hill 141. His plan made and instructions relayed, via the *River Clyde*, to the supporting ships, he retired to watch the bombardment from one of the corner turrets of the captured fortress. The drama of V Beach was about to enter its final act.

Chapter 23

'The Lads Came on Like Devils'

During a morning of relentless pressure the Turks above V Beach had displayed fortitude beyond the call of duty. Outnumbered and outgunned, handfuls of men had disputed every yard of rubble-heaped ground to reduce to a crawl the British advance through Sedd-el-Bahr. But now it was the turn of the defenders on Hill 141 to once again bear the brunt of the Royal Navy's firepower.

At 1252, in answer to Doughty-Wylie's request, the guns of the *Albion* swung away from the village to target enemy positions 'seen on [the] left of the castle'.[1] *Cornwallis* and *Lord Nelson* joined in until the heights were swallowed by a seething cauldron of smoke and flame. Through the pall Turkish defenders could be seen running from their smashed trenches. The firing grew 'heavier and heavier'[2] with machine guns and riflemen aboard the *River Clyde* joining in the barrage of shot and shell. 'Not an inch of ground remained which was not being shelled either by the shrapnel of the fleet or by the many machine guns of the infantry,'[3] wrote Mahmut Sabri. The plight of the Turks above V Beach had become hopeless. Sabri admitted:

> There was no possibility now of soldiers or animals moving between Kirte and Seddulbahir [*sic*], for the enemy fleet was combing this area with fire to stop help coming. Therefore there was no other course but to stand firm until the evening, and word was passed round that every care must be taken not to waste the existing ammunition.[4]

By early afternoon every last bullet had been rushed forward into the front line and there was no chance of any more. The crisis point had been reached if not passed. The Turks were now being squeezed from western and eastern flanks. Casualties were increasing and ammunition diminishing. Reports from the forward positions carried the same bleak

250

message: 'that resistance could not be kept up much longer'.[5] One officer, his post choked with dead and wounded, struggled back to headquarters to report the parlous situation on the heights above V Beach. Suphi Effendi made his way back with the promise of two more sections from Sabri's dwindling reserve and with instructions 'not to leave his trenches without an order'.[6]

A few hundred yards away, a burly, red-tabbed staff officer looked on with grim satisfaction as the shells ploughed the ground around Hill 141. 'Dick' Doughty-Wylie appeared calm and unruffled as he discussed his plan of attack with Guy Nightingale. After all the travails of the day before and the stiff fight for the village that morning, he appeared to harbour no doubts about the outcome of the operation. As Nightingale later wrote:

> He decided that the remnants of the three battalions should assault simultaneously immediately after the bombardment. He was extraordinarily confident that everything would go well, and the hill be won by sunset, and I think it was due much to his spirit of confidence that he had been able to overcome the enormous difficulties with only such exhausted and disorganised troops as he had to deal with. His sole idea and determination was that the hill should be taken that day at all costs; for he realised that it was impossible for us to hold any position between the high ground and the edge of the cliff where we had spent the previous night. As the time was getting near for the bombardment to cease, the Colonel gave his final orders to the few remaining officers before the assault. Major Grimshaw [sic] was to lead the Dublins. Simultaneously the Hampshires were to assault from the far end of the village and come up on the far shoulder of the hill, while the Munster Fusiliers were to advance on the left of the Dublins, and at the same time.[7]

As the moment drew close, Doughty-Wylie left the fort and headed up through the village to where his men were forming up, 'under some garden walls in a small orchard'.[8] A working party of sappers was busy amid the ruins of Sedd-el-Bahr, building barricades to counter the last remaining snipers. But Doughty-Wylie was no longer interested in the village. His sole focus was the attack on Hill 141.

Pausing briefly to talk with Beckwith, whose Hampshires were in the process of ejecting some Turks from the northern edge of Sedd-el-Bahr, he then met with Grimshaw. In those final moments, counting down to the assault, the senior surviving officer of the Dublins exhorted his weary men to one last effort. Evoking a memory of happier times, Grimshaw barked: 'Do you want to go back to Nuneaton?'[9] It was hardly the stuff of Shakespeare and King Hal, but it did the trick. 'Aye' came the reply and a cheer rose from the ranks. 'Very well, then,' he responded, 'make a brilliant charge and may the best men live to return to Nuneaton.'[10]

At 1324, the ships' guns fell silent 'at [the] request of the military'.[11] The fire from the *River Clyde* lasted a little longer. According to Major Carr, Wedgwood's machine gunners and an assortment of sharpshooters continued to target the redoubt until they saw the troops 'fix bayonets and charge'.[12]

The exact time of the assault is unclear. Surviving records are at variance on the matter: most have it starting around 1400, some a good deal earlier while a few put it as much as an hour later.[13] Clement Milward, who was watching events from the bridge of *Euryalus*, timed it at 1400. In his diary, he excitedly wrote:

> I saw a cloud of men, who had come from the upper houses of Seddul Bahr [*sic*] and had been lining a bank for some time, suddenly fling themselves forward and rush uphill and swarm over the Old Castle [Hill 141]. At the same time others came from Hill 138. All were running as hard as they could, as though they were under heavy fire …[14]

Making their way up from the beach towards the first belt of barbed wire were the scattering of Munsters hastily organised into a single force by George Stoney. They included about forty non-commissioned officers and men collected after 'a great effort'[15] by Second Lieutenant Hugh Brown.

Among them was the towering figure of William Cosgrove. At 6ft 6in tall, the twenty-six-year-old corporal was a commanding presence in the ranks of a battalion he had served faithfully if unspectacularly for a little over six years. Naturally reserved, he was a strongly built man who led by example. One of his comrades, a nineteen-year-old Private Edward O'Brien, later wrote:

> He was a quiet sort of fellow. Not good as a mixer … He was not a man to make friends with many of his comrades. Nevertheless a good soldier … determined in all his actions. He was not a fellow I would like to cross or lock horns with.[16]

O'Brien recalled an incident during the unit's passage to the Dardanelles. A fight broke out but Cosgrove swiftly put a stop to it by simply 'muscling in and bashing their heads together'.[17] It had been a powerful demonstration of the young Irishman's strength of character as well as his physical prowess. However, now a greater test lay ahead, one that Cosgrove did not anticipate he would survive. As a member of the small party tasked with cutting a path through the wire, he knew he would be in the forefront of the charge up the slopes and, as a result, a prime target for the Turks on top of the hill. As he later related:

> I thought, when I heard the work I was detailed for, that I would never again have the opportunity of a day's fighting. However, the work was there; it had to be done, for on its success rested the safety of many men, as well as the opportunity it would afford them of helping to throw back the Turks.[18]

The cutting party was led by Company Sergeant Major Alfred Bennett and to reach the 60-yard curtain of 'thickly constructed barbed wire entanglements'[19] they had to cross a bare stretch of ground covered by machine guns and snipers. They had hardly set off when 'a storm of lead'[20] burst around them. Bennett was almost immediately shot through the head and killed outright.[21] Cosgrove straightaway took charge:

> I ... shouted to the boys to come on. From the village near at hand came a terrible fire to swell the murderous hail of bullets from the trenches ...[22]

Urged on by Cosgrove, they made as fast as they could for the wire and threw themselves down in front of it. They had covered about 40 yards, though it felt more like a hundred to Cosgrove. 'I don't know whether I ran or prayed the faster,'[23] he later remarked. Accounts of what followed vary in detail but not in substance. Whereas Brown claimed they only possessed one pair of cutters between them, Cosgrove recalled there being more. Either way, progress was painfully slow and the pliers of little use against wire so thick that 'a bird could not go through it'.[24] As Cosgrove remarked:

> You might as well try and snip Cloyne Round Tower with a lady's scissors ... The wire was of great strength, strained as tight as a fiddle-string, and so full of spikes or thorns that you could not get the cutters between. 'Heavens,' said I, 'we're done'; a moment later I threw the pliers from me.[25]

Cosgrove was angry rather than defeated. O'Brien, who was nearby firing as hard as he could, believed he was maddened by the 'useless slaughter'[26] around him. What followed was an extraordinary feat of physical courage almost certainly born of sheer rage and frustration. Utterly careless of the bullets zipping around him, he lifted his giant frame to his full height, grasped hold of the nearest wooden stake that was holding up the wire and began shaking it out of the ground.

> 'Pull them up,' I roared, 'put your arms round them and pull them out of the ground.' I dashed at the first one; heaved and strained, and then it came into my arms and same as you'd lift a child. I believe there was wild cheering when they saw what I was at, but I only heard the screech of the bullets and saw dust rising all round from where they hit.[27]

Cosgrove had no idea how many posts he uprooted before others joined in. Brown credited him with single-handedly clearing a gap 30 yards wide. But all Cosgrove cared about was that the barrier had been breached. The moment the wire was down 'the rest of the lads came on like 'devils".[28] Their wild charge was matched on the right by the ruck of men surging from the ruins of Sedd-el-Bahr. Guy Nightingale later wrote:

> When the order came to fix bayonets ... the men scarcely waited for any orders, but all joined up together in one mass, and swept, cheering, up through an orchard and over a cemetery, Hampshires, Munsters and Dublins, to the first line of wire entanglement, through which was the way out leading past the deserted Turkish trenches to the summit of the hill.[29]

To his sister, he added:

> My company led the attack with the Dubliners and we had a great time. We saw the enemy, which was the chief thing, and the men all shouted and enjoyed it tremendously. It was a relief after all that appalling sniping.[30]

They were led most of the way by Doughty-Wylie. Amid the crowd sweeping across the hill, he was visible, waving his stick above his head. Weir de Lancey Williams was among those who saw him. Having made his way back to V Beach, he was just in time to find Doughty-Wylie preparing to lead the final assault. Williams, who noted the plan was little different from the one that had failed earlier in the day, offered to 'whip up the reserve'.[31]

As the charge went in, he followed their progress towards the redoubt, his gaze fixed on his friend. 'I noticed him on two or three occasions,' he wrote, 'always in front and cheering his men on.'[32]

Quite who was first to reach the Turkish position is uncertain. According to survivors' accounts gathered by Williams after the battle, 'Dick' Doughty-Wylie headed the charge until 'the last few yards'[33] when he was overtaken by four or five men. By then they had reached the 20ft deep moat that encircled the redoubt. The only away in was via a narrow entrance that led up and over the ditch. There was barely a pause as the leading party swarmed across. Had the Turks been in any strength, the results of such impetuosity might have been costly. But realising the game was up most of the Turks had already fled before the final onslaught and the rush into the redoubt was virtually unopposed.

The men pushing up from the beach benefitted too from the Turks' withdrawal. As George Stoney wrote:

> We did not come under any very heavy fire, only losing about 4 men wounded. We rushed the line of trenches and saw the Turks clearing out. Not many getting away alive. The place proved to have been held by only a very few men – certainly if there had been more we could not have got up as easily as we did. [34]

The final charge, however, was not an entirely bloodless affair. Among the casualties suffered in the closing stages was the Munsters' own hero of the hour. Having come through the desperate struggle to clear the wire unscathed, William Cosgrove was hit by a burst of fire as he neared the crest of the hill. One of the bullets passed through his body, clipping his backbone before exiting through his right side. 'Strange … though I did not realise it,'[35] he later said. Running on a few more yards, his momentum carried him into an enemy trench, where he collapsed.

As he lay bleeding, a volley of shots chased the last of Sabri's brave 10th Company off Hill 141. Having suffered so badly and for so long at their hands, the Irish fusiliers were in no mood to let them off lightly. As Nightingale recorded:

> The men lined round the top edge of the moat firing down on the retreating Turks, who were retiring down their communication trenches in the direction of Achi Baba.[36]

Watching from the *Euryalus*, Clement Milward could hardly contain himself:

> I rushed down to the General's cabin and told him we had gained the 'Old Castle', so now the whole ridge along the south of the Peninsula was ours.[37]

The battle for V Beach had, indeed, been won, but success came at a heavy price. One of the last to fall was 'Dick' Doughty-Wylie. The staff officer without a specific role had gone aboard 'the Wooden Horse' with the vague idea that he might be of some help to the landing force. In the end, he had been a critical factor in turning defeat into victory. During five hours of intense action that followed a day of bloody and dispiriting failure he had inspired all around by his reckless bravery. But, in his moment of triumph, he had taken one chance too many.

With the hill secured and success assured, he had tarried on the skyline to watch his men take pot-shots at the retreating Turks. It was a fatal misjudgement.

A few of the Turks had taken shelter in a trench to the rear of the position and, for all their precariousness, they could hardly resist such tempting targets. Shots peppered the parapet of their old position. Most of the men lining the redoubt immediately went to ground, but not Doughty-Wylie. For reasons that will forever remain a mystery, he stayed standing, a lonely figure totally exposed on the crest of the hill that would soon bear his name. What followed was a tragic inevitability. One of the Munsters, Private William Flynn, recalled:

> I was laid down with the company and he was stood up alongside of me, with his orderly. They were shouting to him, 'Get down, sir, you'll get hit!' … He wouldn't and an explosive bullet hit him just below the eye, blew all the side of his face out – and his orderly got killed.[38]

Moments later a burst of fire from one of the Hampshires' Maxims over to the right silenced the Turks. But it was too late for Doughty-Wylie. According to Guy Nightingale, the chief architect of the victory at V Beach died 'almost immediately'.[39]

Doughty-Wylie's loss was compounded shortly afterwards by the death 'under similar circumstances'[40] of one of his boldest 'lieutenants'. With the possible exceptions of Garth Walford and Arthur Beckwith, no one had done more to galvanise the remnants of the landing force than Cecil Grimshaw. In many ways his achievement was the greatest of all. Alone of the senior officers who led the successful attacks on Sedd-el-Bahr and Hill 141, he had endured the grim struggle ashore on the first day.

As one of the few Dublin officers to survive a landing in which so many of his battalion had been slaughtered or left physically and mentally drained, he had worked tirelessly to instil fresh heart into men fighting beyond the limits of exhaustion. Heedless of danger throughout, he, like Doughty-Wylie before him, ultimately succumbed to needless risk. According to one of his subalterns, Desmond O'Hara, he 'simply threw away his life by standing up and screaming in the way he always used to do – there was no need for it at all and we could ill spare him but he was a real brave man and no mistake'.[41]

The unnecessary loss of such brave and charismatic leaders was a grievous blow to an invasion force already seriously depleted of senior officers. But there was little time to mourn. While Stoney and Nightingale began the task of consolidating the hilltop redoubt, Beckwith, with a portion of the Hampshires, forged on to reach a ridge studded with windmills from where it was possible to look down on Morto Bay.

There, having disposed of a couple of snipers, they dug in while hundreds more enemy soldiers continued to stream back from the direction of V Beach.

One of those struggling to escape was Mahmut Sabri. The commander of the Turkish around Cape Helles had known for some time that his men were almost at the end of their tether. He had briefly contemplated leading them in one last bayonet charge, but ruled it out as a futile gesture. Instead of self-destruction, he sanctioned a partial withdrawal, issuing orders at 1300 for the 200 or so survivors of the 11th and 12th Companies to pull back to Morto Bay. Even then, he recognised it would be touch and go if they made it. Already pressed on three sides, they were being heavily shelled by the British battleships standing off Sedd-el-Bahr.

As pressure mounted, the messages from the frontline became increasingly forlorn. At 1430, the commander of those troops still resisting around the Hill 141 redoubt brought back depressing news. 'Owing to the intensity of the bombardment,' he told Sabri, 'nothing that could be called trenches remained and that the defenders had been much reduced.'[42] His was not the only grim tiding. Not long after, a report reached Sabri's HQ from the embattled defenders on the 'western front' stating that 'it was impossible to hold on and that the battle could not be continued without [more] ammunition'.[43]

All hope of clinging on until nightfall had gone and, observed Sabri, 'there was no course left but to flee'.[44] But that was no simple task for men fighting for their lives and with the ground behind them swept by naval gunfire. With communication between his HQ and some of his positions all but non-existent just informing his troops of his decision was difficult enough:

> The commander of the battalion belonging to the 25th Regiment was sought [but] could not be found … There was no information from our units, only enemy could be seen at every hand … In fact, our line of retreat had been encircled on right and left …[45]

Waiting until the firing around V Beach slackened, Sabri gave his last order: 'to withdraw up the Kirte and Kanlidere streams … to the second line'.[46] The instruction was delivered wherever possible by messengers sent 'in every direction'.[47] Sabri's final act before leaving was the most heart-breaking of all. As his staff prepared to pull back, he made his way to the dressing station where about seventy wounded men were being treated:

> They were told that those who were able to walk would go with their comrades and those who were incapable would remain where they were. In accordance with the rules of war, the enemy would not do the wounded any harm. Sacks full of bread and two tins of water were left by them.[48]

Many were in tears and some complained bitterly at being abandoned. 'You have been promising us since yesterday that carts would come and now you are going to go off and leave us,'[49] they cried. An emotional Sabri found it 'impossible not to be affected',[50] but beyond offering a few consoling words could do nothing more. As the walking wounded struggled to their feet, rifles were collected and loaded on to a donkey and then they were gone.

A splutter of rifle fire hurried them on their way, but the real danger came from the Navy's guns, which were ranging across the open ground between Sedd-el-Bahr and Morto Bay. Sabri wrote: 'The fire grew fiercer … to comb the whole ground.'[51] It was the start of a nightmare journey, a stumbling retreat along hidden streams with the ground quaking beneath their feet:

> In some places the depth of water in the stream was up to the knees and in others up to the thighs. If one moved out of the water, one would be exposed to the fierce fire of the enemy.[52]

Unable to make out landmarks through the pall of smoke and dust, Sabri's party blundered past the second line. In an effort to find his way,

Sabri scrambled out of the stream and into the fire-zone. But only two of his men were prepared to follow him through the storm of shrapnel. And even those went no further than the nearest shell-hole before seeking cover. Their caution was understandable.

From the crow's nests of the ships lying off V Beach, gunnery observation officers had a clear view of the Turkish retreat. Those perched high above the decks of the battleship *Lord Nelson* reported seeing somewhere in the region of 1,500 men falling back towards Morto Bay. In one group alone, there were estimated to be 400 men. They were immediately targeted with devastating results. 'They got awfully hammered,'[53] wrote Midshipman Fraser MacLiesh aboard *HMS Agamemnon*. 'Occasionally one would see a shell land clean among a bunch of them and as it exploded heads, legs and whole bodies were lifted up and blown sky-high in all directions.'[54]

Sabri was lucky. Emerging from the onslaught miraculously unscathed, he somehow managed to find his way to the Turkish second line where he discovered the remnants of the two companies he had ordered away just before the end. His first thought, though, was for the party he had left behind:

> Two men were ordered to go in rushes as far as the stream and to shout, 'the second line of defence is here. The Major is here. Come on'. [But] although this order was carried out, nothing resulted from it and nobody left the stream.[55]

While Sabri was trying to reorganise his shattered force, the new occupants of Sedd-el-Bahr were already busy transforming the battlefield into a base camp. Hill 141 had hardly been wrested from the Turks than it became a hive of activity as men and materials were rushed up on to the newly captured heights. Among the first to make his way on to the crest was Henry Tizard.

Pre-empting Doughty-Wylie's triumph, he had scribbled a hurried message to 29th Division HQ and taken his first steps ashore even as his troops were enveloping the hilltop redoubt. Leaving the sanctuary of the *River Clyde*, he chose to skirt Sedd-el-Bahr on the right in order to get a clearer idea of the difficulties his men had faced. 'There was still a good many snipers in the village,' he wrote, 'and parties of men had been left at various points to keep this down.'[56]

By the time he reached Hill 141 at around 1430 V Beach was, at last, effectively secured, though small, isolated pockets of resistance remained to be mopped up. Surveying his 'new position',[57] he found that 'the Munsters and Dublins were in possession of the hill and the

Hampshire companies were on the right at the end of the village on a small hill'.[58] Over to the left Cayley's Worcesters, having finally received orders to advance and 'join hands'[59] with the troops 'swarming into [the] old castle'[60] otherwise known as Hill 141, were advancing slowly, 'clearing the ground'[61] between Hill 138 and the ruins of a Turkish hospital.

For the most part, however, the Turks appeared to be interested only in escaping the clutches of the invaders as they continued to drift slowly back, harried by 'shrapnel fire'[62] from the Navy's attendant ships, towards the Krithia Road. Over the course of the next hour or so, a line of sorts gradually took shape across the toe of the peninsula and by 1600, with the junction between W and V Beaches made, British troops occupied positions from the cliffs east of Sedd-el-Bahr through Hill 141 and the redoubts on the western flank to the sandy cove at Tekke Burnu.

This was the scene that greeted a greatly relieved Sir Ian Hamilton half an hour later as the *Queen Elizabeth* made its way back to Cape Helles from Gaba Tepe where she had spent most of the day adding her firepower to the support of Birdwood's Anzacs. The first to realise the change in fortunes at V Beach was Jack Churchill. From his lofty position in the ship's crow's nest, he suddenly noticed the tiny figures of men standing 'in the open'[63] at the back of the 'old castle'. He wrote:

> There could be no doubt, only English soldiers would stand about like that. Clearly the ridge behind Seddel-Bahr [sic] was ours. And if so – then V Beach was relieved from pressure ... Sir Ian came up from tea and as he passed asked whether there was anything new. I told him what I could see and that I believed the coast line was all ours. He was very excited and doubtful of any such good fortune. But the position was soon clear. A few minutes later the whole plateau above Helles and Seddel-Bahr [sic] came into view. It was covered with men standing up and walking about, in spots where three hours ago I had seen skirmishers crawling under fire. The amphitheatre had been taken and the whole of Seddel-Bahr [sic] was in our hands.[64]

'Ah, well,' Hamilton noted in his diary, 'that is a load off our minds: every one smiling.'[65]

Ashore, consolidation rather than exploitation was the main focus. To that end, Hunter-Weston ordered Mynors Farmar to cross to V Beach to ensure that the dispositions made by Tizard 'along the right of the line were sound'.[66] Tizard, meanwhile, was busy strengthening his position. 'Parties were sent down to the beach to bring up tools, ammunition and water,' he wrote, 'and the force under my command were given their line on which to entrench.'[67]

From the beach, there flowed a constant stream of men, offering support and succour. Harry Carr's detached party of Worcesters spent an hour collecting casualties and carrying them back to the *River Clyde* before lugging thirty boxes of ammunition back up the slopes. Only then, some thirty-three hours since they had become separated, did they finally rejoin their battalion on the left of Hill 141. The ground around them was littered with the detritus of conflict; fly-covered corpses and fragments of abandoned equipment.

As David Fyffe made his 'toilsome way'[68] up a slope ablaze with poppies and yellow and white marguerites he was struck by the sight of the men heading in the opposite direction. One of a small party led by Josiah Wedgwood despatched from the *River Clyde* with two Maxims to help consolidate the newly won ground, he skirted the village while 'little driblets' of wounded trickled past them:

> Men who, supported by friends on either side, hopped slowly along trying to keep one foot, swathed in blood-stained bandages, off the ground and uttering strange words when their supporters stumbled over the stones. And sometimes there were bearer-parties with a loaded stretcher that they carried with scrupulous care, and when these silent parties passes, the little group of soldiers sitting chattering and smoking by the wayside ceased their talk and gazed with pitying eyes at the still figure that lay, half covered by his overcoat on the swaying stretcher.[69]

The naval machine gunners found their way into a small orchard at the top of the village. It was there, amid the ruins of Sedd-el-Bahr, that the savagery of the fighting was most apparent. Wedgwood later wrote:

> If you have never felt afraid, try crawling up a gutter, crawling over dead men, with every wall and corner hiding a marksman trying to kill you. We got the guns into position, and then cleared that village, peering into dark rooms and broken courts in the growing twilight. Everywhere were our dead Munsters and Dublins, some horribly mutilated and burnt ...[70]

George Davidson discovered similarly shocking scenes after being summoned to Hill 141 by a false report that Doughty-Wylie and Grimshaw were 'badly wounded'.[71] Finding them dead, he made himself useful treating some wounded in a garden at the top of the village. Curiosity then got the better of him. He decided to head back to the *River Clyde* via Sedd-el-Bahr, which he had been assured was now safe though the occasional crack and whine of bullets suggested otherwise. He was alone and armed only with his service revolver. Just recalling that 'mad'[72] journey was enough to make him 'shiver':[73]

> I peered into a number of wrecked houses – every house had been blown to bits – and I had not long returned when sniping commenced from a prominent corner house I had just passed. The only living things I saw in the village were two cats and a dog. I was very sorry for a cat that had cuddled close to the face of a dead Turk in the street, one leg embracing the top of his head. I went up to stroke and sympathise with it for the loss of what I took to be its master, when I found that the upper part of the man's head had been blown away, and the cat was enjoying a meal of human brains. The dog followed till I came upon three Dublin Fusiliers, who wished to shoot it straight away when I pleaded for it, but one of them had a shot at it when my back was turned and the poor brute went off howling. I had done my best, when going along the fosse of the 'Old Fort', to save a badly wounded Turk from three of another battalion who were standing over him and discussing the advisability of putting an end to him, but I am afraid my interference was in vain here also.[74]

Walking on through the village, he stumbled across the body of a young Dublin officer, 'all huddled up among long weeds and nettles'.[75] The last time they had met was over a meal on the *Ausonia* a few days before. Theirs was not the only poignant meeting that afternoon. Following in the wake of the gallant charge that had driven the Turks from their last stronghold above V Beach, Weir de Lancey Williams found 'Dick' Doughty-Wylie 'lying dead inside the 'Castle' [*sic*] on top of the hill'.[76] He later wrote:

> The men round about were full of admiration and sorrow … I took his watch, money and a few things I could find and had him buried where he fell. I had this done at once having seen such disgusting sights of unburied dead in the village that I could not bear to leave him lying there. This was all done hurriedly as I had to reorganise the line and think of further advance or digging in; we just buried him as he lay and I said 'The Lord's Prayer' over his grave and bid him goodbye.[77]

262

Chapter 24
'We Have Achieved the Impossible'

The capture of Hill 141 gave Tizard command of the shore and safety from all but a few diehard defenders holed up in ruined houses or hidden in rocky lairs. But, as the men toiling to bring order to the beachhead quickly discovered, it afforded little security from long-range bombardment. The arduous work of clearance and consolidation had barely begun when Turkish guns on the Asiatic shore opened fire. Having resumed his primary role as Military Landing Officer, George Stoney was an uncomfortable witness to the burgeoning base's vulnerability to shelling:

> They have never sent over so many. How on earth nobody was hit, it is hard to understand. One could hear them coming along some time before they fell.[1]

Not for the first time, nor for the last, the *River Clyde* appeared to be the focal point for the Turkish batteries. The collier already bore the scars of a number of direct hits during the landing. Now her holed and splintered decks were shaken again as shell after shell burst around her. Luckily the gunners' aim proved wayward. Tizard wrote of the 'blind'[2] bombardment recommencing shortly after fighting ceased on V Beach and lasting for 'about half an hour without much result'.[3] Of the eighteen or so shots on 26 April that appeared to be aimed in the general direction of the beached ship, George Davidson recorded only one direct hit.

In the days that followed such bombardments would become so commonplace that men would learn to judge the fall of shells by their sound as they shrieked over the Dardanelles. But even on that second day, when the experience was still relatively novel, the disruption was small. Wilfrid Malleson, who had rejoined his 'somewhat thinned out beach party',[4] maintained that the work of unloading ammunition and water lighters was only 'interrupted slightly by 4.7 inch or 5 inch common [shells] from Asia'.[5] He, like many others on V Beach that day, was anxious to make up for lost time. None more so than Edward Unwin.

The captain of the *River Clyde* was well aware that only half of his mission had been accomplished. And having delivered a 'skimpy'[6] progress report to Wemyss aboard *Euryalus* he was eager to turn his attention to the second part of the plan: converting the 'Wooden Horse' into a 'useful base for assisting the troops we had landed'.[7] The idea, as Wemyss had made clear, was for the collier to act as both depot and shelter, 'where wounded might receive attention and as a pier from which, with her good derricks, guns and stores might be landed'.[8] More immediately, she represented the greatest single source of fresh water with the wherewithal for condensing many gallons a day to make up for shortages ashore.

Water was a priority. The troops had had none since the day before and, according to Stoney, 'they wanted it badly'.[9] Unwin was determined not to let them down. Just as soon as the danger from rifle fire ceased, he set to work:

> I had got two 500 gallon tanks ready beforehand, each with 48 taps to them, so that the troops could fill their water bottles in the shortest possible time. These tanks were now got ashore and hoses run along the lighters to the beach, and into the tanks, and soon the troops were supplied; British and French troops used this means of supply for several weeks ...[10]

Assisting him to meet the Army's demands were a team of naval engineers despatched from *Cornwallis*. Among them was Chief Engine Room Artificer T. Stevens, who had originally been sent to mend the ship's main steam pipe which had been shot away during the landing, thus disabling the forward winches. Returning with a larger party, he joined efforts to improve on the 'crude'[11] and 'entirely inadequate'[12] distillation system on board. It proved an eventful assignment:

> As we arrived with our tools and material, *River Clyde* was having a rough time from the Turkish shells on the Asiatic coast. They were falling thick and fast, the ship was getting badly battered, and daylight could be seen through her in many places.
> Steam was heard escaping from the interior, and on examination I found that quite a number of pipes had suffered; and we got to

More than 60 years later, the *Victor* comic of 31 January, 1976, featured the story of Doughty-Wylie's heroism on its front and back cover.

Above: A cross marks the graves of Captains Walford and Addison who were killed close together as troops from the *River Clyde* pushed up into the village.

Below: The burial of Arthur Coke on 3 May, 1915. Coke had commanded the machine-guns in the f'c'stle of the *River Clyde*, a position he regarded as 'his seat in the stalls'.

Above: A view of V Beach as it is today, as seen from the headland on which Fort Ertugrul is located. In the middle distance is V Beach Cemetery, with the village of Sedd-el-Bahr just beyond and the old castle in the distance. (Historic Military Press)

Below: A closer view of Sedd-el-Bahr and the castle (which is also known as Sedd el Bahr Kale or *Eski Kale*, literally 'Old Castle'). The location of the spit of rock and improvised piers that, in time, linked the *River Clyde* with the beach can just be seen. (Historic Military Press)

Above: The interior of Fort Ertugrul. Whilst the British designated the castle as Fort No.3, Fort Ertugrul was named Fort No.1. On the outbreak of war, Fort Ertugrul was equipped with no less than ten artillery pieces, including a pair of 240mm Krupp L/35 guns. (Historic Military Press)

Below: A surviving 240mm Krupp L/35 gun at Fort Ertugrul. Prior to the landings on 25 April, Fort Ertugrul had been bombarded by the Royal Navy on 25 February, 1915, when much damage was done. (Historic Military Press)

Above: Reconstructed Turkish trenches on the headland overlooking V Beach. Fort Ertugrul is to the right of the photographer. In the distance, beyond Sedd-el-Bahr castle, is the opening of the Dardanelles. (Historic Military Press)

Below: Looking down on V Beach from the walls of Sedd-el-Bahr castle. The Helles Memorial can be seen on the horizon, whilst just in front of it is Fort Ertugrul. (Historic Military Press)

Above: The narrow strip of beach at Sedd-el-Bahr – note the small bank on the left. The *River Clyde* was located roughly in the area where the nearest white boat can be seen. (Historic Military Press)

Below: Looking up at Sedd-el-Bahr castle from the remains of the sand spit which marks the spot where the *River Clyde* was beached on 25 April.(Historic Military Press)

Above: The postern gate where Garth Walford was killed leading the charge into Sedd-el-Bahr village as it is today, albeit now bricked up. (Historic Military Press)

Below: 'Dick' Doughty-Wylie's lone grave on the summit of Hill 141, marking the very spot where he was killed. Note the Commonwealth War Grave Commission grave marker. (Historic Military Press)

Located right on the shore at V Beach, is V Beach Cemetery. There are now 696 servicemen of the First World War buried or commemorated in this cemetery; 480 of the burials are unidentified. Special memorials commemorate 196 officers and men, nearly all belonging to the units which landed on 25 April, known or believed to be buried among them. (Historic Military Press)

work forthwith, and did the best we could under limited circumstances. A large shell suddenly passed down through the deck above, cutting a huge hole in the waste-pipe, and, taking with it eighteen inches of the auxiliary steam-pipe, went through the fore and aft bulkhead, finally ending its career in a heap of coal-dust, where our little forge was standing. Fortunately, it did not explode. The following day three more shells passed clean through the ship above the water-line, taking one man's head off and wounding four others.[13]

V Beach, as Engineer Commander W. H. Crichton testified, was 'a lively spot, especially towards sunset, when the light seemed to favour the Turkish gunners, and several rounds of small shell plopped about in the water and mud'.[14] The work, however, continued uninterrupted with the naval party, in Crichton's words, displaying 'a delightful nonchalance'.[15] Then, with the new arrangements in place, Unwin got on with his next task:

> As soon as I had got the water in full swing, I got a party of shipwrights from the Admiral, and we got underweigh [sic] with making a permanent landing stage from right aft on the *River Clyde* to the shore. This was effected in one day and ships of 16 and 17ft came alongside to discharge stores and troops.[16]

The industry aboard the 'Wooden Horse' was matched ashore, where naval beach parties worked ceaselessly to clear the debris of battle and to land vitally needed stores. Included among them was Howard Weblin, the young midshipman from *Cornwallis*, who had played such a valiant part in the landing. The teenager spent his first night ashore helping disembark French reinforcements shipped over from Kum Kale on the opposite side of the Straits. Though hardly recovered from his exertions, he straightaway joined Unwin, Stoney and a Turkish prisoner of war on a tour of Sedd-el-Bahr, seeking out freshwater wells and collecting identity discs from fallen troops along the way. He wrote:

> We were living on dead men's rations. For the next few days we were employed landing French troops and guns, and cleaning out and repairing the riddled boats, also picking the dead bodies from the bottom by grapnel. The third day I was sent round the trenches with General Hunter-Weston to run messages, etc. And Forbes and I were given a party by Mr Morse to go and unship the Turkish pompoms and bring them down. We found the French in possession

of them, but soon cleared them out and got our own party onto the
job.[17]

In a scattering of outposts and trenches marking the new frontline above
V Beach, the mood was one of relief mingled with incredulity.
Scrambling through Sedd-el-Bahr in the twilight of 26 April, George
Smith was appalled by the 'awful damage that had been done both to
the village and to our men, of whom there were hundreds lying about'.[18]
The young sapper later remembered:

> By the time we reached the top of the cliff it was getting dark … and
> at last we stood in the Turkish trenches and could look down on the
> beach below and it made one wonder how we had managed to get on
> shore at all, let alone get up to where we were. Out at sea we could see
> the ships of the fleet, the silence occasionally broken by one of them
> firing over our heads right into the middle of the Peninsular [sic], and
> I thought to myself that if we were driven off, it would be a deuce of
> a long way to swim … Well, we had done what the Turks had been
> told that we could not do … We had done the impossible …[19]

Others marvelled too. Convinced that he had helped rout '2,000 Turks',[20]
rather than a few hundred, from the wired redoubts above V Beach,
Guy Nightingale told his mother:

> The German officers whom we have taken prisoner say it is
> absolutely beyond them how we ever effected a landing at all. If
> there was one place in the whole world that was impregnable it was
> this peninsula and they say no army in the world except ours could
> have seen half its numbers mown down and still come on and make
> good a landing.[21]

It was a wonderment shared by his senior officers. Ignoring all the
shortcomings in their planning – not least their over-estimation of the
Navy's ability to destroy the defences and their under-estimation of
Turkish courage and resolve – they chose to focus on the positives. In so
doing, they glossed over the disaster at Y Beach while rendering the
near-disaster at V Beach as a magnificent feat of arms secured by a
combination of British pluck and ingenious planning.

Hunter-Weston, who had argued in favour of a daylight landing with
all its inherent risks rather than face the uncertain aggravations of a
potentially confused night assault, was elated. In his first letter home
after securing the beachhead, he declared:

My men, God bless them, have effected the impossible and have effected a landing in the face of severe opposition from defences that were apparently impregnable ... if we keep up this form nothing can stop us.[22]

In another letter, he added ecstatically:

We have managed it, we have achieved the impossible! We are stabilised at the South end of the Gallipoli Peninsula. Wonderful gallantry on the part of regimental officers and men has done it ...[23]

It seemed to him 'hardly credible'[24] that they should have succeeded. 'I take my hat off to the marvellous men who did it,'[25] he wrote and added:

We have terrible tough fighting before us, but nothing to equal the first difficulty of being shot down before the boats could reach the shore, by machine guns, rifles and pompoms; and when on shore to get over, under this fire on an open beach, thick lines of barbed wire. We hadn't a four to one chance, but we have pulled off that one to four event![26]

'Rosy' Wemyss was no less dumbfounded. Writing to his wife on 27 April, he said:

I can hardly believe it, and I know now that I never really believed that we should succeed. So far as I was concerned I was determined that everything should be done to avert disaster, and thank God everybody in that was alike and the result is that the apparently impossible has been attained. Look at the map, and then try and imagine that we actually landed 6,000 men on 2 small beaches at the end of the Peninsula in a few minutes. On beaches which were one mass of barbed wire entanglements and covered from every quarter by maxims and well-concealed rifle fire from trenches which were invisible.[27]

He highlighted the performance of the Lancashire Fusiliers. They had 'covered themselves with glory'[28] at W Beach. Then, he turned to V Beach, where 'the first lot landing were practically annihilated, and sinking boats with nothing but dead in them were the result':[29]

Luckily, thank God, I had fitted up an old Collier to hold 2,000 men, and she was run on shore on the beach, but the fire brought to bear

was so absolutely annihilating that the men couldn't get out. All the
first ones that tried were killed. Eventually they remained in till dark
when they were able to land. Had it not been for this I really doubt
if we should have captured the end of the Peninsula and been where
we are now ...[30]

Four days later, after making his first trip ashore to inspect the Turkish
defences, he wrote again:

I don't think people in England can possibly grasp the magnitude of
the job we have undertaken. I don't expect that they grasp that we
have done the almost impossible. An order of Liman von Sanders'
was found on the body of a German officer today in which he said
that the Peninsula had been made impregnable and that no troops
could ever effect a landing. Truly the British Soldier (and Sailor) is a
marvellous creature. I have been looking at some of the trenches
today. They are wonderfully cleverly made and each beach is so
defended that one can only marvel at the result ...[31]

As with Hunter-Weston and Wemyss, so Sir Ian Hamilton's response to
the bloody landings around Cape Helles veered from the panegyric to
the self-congratulatory. To Sir John French, the Commander-in-Chief
of the BEF and an old comrade from their campaigning days together
in South Africa, he adjudged the invasion 'a magnificent success – first
of all, in the quality of the staff work put into by Braithwaite; his
assistants and a scratch pack of Naval Transport Officers whom we
educated. [And] secondly, in the astonishing valour of the troops'.[32] He
added:

What has come over our fellows I really don't know. Had our men
fought like this in South Africa the war would not have lasted a
month. When you think of steam pinnaces bringing strings of boats
ashore, of which the leading two or three were filled with corpses.
When you think of men seeing the Turks running down into their
trenches to fire at them, and not speaking a word or making a sign
until they get a chance to jump out into the water to their middles
(or sometimes overhead, when they were drowned), and then, as
each small boatload got footing on terra firma, fixing bayonets,
however few their number, and going head down for the enemy,
however great their number! Really it was fine and, as for the old
Turks themselves, I must say they, too, fought with the greatest
courage.[33]

Hamilton had known from the outset that the heavily defended southern beaches would, to use his terminology, be tough nuts to crack. But writing to Lord Kitchener on 30 April, following his first visit to the beaches the previous day, he appeared more surprised than he ought to have been by the strength of the enemy defences:

> Had I been taken round V Beach on land previous to the action instead of merely looking at it through a telescope from a mile's distance – a very different thing! – I would have bet anyone a thousand to one that no party of men landed in the middle of that amphitheatre would ever force their way up. The thing simply did not seem humanly possible.[34]

In an attempt to give an idea of the scale of their achievement, he alluded once more to the South African War, drawing comparison with one of the bloodiest of all struggles fought on the veldt:

> Imagine that the River Tugela was the sea, and that a party was going to land in boats at Colenso. Reduce the scale by one-twentieth, and fill all the amphitheatre with pom-poms, machine guns, galleries, subterranean passages, barbed wire and pitfalls – then you may have some sort of an idea. Instead of, as at Colenso, entering in battle formation, these poor devils entered in boats![35]

He appeared to suggest that the failure to achieve all of his first day objectives was not the fault of mistakes or miscalculations on the part of his senior commanders or himself, but of Turkish malevolence. Dastardly foes that they were, they had had the effrontery to place 'every sort of imaginable pitfall and trap'[36] in the way of his main landing. As he explained to Sir John French:

> Had it not been for these inventions of the devil, machine guns and barbed wire entanglements, we would have swept everything before us inland in our first rush, and gained a commanding position and some elbow room. As it was our effort, made with tired and decimated troops, was either hung up altogether … or, progressed but a thousand yards or so …[37]

Hamilton was either in denial or seriously deluded. Continuing to pay little heed to Turkish skill and resolve in country that suited defence, he maintained that the addition of another brigade on the second day would have tipped the balance and 'carried everything before it'.[38]

Instead, he wrote, 'we could do nothing'[39] for the simple reason that success in what he called 'a really desperate encounter'[40] had come at too high a price. 'I fear you will be horrified by the losses,'[41] he wrote to his 'pacifistissima [*sic*] sweetheart'[42] of a wife on 30 April. 'They have been terrible but the thing could not have been carried out without them … Such a feat of arms could only be bought at a heavy cost – cost in lives, cost in officers, cost in energy, cost in discipline.'[43]

Necessary or not, they dealt a savage blow to his ambitions. By 29 April, after a disastrous attempt to carry the heights of Achi Baba the day before, Hunter-Weston was blaming his division's failure on exhaustion and the excessive number of casualties suffered. Writing home, he stated:

> If my troops had been fresh and at full strength, we should have captured the heights, but the landing and subsequent continuous fighting has made them very exhausted, and has reduced their numbers in the case of many battalions to less than half (In one battalion there is only one officer left).[44]

That battalion was the Dublins. The first four days on the peninsula had cost it dear: ten officers, including its commanding officer, together with 152 men had been killed or fatally wounded and a further thirteen officers and 329 men wounded with twenty-one reported missing. Quite how many of them were sustained during the landing itself is uncertain. Tizard gave an overall figure of about 600 men killed or wounded on top of the officer casualties while the *River Clyde*'s gallant surgeon, himself a casualty, was reported to have treated 750 wounded before being evacuated on 27 April.

What is irrefutable is that by the end of the month the battalion was a shadow of its former self, having shrunk to fewer than 380 men under a single officer, Desmond O'Hara. Since walking off the *River Clyde*'s flimsy gangways in charge of a platoon, the twenty-two-year-old subaltern had been successively a company and then a battalion commander, all within the space of four incredible days. 'It was an awful time,'[45] he later wrote. Fighting 'of the most desperate kind [with] very little quarter on either side'[46] had gone on day and night with 'appalling'[47] casualties. He had gone without food for the first thirty-six hours and without sleep for another thirty-six hours on top of that. 'We are absolutely worn out, mind and body.'[48]

The Munsters were in only marginally better shape. 'Hell it has been, with a vengeance,'[49] wrote Guy Geddes. Reflecting on the nightmarish scenes and appalling losses, he added:

The men who were at Mons and La Bassee say it was sheer child's play to what we've gone through here … As I write we have only six officers and just over 300 men left, out of 28 officers and 900 men … Flanders is a picnic to this and its [*sic*] the most inhuman show that has ever been known – its [*sic*] simply downright murder![50]

It is not possible to be precise about the number of casualties sustained by the battalion during the landing or in the days that followed. The regimental and brigade records both give different tallies and Geddes' figures are at variance with both. But it would appear that the unit lost between 40 and 60 per cent of its original strength of twenty-eight officers and 1,002 men by the end of April. The casualties included Buller, the battalion's bull terrier mascot, injured in the landing and subsequently evacuated. Writing home on 1 May, Guy Nightingale admitted:

It has certainly been a tough job. The heaps of dead are awful, and the beach where we landed was an extraordinary sight the morning they buried them. I buried Major Jarrett just before dawn and have his few personal belongings which I hope to be able to send to his people soon … We lost more men and officers in this battalion in the first 3 days here than we lost in 3 years in S Africa![51]

The evidence of the slaughter was still plainly visible on 27 April when Captain John Gillam led a small party from W Beach to make an inventory of the remaining stores at V Beach. Their journey took them past the badly damaged Helles lighthouse, following the line of a Turkish trench to the fort where two huge guns 'of very old pattern'[52] bore the scars of the naval bombardment. From there, they dropped down towards V Beach and headed towards the sea, at which point Gillam saw 'a sight I shall never forget all my life':[53]

About two hundred bodies are laid out for burial, consisting of soldiers and sailors [he wrote in his diary] … never have the Army and Navy been so dovetailed together. They lie in all postures, their faces blackened, swollen and distorted by the sun. The bodies of seven officers lie in a row in front by themselves. I cannot but think what a fine company they would make if by a miracle an Unseen Hand could restore them to life by a touch. The rank of major and the red tabs on one of the bodies arrests my eye, and the form of the officer seems familiar. Colonel Gostling, of the 88th Field Ambulance, is standing near me, and he goes over to the form,

271

bends down, and gently removes a khaki handkerchief covering the face. I then see that it is Major Costaker [*sic*], our late Brigade Major. In his breast pocket is a cigarette-case and a few letters; one is in his wife's handwriting. I had worked in his office for two months in England, and was looking forward to working with him in Gallipoli. It was cruel luck that he even was not permitted to land … I notice also that a bullet has torn the toes of his left foot away …[54]

A few hundred yards away, Guy Nightingale was still marvelling at his own survival. By his own reckoning he was one of only eight out of twenty-eight officers who had come through the landing unscathed. 'I have had some extraordinary escapes, but haven't been touched yet,'[55] he wrote. His ordeal, however, was far from over:

That night we were attacked at intervals all through, but we held our own till 1000 French reinforced us. The next day we were moved up and dug ourselves in again while 2 other brigades advanced a mile. The next morning we were told to move up to the advanced line, and act in reserve, but by the time we got up to it, the firing line was so hard pressed that we had to go straight up into it. We had a very heavy day's fighting being under fire continuously from 8 am till dark. We had to fall back ½ a mile in the evening, owing to heavy reinforcements to the Turks. We spent another very bad night, very wet and cold and no coats or food. The next morning we advanced about 100 yards in and the whole division dug itself in, in a long line across the peninsula from sea to sea. We are still holding this line having got 3½ miles of the peninsula now. The base is being formed, and all the guns, stores and transport being landed under cover of our line of trenches. We get shelled all day, and sniped at and attacked all night, but are very cheery …[56]

Not everyone shared his optimism. After more heavy fighting a sanguine Desmond O'Hara wrote to Captain David French, one of the first day casualties, in hospital:

I hope your wound is getting better. You were reported as very cheerful – is there any chance of you coming back – for your sake I hope not – this is absolute hell this show with precious little chance of coming out alive …[57]

The realisation among the survivors that their hard-won victory at V Beach marked not the end of their suffering but merely the beginning of an even more gruelling and protracted struggle came quickly. O'Hara's letter was written some three weeks after the landing, during which time the fighting swayed back and forth with neither side able to break the deadlock.

The 29th Division was 'physically spent'[58] even before the first set-piece attempt was made to push out from the beachhead on 28 April. Three days of fighting and four consecutive nights without sleep had taken their toll. 'Many,' wrote staff officer Mynors Farmar, 'were in an abnormal state from their experiences and little sleep.'[59]

What became known as the First Battle of Krithia was, in Farmar's words, 'a difficult and disjointed show'.[60] It had as its limited goals, the capture of Sari Tepe on the Aegean coast, Hill 472 and Krithia in readiness for an assault on Achi Baba, Hunter-Weston's first-day objective. But it achieved nothing other than a further haemorrhage of men. The 29th Division alone suffered 2,000 casualties, almost a quarter of its already much-diminished fighting strength.

'It is hard to resist the conclusion that too much was expected of the men,' observed the official historian of the 2nd Hampshires, 'that those who had forced a landing could hardly be expected to exploit it immediately and that the plan was too ambitious for the force actually available.'[61] Having sustained around 350 casualties, 100 of them killed or missing, the battalion ended the day back where it had started. Among the wounded were two of the leaders in the fight for Sedd-el-Bahr, Arthur Beckwith and Richard Spencer-Smith. One of the few to survive the beach landing unscathed, a 'very weary'[62] Spencer-Smith was again fortunate. He recalled:

> We advanced ... and ... soon came on quantities of the enemy, and a regular pitched battle began. Pakenham was hit in the hand almost at once. I went up and down the company once and tried to control the firing, and to locate the enemy through my field glasses, and was eventually hit, but after the first shock it did not hurt much.
>
> I could not raise myself, so had to lie still, but could talk to the men near me, and finally got a message to go to the dressing station. I passed a good many wounded but could not help them, and could only give directions as to where they were to be found. When I got to the dressing station all people who could walk were sent back (to the beach) as the firing was pretty heavy. I was dragged most of the way by a private, and had to go in stages, resting every 300 yards or so.
>
> Eventually the Padre met us, who took me the rest of the way to the beach, where I was dressed and given a shirt, my own having

been cut off. After waiting a bit I was taken with some others to a mine-sweeper, and the doctor on board gave me his bunk.

I was absolutely exhausted, and must have slept for two hours, as when I woke we were near the hospital ship …[63]

Among the flow of men leaving the peninsula that day was a casualty of a different kind.

Henry Tizard, the commanding officer of the Munsters temporarily in charge of the Covering Force following the death of Herbert Carington Smith and the wounding of Steuart Hare, had spent the previous day and a half reorganising his troops in preparation for handing over V Beach to the French. Restless as ever, he appeared more than a little agitated. Mynors Farmar, who met him late in the afternoon of 26 April, found him 'quite buzzed'.[64] He seemed 'willing to go anywhere and to fight anybody, but incapable of commanding'.[65] In all probability, he was exhausted, worn out by the strain of command and a lack of sleep. Farmar, however, concluded he was simply 'not up to the situation'.[66]

The next evening Tizard was summoned to a meeting with Hunter-Weston. Before heading off, he gave orders for the various units under his command to retire as soon as the French had completed their takeover. Then, on the morning of 28 April, he departed V Beach for *Euryalus* never to return. At 0800, as a desultory bombardment heralded the beginning of the ill-starred advance on Krithia, the man who had overseen the landing from the *River Clyde* was summarily dismissed and ordered home.

His departure came as little surprise to either Unwin or Nightingale. 'He was no coward,' wrote Unwin, 'but simply was not the man for the part.'[67] Nightingale agreed. In a letter to his mother written nearly a month later, he stated:

As we had all expected, our Colonel did not manage to survive more than 2 days of this show before being fired out for incompetency [sic]. I am sorry for him, but I think it is just as well for our sakes …[68]

Guy Geddes was more forgiving. Hearing of Tizard's fall from grace aboard the *Alaunia* where he was receiving treatment for his wounds, he scribbled in his diary:

The Colonel went off for home, *stellenbosched* – for what heaven knows as he couldn't have done anything but what he did … it's a case of someone being made the scapegoat of it all.[69]

Chapter 25

'Marvels of Work and Valour'

Just as he was swift to act over Tizard's apparent shortcomings, so Hunter-Weston was quick to recognise the gallant band of men who he considered were largely responsible for having rescued the landing at V Beach from imminent disaster. In his first report on the operation, written late on 26 April and sent to Hamilton shortly after midnight, the GOC 29th Division praised Commander Unwin and Midshipman Drury [*sic*] for having performed 'marvels of work and valour'[1] on a day when 'the 'Wooden Horse' *River Clyde* had saved the situation'.[2] He also lauded the achievement of Lieutenant Colonel Doughty-Wylie in 'very gallantly'[3] leading the second day's assault that was 'entirely successful'.[4] It was to him and Lieutenant Colonel Williams, he declared, that 'the success of the attack was due'.[5]

Writing to his wife the next day, Hunter-Weston added another name to the list of those he thought worthy of recognition: Garth Walford, the 29th Division Artillery Brigade Major he had personally sent to the *River Clyde* with instructions to urgently press home the attack. He wrote:

> Owing to the action of Colonel Doughty-Wylie and Captain Walford we seized the south end at Sedd-el-Bahr and were safely established. A most glorious and wonderful performance. Alas that Walford (and Doughty-Wylie) should have been killed. I am going to try my very hardest to get him the VC but it is not easy and I may not succeed.[6]

In fact, Hunter-Weston considered them both equally deserving of signal recognition. Walford, he said, had died 'gallantly, very, very gallantly',[7] but it was their joint gallantry that had 'saved the situation and … written their names on the pages of history':[8]

> They achieved the impossible. They showed themselves Englishmen
> of the grand old mould. I esteem it an honour and a privilege to have
> known such gallant men … No honour could be too high for them.[9]

Hunter-Weston was determined to do his level best to ensure both received 'a suitable posthumous reward'.[10]

But what of Williams and others, such as Cecil Grimshaw and Arthur Beckwith, whose bravery had helped transform the 29th Division's fortunes at Sedd-el-Bahr? Unwin was of the view that 'whatever Doughty-Wylie did Williams did',[11] while Nightingale maintained that Grimshaw 'deserved the VC if anybody did'.[12]

In spite of the heavy losses, Grimshaw was actually put up for a gallantry award by the Dublins' last officer standing, Desmond O'Hara.[13] What became of the recommendation is not clear, but no such posthumous distinction materialised. Nor, despite Hunter-Weston's initial acclamation, was there any medal for Williams. Though he emerged from the landings with an enhanced reputation, and with a brevet colonelcy to come, Unwin, for one, felt his omission from the V Beach honours list was an injustice. Writing years later, the captain of the *River Clyde* declared:

> Colonel Williams has never been given credit for his share in this
> attack; he was every bit as gallant as Doughty-Wylie. They were both
> magnificent, but unfortunately Williams was the historian and had
> to omit his name.[14]

Of the other leading participants in the capture of Sedd-el-Bahr, Beckwith was the only one, apart from Doughty-Wylie and Walford, who was not overlooked. His name featured in the Mediterranean Expeditionary Force's first list of honours gazetted on 3 June. The brief citation for his Distinguished Service Order recognised his 'brilliant and gallant'[15] leadership during the fight for the fortress and village as well as his 'exceptional coolness and efficiency'.[16]

It was one of three such awards shared equally among the three infantry units forming the Covering Force at V Beach. The other recipients were Guy Geddes of the Munsters for 'gallantly leading his men into lighters', 'swimming ashore under heavy fire'[17] and hanging on until nightfall despite being wounded early on and Desmond O'Hara, the young subaltern of the Dublins who took command of his battalion when all the other officers had been killed or wounded.

There was a gap of twenty days before *The London Gazette* of 23 June announced the award of the campaign's first Victoria Crosses to 'Dick'

Doughty-Wylie and Garth Walford. By then, Doughty-Wylie, labelled by Hamilton as 'the Mr Greatheart of our war',[18] had already been feted a hero in the English press. Reports of his exploits began circulating in early May. Based on accounts given to journalists by wounded soldiers in Cairo, they spoke of the inspiring leadership of Major Grimshaw and an unnamed 'colonel with a cane in his hand'[19] who went among the troops, encouraging them. The story continued:

> It was he who led the men in their bayonet fight up the hill. The British completely routed the Turks and established themselves on the hill, but the brave colonel and gallant Major Grimshaw, who had done so much to ensure the success of the attack, were found dead on the field of battle.[20]

Nine days later, the 'Nameless hero of Sed-El-Bahr' [sic], hailed in headlines as the 'Bravest of the Brave', was identified as 'Major' Doughty-Wylie, 'a distinguished Suffolk officer'.[21] The report from Cairo, by-lined Press Association War Special, noted:

> An officer speaking about the major said that no braver man ever lived. He had no business to be there as he was a staff officer, but the loss amongst officers in landing had been so great and the necessity for making headway quickly was so essential, that Major Doughty-Wylie felt that his duty lay in leading the men, and so he went forth fearlessly to his death, and the hill will be a lasting monument to his self-sacrifice and great valour.[22]

Walford's name was absent from all of the media coverage, but his family was aware of his exploits and the efforts to honour him. A few days after his death, Betty Walford received a letter from her husband's commanding officer, Brigadier-General Richard Breeks, in which he described Walford as his "mainstay and prop"[23] and observed:

> He died bravely like the gallant gentleman he was, leading infantry in the attack of [sic] an obstinately defended village where he had gone at General Hunter-Weston's request to help an Infantry Brigade who had already lost their Brigadier and Brigade Major...[24]

A fortnight later, a further letter from Walford's friend and deputy, Captain John d'Apice, Staff Captain, 29th Division Artillery, underscored his courage and contribution to the army's lodgement on Turkish territory. He wrote:

277

His was indeed a noble and a soldier's death. He died - was shot - just after the force with whom he was acting had captured a very strong position. He personally helped to a very great extent in getting this position, Sedd-el-Bahr, the capture of which was of vital importance to the success of our landing on this peninsula.[25]

By comparison with the purple prose of the press reports and the sentiment contained in friends' correspondence, the rather woolly joint citation published in *The London Gazette* did scant justice to their magnificent achievement. As well as avoiding all mention of the not insignificant contributions of Beckwith, Grimshaw and Williams, it ended with the erroneous statement that both men had been killed 'in the moment of victory'[26] when, in fact, Walford had been dead several hours before the village, still less the beach, had been secured. Yet, flawed though it was, it did at least reflect a desire on the part of the military authorities to speedily recognise the great bravery displayed at V Beach.

The same could hardly be said for the Navy's efforts to reward the myriad acts of courage displayed by seamen of all ranks during the landing. Inexplicably, the men whose selfless heroism had been so widely witnessed twenty-four hours before the attacks that cleared Sedd-el-Bahr would have to wait at least another seven weeks for their deeds to be officially acknowledged.

Such indeed was the delay that Hunter-Weston, fearing that something had gone amiss with the awards process, submitted his own Victoria Cross recommendations with regard to Commander Unwin and Midshipman Drewry.

In a break with convention, he wrote on June 10: 'These names were not submitted with my first list of recommendations as I was under the impression that the Admiral [Wemyss] was going to forward them.'[27] There was no shortage of eyewitness accounts to support the awards. Commodore Keyes observed:

The general told me at least half a dozen dirty scraps of paper reached him from comparatively junior officers which bore testimony to Unwin's devoted heroism, some written in the heat of action by officers who did not survive it.[28]

Included among them were scribbled notes written by two members of Brigadier Napier's staff who were pinned down on the barges while Unwin and Drewry performed prodigies of heroism in the face of 'almost certain death'.[29] Others who testified to their selfless valour included Weir de Lancey Williams, Guy Geddes and Arthur Beckwith.

The Hampshires' senior surviving officer commented:

> When touch with the shore was temporarily lost, owing to the
> swinging of the front lighter connecting the *River Clyde* with the
> beach, Commander Unwin at the greatest personal risk got a hawser
> on to the other lighter, pulled her round towards a rocky spit on the
> ship's starboard bow and made her fast. He then got one of the
> ship's boats and placed it between the lighter and the rocky spit and
> so established communication again with the shore. All this was
> done under an extremely heavy fire. Later he picked up and got into
> a boat several men lying wounded on the rocky spit. These were
> only two incidents among many in which he was engaged ...[30]

Hunter-Weston considered Unwin's heroism to have been 'of the highest
order'.[31] Both the captain and second in command of the *River Clyde* had
displayed 'conspicuous gallantry'[32] throughout the operation, but Unwin's
performance had been in a class of its own. The general added: 'It was
greatly due to his exertions that the landing on V Beach was successful.'[33]

Unconventional and unusually unrestrained in its acclamation of
men belonging to another service, the submissions were ultimately
unnecessary. Even as they were being forwarded to the Admiralty for
consideration, formal recommendations were slowly navigating their
way through the Navy's official channels.

'Rosy' Wemyss had, in fact, started the process within days of the
landing, telling his wife on 29 April:

> Thank God, I shall have the pleasure of getting 2 of our officers the
> VC for acts of gallantry and self-abnegation seldom if ever equalled.
> There must be many such, but only those 2 [presumably Unwin and
> Drewry] have so far come under my action [*sic*].[34]

As more information came to hand, so the list of men considered worthy
of recognition grew. Indeed, the report Wemyss drafted on the landing
operations on 5 May while still aboard the *Euryalus* was a veritable
chronicle of daring deeds in the face of adversity. It concluded:

> I wish specially to bring to your notice the extraordinarily gallant
> conduct of the following Officers and Men at V Beach:
>
> Commander Edward Unwin, RN
> Lieutenant John A. V. Morse, RN
> Midshipman George L. Drewry, RNR

Midshipman Wilfrid St A. Malleson, RN
Petty Officer J. H. Russell, Royal Naval Air Service
Petty Officer Rumming, Royal Naval Air Service
Able Seaman W. C. Williams, RFR
Able Seaman Geo. McKenzie Samson, RNR

These officers and men showed the utmost gallantry, and absolute disregard for consequences, and worked indefatigably at securing the lighters, etc, to form the bridge from the *River Clyde* to the shore under a murderous fire. Undeterred by the fact that almost every man who was attempting to pass over the bridge was hit, they worked on.

I have since spoken to more than one Military Officer who was in the collier, and they have assured me that the gallantry and cheerful resource of these Officers and men, in most trying circumstances, were beyond the measure of any language they could use …

I consider that the conduct of both Officers and men who manned the boats of the attacking force, is beyond praise. These men, without hesitation repeated the operation of landing troops a second time, under a fire, which, although diminishing, was by no means negligible, and the losses in killed and wounded sustained in the first attack had no effect in diminishing their zeal and ardour.

I regret that I am unable to pick out any special cases for recommendation, but the fact is that, where all showed so much gallantry and determination, it would be difficult to differentiate. Since no individual cases have been brought to my notice, I can only observe that the general dash and daring are worthy of the very finest traditions of the Navy.[35]

As in the case of the recommendation for Doughty-Wylie and Walford, Wemyss' report was not entirely accurate. Neither Russell nor Rumming had been involved in any of the attempts to establish the bridge of lighters between the *River Clyde* and the shore, while Samson was only fleetingly involved. Their actions had been focused on saving lives by removing wounded from harm's way rather than helping more men make it on to the beach. Yet the rescue effort witnessed by so many was not mentioned at all. Nor was it clear from the report what awards Wemyss felt those men cited should receive, though that may have been addressed in a separate note. For in a letter to his wife written the same day he made reference to having been busy writing reports and letters recommending '4 fine fellows for the VC'.[36] 'It has been a great pleasure doing so,' he added, 'but very difficult to find suitable language without being gushing.'[37]

Gushing or not, by the time his report was subsumed into de Robeck's record of the landings on 1 July, the four Victoria Cross recommendations had become five: with young Malleson of the *Cornwallis'* beach party added to the names of Unwin, Drewry, Williams and Samson all from the *River Clyde*, though officially rated to the *Hussar*. Given the size of the naval contingent engaged at the sharp end of the assault, it was a staggering figure. Till then, only two awards of the VC had been made to the Royal Navy, with another yet to be gazetted, during almost nine months of global warfare. De Robeck, however, felt the operation at V Beach to be a special case, unique even among the contested landings elsewhere on the peninsula and unlike anything the Navy had thus far attempted. By way of explanation for such apparent largesse, he wrote:

> The capture of this beach called for a display of the utmost gallantry and perseverance from the officers and men of both services – that they successfully accomplished their task bordered on the miraculous.[38]

Of the others featured in Wemyss' list, Morse was put up for a DSO, and Russell and Rumming, both of whom had been cited by Wedgwood for VCs, had their recommendations downgraded to the next highest award for which they were eligible, the Conspicuous Gallantry Medal. To these were added further recommendations for a DSO to *River Clyde*'s indefatigable surgeon, Peter Burrowes Kelly, and CGMs to Petty Officer Frederick Gibson and RFR, Ordinary Seaman Jesse Lovelock, RN, who were both among the volunteers from HMS *Albion* who helped link the collier to the spit of rocks, and Able Seaman Lewis Jacobs, a member of one of the boats' crews supplied by HMS *Lord Nelson*.

De Robeck's long list of 'special recommendations'[39] in regard to the V Beach landing included three more of *Albion*'s volunteer party. Able Seaman Samuel Forsey, Seamen Henry Morrison and Daniel Roach were cited for Distinguished Service Medals along with five more of *Lord Nelson's* boat crews of whom only two, Able Seamen Albert Bex and William Rowland, survived to receive them. Among those commended for their services were Captain Robert Lambert, the beachmaster, his deputy, Commander Neston Diggle and Commander Hector Watts Jones, acting captain of the attendant ship *Albion*.[40]

Having taken almost nine weeks to compile, it would be another six weeks before the Navy's first list of awards for the landings was actually announced. They were published as part of a special supplement in *The London Gazette* of 16 August that was devoted to de Robeck's dispatch on the Navy's part in what was already being described as the 'immortal'[41] landings on the Gallipoli peninsula. Under the headline 'A story of heroic deeds', the roll-call of gallantry filled almost a page of the next day's edition of *The Times*. Pride of place in the epic saga went to the heroes of the *River Clyde*. Not since the siege of Lucknow almost fifty-eight years earlier had one ship's company earned as many as four Victoria Crosses in a single action.

Where *The Times* majored on Edward Unwin's 'heroic labours',[42] the more populist *Daily Mirror* focused on the collier's young midshipman – George Drewry, or 'River Clyde Drewry' as he had become known to his friends in the Dardanelles. His story appeared beneath an 'exclusive' picture covering half a page that showed him seated on a rocky beach, his head swathed in bandages and a 'haunted look in his far-focused eyes'.[43] An embarrassed Drewry was unimpressed by his celebrity status. 'When I showed him all the newspaper cuttings about him that we had kept,' his brother Ralph once remarked, 'he told me to put them in the toilet.'[44]

Drewry was serving again on HMS *Hussar* when the awards were announced. He had just returned from an exhausting few days spent helping to land troops at Suvla Bay, the new front north of Anzac that had been opened. This time there had been no 'Wooden Horse' and no bloodbath. Instead, a fleet of motorised lighters marshalled by the tireless Unwin had ferried the first wave ashore at night against negligible opposition. Unwin stayed on at Suvla as beachmaster and it was there that he received news of his VC. 'I can't help feeling somewhat elated and I've had a heap of nice messages,' he wrote his wife. 'The VA [Vice-Admiral] told me no officer had ever had more recommendations. 15 soldiers recommended me. Well, there it is ...'[45]

Unwin took almost as much satisfaction in the award of a Victoria Cross to William Charles Williams, the Welsh reservist who had unhesitatingly followed him into the holocaust of V Beach. Describing him as the 'bravest sailor I ever knew', he insisted: 'Williams was the man above all others who deserved the VC at the landing.'[46] Williams, who had been commended for his gallantry some fifteen years earlier while serving with naval brigades in South Africa and China, became the Royal Navy's first posthumous VC recipient. A man of few words, Williams had evidently disclosed nothing to his family about either his work on the *Hussar* or about his impending participation in the operation that would cost him his life. The last any of his relatives had heard of him was shortly after the outbreak of war when he wrote asking his sister to send him the papers for a naval pension that he would never receive.

The only one of the *River Clyde* heroes who was in Britain at the time the awards were announced was 'Geordie' Samson. After spells in hospital in Port Said and Portsmouth, he was convalescing in Aboyne when a telegram from his mother reached him. The terse message read: 'Come home at once; won VC.'[47] His first reaction was to dismiss it as a joke. 'I really thought there was someone in the family telling me a whacker,'[48] he told the local press.

When the truth finally dawned on him, he was dumbfounded. 'It wasn't my faut [*sic*] I got it,'[49] he reportedly said. A guard of honour was on hand to greet him when his train pulled into Carnoustie. From the station, he made his way through cheering crowds to the town hall for a civic reception to the accompaniment of the local band's version of 'The Red, White and Blue'. Shuffling shyly on to the balcony, he struggled to address the large gathering. 'I dinna ken hoo you start,' he said before adding: 'I never tried to make a speech in my life.'[50]

In the days that followed, he would grow more accustomed to such displays of public adulation. Showered with gifts and feted almost everywhere he went, 'Geordie' Samson became quite the star turn at local recruiting rallies.

However, not everyone recognised a hero when they saw one. While travelling on a train out of uniform, a young woman reached across to him and pressed something into his hand: it was a white feather!

As the celebrations continued in Scotland, Ireland rejoiced in its first Victoria Cross hero of the Gallipoli campaign. Nine days after the splurge of publicity accompanying the naval awards, the announcement of Corporal William Cosgrove's honour prompted more media attention. Journalists beat a path to the tiny fishing hamlet of Aghada, where he was staying with his sister while recuperating from his injuries sustained in the assault on Hill 141. They found a young soldier uncomfortable with his new-found fame. One reporter described him as being 'in terror that he will be made a fuss about'.[51] His efforts to belittle his part in the action made no difference. The story of his titanic struggle and unorthodox methods to clear a way through the Turkish barbed wire made him the talk of Cork. But, to the frustration of the press, he remained forever the reluctant hero. At one garden party staged in his honour, he beat a hasty retreat only to be discovered outside, playing with some local children. One of them later recalled: 'He was a very shy man, who hated to be fussed over.'[52]

Peter Kelly, whose award was confirmed the same month, was similarly anxious to downplay his distinction. In a letter to a friend back in Ireland, he listed the honours granted to the *River Clyde*'s volunteer crew and added:

I need hardly say I am rather lucky at having been with such a crowd. I suppose you will naturally be glad to know that I got one of those DSOs, but I fear it was most undeserved. However, my mother will be delighted and many others in the 'Short Grass' [the nickname for County Kildare], and that's the main thing.[53]

The trickle of awards continued with little rhyme or reason. On 6 September, *The London Gazette* confirmed awards of the Distinguished Conduct Medal to Cosgrove's fellow Munster Fusilier, Sergeant Patrick Ryan, and to Sergeant Christopher Cooney of the 1st Royal Dublin Fusiliers. Ryan, who had been a tower of strength on V Beach during the early stages of the landing, was back home in Ireland when the award was announced. However, Cooney was not so fortunate. Having survived the landing and the struggle for Sedd-el-Bahr, where his reckless courage helped galvanise those around him, he continued to display a marked devotion to duty until 5 July, when his luck ran out and he was killed. His award was the second to the Dublins, the first having been announced to Private Thomas Cullen a month earlier.

More honours followed. October brought a DSO for Mynors Farmar, who began 25 April as a staff captain and ended it as acting brigade major, having supplied Hunter-Weston with the first accurate picture of the tragic events that threatened to overwhelm the V Beach landings. A month later, the same distinction was belatedly bestowed on Josiah Wedgwood. In an ironic twist, the MP's award was announced in the Guy Fawkes' Day edition of *The London Gazette*.

Others had to wait longer to receive their just deserts. Guy Nightingale learned that a Military Cross that he thought been awarded in July had finally been granted on 14 January 1916, five days after the last troops left the peninsula. He initially put down his lack of recognition to the unusually high casualty rate among senior ranks. In a letter to his mother, he explained: 'I think the reason there were so few awards to the Dublins and ourselves, or to all the landing party, was because there were no senior officers left to report what happened.'[54] In fact, he had been mentioned in despatches and recommended for 'anything that was going',[55] but nothing had come of it. Only after Guy Geddes intervened on his behalf months later was his case re-examined.

A new recommendation made on 1 November cited 'exceptionally conspicuous acts of gallantry'[56] spanning six months beginning with the landings. Geddes, who by then had recovered from his wound and taken command of the battalion, believed Nightingale's consistent bravery worthy of a 'reward of the highest merit'.[57] Writing in support of the recommendation, Geddes quoted from the diary of an unnamed officer who had 'an intimate knowledge of his services':[58]

> 25 April: He landed that morning from the *River Clyde* with half of his Compy, was sent back by his Company Commander with a report to stop the further landing of Troops, and again rejoined his half Company ashore. That night he took Command of his Company, his Coy Commdr being Killed.

> 26 April: This day he showed conspicuous gallantry and ability of the highest order in the attack and capture of Sedd-el-Bahr Village and Fort 141 (Doughty-Wylie Hill). He acted as Staff Officer to Colonel Doughty-Wylie, assisted him in organising and carrying out the attack on Hill 141 and was with him when he was killed. From what Colonel Doughty-Wylie said before his death, I am of opinion that Captain Nightingale would have been strongly recommended for the VC.[59]

Over time other oversights were rectified. On 14 March 1916 three more of *Cornwallis'* intrepid band of 'snotties' were, at last, recognised for their gallantry during the landing. Midshipmen Haydon Forbes, Maurice Lloyd and William Monier-Williams all received richly deserved Distinguished Service Crosses. Ten weeks later, their commander had his original commendation converted to a Distinguished Service Order. Captain Robert Lambert, the beachmaster marooned on the *River Clyde*, had set 'a magnificent example … in a most difficult and dangerous position'.[60]

Not all were as fortunate. The CO of 89th (Highland) Field Ambulance was still bemoaning a lack of awards to the men under his command six months after the landings. Writing on 16 October, Lieutenant Colonel Thomas Fraser declared:

> I wish to put on record that this unit has received no recognition up to now of its heroic work …
>
> Two officers and three NCOs and 108 bearers of this unit were on the *River Clyde* when this ship was beached at V Beach. They did magnificent work at the capture of Sedd-el-Bahr on the 25th and 26th April and on succeeding days – this is acknowledged on all hands – but so far, the only award or recognition has been one officer, Capt G Davidson, mentioned in despatches.[61]

The question of awards remained a contentious one long after the campaign was over. Among the correspondence held in Sir Ian Hamilton's papers are numerous letters from relatives or would-be recipients seeking recognition for brave or distinguished services at Gallipoli. A few of these personal appeals bore fruit. Most did not. One of the most persistent lobbyists was John Redmond, leader of the Irish Parliamentary Party in the House of Commons and an ardent nationalist. He was convinced that the selfless actions of Father William Finn on V Beach were worthy of the highest posthumous honour and wrote of the 'deep resentment'[62] felt in Ireland at the lack of official recognition. Persuaded to support his claim, Hamilton wrote to Hunter-Weston in March 1916 urging him to forward him a recommendation to which he promised to give 'a fair wind'.[63] The following month, he returned to the subject, telling Hunter-Weston:

> I think it would be better in every way from the point of view of our Army and of our Empire if you put these witnesses evidence into the shape of a recommendation for the Victoria Cross and send it to me for endorsement.
>
> Were this the case of a fighting man I am, I hope and believe one of the last men in the world to be influenced by any political bias in considering whether he deserved a recommendation or not. But here we are faced by a totally different set of considerations. Father Finn was a man of peace … If after hearing these arguments in favour of honouring Father Finn you and the battalion see your way to send his name up to me I will gladly submit it with my recommendation.[64]

Hunter-Weston was not convinced. Replying to Hamilton, he declared: 'I do not see how, by any stretch of the imagination, we could make Father Finn's case into one that merit's a VC.'[65] He suggested instead submitting a recommendation for a Military Cross as soon as the rules, which at that time precluded lesser awards being made posthumously, were changed. He added: 'We are all full of desire to honour the loyal Irish, for whom all English and Scotch soldiers have a very high regard and affection.'[66]

Later that year, under the misapprehension that the rules had been altered, Hamilton, at Redmond's behest, again sought to honour Finn's 'extraordinary valour'.[67] Endorsing the renewed claim, he dispensed with a formal recommendation and forwarded Redmond's appeal to General Sir Francis Davies, Military Secretary at the War Office, describing it as an 'exceptional'[68] case. But his efforts were all in vain.

Davies replied, explaining that there had been no change in the rules and as a result a Military Cross could not be granted. 'I can only say d——!'[69] a disconsolate Hamilton wrote to Redmond on 18 November. He ended his letter with the vaguest of hopes:

> All I can say to you is that in the remote eventuality of my ever getting back into power I hereby engage to do my level best to get due recognition of Father Finn's memory.[70]

Neither was to happen. Hamilton would never again be given an active command and William Finn's sacrifice would receive no official recognition.

Marian Tisdall was no less persistent than Redmond, but rather more fortunate in her attempts to gain some distinction for her son. In the wake of the landing, she had received numerous letters about his actions at V Beach. Henry Foster, the chaplain who had been a 'constant companion'[71] during the run-up to the invasion, wrote of hearing rumours that 'Pog' was 'to be mentioned for the Victoria Cross'[72] for his efforts to save the wounded. 'He rescued men three times under heavy fire, at the risk of his own life,'[73] wrote Foster. Others had also heard tell of his gallantry and of speculation that he was in line for some high award, but, crucially, none of them had actually been witnesses to the extraordinary deeds they described. As weeks turned to months without official word Mrs Tisdall grew increasingly perplexed. The final straw came with the publication of de Robeck's despatch with its long list of naval awards containing no mention of her son.

Stirred into action, she wrote to Edward Unwin, congratulating him on the 'splendid way in which you won your VC'[74] and asking if he knew anything about a 'recommendation for bravery'[75] for her son, 'of which we have been repeatedly informed by word of mouth, as well as by ... letters'.[76] A few days later, she followed up with a direct appeal to Sir Ian Hamilton. As well as supplying copies of the correspondence that she felt supported her case, she urged enquiries to be made to find out 'why and how'[77] any recommendation might have been stopped and 'if possible'[78] to have it resuscitated to 'let our dear son have the honour due to him'.[79]

Hamilton's response was not unsympathetic, but hardly encouraging. As gently as possible, he explained that no such recommendation had come his way and that convention dictated it would have to come from Tisdall's senior officer, in this case Major General Archibald Paris, GOC Royal Naval Division. 'I ... am anxious that everyone should receive their full due,' added Hamilton.

'Unfortunately in the case of honours or awards, this aspiration is impossible as ten gallant deeds are done for one that can be rewarded.'[80]

However, Mrs Tisdall was not to be put off. With the bit firmly between her teeth, she appealed to General Paris, outlining her case once more, only with additional supporting evidence from her son's former commanding officer, Commander Harry Moorhouse. This time her efforts paid off. Paris was moved to order an investigation, entailing gathering statements from surviving witnesses. One of those approached was Peter Burrowes Kelly, who confirmed seeing 'an officer of RND'[81] using a boat to pick up wounded from the shore. 'I never ceased trying to find out who the officer was,' he wrote and added: 'As we only had one RND officer on board *River Clyde* going in, I take it there can be no doubt that Sub Lieut Tisdale [*sic*] was the officer ...'[82] Five weeks later, there came even stronger affirmation from Josiah Wedgwood. Writing to Paris on 21 December, he recalled the day of the landing:

> About 11am, the wounded crying out on the beach and rocks, Commdr Unwin went ashore alone with a boat and tried to get in the wounded. He got, as you know, the VC, and one of my men who went in to help him also got the Distinguished Gallantry Cross [actually the Conspicuous Gallantry Medal]. About 10 minutes later Lieut Tisdall, and another of my men, went to the same place with a boat and they got back 4 wounded. Lieut Tisdall was hit with a splinter but continued his duty; my man got the DG Cross [CGM] ... Commander Moorhouse recommended him for some distinction ... But he did not see his heroism, I did. Owing to his anomalous position I believe he missed the VC, and now, however late, I should like to bear my testimony ...[83]

By then, however, Paris had made up his mind. Swayed by the compelling evidence of Kelly and two members of Tisdall's platoon on *River Clyde*, Paris had already recommended his actions be rewarded in the certainty that the young officer 'did perform a gallant act'.[84] He also urged recognition for those Anson men who had supported him.

Further corroboration was sought from Tisdall's assistants and, by the end of January 1916, Charles Walker, the Assistant Secretary at the Admiralty, was in full agreement with Paris. 'The gallantry of Sub-Lieutenant Tisdall,' he wrote, 'appears to be established beyond all dispute.'[85] It only remained to assess the 'relative degrees of gallantry'[86] shown by the men who had helped him. Finally, on 15 March, Walker presented the case to the Admiralty. 'If the story as pieced together had been represented at the time,' he declared, 'doubtless rewards would have been given, possibly a VC to Sub Lieut Tisdall and CGMs to the four men.'[87]

Almost a year had gone by since the action Paris was now seeking to reward and Walker hoped it was 'not too late now to do so'.[88] Either way, he thought some kind of recognition was warranted. He, therefore, wrote:

> It is proposed that, whether rewards are given or not, the services of Sub Lieut Tisdall and the four men should be recognised by gazetting their names and that a special letter should be written to the relatives of the Sub-Lieutenant.[89]

In the end it did not come to that. For on the last day of March 1916 it was announced in *The London Gazette* that a ninth Victoria Cross, and the seventh to the men of the *River Clyde*, had been awarded for dauntless valour on V Beach. The same publication also carried the news that awards of the Conspicuous Gallantry Medal had also been made to Chief Petty Officer (now Sub-Lieutenant) Perring, Leading Seaman James Malia and Able Seaman Jim Parkinson. It was no more than any of them deserved, but for 'Pog' Tisdall and his fourth assistant, Fred Curtiss, recognition had come too late.

Chapter 26

'Too Horrible for Words'

The last news from 'Pog' Tisdall came in the form of two postcards sent home from the Helles beachhead. Neither made any mention of the landing operation or his part in it. But nor did they attempt to mask the grim nature of the fighting. The first, dated 27 April, stated:

> Have been under fire and are now ashore; all day spent in burying soldiers. Some of my men are killed. We are all happy and fit. Plenty of hard work and enemy shells, and a smell of dead men. Will tell you more when possible ...[1]

The second, undated but postmarked 7 May, noted:

> We are in the firing line now, and spend the night being sniped at and missed. For nearly a week we had to unload barges for other people under heavy fire, which made a lot of dirt, and frightened our Allies and mules. When not working, we sleep and eat ...[2]

In the intervening period between the two postcards much had happened to the men who had struggled ashore on V Beach. The poorly co-ordinated advance towards Krithia on 28 April was followed by two Turkish attempts in the space of three nights to drive the invaders back into the sea. Both took the form of massed frontal attacks and both were bloodily repulsed, though only after more hard and costly fighting.

Among those caught up in the struggle were the volunteer naval machine gunners from the *River Clyde*. Wedgwood's party had been helping plug gaps in the front line since the beach was secured. It was a role few of them had contemplated when they joined the collier. One of those who landed on the second day wrote:

It was bitter cold during the night and as we are in thin khaki clothes we were shivering and our teeth chattering all night long, except a few times when the Turks tried to break through our lines when we would fire away like hell for a short time and then start teeth chattering again. In the morning I thought I wouldn't have another night like that so I went into the village and got an overcoat and rubber sheer off a dead man. Our dead were lying all over the place in all sorts of attitudes … I didn't like taking things off dead men but I soon got over that and now throw away what I don't want and pick up anything off the dead as we go along … I like it alright here in the day but in the trenches at night it is not very nice, especially as we don't know anything about the job at all … We expected when that landing job was over we should do our own work with cars, but we have been dragged into this and expect to keep on doing it for some time although we are not fit for it …[3]

It didn't help morale that the remainder of the unit, still aboard the *Inkosi*, had been diverted to Malta to pick up stores, leading the same correspondent to complain:

Those who stopped behind … are living like lords on the boat while we are doing the dirty work.[4]

It was a case of simple necessity. Sub-Lieutenant Douglas Illingworth wrote:

One section was in the trenches each day … while the others rested, but as a matter of fact the fighting was much too fierce to keep to this rule. I have only been in the front trenches two nights and it is enough, if they are an example of what is usual. The most terrible one was last Saturday night [1 May] when we were attacked all along the line most persistently from 10 pm to 7 am Sunday morning. It was indescribable. Countless rapid fire from every rifle and gun. No one can imagine what it is like who has not been in it. I was indeed thankful when daylight came and they were driven off.[5]

The Turkish dead were heaped in front of their guns, but the successful defence came at a price. Around dawn, just as the Turks were pulling back, a shell landed near the armoured car party's base, killing Lieutenant Arthur Coke. It was a cruel misfortune. Foremost in efforts to support the landing on the first two days, he had played a leading role in consolidating the beachhead only to fall victim to a stray shell behind the line. In great spirits throughout the landing, he seemed undaunted by the fighting ashore.

Recalling his exuberance, the *Clyde*'s indefatigable surgeon Peter Kelly remembered seeing him when he returned briefly to the collier on 27 April for a much-needed 'hose bath' to wash away the grime of nearly three days' continuous fighting:

> He was in great form, covered with mud, and he told me that night he had been through hell. He said it was a straight march through to Constantinople. He bade me goodbye about 11 am and took all his belongings and went off.[6]

Sent back from the front-line shortly before the Turkish attack on the night of 1 May, he had immediately despatched a runner, offering to return with his section. 'That was the last I heard of him,'[7] wrote Wedgwood. According to one account, he was 'watching the fight and dodging the bullets'[8] near Hill 141 when he was struck in the head by a shard of shrapnel. So died, in the words of one of his men, 'the best man we had got'.[9]

Commiserating with his widow, Wedgwood wrote:

> I think if he could have had his choice he would have died like that. He is buried a few yards from where I sit on the spot where he fell, on the top of a cliff looking out over the battlefield, 'his seat in the stalls' as he called it ...[10]

The unit's first officer casualty was closely followed by a second. Douglas Illingworth was 'clouted'[11] in the neck by a piece of shrapnel as he was walking back to base along a road that had become 'a death trap'.[12] Though his injuries were not fatal, they were serious enough for him to be evacuated. He was not sorry to leave. From aboard a ship carrying him to hospital in Egypt, he wrote:

> The relief to have an honourable respite for a short time is beyond words delicious ... I know what it is that makes the wounded men cheerful. It is the relief from the terrors of this ghastly hell which rages and tears at one's vitals.[13]

His letter was dated 6 May, the same day that the reinforced British and French armies renewed their efforts to break out of the beachhead. The Second Battle of Krithia opened with a thirty-minute bombardment and was followed at 1100 by an attack by a combined force of around 25,000 men, including the *River Clyde*'s machine gunners.

By then, Wedgwood's command, which was attached to 2nd Naval Brigade, had swollen to thirty maxims, including ten from the Anson and Hood Battalions, which were attacking alongside the French on the right. As with the failed advance eight days earlier, arrangements for the push left much to be desired. According to Wedgwood, 'there was no artillery preparation, no enemy to be seen, no objective set that I ever heard of. We just went forward'.[14] What one officer called 'a mad adventure' soon faltered in a fog of confusion.

Wedgwood struggled on for 500 yards before ordering his men to halt and dig in to escape scything machine gun and shrapnel fire. 'I ran from gun to gun, a hen with too many chickens,'[15] he wrote. Behind him he noticed some of the Naval Brigade's machine gunners apparently hanging back. He started to run towards them in the belief that they might need 'some persuasion to go forward',[16] but he hadn't gone far when he was 'pole-axed'[17] by a bullet that tore through his left groin. Sub-Lieutenant Parkes and another man leapt out from cover to help him, but Wedgwood, aware of the danger and conscious of having just refused permission to carry another wounded man back, ordered them away. 'He could wait and so I waited,' he wrote, 'wondering if I was bleeding to death.'[18] Eventually, panicked by bullets chipping at stones on the ground near where he lay, he began to crawl back.

It was a little after 1430. Not far away, at the sharp end of the 2nd Naval Brigade thrust, 'Pog' Tisdall was leading his platoon through the scrub against ever fiercer fire from an unseen enemy. In a fortnight of almost unremitting action, the twenty-four-year-old officer had been a constant inspiration, always leading by example. On one occasion he scorned safety to guide an ammunition carrying party through a welter of shells to reach the front line. Another time he helped avert a potential disaster by plugging a gap after French colonial troops abandoned their position. His courage was a source of pride to his men and anxiety to his fellow officers. One later wrote: 'He never would take cover.'[19] It was a trait that was to prove his undoing.

Around 1500 his platoon reached a ditch on the extreme right of the battalion's advance. The enemy fire was 'severe'[20] and he had lost touch with his senior officer, Lieutenant Commander Gerald Grant, DSC. As usual, his first thought was for the safety of his men. Telling them to take cover, he sprang up on to the lip of the ditch to try and locate the enemy position. Moments later, he was seen to crumple and fall. According to one of his men, he had been shot through the chest. 'Pog'

Tisdall, the selfless and self-effacing hero of the first day's rescue effort, died without uttering another word.

But even as one man's luck ran out fortune continued to favour another of the *River Clyde*'s brave-hearts. With the fight waning but not yet finished, Josiah Wedgwood, sick with pain, struggled back whence he came. Along the way he found two men and, with one either side of him as human crutches, he hobbled into his old position. Carried 5 miles to a tented hospital at W Beach, he was patched up and visited by Sir Ian Hamilton prior to being evacuated. Fragments of the bullet that struck him were still lodged in his leg thirteen days later when he wrote home from Malta:

> I have made one great discovery. It is that soldiers going to fight are the most frightened scared things on earth. If they have been there before they know what is coming. If they haven't they see the other poor things coming back. The dear patient dumb things go to my heart. They just go on to get killed or horribly wounded, knowing that it is coming. They are not even allowed to lie down and hide … for some terrible officer will come along and kick them up.
>
> So you will know what a glorious battle is in future – two vast hordes of terror-stricken men, obeying orders as long as they must, not anxious to kill anybody or do anything only to lie very still if possible behind something.[21]

The blood sacrifice was unremitting. Such were the losses that the 86th Brigade temporarily ceased to exist. Meanwhile the remnants of the Dublins and Munsters were merged to form a makeshift unit, 770-strong, known as the 'Dubsters'. The Turks were little better off and within a fortnight of the landings the two armies had fought themselves to a virtual standstill. On 10 May, Guy Nightingale, by then a company commander in charge of 200 Dublins, admitted:

> This is now degenerated into a kind of trench warfare. We can't possibly advance, nor can the Turks. If we had only had enough troops at the beginning to keep them on the run - we would have the whole peninsula by now.[22]

The stalemate appeared unbreakable. A fortnight later, Nightingale wrote again:

> We are at an absolute deadlock here … I don't know what will happen. The whole thing has been thoroughly mismanaged from

the time they began to bombard the Forts in February without being backed up by a military force. I suppose they will have to see the thing through now but how they are going to manage it goodness only knows … I don't see what good we can do now except to be used as a containing force to occupy the Turkish Army while another large force is landed elsewhere … We are faced by positions which are absolutely impossible to be assaulted, and can only be starved out.[23]

How utterly changed the mood was from two months earlier. Then, the men of the 29th Division had been cheered off to war by exultant crowds amid scenes of great expectation. Now, as they trudged out of the line for their first real rest in weeks, they were almost unrecognisable as the confident force that had made such an indelible impression on the people of Warwickshire and North Oxfordshire. Hunter-Weston, however, could not have been prouder of their sacrifices or their endurance. Writing to his wife on 15 May, he said:

I went round and spoke to all of them and told them how highly I thought of them. All of them – that is to say the survivors: viz of the Infantry 90 officers and 4,891 other ranks out of 312 officers and 12,000 other ranks. That is all I have left; much less than one third of my Infantry officers and only a little more than one third of my Infantry NCOs and men … In the one day's landing and subsequent fighting for 24 hours I lost nearly half my Infantry. Glorious fellows, they accomplished the impossible …[24]

The appearance and spirit of the men in those thinned ranks weren't the only things that had changed. When Guy Nightingale returned to Sedd-el-Bahr, he could hardly believe the transformation. From a dugout burrowed in the side of a hill, he wrote:

We look straight down 100 ft on to V Beach, with the *River Clyde* at our feet, and opposite, facing us, the Old Castle where Jarrett's grave is, and Sedd-el-Bahr village, while behind are the Plains of Troy, Mount Ida and Kum Kale Fort, with glimpses of the Dardanelles separating us from the Asiatic side. Our camp is the Fort here. The French are using the Beach as a landing place and depot. It is so different now. Not a blade of grass left, only rows and rows of tents and horses with a great round patch of cornfield and poppies in the middle, surrounded by barbed wire - the grave of 430 Dublins and Munsters and 14 officers of these two regiments who were killed at the landing on V Beach. We still get shelled here. 'Slippery Sam', a well-known gun from Achi Baba, never fails to give us ½ dozen high explosives morning and evening – while 'Asiatic Annie', a most attentive howitzer from the Asiatic side of the Straits, is perpetually keeping us on the lookout and accounts for many horses daily. The old *River Clyde* is just the same, but now inhabited by two middies, a Naval doctor who has been on since 25 April and the landing staff. We are often there and always greeted as the proper owners ...[25]

Even as he penned those lines, orders were received for another 'big attack on Achi Baba'.[26] With a prescience born of bitter experience, he predicted it would 'probably end up in a kind of Neuve Chapelle'[27] before adding fatalistically: 'We are bound to lose heavily, but it's got to be done.'[28]

Nightingale was to be proved correct on all counts. Like the British offensive on the Western Front to which he alluded, the Third Battle of Krithia, which opened on 4 June, also held the tantalising promise of a breakthrough. One brigade of Lancastrian territorials penetrated four lines of Turkish trenches, advancing more than 1,000 yards to reach the outskirts of Krithia. But costly failures on the flanks undermined success in the centre. And in the heavy fighting that followed the Turks regained much of the ground they had lost in the first few hours. By 6 June a small bulge in the middle of the Turkish front line was all that remained of the first day's advantage. As one veteran later commented, 'It was little enough for what it had cost in death, wounds and heroic endeavour.'[29]

The British and French armies had lost another 6,500 men for no appreciable gain. They included yet more of the *River Clyde*'s gallant complement. Leading Seaman Fred Curtiss, who had taken part in the valiant efforts to rescue the wounded on V Beach during the landing, was among more than a thousand men from the Royal Naval Division killed or wounded during the attack on 4 June. Precisely where and how the thirty-five-year-old married man from Liverpool died is not known. His body was never found.[30]

Petty Officer Geoffrey Rumming was rather more fortunate. Another of that gallant band of men who risked their lives to help the wounded on V Beach's blood-rimmed shore, Rumming fell victim to the very type of operation that had been so derided and which led to Wedgwood offering their services to the *River Clyde*: an attack on the Turkish defences by armoured cars! The first and last sortie of its kind attempted on the peninsula, the operation, involving eight Rolls-Royce armoured cars, was of the more novel aspects of the June offensive.

Rumming was among a number of men from the volunteer party aboard the *Clyde* who reverted to the role for which they had trained. Their commander, in the absence of the evacuated Wedgwood, was Francis McLaren, the same officer whose impetuosity had cost him a place in the converted collier for the landing. Rumming joined him as spare driver and second maxim hand in a car called 'Cleopatra'. Their involvement in the attack was something of an experiment. But despite the fact that the cars were neither 'intended or designed'[31] for trench warfare, McLaren considered their employment could be justified on at least two grounds:

> 1 It ought to frighten the Turks a bit to see 8 armoured cars making for them;
>
> 2 ... when our troops have the terrible task of jumping out of our trenches and going for the Turkish lines I think it will encourage them a bit to know that there is a car alongside. I know it would if I were in their place.[32]

Before setting off, he wrote:

> It will be interesting to see if our armour is bullet proof. I think it will keep out shrapnel but a direct hit from common shell would be unpleasant.[33]

In the event, the attack proved an abject failure. None of the cars made it across no-man's-land. Some didn't even make it as far as the British front line, one car toppling over on its side into a roadside trench and another losing its turret as it crashed down into a depression. McLaren's car bumped its way to within 30 yards of the firing line, with Rumming struggling 'with all his might'[34] to prevent the turret from being shaken off. But at the sixth of seven trench bridges 'Cleopatra' missed the crossing and became wedged. McLaren wrote:

> The row was indescribable; the whole of the English and French artillery were firing rapid over us, and it seemed as if the Turkish batteries were concentrated on us. Well, I was near enough to fire, so I began to fire at the Turkish redoubt in front, over the heads of our fusiliers, who jumped out to attack. Then the damned gun began to jam ... I persevered a bit with some loss of temper, loosed off a good many shots and then had another burst case, fixed so hard that the

extracting tool had to be used – a matter of a minute. I said to Rumming, 'Get this right and I'll see if I can get the car out.'[35]

It was all to no avail. So, shielding his head with 'an iron plate',[36] McLaren climbed out of the car and dived into a nearby sap to take a closer look. One of the back wheels was dangling over the edge of the bridge. And the fire was too heavy for anyone to risk trying to level the trench. McLaren was still pondering his next move when someone shouted, 'Your man's hit':

> I jumped out of the sap into the car and saw poor Rumming – his head one mass of soaking blood. I thought he was dead at first, but then he opened his eyes and smiled faintly. We rigged up a sort of bandage and then bundled him over the edge of the car into the sap.[37]

While McLaren and his driver dismantled the car's gun, two men carried Rumming away, though only as far as a communication trench. There they stopped for the simple reason that neither of them knew where the dressing station was located. A frantic McLaren dashed off in search of it, but nobody knew:

> I then ran through a maze of trenches to see if I could reach Parkes' car. He couldn't approach my car as the shells were pitching all round it; one of them, just after I left to follow Rumming, fell where I had been sitting and killed 8 men. I made a dash for Parkes' car, got in, and we backed down to the 5th bridge. I got out again with his two men and between us we carried Rumming and another wounded officer through a sap into the car. There was no room for me, so I sent them home and went back to watch my car … They subsequently tell me that Rumming has just a chance. It is a bad shrapnel wounded through the top of his skull. Owing to our cars, I believe, he was the first wounded man to get into the operating room, and this promptitude may save his life. Poor fellow! He was so keen to come; so cheerful on the way up, and such a terrible sight on the way home![38]

McLaren eventually made it back 'covered with blood, sweat, mud and the smell of old corpses'.[39] By the time 'Cleopatra' was recovered under cover of darkness her radiator had been pierced in two places and her armour scarred by 120 separate bullet hits.

Rumming survived to be evacuated and, after undergoing further treatment in England, was discharged as unfit for further service. Refusing to accept his war was over, he re-enlisted and, in July 1916, was accepted as an officer cadet in the Machine Gun Corps. He was still training when a series of epileptic fits brought on by his wound led to him being discharged again. Five months later, Geoffrey Charlton Paine Rumming passed away in hospital. He was twenty-nine.

With little let up in the fighting, the number of men who had landed from the *River Clyde* continued to dwindle. The Hampshires fared badly in the early June fighting. Then, it was the turn of the reconstituted Dublins and Munsters to suffer all over again during an attack on Gully Ravine. The struggle straddling 28–29 June cost the Munsters another 159 casualties and the Dublins, only recently boosted by the arrival of reinforcements, were reduced from 850 men to eight officers and 595 other ranks. Their dead included one of the heroes of the battle in the ruins of Sedd-el-Bahr's fortress. Shot in the face and mentioned in despatches for his single-handed assault on a machine gun nest, twenty-one-year-old Lawrence Boustead had only recently rejoined the battalion after convalescence in Malta. He was joined on the unit's lengthening roll of honour two months to the day later by another of W Company's originals.

Fulfilling his own bleak prophesy, Lieutenant Henry Desmond O'Hara succumbed on 29 August. 'This whole business is too horrible for words,' he had written in a letter to his fiancée back in May. 'I don't expect to come alive through it for an instant – it is a miracle for anyone who does.'[40] To his comrades he had appeared indestructible, charmed and charming in equal measure, and quietly brave with it. Guy Nightingale thought him 'an awfully decent fellow and very amusing'.[41] But the laughter was merely a mask to cover the strain that had brought him near to breaking point. His letters home revealed a despairing reality. 'I don't think my nerves will stand it much longer,'[42] he admitted in early June.

A few weeks later, following the attack on Gully Ravine, he observed: 'The survivors of us were in a condition bordering on lunacy when it was all over.'[43] Sent to Egypt for ten days' rest and recuperation, he returned, according to Nightingale, 'a different person'. 'You would hardly know him for the same person,' he noted, 'he looks so much better.'[44]

O'Hara arrived just in time to join in Sir Ian Hamilton's vaunted but ultimately vainglorious August offensive. Seriously wounded, he was hovering between life and death when he was evacuated, bound for England. He never made it. News eventually filtered back to the peninsula that the popular young subaltern, who had commanded a battalion, earned a DSO and suffered a near nervous breakdown all before his twenty-fourth birthday, had died on the hospital ship *Arcadian* as it approached Gibraltar.

By then, one of the leading players in the original V Beach drama had also departed the scene. General Hunter-Weston had been taken ill while out riding with Jack Churchill on 17 July. Diagnosed as suffering from sun-stroke, his condition steadily deteriorated and, following a spell in hospital in Mudros, he was evacuated on 25 July, first to Malta and then to England. He arrived 2½ stone lighter and scarcely able to walk or talk following a fever that lasted eighteen days.

During his three months on the peninsula he had failed repeatedly to gain the objective he had optimistically hoped to reach by the end of the first day. Yet his confidence in his own ability had never wavered. Every setback was viewed merely as vindication of the earlier misgivings he had relayed to Hamilton prior to the landings. His reaction to the Army's misfortunes on 4 June was typical. In a letter to his wife, he wrote: 'It proves, if indeed proof be needed, that my forecast in my "appreciation" of a long slow job was but too true.'[45] A realisation, however, that the expeditionary force possessed too few men, heavy guns or high explosive shells to carry out the task set for it did not prevent him demanding further useless sacrifice.

His final action had gone the way of all the others: a limited advance achieved at great cost, followed by renewed deadlock. No less predictable than the results of those futile attacks made on 12 July was his response. 'Another battle and another success,' he declared in a letter home, 'but oh for the necessary howitzers and ammunition to enable me to make it a real success, breaking through the line and having a decisive effect.'[46]

Right to the end, he remained convinced that the campaign could be won, but only if the Government and the High Command were prepared to commit the necessary reserves and resources to supporting the expeditionary force. In one of his last acts before departing, he set out his views in a long letter to Major General Callwell, the Director of Operations at the War Office. He argued that urgent action was needed before bad weather combined with Turkish bombardment and German submarine activity to render the expeditionary force's already precarious position 'nearly impossible'.[47] Without more howitzers, high explosive shells and 'a constant flow of reinforcements',[48] he insisted, progress would continue to be too slow. 'You know how our divisions are melting away and losing their value as fighting machines,'[49] he wrote. His conclusion was succinct:

> It must ... be faced and decided whether this Expedition is to be supported at the expense of our troops in Flanders or to be abandoned. If the latter, not another man or round should be sent here. If on the other hand, it is to be supported, it must be so supported as to ensure success before the bad weather comes ...[50]

Ultimately, the Government and General Staff chose evacuation over continuation, though not before Hamilton joined Hunter-Weston in England. Further failed attempts to break the stalemate, following the opening of another front at Suvla Bay, combined with his reluctance to even countenance an abandonment of the peninsula were more than enough to seal his fate. On 14 October the Dardanelles Committee agreed to dismiss Hamilton and replace him with General Sir Charles Monro.[51] The days of the Mediterranean Expeditionary Force were numbered, but the depletion of its exhausted units would carry on for a while yet.

On the same day that the War Council wired its decision to Hamilton's headquarters, the faltering campaign claimed another of the heroes of the V Beach landing, Lieutenant Colonel George Butler Stoney. At around 1000 on 15 October shells fired from the Asiatic shore began to fall across the back area of the Helles sector where men of the 1st King's Own Scottish Borderers were resting. One of them landed barely 15ft from where Captain A. M. Shaw lay, smothering him with earth and peppering his blanket with bomb fragments. Miraculously unhurt, he had just begun cleaning himself up when another 'monster shell'[52] slammed into a nearby dugout, fatally wounding Stoney, his commanding officer, and scattering his possessions across so wide an area that it took his batman hours to collect them.

The death of Stoney was a 'dreadful calamity'[53] to his regiment and a grievous blow to the 29th Division. Few had rendered greater or more varied service since the campaign began. From the moment he clambered aboard the *River Clyde*, amid a hail of bullets on the first morning of the landing, to his last morning at Helles, he had been unstinting in his efforts to make a success of the operations on the peninsula. If his crowning achievement was the rallying of weary troops lining the foreshore on the second day to help drive the last Turks from the heights above V Beach, his tireless efforts as military landing officer in the days that followed were hardly less noteworthy.

Surgeon Kelly of *River Clyde* fame described him as 'the bravest of the brave'[54] and his charge up the slopes of Hill 141 as 'a sight never to be forgotten'.[55] Yet it was his demeanour when he returned to the ship that struck him most forcibly. 'He was just as usual,' wrote Kelly, 'same as if nothing had happened.'[56] Mystified by his lack of recognition for the landing, he admitted: 'We don't know why he did not get the DSO.'[57]

That honour would come later, but only after he had achieved his greatest ambition of commanding a battalion of his regiment. Having button-holed his commanding officer and told him how anxious he was to return to his regiment, he fired off an application and within two days received orders to join 1st KOSB. He took over as commanding officer on 18 May. 'You can imagine how happy I am to be with the Battn,' he wrote home, 'and to be comdg them is more than I deserve.'[58]

His performance thereafter was exemplary. Kelly later wrote:

> Our loss was his regiment's gain. How he led the KOSB wants no telling. All I can say is that his name became famous all over our portion of Gallipoli and I have no doubt many of the enemy knew him just as well. His visits to our beach and the *Clyde* afterwards were looked upon as an honour to us.[59]

His reputation continued to grow. The Rev Jack Peshall, chaplain on the *Cornwallis*, wrote of him:

> From the very first one heard about his doings, and while he was in command of his regiment, no one from all accounts, could have done better. He was obviously the life (literally) of his regiment …[60]

The award of a DSO on 25 August recognised not only his 'conspicuous gallantry'[61] in the attacks in front of Krithia in early June but also his 'gallant conduct during the operations up to 5 May'.[62] In the words of the official citation, he had demonstrated 'great coolness and good leading'[63] of a battalion that had 'suffered greatly'[64] at the outset of the campaign.

Those qualities held true to the end. 'He lived for the regiment which was his sole thought,'[65] wrote Shaw. And that devotion was reflected in the turnout for his funeral. With pipers playing a plaintive dirge in the grey after-light of an Aegean evening, Shaw saw silhouetted in the moonlight 'the figures of hundreds of the Battalion grouped around to pay a last tribute of respect to a fine commander'.[66]

Chapter 27

'Stealing Away'

The talk was no longer of great victories and a glorious march to Constantinople. Ravaged by injury and sickness, desperately short of shells and essential equipment, the Mediterranean Expeditionary Force was a pitiful shadow of its once proud self. There was hardly a unit that was not gravely below strength and most of the men who remained were utterly worn out. Among them all there grew a weary acceptance that the game was up. A tour of the three sectors was enough to convince General Monro that an evacuation was the only viable option. By the end of October he had telegraphed his conclusion to Kitchener.

The following month the Secretary of State for War came to see for himself. Fearful of the impact an abandonment of the peninsula would have on British prestige in the Near East, Kitchener hoped against hope of coming up with an alternative. But there was none. Over the course of three days, from 12–14 November, he witnessed both the precarious nature of the expeditionary force's position and the virtual impregnability of the Turkish defences. Reluctantly, he accepted Monro's conclusions, though his recommendation was for a limited evacuation only. While willing to give up Anzac and Suvla, he sought to hang on at Helles, partly as a face-saving consolation and partly to assuage naval concerns.

Kitchener telegraphed home his impressions on 15 November. That same day the weather broke. The first of a band of south-westerly squalls blew in, making life on the peninsula yet more miserable. Thunder and lightning followed as the storm set in.

Two days later, with a shrieking wind threatening worse to come, a Royal Marine attached to 8th Army Corps HQ was surprised to see, 'a young middle-aged woman in medium grey clothes walking up the gentle slope to the track to Sedd-el-Bahr'.[1] He asked a nearby soldier if he knew who she was and was told she was the widowed sister of Mr Bonar Law (the then Secretary of State for the Colonies in the Asquith Government) come to lay a wreath on her son's grave. It turned out he was wrong. According to the scant evidence available, it seems more likely that the woman was actually Lily Doughty-Wylie come to pay her respects to her gallant husband.

Word of 'Dick' Doughty-Wylie's death had reached Lily at the Anglo-Ethiopian Red Cross Hospital at St Valery-sur-Somme where she was *directrice* on 1 May. In her diary she wrote:

> The shock was terrible. I don't quite know what I did for the first sixty seconds. Something seemed to tear at the region of my heart. All my life was so much of his life, all his life mine. I suppose I shall have to pick up the pieces of a spoilt life, too old to start again, just a lonely widow, nothing to look forward to, nothing to work for – a blank ...[2]

Though she had talked of committing suicide in the event of her husband's death, she proved herself every bit as 'brave and strong-minded'[3] as he had foreseen. Even before his death had been reported she had lobbied to be allowed to establish a hospital in the Dardanelles. Now, in her desolation, she made renewed efforts in order to be closer to the man who continued to visit her in her dreams. Convinced of her husband's supernatural ability to sway the military authorities into supporting her scheme, she noted: 'We have always run our shows together and finished them together and I really don't see why this should be an exception.'[4]

Despite vague promises from the French, her idea came to nothing. But if subsequent reports are true she did not stop there. She merely sought an alternative means of reaching the Dardanelles, exploiting her contacts in France to secure approval for a visit to a part of the Helles sector that had been under French control almost since her husband had been instrumental in securing V Beach.

Such an act, while being the subject of enduring speculation, was entirely consistent with Lily's formidable character. Brian Doughty-Wylie, 'Dick's' godson, described her as 'a most determined person'[5] who 'usually got her own way'.[6] And while no official papers have been found that make mention of her visit, reports soon began to circulate that she had, indeed, landed on the peninsula, the only woman to do so during the entire campaign, and had made her way up Hill 141 to see her husband's last resting place with its simple cross marker made by the *River Clyde*'s ship's carpenter.

Mirroring a report that appeared in a French newspaper, Surgeon Kelly recorded Lily Doughty-Wylie's presence at V Beach in his diary, stating:

> She had [a] reception from the French, and it is interesting to note that on that day the enemy fired neither bullet nor shell.[7]

Five days later, Kitchener formally submitted his recommendation for a partial evacuation. In accepting his conclusion, the War Committee went further, advising a complete withdrawal. But the Government continued to procrastinate for another fortnight before finally deciding to back Kitchener's original idea of abandoning only Anzac and Suvla for the time being. Not until after the astoundingly successful evacuations of those two beaches were completed over the course of two nights in mid-December did the Government agree to the Army pulling out of Helles as well. By then, preparations for a final evacuation were already under way.

The plan that was eventually adopted called for a gradual thinning of the garrison culminating in the withdrawal, in three waves, of 17,000 men on a single night. Of those, all bar 400 men, who were to be taken from Gully Beach, were to be lifted from W and V Beaches. The operation was a model of meticulous organisation. And, so far as the evacuation from V Beach was concerned, there was about the arrangements a strange symmetry: for just as she had been a critical factor in the original landings 8½ months earlier, so would the *River Clyde* feature prominently in the expeditionary force's departure.

Since Edward Unwin left her back in May, the *River Clyde* had fulfilled all of 'Rosy' Wemyss' hopes. From depot ship to reservoir and landing stage, she had become pivotal to the Helles logistical hub. Her rusting hulk formed one arm of an improvised harbour, which was completed by creating further breakwaters out of an old French battleship and a large steamer that were deliberately sunk off Sedd-el-Bahr. Thus protected, the southern tip of the peninsula was transformed into a network of quays and jetties that, while never entirely free from shell fire, enabled the relatively smooth transfer of men and equipment to proceed night and day for the remainder of the campaign.

Those same piers and breakwaters that had suffered badly in the November storms were now restored and temporary jetties added. At V Beach the *River Clyde* was central to the evacuation plan. While lighters were to be used to ferry small bodies of men and equipment, the bulk of the troops were to march along a stone pier that led directly into the empty body of a specially stripped out *River Clyde*, from where they would be able to embark directly on to waiting trawlers.

Among the first to leave were the sad remnants of the 29th Division. Evacuated from Suvla Bay, where their ranks had been further decimated by disease and the elements, they had been brought back to Helles to help fill gaps left by the departing French. However their stay was short. On 2 January they left the peninsula for good, the Munsters and Dublins clambering aboard a trawler and tug drawn up alongside the ship with which their units had become synonymous. But of those that had stormed ashore from *River Clyde*'s cavernous holds eight months earlier there were few to bid her a last farewell. There were only ninety-one originals among the Dublins and of those fewer than a dozen had survived the campaign unscathed.

The final days at Helles were anxious ones. Bad weather and increasing interference from long-range shelling hampered operations. Inter-service wrangling added to the tension. At the centre of it all was Roger Keyes. Frustrated by what he saw as a lack of drive, de Robeck's chief of staff was desperate to take personal charge as beachmaster 'and drive the mules, horses and soldiers into a little more activity'.[8] Failing that, he wanted a man after his own heart; a man of action, a man of forceful personality. A man, in fact, not unlike the erstwhile commander of the *River Clyde*. 'I would give a good deal for Unwin VC as beachmaster,'[9] he told his wife in a letter home on 5 January. Captain Cecil Staveley and Lieutenant Commander George Mulock, who had been appointed principal and assistant beachmasters at Helles having performed the same roles with marked success at Anzac, were both, in his opinion, perfectly sound officers, but neither of them was another Unwin:

> The former is very good at making out detailed plans and he works very well with Davies' Staff, but we want a few Unwins to hustle things, and Unwin is on his way to Egypt. When I saw Byng after the evacuation he told me that on the way off in the last boat from Suvla, a soldier fell overboard and Unwin jumped in and saved his life. He said, 'You must really do something about Unwin; you should send him home; we want several little Unwins'.[10]

Obsessed with galvanising the operation, he pressed for more ambitious schemes to hasten the withdrawal and conducted his own tour of the evacuation beaches. Riding out in the midst of a 'spirited' artillery duel, he travelled as far as Gully Beach before finishing up at the *River Clyde*, where a naval party had made its base:

The lieutenant in charge was from *Zealandia* and had recently arrived. I asked him if he did not think it was better than the North Sea. He grinned and evidently thought so; they had just had a good shelling from Asia, and every now and then Asia dropped a few shells among the working parties. It was extraordinary how little attention was paid to them.[11]

No less remarkable was *River Clyde*'s continued charmed existence. For more than eight months, she had withstood everything the Turks had thrown at her. All that mattered now was that she survived long enough to fulfil her final duty. After that, with her usefulness at an end, the future was altogether less certain. If Keyes had his way, the 'Wooden Horse' of the landings and the work horse of the subsequent operations would be 'drenched with petrol'[12] and destroyed in a final display of defiance as the expeditionary force sailed away.

Eager to deny the enemy satisfaction of salving any of the blockships at Helles, he considered demolition teams blowing up the vessels once the last troops had been taken off. In most cases, he concluded the risks out-weighed any advantage, since most of the vessels were already little more than wrecks. But the *River Clyde* was a different matter. In a report utterly devoid of sentiment, he proposed on 2 January removing what little metal remained from the ship and then putting in place a plan for her fiery destruction. 'One or two drums of petrol might be kept at Seddul Bahr [*sic*],' he wrote, 'and taken onboard her at the last moment to be fired by a shell later.'[13]

Whether or not Keyes' proposal was rejected is unclear, but it was certainly not acted upon. Meanwhile, his concerns about the organisation of the evacuation proved totally unjustified. Despite intermittent shelling, an alarming Turkish attack on the eve of the final withdrawal and deteriorating weather during it, the British departure from Helles went more or less to plan. That is not to say the evacuation was not without its moments of tension.

Soldiers afterwards recalled the curious alternation of silence and deafening noise as they trekked away from the trenches in the shadow of Achi Baba. Those making for V Beach made their way past a scattering of graves and cemeteries before slipping by the ruins of Sedd-el-Bahr to reach the shore. There, they lay up beneath the broken walls of the castle, waiting their turn to be called, just as eight months earlier another crowd of men had done on the first night after the great landing. Before them stood the *River Clyde*, immutable and, in its own way, imperious. A salvation to hundreds back in April, she now represented a gateway to escape, albeit one that left some of the evacuees feeling deeply uncomfortable. Ordinary Seaman Joe Murray of the Hood Battalion quit the support line a little after dusk to begin the long trek to V Beach:

> I thought to myself 'I don't like sneaking away like this after all this bloody trouble.' I was really distressed in my own mind. I thought to myself, 'We're stealing away. We stole away from Blandford, stole away from Egypt and now we're stealing away from Gallipoli.'[14]

His was a weary retreat that quickened only slightly as the shore drew nearer. The night was dark and there was an eerie stillness broken by the crump of an occasional shell. In his diary, he later noted:

> As we climbed the slight slope leading to the cliffs, we heard the bugler at the fort on Sedd-el-Bahr sound a long 'G'. He had observed the flash of the firing of 'Asiatic Annie'. We had little less than half a minute to take cover but as we were on open ground there was nowhere to shelter. We plodded forward towards where we knew the shell was probably aimed. With a resounding thud it fell directly ahead of us over the brow of the hill. If the shelling was of the usual type we should have reached the shelter of the cliffs before the next shell arrived.
>
> When we reached the cliffs we sat awaiting our turn to leave. The bugler again sounded his warning note and more weary men came to the cliffs for shelter. The shell fell close to the rickety pier and hurrying figures disappeared in the darkness. There was another warning note and another crash; more hurrying figures and more waiting.
>
> It was past midnight when my party was ordered to make for the pier and to board an iron lighter under the shadow of the *River Clyde*.[15]

Among the hundreds of others who followed similar paths that night was Lieutenant Colonel J Young of the 1/3rd Lowland Field Ambulance. Part of a large procession of men from the 52nd Division filing along tracks that wound down from the front-line to the beach, he remembered flares rising from the unsuspecting Turkish lines and the flash of 'Asiatic Annie' followed, eleven seconds later, by the shriek of a shell bursting in the sea 30 yards away.

Most of the shells adding to the night's tension overshot to burst harmlessly over the dark water, their reports echoing round the bay. The 52nd Division's historian thought they were 'probably … intended for the *River Clyde*, where waiting men could hear the rumble of the wheels of French 'seventy-fives', British 60-pounders, and other guns'.[16] Whatever the target, the luck that had accompanied the Scots out of the trenches stayed with them as they tramped by the old 'Wooden Horse'. Young recalled:

> With one last look at the famous old tattered liner [*sic*] we passed on. We continued our course past V Beach to the rocking, ramshackle wooden pier and thence along the breakwater to where we could just make out in the darkness a torpedo boat destroyer tossing on the sea.[17]

The wind had freshened and there was an ominous swell that began to pound the makeshift harbour. Joe Murray's last memory was of the lighter that was taking them away pitching violently as more shells added to their discomfort. 'The rolling increased,' he wrote, 'and a mass of exhausted humanity left the shore they could not see; a load of garbage to be dumped somewhere and forgotten.'[18]

So, the evacuation hurried on until at 0355, to the planners' 'intense relief',[19] bonfires made from heaps of abandoned stores began to light up the shore signalling that the last man had been spirited away. From the bridge of the light cruiser HMS *Chatham*, Keyes watched the pyrotechnic display that followed with a kind of grim satisfaction:

> At last the enemy realised that we were really going, scores of rockets shot into the sky from Asia and Gallipoli. Every gun burst into flame and the beaches and piers, which half an hour before were crowded with men, were smothered with hundreds of bursting shells. Our ammunition dumps all over the Peninsula, exploded by time fuses, contributed to the confusion ...[20]

A few minutes later the main magazines at Cape Helles erupted 'with a thunder that was heard above the diapason of the bursting shells'.[21] The shore from Cape Tekke to Sedd-el-Bahr was a mass of flames that 'lit the heights ... and flickered over the surrounding waters'.[22] Like a vast funeral pyre, the fires that would burn for two days cast their fierce light across the battered breakwaters and jetties. In the midst of it all, silhouetted by the conflagration, lay the *River Clyde*.

For so long a symbol of British defiance and determination, she remained stuck fast to the beach as a rusting memorial to British defeat.

Chapter 28

'One Almighty Might Have Been'

'Rosy' Wemyss was about to turn in for the night when an aide knocked on the door of his railway cabin in the middle of the Foret de Compiègne. After days of to-ing and fro-ing, the German envoys had, at last, received instructions from Berlin. A meeting was liable to be called soon. Shrugging off the prospect of sleep, the First Sea Lord lay down on his bed alone with his thoughts.

The speed of events might have found an echo in those long days of hustle and haste that preceded the historic landings on Gallipoli. So much had happened in the three and a half years since that gargantuan effort, three and a half years crammed with heavy responsibility and high endeavour. A knighthood and promotion to command of the East Indies Station had been his reward for overseeing the Army's near miraculous evacuation from the peninsula. However, his long-cherished hopes of becoming Commander-in-Chief, Mediterranean, which for a second time in his career seemed tantalisingly close, were unrealised. Instead, Wemyss found himself serving his country behind an Admiralty desk, first as Second Sea Lord, then as Deputy First Sea Lord and, finally, in December 1917, as First Sea Lord in place of Admiral Sir John Jellicoe.

It was from this most exalted of offices that he had given his support and enthusiastic encouragement to another audacious naval enterprise: the daring operation to block the ports of Zeebrugge and Ostend that would prove the crowning glory of another 'old Gallipoli hand', Admiral Roger Keyes. And it was in this role that the former Governor of Mudros found himself in a forest outside Paris waiting for the curtain to fall on more than four years of war. The Turks had, at last, grown sick of the conflict, just as he had once hoped they would.[1] It had simply taken three years longer, and disastrous defeats in Palestine and Mesopotamia, for them to admit it. Now, ten days on, it was Germany's turn to acknowledge that it was all over, even if the absence of a decisive naval victory left him with 'a feeling of incompleteness'.[2]

Around midnight, his train of thought was broken by the call he had been awaiting for the best part of two days. Minutes later, the German deputation emerged from their train, walked the 200 or so yards across a carpet of wet leaves and climbed aboard the carriage where Marshal Foch sat waiting for them. The resumed discussions lasted a little under five hours before Britain's senior representative added his name to an Armistice agreement due to come into effect on the eleventh hour of the eleventh day of the eleventh month of 1918.

With that, the man who had once hankered after the governorship of Constantinople, and had given his blessing to the 'Wooden Horse' project as a means to achieving that end, departed for a quiet stroll through the forest. 'It was a queer feeling that I had that the war was at last over,' he wrote, 'and that bloodshed would cease at 11 o'clock.'[3]

For many of the men who survived the slaughter on V Beach the end came too late. The Somme, Passchendaele and countless other killing fields ensured that the ranks of those who escaped the misery of Gallipoli were further thinned by the time Wemyss put his name to the Armistice. And of all those men who lived through the horror of that ghastly landing only to succumb elsewhere none died more bravely than Maurice Lloyd.

One of that gallant band of young midshipmen who were instrumental in restoring the bridge of lighters linking the *River Clyde* to the shore, he spent almost ten weeks recovering from wounds to his back and right ankle before rejoining the *Cornwallis*. Decorated, promoted and hospitalised again (with enteric fever), the youngster represented something of a conundrum to senior officers. They found him variously 'lazy', 'careless and apathetic' and 'unreliable'.[4] One reckoned he was 'useless' as a watch-keeper, adding: 'He cannot be trusted to do the simplest thing correctly'.[5]

The causes of his erratic behaviour may only be surmised, though one commanding officer was a little more forgiving, pointing to a lack of training 'owing to wounds and sickness'.[6] Overall, he was considered no better than 'average' and sometimes 'below average' as an officer whose conduct was assessed as never more than 'satisfactory'.[7] But such damning verdicts counted for little when it mattered most.

When the commander of a block ship earmarked for the raid on Zeebrugge was forced to drop out with illness only days before the operation, Lloyd seized his opportunity. He had already volunteered and been turned down once. But now Keyes relented and offered the twenty-year-old sub-lieutenant the junior officer vacancy on the

Iphigenia. On a night drenched with heroism, the youngster considered to be weak and unreliable performed his duties admirably as his ship swept into the mouth of the fire-swept harbour. Finally, in an act of youthful defiance, he snatched the ship's ensign and wrapped it round his waist before leaping aboard a rescue launch. Wounded as the boat made for the open sea, the flag he had sought to save became a blood-saturated bandage barely keeping him alive long enough to reach Keyes' flagship. 'I think that he knew his number was up,' Keyes later wrote, 'but he was perfectly happy and fearfully proud of having been able to bring away the ensign, which I told him he could keep.'[8]

Keyes did not stop there. As soon as he was ashore, he telephoned the Admiralty and spoke with 'Rosy' Wemyss. He gave the First Sea Lord a brief report of the night's actions before urging him to grant immediate recognition to two brave officers thought to be on the verge of death. Wemyss took the matter up and later that same day Keyes informed Lloyd he now had a Bar to go with the DSC he had so gallantly earned at V Beach. This time, however, there was to be no happy ending. Maurice Lloyd was dead before the day was out. For his burial in Dover, Keyes sent a wreath of red roses with the message: 'In proud and grateful memory of a very gallant officer who died for England on St George's Day.'[9]

Other losses among the men of the *River Clyde* were more prosaic. John Russell, who had quit his studies to enlist, recovered from the wound he suffered rescuing injured soldiers from the spit of rocks only to die in a flying accident. Following armoured car service in North Africa, the young Scot had transferred in November 1916 to the Royal Flying Corps. A year later, while flying in formation above Wallington, Surrey, his Sopwith Camel collided with another. Both pilots were killed as their aircraft plunged 5,000ft to the ground.

Nine months later, another mishap ended the calamitous short life of 'River Clyde' Drewry. In the cruellest of ironies, the 'boy hero' of Gallipoli, who had dodged death by the narrowest of margins on so many occasions, suffered fatal injuries in the supposedly safe haven of Scapa Flow. By then a twenty-three-year-old lieutenant in command of the armed trawler *William Jackson*, he was supervising the loading of his vessel on 2 August 1918, when a concrete balancing block fell from a derrick, fracturing his skull and breaking his left arm. He died the same night and his body was brought back to London for burial in the family plot in Manor Park. Newspapers reported the funeral, but the coverage was in marked contrast to the headline-grabbing treatment three years' earlier. One even contrived to use a picture of Wilfrid Malleson in place of Drewry. But by then, of course, Gallipoli and the landings on V Beach were old news and the death of one more young hero scarcely merited a second glance.[10]

Even peace, when it eventually came, brought no end to the sad roll call of deaths among the men of the *River Clyde*. Among the first to fade away was the ship's surgeon, Peter Burrowes Kelly. The Irishman, who had carried on treating the wounded despite being hit in the right leg early on and then 'pinked'[11] in the left foot, continued to serve on Gallipoli till mid-June 1915, by which time he had 'given up all hope of ever leaving the ruddy place'.[12]

In spite of his injuries, he appeared in rude health. 'I have now a flat foot and no upper teeth,' he told a friend, 'but never felt better in my life.'[13] Haunted as he was by that 'terrible day'[14] when the *River Clyde* ran ashore and the Irish fusiliers she carried were 'almost annihilated',[15] he showed no sign of buckling under the strain. 'Like all others who have been through the real thing,' he wrote, I want to see the war finished but on condition that things are satisfactorily settled, otherwise there can be no peace.'[16]

After a spell aboard a minesweeper, he was sent to Madras for a rest before returning to the Dardanelles, where he saw out the rest of the campaign. His last wartime appointment was at the Royal Naval College, Osborne, where he was part of a medical staff stretched to the limit treating the victims of the influenza pandemic that swept the world as the conflict drew to a close. By the end of the war, Kelly was exhausted and his normally robust health beginning to fail. Ignoring the signs, he started his own private practice in London. The strain, however, eventually took its toll. According to the obituary published in *The British Medical Journal*, 'his health rapidly declined'.[17] He headed back to his native Ireland and it was there, while staying with his brother in Ballytore, County Kildare, that one of the *River Clyde's* most notable characters died on 6 April 1920. He left a widow and one child.

'Geordie' Samson VC, who in Kelly's words had 'effected many daring rescues'[18] and been 'prominent in the close fighting'[19] that followed, did not long outlast him. Since being invalided home, the much-travelled seaman, who had talked his way aboard the *River Clyde*, had married and had a son. Although still in pain from his injuries, he continued to serve, rising to the rank of chief petty officer. Rejoining the Merchant Navy after the war, he was serving aboard the SS *Docina* in the Gulf of Mexico when he was taken ill. Carried to Bermuda for urgent medical treatment, he was diagnosed with pneumonia and died on 23 February 1923. The Scot with a wanderlust, who had worked as a cowboy in South America, plied the Arctic as a whaler and driven trains in Turkey was laid to rest, with full honours, in the island's military cemetery.

Guy Nightingale's charmed life on the peninsula gave way to a more troubling post-war existence. As a brevet-major he had commanded the cadre of his demobilised battalion in May 1919 before joining another Churchillian folly as a volunteer with the North Russian Relief Force. Following the dissolution of the Royal Munster Fusiliers in 1922, he transferred to the Lincolnshire Regiment and soldiered on for another four years, serving in Poland, the Middle East and Africa. He retired to Somerset, a major on half-pay, but found it hard to settle into civilian life. Rudderless and lonely, he drank heavily and slipped into a deep depression. Finally, on 18 April 1935, a week before the twentieth anniversary of the landing at V Beach, he rid himself of his demons by taking his own life. He was forty-three.

The passing of one of the Munsters' longest-serving officers of the Gallipoli campaign was followed a year later by the death of the unit's greatest hero of the landing: William Cosgrove VC, the so-called giant of East Cork. Like Nightingale, Cosgrove had chosen to remain in the British Army after the disbandment of his old regiment. Serving first with the Royal Northumberland Fusiliers and then the 6th (Burma) Battalion, University Training Corps, based in Rangoon, he was a respected instructor until his retirement in 1934. Thereafter, his health declined rapidly. A medical examination found he had been carrying pieces of shrapnel in his body since the assault on Hill 141 twenty years earlier. The wounds sustained helping secure V Beach ate away at his strength, causing muscle wastage, which regular treatment slowed but could not halt. Cosgrove's ten-month battle against ill health ended with his death in Millbank military hospital on 14 July 1936. Three hundred veterans from the Munster Comrades Association provided a guard of honour as his body was brought back to Cork for burial on a hilltop above Upper Aghada. There, in the fullness of time, an imposing Celtic cross was built in memory of 'a great Irish soldier'.[20]

Whereas, for some, the landing from the *River Clyde* was the high-water mark in otherwise unremarkable lives, for others, it proved merely another rung on a ladder of success. Arthur Beckwith, who took charge of the 2nd Hampshires following the death of his commanding officer, and Weir de Lancey Williams, the General Staff liaison officer, who helped to plan and lead the assault that made the beachhead safe, both rose to general rank.

Beckwith ended the war a brigadier-general on the Western Front, having been four times wounded and six times mentioned in despatches. Williams went one better, commanding the 30th Division in France from 1917–19 as a major general. For a brief spell in June 1915, the two distinguished 'Hampshires' had taken it in turn to command the 2nd Battalion. Beckwith eventually retired in 1924, with a CB and a CMG to add to his DSO. He died eighteen years later, with another world war raging. Williams outlived his old comrade-in-arms by a further nineteen years, dying on his native island of Guernsey in 1961 at the grand old age of eighty-nine.

Guy Geddes was another whose career prospered in the aftermath of the slaughter on V Beach. The only Munster officer decorated for his courageous leadership at the landing, he returned to the peninsula after his wounds had healed to take charge of what remained of his unit. Nightingale described him as the 'first sound commander'[21] they had. The strain, however, was evident. Nightingale wrote: 'Geddes is a ripping commanding officer to work with but he is frightfully worried and his hair is nearly white! I've never seen fellows get old so quickly.'[22]

His 'temporary' commanded lasted six months until he fell sick in November 1915, and was ordered to leave. Geddes served the rest of the war mainly on brigade and divisional staffs at home and abroad. Resuming his regimental career, he transferred to the East Yorkshire Regiment when the Munsters ceased to exist and went on to command a brigade in the 1930s, shortly before his career drew to a close. By then, he was married and had two sons. His retirement was interrupted by the Second World War, during which he found himself commanding a battalion again, this time in Guildford's Home Guard. He lived on into another peace, eventually dying, aged seventy-four, on the eve of the fortieth anniversary of the action he always regarded as the most 'desperate venture'[23] of his long military service.

Harry Carr, who followed Brigadier-General Napier on to the bridge of lighters and spent most of the first day of the landing desperately trying to avoid his fate, also enjoyed a successful career. Wounded and awarded the DSO for his services on the peninsula, he was awarded a brevet lieutenant colonelcy for his services on the Western Front in 1918. He retired in 1921 after twenty-eight years of unbroken service with the Worcestershire Regiment that culminated in his command of the 2nd Battalion. Like Geddes, he came out of retirement during the Second World War and was placed in charge of the Eastern Command, Forces Information Bureau. Having served no fewer than four sovereigns, the veteran of the Boer War and two world wars died peacefully at his home in Northumberland in 1951 at the age of seventy-eight.

The fate of Henry Tizard was altogether more wretched. Sent home in disgrace by Hunter-Weston, the man who had taken charge of the *River Clyde* landing in the most harrowing of circumstances never had a chance to restore his tarnished reputation. Given the sop of commanding a reserve battalion of the East Lancashire Regiment in

England in September 1915, he was replaced the following June. With his career effectively over, the officer Guy Geddes considered to have been made a scapegoat for the failure to secure V Beach on the first day retired a month later. A long illness added to the pain of his humiliating fall from grace and he died, all but forgotten, in Srinagar, Kashmir, on 19 December 1943.

Years later, reflecting on the landing that had cost Tizard his command and his career, Tony Morse struggled to make it sense of it all. 'So much happened in such a short time,'[24] he wrote in a letter to Edward Unwin.

With the exception of Unwin himself, no one had struggled harder or longer to rescue the *River Clyde* captain's scheme from disaster than Lieutenant John Anthony Vere 'Tony' Morse. His survival had been a source of some astonishment. Such, indeed, was the inferno of fire into which he repeatedly ventured that Roger Keyes had 'never expected to see him again'.[25] But, by some miracle, he had come through it all with barely a scratch to fight on not just in that war but through another world war.

Twenty-six years after commanding the *Cornwallis* beach party at Cape Helles, he distinguished himself all over again in a further desperate service, planning and executing the evacuation of British Commonwealth forces trapped on Crete. He ended the war a be-knighted rear-admiral, showered with honours to add to his V Beach DSO. Advanced to vice-admiral, he was placed on the retired list in 1947. An extraordinary life ended abruptly in May 1960 when he was killed in a road accident in Southern Rhodesia (now Zimbabwe). A few months later his ashes were scattered in the South Atlantic, close to the scene of the River Plate battle twenty-one years earlier in which his son had been killed while serving aboard HMS *Exeter*.

At eighteen the youngest of the V Beach Victoria Cross recipients, Wilfrid St Aubyn Malleson spent the rest of his life playing down his involvement in the landings. He wrote sparingly of his exploits, which he thought had been greatly exaggerated, and shied away from any form of public adulation. His only detailed account of the operation, which he wrote after recovering from a bout of rheumatic fever that was said to be a legacy of his actions, was secretly squirreled away by his family for fear that he might destroy it. According to his younger brother, Hugh, his modesty was 'very real':

> He reckoned that he and his companions trying to replace the landing barges at V Beach … were available for any odd jobs, and this was an emergency. Of course, he was frightened, as were the

others, but like truly modest men, he seemed to prefer keeping his reflections on the action to himself. The hours spent in the water trying to get lighters back into position, under heavy fire was one thing, but the visible execution of hundreds of our soldiers before slipping into the water might well have un-nerved others. On this subject, therefore, Wilfrid's reluctance to talk or join in celebrations about VCs was initiated by his illness ... and prolonged by the curious.[26]

Like many others before and since, Malleson may also have found the distinction he had gained so early in his career a burden. Certainly the rest of his career, while not entirely devoid of note, was, perhaps inevitably, an anti-climax. Following a spell on the *Lord Nelson*, where his fellow midshipmen included his younger brother Rupert, he transferred to submarines. His first command, in 1923, was an H-class submarine as was his next, four years later. Thereafter, he alternated staff duties with 'big ship' appointments.

Regarded as 'a bit unpredictable' and 'fiercely forgetful',[27] 'Mad Malleson', as he became known, had the swarthy, hooked nose look of a pirate. It was said of him that he spoke little, but when he did he was prone to having 'rather definite views'.[28] Serving as a commander at the outbreak of the Second World War, he joined the Retired List in 1941 only to be 'recalled' and appointed Assistant Captain of Malta Dockyard. He remained in Malta until 1948, when he retired as King's Harbour Master.

Still in his early fifties, the former naval officer tried his hand at running hotels and caravan sites in Scotland and the West Country, before finally settling into the relative obscurity of Cornish village life. Having taken to wearing a monocle, he became a notable local character, though few of his neighbours had any inkling as to his heroic past. When a family friend surprised him by presenting him with a painting of his VC action, it was politely accepted and promptly 'tucked away from the gaze of visitors'.[29]

The last and most determinedly little-known of the V Beach Victoria Cross holders died on 21 July 1975 in the quiet little Cornish village that had been his refuge for the last twelve years of his life. In keeping with his wishes, his ashes were scattered in the sea off Falmouth, with the minimum of ceremony and with scant regard to the gallant action he preferred to forget.

Edward Unwin, unsurprisingly, took a different view of the struggle that had rescued him from anonymity. As the originator of the *River Clyde* scheme, he took great pride in the achievements of his volunteer crew and the men who were landed at such heavy cost and never ceased to honour their memory.

Speaking at a memorial dedication ceremony in Eltham in 1926, he declared: 'Both officers and men were splendid. They did astonishing things ... The charge at Balaclava was honoured in verse. What the men at Balaclava did was in no way comparable with what was done by the men of the 29th Division.'[30]

However, his tributes to their courage and sacrifice were often clouded by a feeling of injustice, of having been let down by military and political leaders who had failed to adequately resource the operations at Gallipoli. At the 29th Division's annual memorial service in 1938, he insisted: 'If the campaign had been properly managed, Constantinople would have been taken, for no nation has sent forth to battle braver troops.'[31]

His views did not alter, still less soften, with the passage of time. While some veterans began to question the viability of the campaign and its subsequent direction, Unwin stayed true to his belief that the landings on Gallipoli were 'a heaven-sent idea'[32] which only failed as a result of a lack of support. 'A few more guns,' he once remarked, 'and the men would have got there.'[33]

The peninsula campaign remained the high point of his career. From start to finish, he left an indelible mark on the conduct of naval operations in support of the Army; from the landings at V Beach and Suvla Bay through to the final evacuation. His individual contribution was immense and without parallel. What followed was humdrum by comparison. Command of the light cruiser *Amethyst* on the distant South-East America Station gave way to shore duties as Principal Naval Transport Officer in Egypt and, then, in the whole of the Eastern Mediterranean. More promotion and honours followed in their wake, but no more action. The only man to be decorated for acts of heroism performed both during the initial landing and the evacuation from the peninsula, he retired for the second and last time in 1920 as a captain, with seniority backdated to Armistice Day 1918 as a reward for his distinguished war service, and a CB, a CMG, an Order of the Nile and a Legion d'Honneur to add to the Victoria Cross and Royal Humane Society medal earned at Gallipoli.

Never one to indulge in endless navel gazing, Unwin seems to have devoted little time to analysing how his 'Wooden Horse' scheme came to go awry. A rare exception was when he responded to a request from 'Rosy' Wemyss to write an account of the landing in order to help his former chief with a book he was writing about the Navy's role in the

Dardanelles campaign. His vivid narrative concluded with some pithy observations that were the nearest he came to self-criticism:

> In all accounts I have read of the *River Clyde* it has always been stated that owing to the current I beached the ship in the wrong place. I beached the ship exactly where I intended to, and where you ordered me to.
>
> The picturesque part of my show was spoilt by the failure of the hopper to continue my line, a perfectly simple thing to do. Some years later, I was walking in the VC procession to Buckingham Palace with Samson next to me. I said, 'Samson, I never said anything at the time, but why did the hopper go adrift like she did.' He said, 'It was them bloody Greeks. As soon as the firing began they went full speed astern'. This would, of course, account for it.
>
> My only real mistake was that I ought to have cut the exit in the extreme eyes of the ship. This would have saved all the staging that I had to put in, but there would still have had to be an exit and on that the Turks would have concentrated just the same, with the same result – the enfilading of the troops inside. Speaking after the event, I think we should have run an hour before dawn, or possibly two hours, then we could have got all the troops ashore before the enemy could distinguish our exit. What I do claim is that the old *River Clyde* saved hundreds of lives that would have inevitably been lost had the troops she carried landed or tried to land in boats, for they would all have been killed ...[34]

Unwin adapted well enough to peace. In a busy retirement, he combined civic duties with sporting pursuits while also supporting a myriad of veterans' organisations. However, the man with a reputation for being the greatest hustler in the Eastern Mediterranean proved singularly unsuccessful in his efforts to revive the fortunes of his family's Derbyshire estate. Forced to sell up after a number of failed ventures, he headed south in 1936 to Hindhead in Surrey. It remained his home for the rest of his days. On 19 April 1950, while on his way to his local barber for his customary early morning shave, the man whose name above all others was synonymous with the 'Wooden Horse' of Gallipoli dropped dead.

Seven years earlier, in the midst of another war, his thoughts had drifted back to the *River Clyde* and the desperate efforts to make good a landing that had gone so disastrously awry. The Allies had just landed in Sicily and the newspapers were filled with reports testifying to the vast scale of the amphibious operation. From Ling Cottage in Hindhead, he rattled off a letter to the commander of an earlier Mediterranean Expeditionary Force. The note to an eighty-nine-year-old Sir Ian Hamilton had a familiar ring to it:

> I am supposing that the events in Sicily are being viewed by you much in the same way as they are by me, that is to say, regretting that we did not have the same attention in 1915 as was given to the attack on Sicily. Had you had anything approaching what was meted out to this landing, with a like number of troops plus reinforcements you would have been through, as it was, starvation was our portion. Had Kitchener been as he was at Omdurman, he would have said that as he had now given the expedition his blessing, it had got to succeed, and French would have been ordered to send you what troops you asked for... I was only one of those who sweated and toiled on the beaches and saw it all go for nought. Whereas if we had only half what was given to the Sicilian campaign we could have sailed through ...[35]

To his dying breath in Grayshott, Edward Unwin remained resolute in his conviction that the campaign waged on the Gallipoli peninsula, from the heroic landings at V Beach through to the miraculous evacuation, was a saga of squandered heroism and 'one almighty might-have-been'.[36]

Chapter 29

'Something Sacred'

Rain was falling and a chill breeze blowing as a small naval launch drew alongside the *River Clyde* on the morning of 9 January 1919. On board, a solitary passenger was alone with her thoughts. Fifty-nine days had passed since the signing of the Armistice, but Lily Doughty-Wylie's mind was focused on an altogether bleaker time after her husband's death on the heights above Cape Helles.

Since then, she had filled the aching void with work; the work he, in his last wish, had urged her to carry on with and which continued to wed her to his memory. She had set up hospitals for the Royal Naval Air Service, including one at Mudros, from where 'Dick' had embarked on his last adventure. As matron in charge of nursing and later hospital commandant, Lily spent more than a year on Lemnos before moving on to the more remote island of Thasos, where she established and ran another hospital serving the officers and men of a naval air detachment based there. And amid the desolation of her eternal grief, she found solace in the conviction that one day, whenever fate decided, they would be reunited 'in the next world'.[1]

Now, content that she had 'carried out Dick's orders to the letter',[2] she sought a different kind of reunion by revisiting the grave she had last seen more than three years earlier. Leaving behind 'a suite of apartments built out of aeroplane packing cases',[3] Lily had taken passage to Chanak with a view to journeying on to Helles. After a night spent in a casualty clearing station, persuasive as ever, she had hitched a ride across the Straits to reach the 'Wooden Horse', still where she was when 'Dick' had sallied forth on that first uncertain night of the invasion.

As the launch bumped against the *River Clyde*'s flaking hull, Lily needed the help of a few sailors to scramble through one of the holes cut in her side. The ship was in a sorry state. Shells had ripped through the starboard forward corner of No 1 hatch and the poop deck, removing the steering gear and leaving a gaping hole in the deck. Elsewhere, her ruptured funnel and shell-punctured super-structure were scarred with smaller shrapnel holes so as to resemble a pepper pot. Writing in her diary, Lily noted:

> The *Clyde* has been completely gutted. Not a fragment of wood work remains. There is some talk of salving her, but really I don't think she could be worth it – in these days one hasn't much room for sentiment.
>
> Two Poilus were peacefully fishing through one of the holes in her side and they eyed us curiously as we passed. We walked down a gangway on the shore and then straight on up to the fort.[4]

There was little to recognise as she made her way towards her husband's last resting place:

> Things are much changed since my last visit. Everything is in ruins. The gate of the old fort is demolished and we got in over the remains of the wall at the back. Dick's grave has sunk very much at one end, which accounts for the breaking up of the cement. I am rather afraid to make a decent tomb we shall have to disinter as one can't do much with a grave on the slope. If so we won't touch it now but wait till the memorial is building and bury him under the Altar.
>
> I saw one British subaltern wandering about. He belongs to the Graves Commission and told me Dick's grave was the only one left on the Peninsular [sic]. Every cross had been moved and it was impossible to locate anybody. Oh how glad I am I came out here and arranged through the American Embassy that the Turks should see no harm came to it. They gave me their word and kept it. The two crosses at his feet marking French graves have gone.
>
> The French are busy making sham cemeteries. They enclose the ground, make nice little mounds, put up crosses and send the photographs home to France. It's one way of doing things …[5]

Lily left Helles three days later uncertain about what the future held either for 'Dick's' grave or the *River Clyde*.[6]

The collier was still lying beneath the ruins of Sedd-el-Bahr when a ship carrying British troops home from Transcaspia via the Black Sea and Constantinople steamed through the Dardanelles in the early morning light of 29 April.

On board was a thirty-year-old Army chaplain and squirreled away in his pack was the manuscript of a novel that would help cement the legend of the *River Clyde* like no other. Fresh from a quixotic adventure on the shores of the Caspian, Ernest Raymond, shortly to become famous as the best-selling author of *Tell England*,[7] had not set eyes on the peninsula in over three years. But now, in the 'lovely pellucid Grecian air',[8] its familiar outline seemed almost within touching distance:

> My heart nearly stood still as we came in sight of the Allies' sector beneath old Achi Baba – Achi Baba no more than a gentle swell – and the scrubby ground, the 'few acres of scrub', where I had so often ridden, dodging shells from Achi Baba or Asiatic Annie.
>
> I was proud to be the only one among the men around me who had been on the Peninsula and to be pointing out the places of interest to an audience enthralled: Achi Baba, the French dug-outs, the Boyau de la Plage beneath the cliff, De Tott's Battery, Sedd-el-Bahr, the redoubt above Cape Helles, and then – suddenly – red with rust, listing, empty, abandoned, the *River Clyde*, still grounded off V Beach, where we had left her in that midnight darkness four years before ...[9]

Contrary to Lily Doughty-Wylie's expectations, she would not remain there much longer. Despite her decks and funnel having been riven by shells and her mechanical innards brutally cannibalised, the redoubtable old 'Wooden Horse' was considered sound enough structurally to be salved. In June 1919, a team from the Ocean Salvage Company succeeded in refloating the *River Clyde*. She was towed to Mudros, where she was patched up sufficiently to make the precarious passage to Malta with a small 'running crew' made up of Royal Navy volunteers.

The journey, at the end of a trawler's tow-line, was not without hazard. There was 'not a rope, hawser, chain or rail',[10] recalled Seaman Arthur Pearman. With nowhere that was remotely habitable inside the ship, the crew was forced to sit in the middle of the deck, away from the shell-holes. At night, with the darkness splintered only by matches lighting cigarettes, those who were not seasick tried to keep their spirits up with sing-songs. When the sea got up, observed Pearman, 'it was as much as we could do to sit together without sliding off the deck'.[11] After a brief pause at Skyros, trawler and tow pushed on to Malta, which was reached without further incident.

But what next for the Gallipoli campaign's unlikeliest of survivors? Like Lily, Pearman was evidently aware of speculation that there were plans afoot to preserve the *River Clyde* as a permanent memorial or, as he put it, 'a museum piece'.[12] Sentiment, however, played no part in the rescue effort. Salvage and delivery to a dockyard in Malta were merely first steps to finding a buyer. By late 1919, the die appeared cast.

On 18 November, *The Times* reported:

> After being salved at Gallipoli and brought to Malta, it was thought that she would be preserved permanently as a memento. Unless there is a further change in the official view, however, she is to be sold where she lies.[13]

The fate of the *River Clyde* now became a matter for Parliamentary debate. On 18 December, the MP for Horsham, Edward Turnour, 6th Earl of Winterton, asked if the recently salved ship could be brought home and 'moored permanently in the Thames?'[14] Stung into response, the Prime Minister, David Lloyd George, acknowledged the 'great sentiment in favour of bringing this vessel back',[15] but insisted that it was impractical. He said the cost of the tow alone would be around £20,000, with a further repair bill on top that was likely to be 'enormous'.[16] 'If it could be done at anything like reasonable figures,' he added, 'we should do it.'[17]

To the suggestion of having her preserved as 'a great national relic'[18] in Malta, he was circumspect. Aware of the 'great sentiment that centres round this vessel',[19] he held out the vague promise of further consideration even as arrangements for the sale continued.

Sentiment or not, there would be no change of heart. On 28 January 1920 the *River Clyde*, still languishing in a Maltese dockyard, went under the hammer at London's Baltic Exchange. Bidding was initially slow. But from a starting figure of £3,000, it eventually rose to £11,500. The highest bid came from London shipbrokers Harris & Dixon acting on behalf of Spanish ship owner, Arturo Pardo, based in Santander. Among the interested parties at the auction was *River Clyde*'s most famous captain, Edward Unwin. The sale sparked outrage. *The Times* of 29 January was highly critical. In its leader, it declared:

> The news will be received throughout this country with regret, if not with a sense of shame. Let us hasten to add that the sale was not made with the approval of the mass of the British people, of that we are quite sure ... To preserve the memory of the awful ordeal to which the men who scrambled from this modern Horse of Troy to the shore were submitted, the *River Clyde* might have been preserved off Gallipoli, she might have been sheltered at Malta, she might have been made seaworthy again and brought home to rest in the Thames

where millions could see her. But no! A Government which has been profligate enough could not countenance the outlay of the comparatively small sum required to retain her as a national relic … The sense of the nation has, we believe, been misjudged.[20]

There followed brief hope that the ship's departure into foreign hands might yet be averted. *The Times* of 31 January reported that a British shipping manager had sought to repurchase the *River Clyde* 'on terms which would yield the Spanish buyers … a very substantial profit'[21] with the intention of preserving the vessel 'in a British harbour'.[22] But the offer came to nothing. On 12 February, *The Times* stated that the original sale had gone through:

It is understood that the Spanish buyer fully appreciated the sentiment, and was quite willing to relinquish the vessel, provided that a substitute could be secured. So far, although enquiries have been made in the most likely quarters, a suitable substitute has not been found.[23]

Questions were again asked in the House of Commons. But it was all too little, too late. Asked 'why the SS *River Clyde* had been sold to foreigners; why this historic ship could not have been preserved at Malta and whether nothing can be done to re-purchase this ship for preservation',[24] Andrew Bonar Law, the Conservative Leader of the House, was unrepentant:

The *River Clyde* was sold by auction because after very careful consideration it was not thought either that His Majesty's Government would have been justified in incurring the heavy expense involved in bringing her to this country, or that preservation at Malta was desirable … We thought the best way of disposing of property of that kind was by auction and that is why it was done. It was a very old ship, and had it remained at Malta it would simply have rusted away and have been of no benefit to anybody.[25]

Earl Curzon, the former Viceroy of India and a future Foreign Secretary, was unimpressed. Questioning the sale further, he insisted:

When you have a credit account for a very large sum and when the expenses of the Department [the Ministry of Shipping] are enormous, it is ridiculous to sell a ship with these great associations to an alien firm for so small a sum. I, in common with a great many others, would far rather have seen that ship sunk in deep water than … handed it over to an alien firm.[26]

The Parliamentary Secretary to the Ministry of Shipping, however, remained unmoved. Sticking to the Government line, Lieutenant Colonel Leslie Wilson, himself a veteran of the Gallipoli campaign, replied:

One felt … proper sentiment and if it had been possible to have brought this ship back to England it would have been done but the cost was really prohibitive. It was only a shell-riddled hull and there were no engines. She had been brought back to Malta but it would have been quite impossible to bring her through the Bay of Biscay without the expenditure of a very large sum of money, in order, at any rate, to make her seaworthy …[27]

Wilson insisted that the question of leaving her as a memorial in Malta had been considered, but ultimately the Government had felt the best option was to sell her 'for the very considerable sum of money we got'.[28]

It was a decision that would rankle with veterans for years after. Compton Mackenzie, writer and wartime intelligence officer, summed up the dismay felt by many in his 1929 classic, *Gallipoli Memories*. Recalling a journey made fourteen years' earlier in search of a wild flower growing in the cliffs above V Beach, he found himself drifting back and forth between past and present. He remembered having to make his way past the rotting carcases of four dead horses to reach a flower that was actually a caper. Its fragile filaments were fluttering in the breeze above a stretch of water he called a 'hallowed sea which was once stained … by Irish and by English blood'.[29] And the thought of it evoked again an image of the *River Clyde* and a more recent memory that had become a festering wound:

For the sake of a few hundred pounds [*sic*] they were not willing that her plates should slowly rust away in memory of that April morning, rust away in red flakes and like the blood of the men she carried be mingled at last with the sea … I would that the man who signed the order might carry in his nose till death the stench of those four horses.[30]

But the deed had been done and, like it or not, a new chapter in the remarkable story of the 'Wooden Horse' began. Taken to Italy to undergo the major repairs needed to convert her back to her old use, the newly re-christened *Angela* was effectively rebuilt, with three new boilers in place of her original two. Her sea-going career thereafter was largely undistinguished, but possessed the enviable merit of longevity. And her Gallipoli fame ensured that this humble Spanish merchant vessel would continue to attract attention in Britain.

The *Angela* gained press coverage in 1926 when she delivered a cargo of coal to Britain in the midst of the General Strike and she attracted more headlines the following year. While carrying a cargo to Hamburg, she was forced to divert to Lisbon for temporary repairs after springing a leak. Continuing her journey, she was on her way to Sunderland from Germany when she signalled that she was 'in difficulty' off Flamborough Head. A tug was asked to stand by, but *Angela* managed to find a safe anchorage after reaching the river Humber under her own steam.

Ten years after being removed from the beach at Sedd-el-Bahr, the former *River Clyde* changed hands and her name, though not her nationality. Acquired by Gijon-based Gumersindo Junquera Blanco and Vicente Figaredo Herrero, the *Angela* was renamed *Maruja y Aurora* after the owners' two eldest children. But there was no attempt to disguise her past. Following the first pilgrimage to Gallipoli by veterans of the campaign in 1934, William Stanton Hope corresponded with Gumersindo Blanco for a book he was compiling about the tour. In Gallipoli Revisited, the Royal Naval Division veteran observed:

> The *River Clyde*, under her Spanish name, at present trades with coal between Gijon and the Mediterranean ports, principally Barcelona. She carries no passengers.
>
> No repairs involving alteration in the ship's structure have been made. The ship still bears the scars of shell-fire on her hull; and the metal bulkheads and fixtures in the engine room remain bent from impact of the Turkish shells nineteen years ago.
>
> A peppering of shot may be seen on wooden rails and companion ladders. At one time there were rumours of supernatural occurrences in the *River Clyde*, but the Spanish officers serving with the ship have never noticed any unusual phenomena.
>
> Years ago when the *River Clyde*, under the name of *Angela*, was calling at British ports ... the ship was much visited by ex-Service men and others. British tourists in Barcelona and other ports see her under the name of *Maruja y Aurora* and seldom take a second glance.
>
> She looks just an old coasting steamer, and probably few tourists, if any, realise that this was the ship hallowed by the blood of

Britain's youth in the distant War days. Beside her war-time scars, the ship wears a medallion with which she was decorated in memory of great deeds. The plaque was given by a Liverpool ship owner and presented through the Imperial Merchant Service Guild.

It may be some satisfaction to Britons who hold the ex-*River Clyde* as something sacred, that Senor Junquera [*sic*] ... has a very live respect and interest in this world-famous ship.[31]

That mutual respect was exemplified by a chance encounter off Gibraltar two years later between the *Maruja y Aurora* and the Cunard liner *Lancastria*. Travelling on board the British ship were 150 ex-servicemen, including Captain Edward Unwin VC and Admiral of the Fleet Sir Roger Keyes, returning from Gallipoli following the second official pilgrimage to the peninsula. Having sighted the former *River Clyde* on a reciprocal course, the Lancastria's captain sent word to his passengers, who promptly lined the rails. The two ships then manoeuvred so as to pass slowly close by one another. As they did so, the *Maruja y Aurora* dipped its ensign in salute and the *Lancastria* returned the compliment. The veterans' last, emotion-charged glimpse of the 'Wooden Horse' was of her disappearing into the afternoon haze.

Barely two months after their unexpected meeting, the *Maruja y Aurora* found herself having to negotiate altogether more difficult waters as political upheaval in Spain descended into civil war. Initially aligned with the Republican side, the ship fell into Nationalist hands in August 1937 during a failed attempt to assist in the evacuation of anti-fascist forces from its former home port of Santander. The 'Wooden Horse' appears then to have resumed her old warring ways. Operating under the Nationalist flag, she is believed to have served as a naval auxiliary or armed raider, during which time she reportedly captured a Republican ship crowded with refugees fleeing from Gijon.

As one war ended another far larger conflict erupted. The former *River Clyde* was at Antwerp around the time the Germans invaded Belgium and took control of the port. But the veteran of three wars and countless voyages continued to bear a charmed existence even after her usual coastal runs gave way to deep-sea passages across the submarine-menaced Atlantic. Between 1940 and 1944, she maintained regular traffic between Spain and South America before rounding off an eventful Second World War career with a trip to the United States. Returning to more familiar waters, she entered her fifth decade as busy as ever. One of her chroniclers, Denis Stonham, has recorded:

As year succeeded year she plodded faithfully back and forth along the Spanish and Portuguese coasts but as her end drew near she was to be seen more frequently sailing north in the English Channel. In 1962 she was at Ghent, Emden, Antwerp and Rotterdam. In 1964 she called at Emden, Ghent, Antwerp, Bremen and Dunkirk, and ventured into the Baltic, possibly for the first time, when she visited Szczecin in September.[32]

The following year, for the last time, she resumed her coasting runs, mostly out of Aviles, while in Britain commemorations to mark the fiftieth anniversary of Gallipoli contrived to place the former 'Wooden Horse' back in the public eye. The spur for what quickly became another campaign to preserve the old *River Clyde* as a 'living memorial' was an article published in the *Daily Telegraph*. Its author was Ernest Raymond, the clergyman turned best-selling novelist who had written so movingly of his last encounter with the ship forty-six years earlier. Like so many romanticists before and since, Raymond re-imagined a campaign with 'a glamour, a tragic beauty all its own'.[33] He remembered the 'haunting atmosphere'[34] of battlefields awash with legend and a struggle that assumed 'the perfect pattern … of a Greek tragedy'.[35] In particular, he recalled their very own 'Trojan horse',[36] the *River Clyde*, which he had held 'in reverence'[37] ever since. He wrote:

> Some of us have always wondered who dared to sell this old collier, with her glory, and her story to Spain, and why she was not brought back to a berth in the Thames, or in Portsmouth Harbour, or better still perhaps, in the River Clyde.[38]

And then, he posed the question that would set other minds a-thinking:

> Is it too late, even now, to bring her home?[39]

The response came quickly. Five days later a letter appeared in the *Daily Telegraph* from a Randal Allanson, nephew of Major Cecil Allanson, who seized the heights of Sari Bair from where he caught a brief and tantalising glimpse of the Narrows. Having alluded to his uncle's brave stand, he added:

> Many of my uncle's comrades died on V Beach in the *River Clyde* landing. I learned with great surprise, and a sense of shame, that this great vessel is afloat under a foreign flag. I can think of no higher

memorial to the men who died in the Gallipoli campaign than that she should be purchased from her present owners, as Mr Raymond suggests, and brought home to lie forever in an English, or indeed Scottish, river.[40]

Allanson urged anyone who felt as he did to contact him, 'so that ways and means may be discussed and an appeal launched'.[41] Thus was the River Clyde Preservation Trust born.

Armed with offers of support from more than fifty individuals and organisations, Allanson approached the ship's Spanish owners, who appeared 'sympathetic'[42] to the idea of such a venture. Their next communication, however, was less encouraging. Perhaps spotting an opportunity to cash in on their diminishing asset, the owners told Allanson that the vessel was earmarked for scrapping in 1966 and that tenders from Spanish breakers were awaited.

With a bidding war on the cards, it was realised that the Trust would have to come up with a price in excess of the highest of the breakers' valuations, which was anticipated at being in the region of £14,000. Of course, it didn't end there. More money would then be required to bring the ship back to Britain and to fit her out as a floating museum-cum-memorial.

Recognising the need to act fast, Allanson wrote in June to his potential supporters. His River Clyde Presentation Trust headed letter stated:

> Directly negotiations have been completed with the owners a National Appeal will be launched which Lord Attlee and Sir Compton Mackenzie (both veterans) have been good enough to say they would sign. An approach will also be made to the British Government and the Governments of Australia and New Zealand, as well as to associations connected with the campaign.[43]

The National Appeal was to be backed by a formal letter signed by Allanson, Lord Attlee, the former Labour prime minister, Edward Unwin's daughter, Sir Compton Mackenzie and Ernest Raymond. Optimism ran high that, at the second attempt, the 'Wooden Horse of Gallipoli' might finally be saved as a national memorial. However, in August the trust was dealt a major blow. Allanson was informed that the ship's owners had fixed the sale price at £42,500, with a request that the contract should be signed shortly and that the price would need to be guaranteed. According to Raymond's daughter, Lella, hopes of meeting such terms 'were shaken and finally faded'.[44]

A few months earlier, her father had pictured the realisation of a dream to honour not just the *River Clyde* or the men who sailed in her, but all the countless others who had struggled so hard and sacrificed so much to turn Churchill's 'beloved conception'[45] into triumphant reality. In a follow-up article published in the *Daily Telegraph* on 6 May, he commented:

> My idea has always been that she might be berthed in the Thames as a kind of chapel-at-ease to the Imperial War Museum, her holds (which once held the hundreds of men ready to land on V Beach, and in many cases to die) now furnished with the fine diorama, the relief maps, the numerous pictures and other Gallipoli souvenirs at present in the Museum.
>
> What a day it would be for all Gallipoli veterans still alive, and for their children, if the old *River Clyde* with her wounds still visible, came up the Thames towards a last home, saluted by other ships as she went by.[46]

Sadly, it was not to be. With the price way beyond its reach, the Trust had no option but to accept honourable defeat and withdraw from negotiations. A similar effort to rescue the ship's commemorative plaque from the saloon ended in another failure. The second chance of preserving the *River Clyde* as a floating memorial had gone the way of the first. And this time there would be no chance of a last-minute reprieve.

On 15 March 1966, at San Juan de Nieva, in the breakers' yard of Desguaces y Salvamentos, cutting torches began their pattern of destruction on the venerable old ship's rusting hull. Dismembered and discarded on to piles of scrap, the 'Wooden Horse of Gallipoli' followed the ghosts of her gallant company into a Valhalla of epic proportions. Her strangely heroic and Homeric odyssey had passed into legend.

Appendix I

Victoria Cross Citations

The Victoria Cross citations of the men connected with the landings from the *River Clyde* on 25–26 April 1915:

Commander Edward Unwin, RN
HMS *Hussar* attached to the SS *River Clyde*
While in River Clyde, observing that the lighters which were to form the bridge to the shore had broken adrift, Commander Unwin left the ship, and under a murderous fire attempted to get the lighters into position. He worked on until, suffering from the effects of cold and immersion, he was obliged to return to the ship, where he was wrapped up in blankets.

Having in some degree recovered, he returned to his work against the doctor's order and completed it. He was later again attended by the doctor for three abrasions caused by bullets, after which he once more left the ship, this time in a lifeboat, to save some wounded men who were lying in shallow water near the beach. He continued at this heroic labour under continuous fire, until forced to stop through pure physical exhaustion.
London Gazette, August 16, 1915.

Midshipman George Leslie Drewry, RNR
HMS *Hussar* attached to the SS *River Clyde*
Assisted Commander Unwin at the work of securing the lighters under heavy rifle and maxim fire.

He was wounded in the head, but continued his work, and twice subsequently attempted to swim from lighter to lighter with a line
London Gazette, August 16, 1915.

Midshipman Wilfrid St Aubyn Malleson, RN
HMS *Cornwallis* beach party

Also assisted Commander Unwin, and after Midshipman Drewry had failed from exhaustion to get a line from lighter to lighter, he swam with it himself and succeeded. The line subsequently broke, and he afterwards made two further but unsuccessful attempts at his self-imposed task.
London Gazette, August 16, 1915.

Able Seaman William Charles Williams, ON 186774, RFR
HMS *Hussar* attached to the SS *River Clyde*

Held on to a line in the water for over an hour under heavy fire, until killed.
London Gazette, August 16, 1915.

Seaman George McKenzie Samson, ON 2408 A, RNR
HMS *Hussar* attached to the SS *River Clyde*

Worked on a lighter [steam hopper] all day under fire, attending wounded and getting out lines; he was eventually dangerously wounded by Maxim fire.
London Gazette, August 16, 1915.

Sub-Lieutenant Arthur Walderne St Clair Tisdall, RNVR
Anson Battalion, Royal Naval Division

During the landing from the SS River Clyde at V Beach, in the Gallipoli Peninsula, on the 25th April, 1915, Sub-Lieutenant Tisdall, hearing wounded men on the beach calling for assistance, jumped into the water and, pushing a boat in front of him, went to their rescue. He was, however, obliged to obtain help, and took with him on two trips Leading Seaman Malia and on other trips Chief Petty Officer Perring and Leading Seamen Curtiss and Parkinson. In all Sub-Lieutenant Tisdall made four or five trips between the ship and the shore, and was thus responsible for rescuing several wounded men under heavy and accurate fire.

Owing to the fact that Sub-Lieutenant Tisdall and the platoon under his orders were on detached service at the time, and that this officer was killed in action on the 6th May, it has only now been possible to obtain complete information as to the individuals who took part in this gallant act. Of these, Leading Seaman Fred Curtiss, ON Dev, 1899, has been missing since 4th June, 1915.
London Gazette, March 31, 1916.

Lieutenant Colonel Charles Hotham Montagu Doughty-Wylie, CB, CMG
Headquarters Staff, Mediterranean Expeditionary Force
Captain Garth Neville Walford
Brigade-Major, Royal Artillery, 29th Division
On the 26th April, 1915, subsequent to a landing having been effected on the beach at a point on the Gallipoli Peninsula, during which both Brigadier-General and Brigade-Major had been killed, Lieutenant Colonel Doughty-Wylie and Captain Walford organised and led an attack through and on both sides of the village of Sedd-el-Bahr on the Old Castle [sic] at the top of the hill inland. The enemy's position was very strongly held and entrenched, and defended with concealed machine guns and pom-poms.

It was mainly due to the initiative, skill and great gallantry of these two officers that the attack was a complete success. Both were killed in the moment of victory.
London Gazette, June 23, 1915.

Corporal No 8980 William Cosgrove
1st Battalion, the Royal Munster Fusiliers
For most conspicuous bravery in the leading of his section with great dash during our attack from the beach to the east of Cape Helles, on the Turkish positions, on the 26th April, 1915.

Corporal Cosgrove on this occasion pulled down the posts of the enemy's high wire entanglements single-handed, notwithstanding a terrific fire from both front and flanks, thereby greatly contributing to the successful clearing of the heights.
London Gazette, 23 August 1915.

Appendix II

Letter By Commander Henry Montagu Doughty

The following letter was sent by Commander Henry Montagu Doughty, younger brother of 'Dick' Doughty-Wylie VC, CB, CMG, to Garth Walford's widow, some seven months after the landings. At the time, Doughty was commanding the 14in gun monitor *Abercrombie*:

27 November 1915
Dear Mrs Walford,

I sent a photograph of your husband's grave, and I my wife has, I am glad to say, found out your address and sent it to you. She now sends on your letter. I am very glad to be able to tell you what little I know. My ship did not arrive until July so I had to trace matters out.

The attacks on the 25th [April] had failed and after the rightful leaders had been killed and wounded and Colonel Williams was considering taking the remnants of the landing force round and landing at the next beach [W Beach]. My brother, having carefully thought it out, took the final try to take the Castle and village and hill overlooking it in hand. Your husband joined him with the officers that were left.

They charged into the Castle of Sedd-el-Bahr by a breach made by the Naval guns without much loss, but the Turks had posted snipers and hidden men about the walls of the Castle and their main force was in the houses of the town and on the hill of the Old Fort. Hidden maxims were on the other side overlooking the beach. They had to retire several times out of the Castle and signal to the ships to shell it again, but they finally held it fairly securely having killed and driven out the Turks on the walls. The attack started about 9am.

About 1pm they had the castle securely. The next effort was on the town (on the far side of the Castle to the ships).

The main attack was lead [*sic*] through a breach in the walls to the left of the main entrance which is shown in the photograph (as you look at it). Parties of our men had been posted on the wall to fire into and help draw the fire of the houses (behind where the photo is taken from) to the right looking at the photo. Several Turks and Germans were shot in this way. While the main attack was pushing out and working round to the left and up the hill, fighting house to house and street to street. Another party advancing along the street at right angles to the gate (photo) and to the left looking at it. Your husband tried to lead a small party out of the gate in the photo, which is the main entrance to the Old Fort and was shot dead from a house which is just off the right hand edge of the photograph. His grave is thus really where he was killed.

The main attack worked on slowly with further help from the ships' guns up the hill and finally charged and took the Old Fort on the top of the hill. Then the Turks streamed away, but a few remained and my brother and two other officers were shot in the Old Fort.

This is, I think, a fairly true account but it is nearly impossible to realise how after a day and night [of] failure and no heart left in the men, having nobody to lead, the place was taken. I hope this account will be some comfort to you,

Yrs sincerely,
H M Doughty.

One of the officers Doughty spoke with in order to gain a clearer understanding of his brother's actions was Guy Nightingale. In a letter dated 27 July 1915, Nightingale, who had already been in contact with 'Dick' Doughty-Wylie's sister, wrote:

Colonel Doughty-Wylie's brother is out here ... and he asked me to go and stay a few days on board with him and take him over the places his brother had been on the 26th.

Though broadly accurate, the timings in Doughty's letter bear little relation to those in most other accounts written by participants in the advance through Sedd-el-Bahr.

Appendix III

The Last Crusade

Garth Walford penned the following lines of verse to his wife while travelling to the Dardanelles aboard the SS *Aragon*:

The Last Crusade

Once more revives the never-dying War
Of East and West: through this one entry-gate
Between two worlds have armies alternate
Swept forth to conquest on an alien shore
Age after age; varied the garb they wore,
Changing their standards, different their fate;
Their faith was changeless, unappeased their hate:
Each ruled the stranger for a space, no more
Shone Persia's Sun till Zeus his Thunder rolled;
The sword of Alexander shared his tomb;
The Roman Eagle gorged with Asia's gold
Was torn by hungry broods from Asia's womb;
Now from th' unholy bond, Islam controlled
By Thor, we cleanse the soil of Christendom.

27/3/15 GNW.

Appendix IV

Guy Nightingale's Letter

In July 1915, Guy Nightingale was enjoying a month's rest on Lemnos, during which he was able to meet with officers of HMS *Albion* and discuss the supporting fire arrangements at V Beach during the landing from the *River Clyde*. He related his impressions in a letter written to his mother on 25 July:

Dear Mother,

Three calendar months today from the day of the landing! It's gone pretty quickly in some ways, but most awfully like a lifetime in others. I haven't written for a long time I'm afraid. The last time I wrote, we were just about to come down from a spell of 19 days out of 22 in the firing line, and proceed to Lemnos for a month's rest. That was on the 13th. Well, we didn't get clear of the trenches till the 15th after all, and then we went straight to X Beach where we stayed till 7pm and then marched via W Beach to V Beach, where at 10pm we got on to the Torpedo-Destroyer '*Savage*' using the *River Clyde* as a pier. So, 12 weeks and 4 days after landing from the *River Clyde* on V Beach, we left the Peninsular [sic] by the same manner. As we were getting the last few men on board, 'Asiatic Annie' plumped two high-explosive shells within 50 yards, just as a parting shot! Nobody cared a damn then however, as we were off (so we thought) for a month's complete rest at Mudros. The fellows on the Destroyer were awfully good to us, as they are throughout the whole Navy. The name 'Dublin' or 'Munster' is a password anywhere out here among the senior service. We slept in the Ward Room after a scrap of dinner, but we only went to sleep at 2.30am and arrived at 5am at Lemnos. We went ashore at once and were shown the camp we had to go to. As soon as the men were settled down and everything fixed up, I went to sleep under a tree and never woke up till 5.30 in the evening! I then went off with the doctor, and we had a glorious bathe and then came back to dinner. The camp we were in was quite nice and shady. All the ground was covered with white grapes and melons. There were hundreds of plants and some nice cherry and green-fig trees for shade. The quiet was too glorious for words – not a gun or a rifle shot. Between bathing and dinner Williams and I walked into Mudros Town which was most picturesque and quaint. Of course it is doing a thriving trade. There is a new Greek Church there. It was destroyed by the Turks when they bombarded Lemnos in 1911, but since then has been rebuilt. The whole place was full of French and British soldiers, everyone buying the most ridiculous things which no one would ever think of buying under any other circumstances. On getting back to camp, we found Geddes talking to the Commander and No 1 of the Battleship '*Albion*' which had covered our landing on V Beach on the 25th, and had bombarded 'Doughty-Wylie Hill' [Hill 141] the following day and seen the whole assault. They were most awfully interested in finding 3 survivors of that day, so we fixed up an invitation which they insisted on, for 2 of us to go on board the following day and stay to dinner. Williams was to stay in camp, as one of us 3 generally have to (we are the only 3 regular officers left now, Tomlinson and Russell both having gone sick with the strain and gone for a rest), and Geddes and I were to go together with the CO, Adj and Doctor of the Dublins, who, by the way, had no survivors [among the unit's original officers], O'Hara having gone with Turkish prisoners to Alexandria. The next day the Bn did nothing but rest, as Geddes had very wisely given us all 3 days' complete rest, and then he would try to get some organisation in the Bn. At 3pm I and Geddes went off on a pinnace sent by the '*Albion*' to fetch us off the island and arrived in time for tea. Everyone was most kind. I can't say how good the Navy have been to our fellows whenever we've had any occasion to go on a board any of their ships. Do you remember when I went on board the '*Dublin*' how good they were to me? After tea we all had a hot bath in turn in the Captain's cabin. It was a great luxury. After that there was a jolly good dinner, and we drank the 'King' for the first time (for us at any rate) since we left Rangoon. Then we went on deck and spent a most cheery evening. Geddes went off about 11pm but 3 of us were enjoying ourselves much too much, so, as a complete 'bundobast' had been arranged for us in the shape of camp-beds on deck, we remained on and eventually turned in at 2am after a most jolly evening. I was up at 6am after a grand cool night with no dust and then had a cold tub and breakfast, after which followed 'Divisions' during which I went right over the whole ship with the Captain. It was especially interesting to me, as all that day when I was lying under the bank, waiting for dark, and the next day when waiting at the end of the village of Sedd-el-Bahr while the bombardment was going on to allow us to charge up Doughty-Wylie Hill, I was watching the Battleships covering us and wondering what they were doing all day and now I heard everything. There were lots of things seen from the ship which I had no idea had ever been noticed by anyone who was alive now. The Commander took us round, a fellow called Gibson,[1] and he had spent the day [25 April] in the main top where he directed the guns of the ship and saw the whole show best of all. After 'Divisions', it being Sunday, of course we had to stop to Church, one of the most cheery services I've ever been to, plenty of hymns and all that sort of thing and not too much talk and loose chat. After church, we had a few cocktails and were just going off when a whole crowd of Russian officers off a Russian cruiser here, came on for tiffin, so we all had to stop. After lunch we dozed quietly, and finally, after tea, we went off with a whole boatload of 'snotties' who were going for a sail and bathe and landed us after much manoeuvring at our pier. The next day, we commenced work and did some drill and in the afternoon Williams and I went off to a liner called the 'Aragon' and had lunch and saw a lot of people we knew ... The following day at 9.30am we were suddenly told that the 86th and 87th Bdes of the 29th Division would begin embarking immediately for Cape Helles! It was a blow. We went off at 2pm on the Destroyer 'Basilisk'. As usual they were awfully good to us. Though we reached Cape Helles at 10pm we did not disembark till 4am and then marched straight to Gully Beach which is between X and V Beaches ...

Lots of love from your loving son,

Guy.

Appendix V

Positions at the Beach

Among the more contentious issues associated with the *River Clyde* landing operation were the positioning of the steam hopper and the decked lighters which were to form the 'bridge' between ship and shore. As well as the different arguments for why the *Argyle* ran off course, survivors of the V Beach fighting had different recollections when it came to describing the number of lighters that were used and where they were actually situated.

Here, I present just a few of the varying versions supplied by survivors together with their own sketch plans of what they remembered.

The earliest one dates back to 1926 and was written by Tony Morse, the leader of *Cornwallis'* beach party. It was evidently sent to Edward Unwin in reply to his own questions on the matter. Based on his memories, Morse wrote:

> 1 Bridge connecting *Clyde* and shore to the best of my knowledge was never completed until the spare lighter from Starboard bow of RC was brought up. Assuming RC grounded at 7am I brought up spare lighter about 8 or later …

> 2 The original breakaway I have always believed was due to RC not hitting the Beach exactly where you meant [a point disputed by Unwin]. The Hopper went on and I thought parted the line connecting with lighter.

> 3 A One lighter lashed on Port bow RC.

> B Lighter secured to A which had been secured to Hopper and of which Tow parted when RC grounded and Hopper went on.

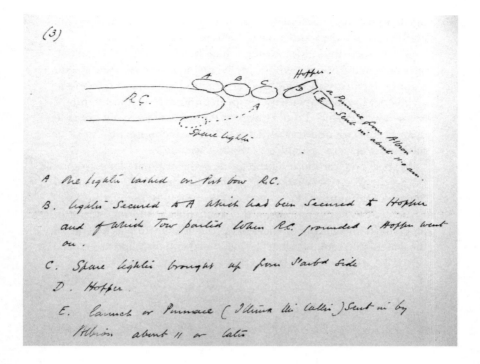

Tony Morse's sketch plan

C Spare lighter brought up from Starboard side.

D Hopper.

E Launch or Pinnace (I think the latter) sent in by *Albion* about 11 or later.

The next account from Wilfrid Malleson, one of the six recipients of the Victoria Cross during the V Beach landing, was based on even more hazy memory. It was written in 1967 in response to Captain Eric Bush's appeal for information for a book he was preparing on the Gallipoli campaign. Given the passage of time, he was suitably circumspect about his recollections:

> Memories of over 50 years ago are necessarily suspect. However, for what they are worth! Our beach party from the 'Cornwallis' under Tony Morse, then a Lieutenant, landed via a picket boat with pinnace in tow. My recollection is that my section landed on Lighter

B, where we were immediately and violently abjured by those lying on the lighter's deck still alive to lie down and stay there.

Meantime, Tony Morse, who had been in the picket boat, appeared in the hopper, whose engine casing provided some shelter from bullets. Having sized up the situation, he sang out to me to swim over to the hopper with a rope in order to re-connect lighter C to the hopper, which I did. However, the soldiers were not going to move until dark and it is difficult to blame them. I expect most of their officers were casualties – I did not see any.

I expect you are about right regarding the original plan – to span the gap between the 'River Clyde' and the beach with the hopper and perhaps two lighters. However, as you probably know, the 'River Clyde' had to stop engines on the final run-in, due to a string of lifeboats in tow getting too near her propeller, which was half out of the water. The result was that she lost speed and direction at a crucial

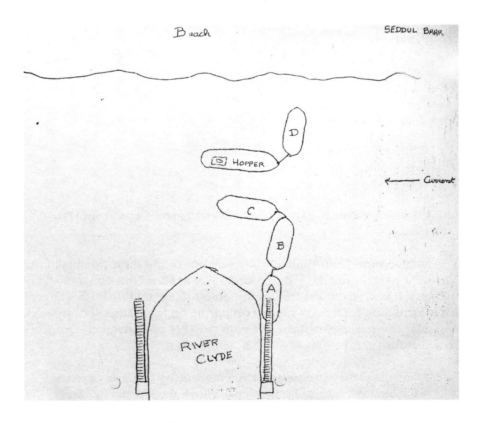

Wilfrid Malleson's sketch plan

period and grounded further from shore and further West than intended. I imagine therefore that lighters from the '*River Clyde*'s port side were joined in the chain. The probable reason for the hopper swinging round was grounding forward and the stern being caught by the current [this was not so, according to Drewry and Samson]. This could also have parted the tow to lighter C.

Having said all this and again looked at my sketch, I am unable to explain why lighter B has not also swung round with the current. Maybe there was no lighter C and that it was lighter B which swung round and lighter A on which we landed. However, I cannot recall crossing over to another lighter before going in the drink. I could not swear to lighter D nor could I explain how it got where I have shown it – just a vague impression that some craft was inshore of the hopper [this was almost certainly Albion's pinnace].

Your photo [sadly missing] puzzles me. I do not remember the ship's launch ahead of the lighter. The other craft looks like a ship's lifeboat, of which there were plenty around then but mostly holed … One can discern some soldiery on their pins … which was certainly not the case while I was there, except for the desperate rush from the boats to the nearest cover.

On re-reading this letter, the only solid piece of evidence produced is that for the presence of the hopper. Not very helpful, I fear – we should have had the Americals [specialised landing craft] there!

As part of the same research, Bush also received another account and sketch from Lennox Boswell, who as a midshipman from the *Queen Elizabeth* helped to rescue some of the Dublin Fusiliers trapped on the Camber. In his account, also written in 1967, he recorded:

I think you're right and the Hopper used power and, in trying to get ahead of the *R Clyde* from its port side, had to stem the current and ended up across the *RC's* bow …

I enclose a plan showing what I mean, but … I've forgotten where the stbd lighter fetched up but I think this is the one that Unwin & Co were trying to place and secure. I wouldn't mind betting that to start with it fetched up where I've shown it, and it then had to be hauled back against the current.

I can't quote my reference, but am pretty sure the 1 Coy Dublins at the Camber were first flight. The other Coys were in the boats that beached on the *RC's* port hand, just after she went ashore, and got badly cut up.

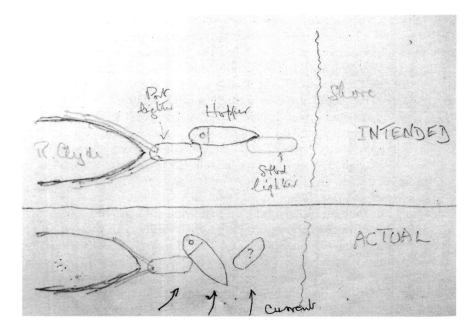

Lennox Boswell's sketch plan

I wouldn't mind betting that the Coy at the Camber had orders 'to join up on the right flank of the Battn landing on V beach'.

This they tried to do … and got shot up. Perhaps their officers got shot up and there was nobody left to lead them up the village street and exploit their success.

Anyhow nobody afloat took in the situation or tried to reinforce them via the Camber. Even when the top brass came round in the *QE* (about noon?) they were all obsessed with the mess on V beach.

Neither the Camber landing or that at S beach (de Tott's Battery) was reinforced and exploited. The world knows about Y beach but the command failure to help the Camber and S beach landings was worse, because the V beach main flight was there all ready [*sic*]. How we missed *Nelson* …

Appendix VI

Brigadier-General Alexander Roper's Critique

Brigadier-General Alexander Roper, CB, the Principal Landing Officer for the Cape Helles operations, witnessed the struggle for V Beach from the troop transport *B3*. Seven years later, he supplied the official historian with a critique of the landing, which is held in The National Archives.

Dated 19 November 1922, the report briefly outlines the plans and composition of the forces engaged and then goes on to examine the suitability of the three main and two minor beaches selected for the southern invasion of Gallipoli.

Having noted that 'all these had been reconnoitred, as far as possible, by Naval officers, from Destroyers and other small craft', the Royal Engineers officer went on to draw the following conclusions based on his experience:

> 9 I think the selection of the most suitable place for landing is one of considerable difficulty. To allow of guns and vehicles being taken straight from the beach, it is essential that the gradient should not be too steep. From this point of view both 'W' and 'V' Beaches seem very suitable – but, when high ground on either side of it and overlooking it is held by the enemy, a beach is apt to prove a death trap to infantry landing there. For the landing of infantry one would, I think, prefer a narrow beach with steep cliffs, so that there is a certain amount of dead ground at the foot – as at ANZAC. Therefore when a landing is likely to be opposed – one should select for choice a place where the infantry can get ashore without much loss to gain possession of the high ground, without too much difficulty and thus protect a suitable beach on which to land vehicles. The point is that the best place for infantry and the best place for animals and vehicles are not necessarily the same.

10 It takes a considerable time to transfer men from one ship to another or from a ship to a boat and this should be practised beforehand.

11 Considerable time was lost at the CAPE HELLES landing owing to our not having sufficient Cutters and Picket Boats. After landing the first lot of men, the Tows had to proceed out to sea and meet the Fleet Sweepers with the second contingent. There should have been enough Tows for both.

12 It was considered very important that the Troops should be given a good hot meal before landing and consequently, in some cases, they were not transferred from the Transports to the Fleet Sweepers till the morning, this took time and caused delay. In other cases they were transferred to the Fleet Sweepers overnight and then it was impossible to give them a hot meal in the morning.

13 The SS RIVER CLYDE was beached and was distinctly useful. Large holes were cut in her sides so as to facilitate access to the gangways, which themselves would give access to lighters towed by the ship and afterwards moored between the ship and the beach.

14 The division of the beach into so called landing places and the allotment of a certain number of soldiers as working party at each landing place seems useless. Infantry coming ashore in cutters, etc, can look after themselves, and much larger working parties are required where it is a case of landing guns or vehicles ...

References and Notes

BL   British Library
CAC   Churchill Archives Centre, Churchill College, Cambridge
IWM   Imperial War Museum
LC   The Liddle Collection, Leeds University
LHC   Liddell Hart Centre for Military Archives, King's College London
NAM   National Army Museum
RHRM Royal Hampshire Regiment Museum
RL   The Robinson Library, University of Newcastle Upon Tyne
RWFM Royal Welch Fusiliers Museum
TNA   The National Archives

Introduction: 'The Rusted Bulk'

1. C. Mackenzie, *Gallipoli Memories*, p.34.
2. ibid, p.77
3. ibid, p.76.

Chapter 1: 'We Shall Have to Land'

1. I. Hamilton, *Gallipoli Diary*, Volume I, p28.
2. ibid.
3. G. Dawnay, quoted by R. Rhodes James, *Gallipoli*, p.61.
4. ibid.
5. E. Bush, *Gallipoli*, p.30.
6. H. von Moltke, quoted by R. Rhodes James, *Gallipoli*, p.3.
7. J. Fisher, quoted by R. Rhodes James, *Gallipoli*, p.3.
8. R. Rhodes James, *Gallipoli*, p.3.
9. W. Churchill, quoted by R. Rhodes James, *Gallipoli*, p.4.
10. H. Kitchener, quoted in M. Gilbert, *Winston S. Churchill, Volume III, Part 1, August 1914–1915*, p.361.
11. S. Carden, quoted by R. Rhodes James, *Gallipoli*, p.28.
12. I. Hamilton, *Gallipoli Diary, Volume I*, p.1.
13. ibid, p.3.

14. ibid, p.5.

15. ibid, p.6.

16. ibid, p.7.

17. ibid, p.16.

18. ibid.

19. O. Williams, quoted by R. Rhodes James, *Gallipoli*, p.55.

20. ibid, p.54.

21. I. Hamilton, *Gallipoli Diary, Volume I*, p.2.

22. ibid, p.14.

23. C. Aspinall, quoted by R. Rhodes James, *Gallipoli*, p.53.

24. I. Hamilton, *Gallipoli Diary, Volume I*, p.17.

25. W. Braithwaite, notes, quoted by I. Hamilton, *Gallipoli Diary, Volume I*, p.17.

26. W. Wemyss, memoirs, quoted in *The Life and Letters of Lord Wester Wemyss GCB, Admiral of the Fleet*, p.197.

27. W. Wemyss, letter to his wife, 3 March 1915, CAC.

28. ibid, 9 March 1915, CAC.

29 ibid, 3 March 1915, CAC.

30. ibid, 7 March 1915, CAC.

31. ibid, 8 March 1915, CAC.

32. W. Wemyss, The Life and Letters of Lord Wester Wemyss GCB, Admiral of the Fleet, p201.

33. W. Wemyss, letter to his wife, 8 March 1915, CAC.

34. ibid, 13 March 1915, CAC.

35. ibid.

36. W. Wemyss, letter to his wife, 18 March 1915, CAC.

37. ibid.

38. I. Hamilton, letter to Sir John French, 19 March 1915, Hamilton Papers, LHC.

39. ibid.

40. W. Birdwood, diary, 22 March 1915, quoted by R. Rhodes James, *Gallipoli*, p.67.

41. I. Hamilton, *Gallipoli Diary, Volume I*, p.42.

42. W. Wemyss, letter to his wife, 14 March 1915, CAC. His chief concern was not whether or not the Navy would break through the Dardanelles, but what they would find in Constantinople when they arrived. 'I am much afraid that when we get through they may burn the city before the Fleet gets there to stop it,' he wrote.

43. W. Wemyss, letter to his wife, 22 March 1915, CAC.

44. I. Hamilton, *Gallipoli Diary, Volume I*, p.46.

Chapter 2: 'My British Division From India'

1. G. Nightingale, letter to his mother, 12 March 1915, TNA.

2. S. Gillon, quoted in *Before Gallipoli* by C. Holland, p.14.

3. G. Nightingale, quoted in Before Gallipoli by Chris Holland, p.14.

4. C. Milward, quoted in *Before Gallipoli* by Chris Holland, p.14.

5. O. Creighton, *With the Twenty-Ninth Division in Gallipoli*, p.15.

6. T. Frankland, note in 86th Brigade War Diary, 25 February 1915, TNA.

7. 86th Brigade War Diary, February 1915, TNA.

8. R. Gillett, interview with Peter Liddle, 1973, LC.

9. H. Harris, memoirs, LC.

10. O. Creighton, *With the Twenty-Ninth Division in Gallipoli*, p.5.

11. ibid, p.13.
12. ibid, p.9.
13. *Rugby Advertiser*, 16 January 1915.
14. *Midland Counties Tribune*, 12 February 1915.
15. ibid.
16. *Nuneaton Observer*, 12 March 1915, quoted in *Before Gallipoli* by C. Holland, p.84.
17. G. Nightingale, letter to his mother, 1 March 1915, TNA.
18. War Diary, 86th Brigade, March 6, 1915, compiled by Brigade Major, Thomas Frankland, TNA.
19. G. Nightingale, letter to his mother, 9 March 1915, TNA.
20. ibid, note to his mother, 13 March 1915, TNA.
21. ibid, 13 March 1915, TNA
22. ibid, 17 March 1915, TNA.
23. G. Geddes, diary, 15 March 1915, IWM.
24. G. Nightingale, letter to his mother, 17 March 1915, TNA.
25. War Diary, 86th Brigade, 16 March 1915, TNA. Frankland stated: 'Vehicles of transport were mostly with units on their ships, except that of Headquarters … and that of 1st R Munster Fus, which was divided between Alaunia and Ausonia. Saddlery was done up in sacks, labelled and intended to accompany drivers and grooms on board the Mercian. Most, however, was stored on the wagons and hence some confusion caused on disembarkation …'
26. Anon, quoted in *Gallipoli* by R. Rhodes James, p.78.
27. G. Davidson, diary, 16 March 1915, quoted in *The Incomparable 29th and the River Clyde*.
28. G. Nightingale, letter to his mother, 17 March 1915, TNA.
29. ibid.
30. A. Hunter-Weston, diary entry, 10 March 1915, BL.
31. G. Nightingale, letter to his mother, 17 March 1915, TNA.
32. G. Walford, letter to his wife, 15 March 1915, LC.
33. ibid, 6 December 1914, LC.
34. ibid, 15 March 1915, LC.
35. ibid, 21 March 1915, LC.
36. A. Hunter-Weston, letter to his wife, 6 April 1915, BL.
37. ibid, 24 March, BL.
38. ibid.
39. ibid.
40. A. Hunter-Weston, diary entry, 25 March 1915, BL.
41. A. Hunter-Weston, 'Appreciation of Situation at the Dardanelles', written on 25 March 1915, BL.
42. ibid.
43. ibid.
44. A. Hunter-Weston, handwritten copy of 'Appreciation of Situation at the Dardanelles', written on 25 March 1915, Hamilton Papers, LHC.
45. I. Hamilton, letter to his wife, 3 May 1915, Hamilton Papers, LHC.
46. I ibid, 9 May 9 1915, Hamilton Papers, LHC.
47. ibid.
48. I. Hamilton, *Gallipoli Diary, Volume I*, p.3.
49. ibid, p.62.

50. A. Hunter-Weston, diary entry, 30 March 1915, BL.
51. A. Hunter-Weston, Note as to the best utilisation of our Forces in the Eastern Mediterranean, March 1915, BL.
52. A. Hunter-Weston, Note with regard to the opinion of Major General Aylmer Hunter-Weston, Commanding 29th Division, as to the best utilisation of our Forces in the Eastern Mediterranean, March 1915.
53. I. Hamilton, *Gallipoli Diary, Volume I*, p.63.
54. A. Hunter-Weston, Note with regard to the opinion of Major General Aylmer Hunter-Weston, Commanding 29th Division, as to the best utilisation of our Forces in the Eastern Mediterranean, March 1915.
55. A. Hunter-Weston, diary entry, 2 April 1915, BL.
56. ibid, letter to his wife, 5 April 1915, BL.
57. ibid.
58. ibid, 6 April 1915, BL.
59. I. Hamilton, *Gallipoli Diary, Volume I*, p.83.
60. G. Nightingale, letter to his mother, 4 April 1915, TNA.
61. G. Geddes, diary, 2 April 1915, IWM.
62. ibid, 3 April 1915, IWM.
63. War Diary, 2nd Battalion Hampshire Regiment, April 1915, TNA.
64. G. Walford, letter to his wife, 5 April 1915, LC.
65. I. Hamilton, letter to Lord Kitchener, 3 April 1915, Hamilton Papers, LHC.
66. A. Hunter-Weston, letter to his wife, 8 April 1915, BL.

Chapter 3: 'A Sailor Out of a Novel'

1. J. Gillam, diary, 15 December 1915, quoted in *Gallipoli Diary*, p.293.
2. W. Wemyss, letter to his wife, 3 April 1915, CAC.
3. ibid.
4. W. Wemyss, letter to his wife, 13 March 1915, CAC.
5. ibid.
6. ibid, 22 March and 25 March 1915, CAC.
7. ibid, 22 March 1915, CAC.
8. ibid, 25 March 1915, CAC.
9. ibid.
10. ibid, 5 April 1915, CAC.
11. ibid, 2 April 1915, CAC.
12. E. Unwin, River Clyde narrative, undated, p.1, IWM.
13. C. Aspinall-Oglander, *Official History: Military Operations Gallipoli*, p.132.
14. ibid.
15. W. Wemyss, letter to his wife, 3 April 1915, CAC.
16. E. Unwin, *The Landing from the River Clyde*, a narrative written for W. Wemyss, undated, p.1, IWM.
17. E. Unwin, River Clyde narrative, undated, p.1, IWM.
18. E. Unwin, *The Landing from the River Clyde*, p.1, IWM.
19. ibid.
20. E. Unwin, River Clyde narrative, undated, p.1, IWM.
21. ibid.
22. ibid.
23. E. Unwin, *The Landing from the River Clyde*, p.1, IWM.

24. ibid.
25. E. Unwin, River Clyde narrative, undated, p.1, IWM.
26. W. Wemyss, *The Navy in the Dardanelles*, p.61.
27. ibid, p.62.
28. ibid.
29. E. Unwin, River Clyde narrative, undated, p.1, IWM.
30. E. Unwin, *The Landing from the River Clyde*, p.1, IWM.
31. E. Unwin, River Clyde narrative, undated, p1, IWM.

Chapter 4: 'The Dirtiest Ship I've Seen'
1. G. Drewry, letter to his father, 12 May 1915, IWM.
2. P.B. Kelly, diary, IWM.
3. ibid.
4. G. Drewry, letter to his father, 12 May 1915, IWM.
5. ibid.
6. ibid.
7. E. Unwin, River Clyde narrative, undated, p.1, IWM.
8. ibid.
9. E. Unwin, *The Landing from the River Clyde*, p.2, IWM.
10. E. Unwin, River Clyde narrative, undated, p.2.
11. E. Unwin, *The Landing from the River Clyde*, p.2.
12. W. Wemyss, *The Navy in the Dardanelles Campaign*, p.62.
13. ibid.
14. E. Unwin, River Clyde narrative, undated, p.2.
15. Ibid.
16. E. Unwin, *The Landing from the River Clyde*, p.2.
17. E. Unwin, River Clyde narrative, undated, p.2.
18. E. Unwin, *The Landing from the River Clyde*, p.3.
19. ibid, p.2.
20. ibid, p.3.
21. G. Drewry, letter to his father, 12 May 1915, IWM.
22. ibid.
23. E. Unwin, *The Landing from the River Clyde*, pp.2-3, IWM. Details of the volunteer crew are, at best, sketchy. I have not been able to discover a full roll of the men who manned the 'Wooden Horse' and even numbers are uncertain. Unwin is imprecise on the matter, while Kelly refers to there being 'about 17 all told' after Unwin departed on 9 May. The most complete crew list that I have found is contained in a post-war letter from an ex-stoker who served aboard HMS *Hussar* from 1914–17 and was among the volunteers on the *River Clyde* during the V Beach landing. The author was F. Thompson, from South Shields, and he was attempting to find out if any of the 'original' naval crew of the *River Clyde* was still alive so that he could renew contact with them. Thompson, who was then unemployed as a result of an injury, concluded his letter with a list of the crew 'as far as I remember': Captain Unwin VC, Lt [actually Midshipman] Drewry VC, Seaman Samson VC, [Leading] Seaman Williams VC, Seaman Ellard, Seaman Cook (coxswain), [ship's] carpenter Lellywin [perhaps more likely Llewellyn], Stoker PO Moore, Stoker PO Dane, Stoker McGrory, Stoker Morris, Stoker Thompson, Stoker Buchanan, and Warrant Eng Huron [actually, Horend]. Another man to be added to that list, according to Unwin's record, is ship's steward

Kerr, the only member of the *River Clyde*'s Merchant Navy complement who served during the landing. Unwin appears to have misjudged the ship's skipper, Captain John Kerr. According to Philip Lecane, in his excellent study of 'The Royal Dublin Fusiliers and the Assault on Gallipoli', Kerr was a highly regarded Merchant Navy officer who went on to enjoy a distinguished war career with the Royal Naval Reserve. Described in one report as 'a loyal, hardworking and reliable officer', he was later awarded a Distinguished Service Cross 'for services in command of a seaplane carrying vessel on the East Indies and Egypt Station during the period 1 April 1916-31 March 1917'. Demobilised in 1919, he moved to Canada where he continued to command merchant ships. The maligned Captain Kerr, DSC, died in 1951.

24. E. Unwin, *The Landing from the River Clyde*, p.3.
25. ibid, p.5, IWM.
26. E. Unwin, River Clyde narrative, p.2.
27. G. Samson, 'Adventures of George Samson: The Cowboy VC', *The Post Sunday Special*, undated (c.1915).
28. ibid.
29. G. Samson, 'George Samson's Adventures with Midshipman Drewry VC', *The Post Sunday Special*, 5 September 1915.
30 G. Samson, 'Carnoustie Seaman Hero Tells How He Won the VC', undated, (c.August 1915).
31. G. Samson, 'George Samson's Adventures with Midshipman Drewry VC'.
32. ibid.
33. ibid.
34. E. Unwin, *The Landing from the River Clyde*, p.3.
35. E. Unwin, River Clyde narrative, p.3.
36. ibid.
37. E. Unwin, River Clyde narrative, p.4.
38. ibid.

Chapter 5: 'A Splendid Crowd'

1. F. McLaren, letter, 13 April 1915, IWM.
2. ibid.
3. ibid.
4. ibid.
5. I. Hamilton, *Gallipoli Diary, Volume I*, p.106.
6. ibid.
7. J. Wedgwood, *Memoirs of a Fighting Life*, p.43.
8. J. Wedgwood, quoted by C.V. Wedgwood in *The Last of the Radicals*, p.100.
9. J. Wedgwood, *Memoirs of a Fighting Life*, p.87.
10. ibid, p.96.
11. A. Coke, letter to his wife, 27 November 1914, Holkham archives.
12. J. Wedgwood, *Memoirs of a Fighting Life*, p.96.
13. ibid.
14. ibid.
15. J. Wedgwood, *Memoirs of a Fighting Life*, pp.96-7.
16. J. Wedgwood, letter to W.S. Churchill 19 February 1915, CAC.
17. J. Wedgwood, *Memoirs of a Fighting Life*, p.97.
18. ibid.

19. B. Isaacs, diary, 9 April 1915, IWM.
20. C. Wedgwood, letter to sister, 11 April 1915, LC.
21. F. McLaren, letter, 2 April 1915, IWM.
22. ibid., 13 April 1915, IWM.
23. J. Wedgwood, letter to W.S. Churchill, 24 April 1915, IWM.
24. F. McLaren, letter, 13 April 1915, IWM.
25. ibid.
26. C. Wedgwood, letter to sister, 11 April 1915, LC.
27. ibid.
28. F. McLaren, letter, 13 April 1915, IWM.
29. ibid.
30. ibid.
31. ibid.
32. ibid.
33. ibid.
34. ibid.
35. ibid.
36. P.B. Kelly, letter to H. Coke, undated, Holkham archives.
37. A. Coke, letter to his wife, 19 April 1915, Holkham archives.
38. ibid.
39. J. Wedgwood, letter to W.S. Churchill, 24 April 1915, IWM.
40. A. Coke, quoted by J. Wedgwood in *Memoirs of a Fighting Life*, p.99.
41. A. Coke, letter to his wife, 19 April 1915, Holkham archives.
42. J. Wedgwood, 'With Machine Guns in Gallipoli', *Westminster Gazette*, p.3.
43. J. Wedgwood, letter to his son, quoted by C.V. Wedgwood in *The Last of the Radicals*, p.104.
44. E. Unwin, River Clyde narrative, p.3.
45. F. McLaren, letter, 16 April 1915, IWM.

Chapter 6: 'A Place I Mayn't Mention'
1. G. Davidson, diary, 17 April 1915, quoted in *The Incomparable 29th and the River Clyde*.
2. G. Nightingale, letter to his mother, 13 April 1915, TNA.
3. ibid.
4. ibid.
5. G. Walford, letter to his wife, 13 April 1915, LC.
6. ibid.
7. I. Hamilton, letter to Lord Kitchener, 10 April 1915, Hamilton Papers, LHC.
8. I. Hamilton, *Gallipoli Diary, Volume I*, p.96.
9. C. Aspinall-Oglander, *Official History: Military Operations Gallipoli*, p.125.
10. I. Hamilton, *Gallipoli Diary, Volume I*, p.95.
11. C. Aspinall-Oglander, *Official History: Military Operations Gallipoli*, p.125.
12. ibid.
13. ibid.
14. I. Hamilton, *Gallipoli Diary, Volume I*, p.96.
15. ibid.
16. I. Hamilton, letter to Lord Kitchener, 3 April 1915, Hamilton Papers, LHC.
17. ibid.
18. I. Hamilton, *Gallipoli Diary, Volume I*, p.98.

19. MEF General Staff War Diary, 1 April 1915, TNA.
20. ibid.
21. ibid.
22. ibid.
23. G. Nightingale, letter to his mother, 13 April 1915, TNA.
24. S. Hare, diary, 18 April 1915, IWM.
25. I. Hamilton, *Gallipoli Diary, Volume I*, p.107.
26. ibid.
27. C.T. Atkinson, *History of the Royal Hampshire Regiment, Vol II*, p.71.
28. ibid.
29. V
30. G. Davidson, diary, 7 April 1915, quoted in *The Incomparable 29th and the River Clyde*.
31. ibid.
32. ibid.
33. I. Hamilton, *Gallipoli Diary, Volume I*, p.108.
34. ibid.
35. I. Hamilton, letter to Lord Kitchener, 15 April 1915, Hamilton Papers, LHC.
36. G. Davidson, diary, 11 April 1915, quoted in *The Incomparable 29th and the River Clyde*.
37. ibid, 12 April 1915.
38. H. Foster, *At Antwerp and the Dardanelles*, p.71.
39. ibid, p.70.
40. ibid.
41. ibid.
42. I. Hamilton, *Gallipoli Diary, Volume I*, p.112.
43. I. Hamilton, letter to Lord Kitchener, 15 April 1915, Hamilton Papers, LHC.
44. A. Hunter-Weston, letter to his wife, 15 April 1915, BL.
45. A. Hunter-Weston, diary, 14 April 1915, BL.
46. I. Hamilton, letter to Lord Kitchener, 15 April 1915, Hamilton Papers, LHC.
47. G. Geddes, diary, 10 April 1915, IWM.
48. G. Davidson, diary, quoted in *The Incomparable 29th and the River Clyde*.
49. G. Walford, letter to his wife, 21 April 1915, LC.
50. ibid.
51. ibid.
52. ibid.
53. ibid.
54. ibid.
55. A. Tisdall, letter to 'A Cambridge Friend', 16 April 1915, *Verses, Letters and Remembrances of Arthur Walderne St Clair Tisdall VC*, p.100.
56. A. Tisdall, letter, 7 October 1914, ibid, p.77.
57. ibid, 9 March 1915, ibid, p.82.
58. ibid, 22 February 1915, LC.
59. I. Hamilton, *Gallipoli Diary, Volume I*, p.57.
60. D. Jerrold, *The Royal Naval Division*, p.70.
61. A. Tisdall, letter to 'A Cambridge Friend', 16 April 1915, *Verses, Letters and Remembrances of Arthur Walderne St Clair Tisdall VC*, p.101.
62. E. Unwin, River Clyde narrative, p.3.
63. H. Tizard, *The Landing at V Beach, Gallipoli*, p.3, IWM.
64. E. Unwin, River Clyde narrative, p3.

65. G. Davidson, diary, 17 April 1915 quoted in *The Incomparable 29th and the River Clyde*.
66. ibid.
67. ibid, 19 April 1915.

Chapter 7: 'An Extremely Dangerous Job'
1. E. Unwin, River Clyde narrative, undated, p.3.
2. E. Unwin, *The Landing from the River Clyde*, p.3.
3. ibid.
4. War Diary, General Staff (GHQ), MEF, Allotment of General Headquarters for the Operations, 20 April 1915, TNA.
5. War Diary, General Staff (GHQ), MEF, 24 April 1915 TNA. Lloyd and Smith were attached to the Anzac landing at Gaba Tepe while Bolton accompanied the troops ashore at W Beach.
6. C. Doughty-Wylie, letter to Gertrude Bell, 20 April 1915, RL.
7. W. de L. Williams, letter to Captain S.H. Pollen, 22 May 1915, IWM. Pollen was Sir Ian Hamilton's military secretary.
8. C. Doughty-Wylie, letter to Gertrude Bell, 20 April 1915, RL
9. C. Doughty-Wylie, letter to his mother-in-law, 20 April 1915, IWM.
10. ibid.
11. W. de L. Williams, letter to Captain S.H. Pollen, 22 May 1915, IWM.
12. ibid.
13. W. de L. Williams, letter, quoted in *Hampshire Regimental Journal*, June 1915, RHRM.
14. Colonel Neville Howse was Assistant Director of Medical Services to the 1st Australian Division. As a young medical officer in the Boer war he had earned the Victoria Cross for braving 'a very heavy crossfire' to rescue a wounded man during a skirmish near Vredefort on 24 July 1900. Among the men he helped saved that day was Captain Charles 'Dick' Doughty-Wylie, who recommended his courage be recognised, noting 'a more clear VC and better deserved I haven't heard of'.
15. War Diary, General Staff (GHQ), MEF, 18 March 1915, TNA.
16. C. Doughty-Wylie, Col Doughty-Wylie's Diary: Summary of telegrams and reports received, TNA.
17. ibid, Report of agent, April 4, 1915, TNA.
18. G. Howell, *Daughter of the Desert: The Remarkable Life of Gertrude Bell*, p.141.
19. ibid, p.142.
20. G. Bell, cited by J. Wallach in *Desert Queen*, p.96.
21. G. Bell, letter to Sir Valentine Chirol, December 1913, quoted by S. Dearden in 'A Journey of the Heart', *Cornhill Magazine*, Vol 177, p.471.
22. C. Doughty-Wylie, letter to Gertrude Bell, 15 January 1915, RL.
23. G. Bell, letter to C 'Dick' Doughty-Wylie, January 1915, RL.
24. G. Howell, *Daughter of the Desert: The Remarkable Life of Gertrude Bell*, p.163.
25. C. Doughty-Wylie, letter to his mother-in-law, Mrs H.H. 'Jean' Coe, 20 April 1915, IWM.
26. C. Doughty-Wylie, letter to Gertrude Bell, 20 April 1915, RL.
27. ibid.

Chapter 8: 'Blowing Big Guns'
1. I. Hamilton, *Gallipoli Diary, Volume I*, p.120.
2. G. Geddes, typescript diary, 20 April 1915, IWM. 'Whole show scandalous and

several fellows cursing like anything,' he noted. In a letter to his mother, Guy Nightingale wrote: 'It was so rough that no boats could put off to fetch us back. We were on the beach from 3pm to 9pm signalling and finally the Inflexible came up with a steam pinnace and 7 cutters and took us back!'

3. ibid.
4. A. Hunter-Weston, letter to his wife, 21 April 1915, BL.
5. D. Illingworth, letter to his mother, 21 April 1915, via Stephen Chambers.
6. R. Gillett, diary entry, 21 April 1915, IWM.
7. ibid.
8. A. Hunter-Weston, letter to his wife, 21 April, 1915, BL.
9. ibid.
10. A. Hunter-Weston, Personal Note in Gallipoli Diary, BL.
11. ibid.
12. A. Hunter-Weston, letter to his wife, 12 April 1915, BL. Hunter-Weston, who had been a personal friend of Wemyss' late brother, Randolph, described the admiral as 'a capital fellow'.
13 W. Wemyss, letter to his wife, 21 April 1915, CAC.
14. J.M. de Robeck, *Naval and Military Operations: Duties and Responsibilities of Admirals,* 2 April 1915, TNA. The same instructions stated that 'should the Vice-Admiral [de Robeck] and the main portion of the Fleet proceed into the Marmora, he [Wemyss] will be in command of the Squadron remaining outside the Dardanelles and responsible for communications and supply of the Fleet and the Army'.
15. Conveyance of flotillas from Tenedos to place of landing, 22 April 1915, TNA.
16. Instructions for landing in Morto Bay, TNA.
17. Orders for River Clyde, 21 April 1915, TNA.
18. G. Walford, letter to his wife, 26 March 1915, LC.
19. Preliminary orders No.1, contained in War Diary, 1st Royal Munster Fusiliers, 21 April 1915, TNA.
20. War Diary, General Staff, 29th Division, Operation Order No.1, Appendix I, 20 April 1915, TNA.
21. ibid.
22. R. Rhodes James, *Gallipoli,* p.89.
23. I. Hamilton, quoted by R. Rhodes James in *Gallipoli,* p.89.
24. Aeroplane spotting during the disembarkation and advance of the Army (29th Division), 20 April 1915, TNA.
25. Hamilton's air support consisted of eleven pilots, 120 men and five 'serviceable' aircraft belonging to No.3 Squadron, Royal Naval Air Service, under the command of Squadron Commander Charles Samson. According to Hamilton (*Gallipoli Diary,* p.110), Samson estimated that he required 'a minimum' of thirty two-seaters, twenty-four fighters, forty pilots and 400 men to carry out such a 'stunt' as the landings. 'So equipped he reckons he could take the Peninsula by himself and save us all a vast lot of trouble,' noted Hamilton.
26. Instructions for artillery co-operation between HM Ships and 29th Division, 20 April 1915, TNA.
27. ibid.
28. ibid.
29. ibid.
30. G. Geddes, diary entry, 21 April 1915, IWM.

31. G. Nightingale, letter to his mother, 21 April, 1915, TNA.

Chapter 9: 'Tis a Grand Adventure'
1. I. Hamilton, *Gallipoli Diary, Volume I*, p.121.
2. R. Keyes, letter to his wife, 22 April 1915, in *The Keyes Papers, Vol I 1914–1918*, p.126.
3. I. Hamilton, *Gallipoli Diary, Volume I*, p.121.
4. G. Davidson, diary, 22 April 1915, quoted in *The Incomparable 29th and the River Clyde*.
5. C. Boxall, letter to his family, 22 April 1915, EC.
6. J. Wedgwood, letter to his son, 22 April 1915, quoted by C.V. Wedgwood in *The Last of the Radicals*, pp.103-4.
7. J. Wedgwood, letter to his mother, undated, quoted in *Memoirs of a Fighting Life*, p.98.
8. W. Wemyss, letter to his wife, 23 April 1915, CAC.
9. ibid. 'If the Allies get Constantinople it must have a very immediate effect on the war, whatever the ultimate complications,' he added.
10. I. Hamilton, *Gallipoli Diary, Volume I*, p.123.
11. ibid.
12. I. Hamilton, letter to Lord Kitchener, 23 April 1915, Hamilton Papers, LHC.
13. ibid.
14. ibid.
15. A. Hunter-Weston, letter to his wife, 23 April 1915, BL.
16. O. Williams, quoted by R Rhodes James, *Gallipoli*, p.95.
17. E. Unwin, *The Landing from the River Clyde*, p.3.
18. P.B. Kelly, letter to H Coke, undated, Holkham archives.
19. G. Drewry, letter to his father, 12 May 1915, IWM.
20. J. Wedgwood, 'With Machine Guns in Gallipoli', *Westminster Gazette*, p.3.
21. G. Drewry, letter to his father, 12 May 1915, IWM.
22. G. Geddes, The landing from the River Clyde at V Beach, 25 April 1915, by a Company Commander in the 1st Royal Munster Fusiliers, 86th Brigade War Diary, TNA.
23. ibid.
24. ibid.
25. ibid.
26. G. Nightingale, letter to his mother, 23 April 1915, TNA.
27. G. Davidson, diary, 23 April 1915, quoted in *The Incomparable 29th and the River Clyde*.
28. ibid.
29. ibid.
30. ibid.
31. O. Williams, quoted by R. Rhodes James, *Gallipoli*, p.95.
32. ibid.
33. G. Davidson, diary, 23 April 1915, quoted in *The Incomparable 29th and the River Clyde*.
34. R. Gillett, diary entry, 24 April 1915, IWM.
35. G. Geddes, The landing from the River Clyde at V Beach, 25 April 1915, by a Company Commander in the 1st Royal Munster Fusiliers, 86th Brigade War Diary, TNA.
36. C. Milward, diary entry, 24 April 1915, TNA.
37. ibid. Colonel Owen Wolley-Dod, DSO, was Hunter-Weston's senior staff officer in the 29th Division.
38. A. Hunter-Weston, letter to his wife, 24 April 1915, BL.

39. ibid.
40. G. Davidson, diary, 24 April 1915, quoted in *The Incomparable 29th and the River Clyde*.
41. ibid.
42. E. Unwin, River Clyde narrative, p.4.
43. ibid.
44. G. Drewry, letter to his father, 12 May 1915, IWM.
45. ibid.
46. ibid.
47. E. Unwin, River Clyde narrative, p.4.
48. ibid.
49. G. Drewry, letter to his father, 12 May 1915, IWM.
50. C. Milward, diary entry, 24 April 1915, TNA.
51. G. Davidson, diary, 24 April 1915, quoted in *The Incomparable 29th and the River Clyde*.
52. ibid.
53. D. Fyffe, diary, quoted by Richard van Emden and Stephen Chambers in *Gallipoli: The Dardanelles Disaster in Soldiers' Words and Pictures*, p.57.
54. P.B. Kelly, letter to H. Coke, undated, Holkham archives.
55. ibid.
56. A. Coke, letter to his wife, 24 April 1915, Holkham archives.
57. 'An Officer's Account of the Landing', *Hampshire Regimental Journal*, July 1915, RHRM.
58. ibid.
59. D. Fyffe, diary, quoted by Richard van Emden and Stephen Chambers, p.57.
60. ibid.
61. H. Tizard, The Landing at V Beach, Gallipoli, p.3.
62. The War Diary of the 1/1st West Riding Field Company makes no mention of the embarkation exercise carried out on the *River Clyde* at Lemnos on 17 April.
63. G. Smith, transcript of interview with Peter Liddle, September 1972, LC.
64. H. Tizard, The Landing at V Beach, Gallipoli, p.3.
65. The distribution of the Munsters is taken from Tizard's narrative account of the landing.
66. G. Geddes, Extracts from Diary kept in the Dardanelles, 24 April 1915, IWM.
67. D. Fyffe, diary, quoted by Richard van Emden and Stephen Chambers, pp.57-9.
68. E. Unwin, River Clyde narrative, p.4.
69. ibid.
70. The figure was probably nearer to 2,100 men, although the total varies in different accounts. Both the Official History and Wemyss refer variously to 2,000 and 2,100 men, while Tizard writes of there being 'about 2,100' men, De Lancey Williams has 'over 2,000' and Wedgwood hovers between '2,400 Munsters, Dublins and Hampshires' and 2,500 men all told!
71. G. Davidson, diary, 24 April 1915, quoted in *The Incomparable 29th and the River Clyde*.
72. G. Drewry, letter to his father, 12 May 1915, IWM.
73. E. Unwin, River Clyde narrative, p.4. His actual instructions, as set out in Rear-Admiral Wemyss' Orders for the Landing of the Expeditionary Force issued on 17 April 1915, stated: 'The collier 'River Clyde' will leave at such time as to enable her to reach a rendezvous 1½ miles S W of Cape Helles one hour before dawn.'
74. E. Unwin, The Landing from the River Clyde, a narrative written for W. Wemyss, p.4.

75. D. Fyffe, diary, quoted by Richard van Emden and Stephen Chambers, pp.59-60.

76. ibid.

77. ibid.

78. ibid.

79. E. Unwin, The Landing from the River Clyde, a narrative written for W. Wemyss, p.4.

80. G. Drewry, letter to his father, 12 May 1915, IWM.

81. G. Davidson, *The Incomparable 29th and the River Clyde*.

82. G. Davidson, diary, 24 April 1915, quoted in *The Incomparable 29th and the River Clyde*.

83. R. Gillett, transcript of talk on the BBC, April 1965, marking the fiftieth anniversary of the landing, IWM.

84. G. Geddes, Extracts from Diary kept in the Dardanelles, 24 April 1915.

85. G. Geddes, The landing from the River Clyde at V Beach, 25 April 1915, by a Company Commander in the 1st Royal Munster Fusiliers, 86th Brigade War Diary, TNA.

86. ibid.

Chapter 10: 'Dad, it Was Glorious'

1. E. Unwin, The Landing from the River Clyde, a narrative written for W. Wemyss, p.4.

2. E. Unwin, River Clyde narrative, p.4.

3. G. Drewry, letter to his father, 12 May 1915, IWM.

4. D. Fyffe, diary, quoted by Richard van Emden and Stephen Chambers, pp.60-1.

5. J . Godfrey, *The Naval Memoirs of Admiral J. H. Godfrey*, unpublished typescript, p.3, CAC.

6. ibid.

7. W. Wemyss, Supplementary report on the landings of 25 April 1915, written aboard HMS *Hussar*, 3 June 1915, TNA.

8. 'An Officer's Account of the Landing', *Hampshire Regimental Journal*, June 1915, RHRM.

9. G. Smith, narrative of the landing, written twenty years after, LC.

10. P.B. Kelly, letter to H Coke, undated, Holkham archives.

11. G. Davidson, narrative, quoted in *The Incomparable 29th and the River Clyde*.

12. ibid.

13. G. Drewry, letter to his father, 12 May 1915, IWM.

14. F. MacLiesh, diary entry, 25 April 1915, CAC.

15. H. Williams, typescript narrative, *Fat's War*, IWM.

16. M. Sabri, *Memoirs of the Battalion Commander Who Opposed the First Landings at Seddulbahr*, p.2, IWM.

17. ibid.

18. ibid.

19. A reference made in the Reports of the captains of the *Albion*, *Swiftsure* and *Euryalus*.

20. C. Maxwell-Lefroy, HMS *Swiftsure*, Report of Operations, 5 May 1915, TNA.

21. ibid.

22. ibid.

23. R. Prior, *Gallipoli: The End of the Myth*, p.101.

24. ibid.

25. A. Thomson, letter to the historian John North, 20 April 1937, IWM.

26. H. Watts-Jones, HMS *Albion*, Report of Operations, 29 April 1915, TNA.
27. War Diary, General Staff, 29th Division, 25 April 1915, TNA.
28. E. Unwin, The Landing from the River Clyde, a narrative written for W. Wemyss, p.4.
29. E. Unwin, River Clyde narrative, p.4.
30. H. Tizard, The Landing at V Beach, Gallipoli, p.6.
31. ibid.
32. ibid.
33. ibid.
34. E. Unwin, River Clyde narrative, p.4.
35. ibid.
36. E. Unwin, The Landing from the River Clyde, a narrative written for W. Wemyss, p.4.
37. ibid.
38. E. Unwin, River Clyde narrative, undated, pp.4-5.
39. In an account written by an officer of the Hampshire Regiment who was aboard the *River Clyde*, the collier made 'two complete circles to starboard' on account of the tows carrying the Dublins being 'a bit late'. He added: 'These circles took her over towards the Asia Minor shore, and we consequently began to receive attention from some guns on that side …' The tows were, in his words, 'still a bit behind' when Unwin set course for the beach. Information from Hampshire Regimental Journal, July 1915, RHRM.
40. D. Fyffe, diary, quoted by Richard van Emden and Stephen Chambers, p.108.
41. ibid, pp.108-9.
42. ibid, p.108.
43. G. Drewry, letter to his father, 12 May 1915, IWM.
44. 'An Officer's Account of the Landing', *Hampshire Regimental Journal*, July 1915, RHRM.
45. E. Unwin, The Landing from the River Clyde, a narrative written for W. Wemyss, p.5.
46. ibid, p.4.
47. E. Unwin, River Clyde narrative, p.5.
48. E. Unwin, The Landing from the River Clyde, a narrative written for W. Wemyss, p.4.
49. Unidentified member of the RNAS, letter, 2 May 1915, Holkham archives.
50. D. Fyffe, diary, quoted by Richard van Emden and Stephen Chambers, p.109.
51. H. Watts-Jones, HMS *Albion*, Report of Operations, 29 April 1915, TNA.
52. Instructions for Artillery Cooperation Between HM Ships and 29th Division, 20 April 1915, Rear-Admiral Stuart Nicholson, commanding Third Division, Eastern Mediterranean Squadron, NA. Nicholson wrote: 'The greatest care must be taken by all ships in identifying any bodies of troops visible … In any doubtful case fire must not be opened without the direct orders of the Commanding Officer of the ship who should consult with the Military Officer on board.' According to Commander Isham Worsley Gibson, *Albion*'s gunnery officer, the order to 'cease fire' came direct from Wemyss in a signal sent at around 6.20am as the first tows were approaching V Beach. In his diary, Gibson noted: 'I don't know why, but so far as I can remember we were stopped firing while troops were landing, a great mistake, we ought to have gone on firing over their heads. The risk was not great.' IWM.

53. G. Davidson, narrative, quoted in *The Incomparable 29th and the River Clyde*.
54. 'An Officer's Account of the Landing', *Hampshire Regimental Journal*, June 1915, RHRM.
55. R. Gillett, transcript of talk given on the BBC in April 1965, IWM.
56. D. Fyffe, diary, quoted by Richard van Emden and Stephen Chambers, p.109.
57. G. Smith, narrative of the landing, written twenty years after, LC.
58. ibid.
59. R. Gillett, transcript of talk given on the BBC in April 1965, IWM.
60. E. Unwin, River Clyde narrative, p.5. In his account to Wemyss, Unwin contradicted this version, insisting 'I beached the ship exactly where I intended to', p.10.
61. W. de L. Williams, letter, quoted in *Hampshire Regimental Journal*, June 1915, RHRM.

Chapter 11: 'Slaughtered Like Rats in a Trap'
1. M. Sabri, p.2.
2. H. Tizard, The Landing at V Beach, Gallipoli, pp.5-6.
3. M. Lloyd, The Landing at V Beach, 25 April, 1915, Account to the captain of HMS *Cornwallis*, IWM.
4. E. Rickus, letter to his sister from RN Hospital, Malta, 7 May 1915, IWM.
5. D. French, letter, NAM.
6. J. Wedgwood, letter to W.S. Churchill, 27 April 1915, IWM.
7. W. de L. Williams, letter, quoted in *Hampshire Regimental Journal*, June 1915, RHRM.
8. P.B. Kelly, letter to H. Coke, undated, Holkham archives.
9. D. Fyffe, diary, quoted by Richard van Emden and Stephen Chambers, p.109.
10. P.B. Kelly, letter to H Coke, undated, Holkham archives.
11. Private Fox, letter quoted in *Torquay in the Great War*, p.34.
12. A. Morrison, letter quoted in *Torquay in the Great War*, pp.34-5.
13. C. Maffett, quoted in *Neill's Blue Caps, Vol III 1914–1922*, pp.30-1.
14. D. French, letter, NAM.
15. ibid.
16. R. Martin, letter, 26 May 1915, quoted in *Gallipoli* by Peter Hart, p.146.
17. J. McColgan, letter to his wife, published in *Cork Examiner*, 20 May 1915.
18. ibid.
19. ibid.
20. N. Diggle, letter to Winston Churchill, First Lord of the Admiralty, 12 May 1915, CAC.
21. A.T. Stewart and C.J.E. Peshall, *The Immortal Gamble and the Part Played In It by HMS Cornwallis*, p.88.
22. Ibid, pp.88-9. Able Seaman William Taylor, who was thirty-nine and from Liverpool, succumbed to his injuries on 15 June 1915. He was one of sixteen men from Cornwallis killed or died of wounds received on 25 April 1915. A further forty-four men from the ship's company were wounded.
23. ibid, pp.90-1. Petty Officer William Medhurst was born in Sussex and was thirty-nine when he was killed.
24. E. Rickus, letter to his sister from RN Hospital, Malta, 7 May 1915, IWM.
25. ibid.
26. ibid.
27. W. Wemyss, Report on the Southern Landing Operations, 25 April 1915, TNA.
28. J. de Robeck, Account of Landing Operations, 25–26 April 1915, TNA.
29. ibid. Writing to Jacobs' mother, the captain of the *Lord Nelson* gave a slightly different

version: 'Your son ... was in one of the boats taking soldiers ashore and from evidence of one of the survivors was standing up in the boat which had grounded, trying to get her afloat under heavy fire. While doing this he was struck and fell and I understand was killed on the spot. It is no doubt unnecessary for me to tell you, his mother, that your son was a gallant man but I do know he was also a fine seaman and one who did his duty at all times and at the end was faithful to death.'

30. G. Nightingale, letter to his mother, 1 May 1915, TNA.
31. G. Geddes, Extracts from Diary kept in the Dardanelles, 25 April 1915, IWM.
32. G. Geddes, The landing from the River Clyde at V Beach, 25 April 1915, TNA.
33. J. Wedgwood, letter to W.S. Churchill, 27 April 1915, IWM.
34. W. de L. Williams, letter, quoted in Hampshire Regimental Journal, June 1915, RHRM.
35. ibid.
36. ibid.
37. G. Davidson, narrative, quoted in *The Incomparable 29th and the River Clyde*.
38. D. Fyffe, diary, quoted by Richard van Emden and Stephen Chambers, p.112.
39. 'An Officer's Account of the Landing', *Hampshire Regimental Journal*, July 1915, RHRM.
40. H. Tizard, The Landing at V Beach, Gallipoli, p.7.
41. ibid.
42. H. Foster, *At Antwerp and the Dardanelles*, p.69.
43. ibid, p.83.
44. ibid, pp.83-4.
45. ibid, p.84. Father Thomas Harker, catholic chaplain to the 1st Royal Munster Fusiliers, believed some of the reports about Finn's bravery were exaggerated. Harker, who was on board the *River Clyde*, wrote to Monsignor Manuel Bidwell, secretary for military affairs to the Bishop in ecclesiastical control of all serving catholic chaplains, stating: 'The newspaper accounts and stories told in panegyric at Hull during Finn's requiem are a fake. Good zealous priest that he was, he needs no lies to endear him among the Dublins.' (Quoted in The Cross on the Sword: Catholic Chaplains to the Forces, by Major Tom Johnstone and Dr James Hagerty, publisher Geoffrey Chapman, 1996).
46. H.D. O'Hara, quoted in *Neill's Blue Caps, Vol III 1914–1922*, p.32.
47. A.W. Molony, quoted in *Neill's Blue Caps, Vol III 1914–1922*, p.34.
48. M. Sabri, p.3.
49. ibid.
50. ibid.
51. H. Forbes, Boats' Crews' Experiences, quoted in *The Immortal Gamble*, pp.110-1.
52. H.C. Wylly, *Neill's Blue Caps, Vol III 1914–1922*, p.34.
53. In another version of de Lusignan's death, Captain John Mood said he was killed trying to save one of his men who was wounded. Writing to de Lusignan's mother from hospital in Cairo, he stated: 'He and I and 100 men had a special job apart from the rest of the Battalion. We had to land round the south side of Sedd-el-Bahr and Captain [Arthur] Johnson to the north of it. I sent him to the left with a party of men to join up with Johnson who I afterwards heard was held up with the [battalion] on the beach and never reached the village at all, while I went right according to orders. By midday we were kicked out of the village back to the fort at the end of it. His party was also outnumbered and a wounded man lay in the middle of the street being sniped to death when the dear old prince tried to pull him back into cover and

was at what no one else dared to do. I feel sure you would like to know the splendid manner of his death. I heard all this from one of his men who survived ...' Quoted in *Beneath a Turkish Sky* by Philip Lecane, pp.160-1.

54. G. Norman, quoted in *Gallipoli* by Eric Bush, p.120.
55. A.W. Molony, quoted in *Neill's Blue Caps, Vol III 1914–1922*, p.29.
56. R. Rooth, notice published on board SS *Ausonia*, 17 March 1915, copied into C. Grimshaw's notebook, quoted by Philip Lecane in *Beneath a Turkish Sky*, pp.98-9.
57. C. Maffett, quoted in *Neill's Blue Caps, Vol III 1914–1922*, pp.30-1.
58. ibid.
59. D. French, letter, NAM.
60. ibid.

Chapter 12: 'The Hardest Haul'
1. E. Unwin, River Clyde narrative, p.5.
2. E. Unwin, The Landing from the River Clyde, a narrative written for W. Wemyss, p.5.
3. G. Samson, 'Carnoustie's Seaman Hero Tells How He Won the VC', newspaper article, August 1915.
4. D. Fyffe, diary, quoted by Richard van Emden and Stephen Chambers, p.109.
5. G. Samson, ibid.
6. D. Fyffe, diary, quoted by Richard van Emden and Stephen Chambers, p.112.
7. D. Illingworth, letter to his brother, 6 May 1915, via Stephen Chambers.
8. G. Drewry, letter to his father, 12 May 1915, IWM.
9. ibid.
10. ibid.
11. ibid.
12. E. Unwin, River Clyde narrative, p.5.
13. E Unwin, The Landing from the River Clyde, a narrative written for W. Wemyss, p.5.
14. E. Unwin, River Clyde narrative, p.5.
15. ibid.
16. G. Drewry, letter to his father, 12 May 1915, IWM.
17. ibid.
18. ibid.
19. ibid.
20. E. Unwin, *The Landing from the River Clyde*, a narrative written for W. Wemyss, p.6.
21. E. Unwin, River Clyde narrative, p.5.

Chapter 13: 'No Finer Episode'
1. G. Geddes, *The landing from the River Clyde at V Beach*, 25 April 1915, TNA.
2. ibid.
3. ibid.
4. ibid.
5. ibid.
6. ibid.
7. D. French, letter, NAM.
8. ibid.
9. D. Fyffe, diary, quoted by Richard van Emden and Stephen Chambers, p.114.
10. ibid.

11. ibid, pp.114-5.
12. E. Henderson, report dictated to Captain H.S. Wilson, 25 April 1915, War Diary, 1st Royal Munster Fusiliers, TNA.
13. N. Dewhurst, quoted in *Norman Dewhurst MC* by H.J. Edmonds, p.26.
14. E. Henderson, report dictated to Captain H.S. Wilson, 25 April 1915, TNA.
15. C. Milward, diary entry, 25 April 1915, TNA.
16. R. Lane, quoted in *The Landing at V Beach Gallipoli* by Lieutenant Colonel H.E. Tizard, p.9, IWM. Henderson subsequently died of his wounds in hospital at Alexandria in Egypt on 20 May 1915. He was Mentioned in Despatches for his gallant leadership.
17. ibid.
18. G. Geddes, letter, 30 April 1915, IWM.
19. ibid.
20. G. Geddes, The landing from the River Clyde at V Beach, 25 April 1915, by a Company Commander in the 1st Royal Munster Fusiliers, 86th Brigade War Diary, NA. Second Lieutenant Timothy Sullivan was a thirty-one-year-old veteran of the Boer war. He had been commissioned while billeted in Coventry where he had married Maud Bates shortly before embarking for the Dardanelles. His best man was Second Lieutenant John Watts. The Munsters' adjutant, Captain Harry Wilson reckoned the sea into which Geddes 'plunged' was about 10ft deep and he confirmed: 'Many of the men who had escaped the rifle and machine gun fire on the gangways and barges followed him, but owing to the weight of their ammunition and equipment were drowned.'
21. W. Flynn, sound record 4103, IWM.
22. ibid.
23. R. Breeks, letter to Betty Walford, 1 May 1915, LC.
24. ibid.
25. J. d'Apice, letter passed to Betty Walford, 15 May 1915, LC.
26. ibid.
27. ibid.
28. G. Geddes, The landing from the River Clyde at V Beach, 25 April, 1915, TNA.
29. G. Geddes, letter, 30 April 1915, IWM.
30. G. Geddes, typescript diary entry, 25 April 1915, IWM.
31. G. Geddes, letter, 30 April 1915, IWM.
32. ibid.
33. G. Geddes, The landing from the River Clyde at V Beach, 25 April 1915, TNA.
34. ibid.
35. ibid.
36. E. Henderson, report dictated to Captain H.S. Wilson, 25 April 1915, TNA.
37. G. Geddes, Extracts from Diary kept in the Dardanelles by Lt-Col G. W. Geddes DSO, IWM.
38. G. Geddes, The Landing from the River Clyde at V Beach, 25 April 1915, TNA. In his diary entry, Geddes noted that Ryan found Sedd-el-Bahr to be 'but lightly held'.
39. E. Henderson, report dictated to Captain H.S. Wilson, 25 April 1915, TNA.
40. H. Wilson, Summary of events compiled on 26 April 1915, War Diary, 1st Royal Munster Fusiliers, TNA.
41. ibid.
42. ibid.
43. ibid.

44. E. Unwin, The Landing from the River Clyde, a narrative written for W. Wemyss, p.6.
45. E. Unwin, River Clyde narrative, p.5.
46. ibid, pp.5-6.
47. E. Unwin, The Landing from the River Clyde, a narrative written for W. Wemyss, p.6.
48. ibid.
49. E. Unwin, River Clyde narrative, p.6. According to Unwin, it was while trying to get Williams on to the lighter that he saw Drewry for the first time since watching the steam hopper veer off course.
50. G. Drewry, letter to his father, 12 May 1915, IWM.
51. E. Unwin, River Clyde narrative, p.6.
52. H Tizard, The Landing at V Beach, Gallipoli, p.8.
53. ibid.
54. ibid.
55. ibid.
56. M. Sabri, p.3.
57. ibid.

Chapter 14: 'Have You Secured the Hawser?'

1. O. Striedinger, Notes of Landing W Beach, 25 April 1915, TNA.
2. ibid.
3. War Diary, 29th Division, 25 April 1915, TNA. The report of troops in Sedd-el-Bahr was probably a reference to the party of Royal Dublin Fusiliers which landed at the Camber and briefly gained a footing in the village before being forced to withdraw.
4. L. Berridge, letter, IWM.
5. H. Watts-Jones, HMS *Albion*, Report of Operations, 29 April 1915, TNA.
6. ibid.
7. ibid.
8. W. Wemyss, Landing of Army on Gallipoli Peninsula: Orders for Fleet Sweepers, 21 April 1915, TNA.
9. ibid.
10. J. M. de Robeck, Orders for Combined Operations: Beach Parties, 12 April 1915, TNA.
11. M. Lloyd, The Landing at V Beach, 25 April 1915, Account to the captain of HMS *Cornwallis*, IWM.
12. H. Weblin, Landing at V Beach, 25 April 1915, Account to the captain of HMS *Cornwallis*, IWM.
13. M. Lloyd, Boats' Crews' Experiences, quoted in *The Immortal Gamble*, p.105.
14. H. Forbes, Boats' Crews' Experiences, quoted in *The Immortal Gamble*, pp.111–2.
15. H. Weblin, Landing at V Beach, 25 April 1915, Account to the captain of HMS *Cornwallis*, IWM.
16. M. Lloyd, The Landing at V Beach, 25 April 1915, Account to the captain of HMS *Cornwallis*, IWM.
17. ibid.
18. ibid.
19. H. Weblin, Landing at V Beach, 25 April 1915, Account to the captain of HMS *Cornwallis*, IWM.
20. ibid.

21. M. Lloyd, The Landing at V Beach, 25 April 1915, Account to the captain of HMS *Cornwallis*, IWM.

22. ibid.

23. M. Lloyd, Boats' Crews' Experiences, quoted in *The Immortal Gamble*, p.106.

24. H. Weblin, Landing at V Beach, 25 April 1915, Account to the captain of HMS *Cornwallis*, IWM.

25. ibid.

26. ibid.

27. ibid.

28. M. Lloyd, Boats' Crews' Experiences, quoted in *The Immortal Gamble*, p.107.

29. G. Drewry, letter to his father, 12 May 1915, IWM.

30. As with all timings at V Beach on 25-26 April 1915, there is some disagreement here. W. Malleson, for instance, has a somewhat later time.

31. A. Morse, letter to E. Unwin, 4 May 1926, IWM.

32. G. Stoney, letter to his brother, 10 May 1915, IWM.

33. G. Drewry, letter to his father, 12 May 1915, IWM.

34. W. Malleson, letter to Eric Bush, 18 July 1967, IWM. Even after linking the lighter to the hopper the troops refused to budge. Malleson told Bush: 'The soldiers were not going to move until dark and it is difficult to blame them. I expect most of their officers were casualties – I did not see any.'

35. W. Malleson, account of the landing at V Beach, written on 21 March 1916, via his family.

36. ibid.

37. G. Drewry, letter to his father, 12 May 1915, IWM.

38. M. Lloyd, Boats' Crews' Experiences, quoted in *The Immortal Gamble*, p.107.

39. M. Lloyd, The Landing at V Beach, 25 April 1915, Account to the captain of HMS *Cornwallis*, IWM.

40. H. Weblin, Landing at V Beach, 25 April 1915, Account to the captain of HMS *Cornwallis*, IWM.

41. G. Drewry, letter to his father, 12 May 1915, IWM.

42. W. Malleson, account of the landing at V Beach, written on 21 March 1916, via his family.

43. ibid.

44. ibid.

45. A. Morse, letter to E. Unwin, 4 May, 1926, IWM.

46. W. Malleson, account of the landing at V Beach, written on 21 March 1916, via his family.

47. G. Drewry, letter to his father, 12 May 1915, IWM.

48. ibid.

49. H. Forbes, Boats' Crews' Experiences, quoted in *The Immortal Gamble*, pp.112-3.

50. N. Diggle, letter to Winston Churchill, First Lord of the Admiralty, 12 May 1915, CAC.

51. H. Forbes, Boats' Crews' Experiences, quoted in The Immortal Gamble, p112–113. Able Seaman Ernest Grose was 30. He left a widow living in Clapham Junction, London. Able Seaman H.G. Smith (RFR) and Ordinary Seaman F.E. Sawyer both survived their injuries.

52. N. Diggle, letter to Winston Churchill, First Lord of the Admiralty, 12 May 1915, CAC.

53. ibid.

54. H. Watts-Jones, HMS *Albion*, Report of Operations, 29 April 1915, TNA.

55. I. Hamilton, Diary, 25 April 1915, Hamilton Papers, LH.
56. I. Hamilton, *Gallipoli Diary, Volume I*, pp.130-1.
57. ibid, p.131.
58. J. Churchill, letter to his brother Winston Churchill, First Lord of the Admiralty, 27 April 1915, CAC.
59. ibid.
60. ibid.
61. ibid.
62. ibid.
63. ibid.
64. R. Keyes, *The Fight for Gallipoli*, p.119.
65. ibid.
66. ibid.
67. ibid.
68. I. Hamilton, *Gallipoli Diary, Volume I*, p.131.
69. ibid, pp.131-2.
70. J. Churchill, letter to his brother Winston Churchill, First Lord of the Admiralty, 27 April 1915, CAC.
71. I. Hamilton, *Gallipoli Diary, Volume I*, p.132.
72. H. Watts-Jones, HMS *Albion*, Report of Operations, 29 April 1915, TNA.

Chapter 15: 'Red With Blood'
1. C.R. Samson, *Fights and Flights*, p.233.
2. ibid, p.234.
3. ibid, p.233.
4. ibid, pp.234-5.
5. War Diary, General Staff (GHQ), Mediterranean Expeditionary Force, 25 April 1915, TNA.
6. H. Tizard, The Landing at V Beach, Gallipoli, p.10.
7. ibid.
8. ibid.
9. In his subsequently published memoir, Norman Dewhurst wrote: 'Captain [*sic*] Pollard was killed before my eyes as he passed through the exit port on to the gangway.'
10. N. Dewhurst, quoted in *Norman Dewhurst MC* by H.J. Edmonds, p.26.
11. ibid.
12. H. Tizard, The Landing at V Beach, Gallipoli, p.10.
13. Letter by 'a brother officer' (Guy Nightingale), quoted in *Stonyhurst War Record: A Memorial of the Part Taken by Stonyhurst Men in the Great War*, p.136. Jarrett was one of six brothers to attend Stonyhurst.
14. ibid.
15. H. Tizard, The Landing at V Beach, Gallipoli, p.10.
16. G. Nightingale, letter to his mother, 1 May 1915, TNA.
17. H.M. Wilson, Appendix 1a to War Diary, 1st Royal Munster Fusiliers, TNA. Wilson gave the time of the second landing attempt as 0800, although with some reservation, as he noted: 'About this time, having been hit in the leg at 7am, I fell asleep for an hour or so and, my watch having stopped, subsequent times are only approximate.'
18. ibid.

19. H. Tizard, The Landing at V Beach, Gallipoli, p.10.
20. H. M. Wilson, Appendix 1a to War Diary, 1st Royal Munster Fusiliers, TNA.
21. H. Tizard, The Landing at V Beach, Gallipoli, p.10.
22. ibid.
23. ibid.
24. ibid.
25. ibid, pp.10-1.
26. ibid, p.11.
27. ibid.
28. Captain Caryl Lermitte Boxall died of his wounds on 27 April 1915. He was twenty-seven.
29. H. Tizard, The Landing at V Beach, Gallipoli, p.11.
30. C.T. Atkinson, History of the *Royal Hampshire Regiment, Vol II*, p.72.
31. I. Hamilton, *Gallipoli Diary, Volume I*, p.132.
32. ibid, pp.132-3.
33. War Diary, 86th Infantry Brigade, 25 April 1915, TNA. The 29th Division General Staff War Diary entry for 0920 on 25 April has the report coming from Major Thomas Frankland, Brigade Major of the 86th Brigade. It stated that Brigade HQ had been established at the lighthouse and that 'reinforcements can land safely under cliff N of W Beach (where the larger portion of Lancs Fusiliers made their way up …)'. The reference to the V Beach landing differs from the entry in the 86th Brigade War Diary with regard to the impression of the number of men still aboard the *River Clyde*. Where the Brigade record states that the 'majority' of the Munsters had yet to disembark, the Divisional entry changes that to 'some'.
34. Hunter-Weston, Landing of 29th Division on the Gallipoli Peninsular, 25 April 1915 in Gallipoli Diary, BL.
35. J. Godfrey, *The Naval Memoirs of Admiral J. H. Godfrey*, unpublished typescript, p.6, CAC.
36. ibid, p.8.
37. ibid, p.9.
38. ibid.
39. ibid.
40. I. Hamilton, *Gallipoli Diary, Volume I*, pp.133-4.
41. W. Wemyss, *The Navy in the Dardanelles*, p.83.
42. ibid, p.84.

Chapter 16: 'I'll Have a Damned Good Try'

1. H. FitzM Stacke, *The Worcestershire Regiment in the Great War*, 1928.
2. ibid.
3. 'An Officer's Account of the Landing', *Hampshire Regimental Journal*, July 1915, RHRM.
4. 'An account by a Private in the 2nd Hampshires Regiment', *The Hampshire Regimental Journal*, July 1915, RHRM.
5. H. FitzM Stacke.
6. ibid.
7. ibid.
8. H. Carr, Additional information about the part played by the 4th Worcestershires at Gallipoli, 25 April–2 May, 1915, in the Official Historian's papers, TNA.

9. B. Ward, *My Tales of the Dardanelles*, an account written from memory while in hospital suffering from enteric fever and dysentery, .

10. H. Carr, Additional information about the part played by the 4th Worcestershires at Gallipoli, 25 April–2 May, 1915, in the Official Historian's papers, TNA.

11. G. Keen, letter, quoted by Peter Hart in *Gallipoli*, p.153.

12. ibid.

13. H.M. Wilson, Appendix 1a to War Diary, 1st Royal Munster Fusiliers, TNA.

14. 'An Officer's Account of the Landing', RHRM.

15. H.M. Wilson, Appendix 1a to War Diary, 1st Royal Munster Fusiliers, TNA.

16. 'An Officer's Account of the Landing', RHRM.

17. ibid.

18. G. Nightingale, letter to his mother, 18 May 1915, TNA.

19. H. Tizard, The Landing at V Beach, Gallipoli, p.11, IWM.

20. ibid.

21. G. Reid, letter to his wife, 30 April 1915, quoted in *The Gallipoli Journal*, No.111 Autumn 2006; *The Landing from the River Clyde in Letters to Stratford-on-Avon* by Michael Caldwell.

22. ibid.

23. ibid.

24. A. Morse, letter to E. Unwin, 4 May 1926, IWM.

25. ibid.

26. ibid.

27. C. Aspinall-Oglander, *Official History: Military Operations Gallipoli*, pp.239-40.

28. ibid, p.240.

29. C. Jeffries, Landing on the 25th, *The Gallipolian*, No.36, p.23.

30. H. FitzM Stacke.

31. G. Reid, letter to his wife, 30 April 1915, quoted in *The Gallipoli Journal*, ibid.

32. H. Tizard, The Landing at V Beach, Gallipoli, p.11.

33. A. Morse, letter to E. Unwin, 4 May 1926, IWM.

34. E. Unwin, River Clyde narrative, p.5.

35. ibid, p.6.

36. ibid.

37. E. Unwin, The Landing from the River Clyde, a narrative written for W. Wemyss, p.6.

38. E. Unwin, River Clyde narrative, p.6.

39. E. Unwin, The Landing from the River Clyde, a narrative written for W. Wemyss, p.6.

40. E. Unwin, River Clyde narrative, p.6.

41. ibid.

42. ibid.

43. ibid, p.7.

44. M. Lloyd, The Landing at V Beach, 25 April 1915, Account to the captain of HMS *Cornwallis*, IWM.

45. M. Lloyd, Boats' Crews' Experiences, quoted in *The Immortal Gamble*, p.108.

46. G. Samson, 'George Samson's Adventures with Midshipman Drewry', *The Post Sunday Special*, 5 September 1915.

47. R. Spencer-Smith, An Account of the Landing on the Beach near Sedd-el-Bahr, Close to the River Clyde, *Hampshire Regimental Journal*, July 1915, RHRM.

48. M. Sabri, p.4.

49. ibid.

50. ibid.

51. H. Foster, *At Antwerp and the Dardanelles*, p.90.

52. ibid. Private Ben Ward, of 'W' Company, 4th Worcestershires, was among those diverted to W Beach under Lieutenant A.W. Roberts. He wrote: 'the little boats we were in [were] four and five inches deep in blood. It was a shocking sight, but the realisation was worse, the poor fellows struggling in the water, making efforts to swim, only to be cut down by the Turks' fire …' He doubted whether a quarter of his battalion would have made it ashore alive had they stuck to their original plan to land at V Beach.

53. ibid.

54. ibid, p.89.

55. ibid, p.89.

56. ibid.

Chapter 17: 'Some Fuss About the Cornwallis'

1. E. Unwin, River Clyde narrative, p.6.

2. ibid.

3. E. Unwin, The Landing from the River Clyde, a narrative written for W. Wemyss, p.7.

4. ibid.

5. ibid. The timing of Lieut Colonel Carington Smith's death is a matter of some conjecture. Henry Tizard's original record written on 28 April, and contained in the 1st Royal Dublin Fusiliers' War Diary, states the time as 10.20am. Unwin gives no precise times, but in both of his accounts has it occurring after Napier was shot and before he embarked on his own rescue effort around midday. An unnamed Hampshire officer has him being killed 'about midday' by 'a sudden burst of fire'. The Official History gives the time as roughly 3pm, while in a letter written on 30 April Captain Reid of the Hampshires, says Carington Smith was killed by 'a beast of a sniper' at about 4pm while he was 'watching for a machine gun which was worrying us badly'.

6. H. Tizard, 'The Landing at V Beach', Gallipoli, p.12.

7. ibid.

8. ibid.

9. D. Illingworth, letter to his brother, 6 May 1915, via Stephen Chambers.

10. J. Wedgwood, letter to W.S. Churchill, 27 April 1915, IWM.

11. J. Wedgwood, 'With Machine Guns in Gallipoli', *Westminster Gazette*, p.4.

12. ibid, p.6.

13. ibid, p.7.

14. P.B. Kelly, letter to H. Coke, undated, Holkham archives.

15. ibid.

16. ibid.

17. Unidentified member of the RNAS, letter, 2 May 1915, Holkham archives.

18. D. Fyffe, diary, quoted by Richard van Emden and Stephen, p.118.

19. 'An Officer's Account of the Landing', RHRM.

20. D. Fyffe, diary, quoted by Richard van Emden and Stephen Chambers, p.118.

21. D. Illingworth, letter to his brother, 6 May 1915, via Stephen Chambers.

22. W. de L. Williams, letter, 10 May 1915, quoted in *Hampshire Regimental Journal*, June 1915, RHRM.
23. ibid.
24. ibid.
25. G. Reid, letter to his wife, 30 April 1915, quoted in *The Gallipoli Journal*, No.111 Autumn 2006, ibid.
26. ibid.
27. 'An Officer's Account of the Landing', *Hampshire Regimental Journal*, July 1915, RHRM.
28. R. Gillett, transcript of talk given on the BBC in April 1965.
29. 'An Officer's Account of the Landing', *Hampshire Regimental Journal*, July 1915, RHRM.
30. P.B. Kelly, letter to H. Coke, undated, Holkham archives.
31. ibid.
32. G. Davidson, narrative, quoted in *The Incomparable 29th and the River Clyde*.
33. ibid.
34. G. Smith, narrative written in 1935 to mark the 20th anniversary of the landings, LC.
35. W. Perring, quoted by Henry Foster in At Antwerp and The Dardanelles, p86. Contrary to Davidson's account, Perring stated that the first shell 'went in the boiler room without killing or wounding anyone'. He said a second shell then hit the ship aft, 'crashed through the upper deck, then on the main deck, port side, and took off the legs of two soldiers.' Both lived for about twenty minutes, according to Perring, before succumbing to their injuries.
36. War Diary, 1/1st West Riding Field Company, RE, 25 April 1915, TNA.
37. War Diary, 89th Field Ambulance, RAMC, entries by Lieutenant J.A. Morris, senior officer in charge of Bearer Subdivision. He reported: 'Two shells entered No 4 hold in which were Bearers, RE and RND.'
38. ibid.
39. W. Perring, quoted by Henry Foster in *At Antwerp and The Dardanelles*, p.86.
40. J. Wedgwood, 'With Machine Guns in Gallipoli', *Westminster Gazette*, p.8.
41. ibid., p.6.
42. R. Gillett, transcript of talk given on the BBC in April.
43. 'An Officer's Account of the Landing', *Hampshire Regimental Journal*, July 1915, RHRM.
44. B. Isaac, diary, 25 April 1915, IWM. Hamilton had been warned of the squadron's weaknesses before embarking for the Dardanelles. In a letter written on March 1, Lieut Col Brancker, Director of Military Aeronautics in the War Office, stated: 'Lord K[itchener] has just told me that he has arranged to send you a naval squadron of 12 aeroplanes under Captain [*sic*] Samson RN. For offensive work and bomb-dropping you will find them excellent, but if you want to get efficient results from their reconnaissance you will have to keep a tight hand on them, as they have very few ideas on the subject, and I would recommend that a few experienced regular officers (3 or 4) should be attached to the naval squadron for observation duties, and that they should insist on the pilots going exactly where required and when required – otherwise you may find aerial reconnaissance somewhat barren in results. I wish we could have sent you one of our military squadrons, but France is making such enormous demands on us that we can only send a few odd machines to other theatres of war ...' Finally, in a cutting dig at Samson's penchant for

publicity, he noted: 'Samson will probably bring his own newspaper correspondent with him!'

45. A. Thomson, letter to the historian John North, 20 April 1937, IWM.
46. ibid.
47. ibid.
48. W. Wemyss, Instructions for landing in Morto Bay, TNA.
49. W. Wemyss, signal to HMS *Cornwallis*, timed 9.16pm, 24 April 1915, CAC.
50. A. Davidson, HMS *Cornwallis*, Letter of proceedings, 29 April 1915, TNA.
51. A. Davidson, reply to signal from Admiral Wemyss, CAC. In his account of the landings published in *The Immortal Gamble*, Davidson stated that the signal, which he timed at 9pm, was confirmation that the 'tentative arrangements' drawn up by him and Lieut Colonel Casson were 'finally and definitely settled'.
52. A. Davidson, HMS *Cornwallis*, Letter of proceedings, 25 April–29 May 1915, CAC.
53. ibid.
54. H. Casson, report to Admiral Wemyss bringing to his notice 'for favourable consideration' officers and men of the *Cornwallis* who assisted the landings at S Beach, 14 May 1915, TNA. Writing of Davidson, Casson stated: 'The whole Battalion was made to feel that come what might they were going to be supported at all costs and this knowledge unquestionably established in all ranks a feeling of calm confidence.' He insisted that his assistance was 'of the highest military value to me' and added: 'I cannot speak too highly of the conduct of this officer.'
55. A. Keyes, personal letter to Admiral Wemyss, 31 May 1915, CAC. Keyes claimed Davidson's lack of judgment was 'a source of continual anxiety and danger'.
56. W. Wemyss, *The Navy in the Dardanelles Campaign*, p.75.
57. ibid. Writing in January 1970, Commander Henry Minchin, who as a lieutenant commanded the naval landing party from *Cornwallis*, recalled the S Beach operation: 'It was expected to be the hardest position of all, but turned out a very easy one. We only lost 12 men, soldiers and sailors … This was the only time I ever took part in a real live bayonet charge.'
58. J. Godfrey, *The Naval Memoirs of Admiral J. H. Godfrey*, unpublished typescript, p.15, CAC.
59. I. Hamilton, *Gallipoli Diary, Volume I*, p.134.
60. A. Davidson, HMS *Cornwallis*, Letter of proceedings, 25 April–29 May 1915, CAC.
61. A. Davidson, narrative, quoted in *The Incomparable 29th and the River Clyde*.
61. ibid.
62. ibid.
63. ibid.
64. ibid.
65. ibid.
66. A. Davidson, HMS *Cornwallis*, Letter of proceedings, 25 April–29 May 1915, CAC.
67. A. Davidson, narrative, quoted in *The Incomparable 29th and the River Clyde*.
68. ibid.
69. A. Keyes, personal letter to Admiral Wemyss, 31 May 1915, CAC.
70. ibid.
71. A. Davidson, narrative, quoted in *The Incomparable 29th and the River Clyde*.
72. E. Unwin, letter to Captain Hughes Lockyer, 21 June 1936, IWM. Lockyer commanded the pre-dreadnought HMS *Implacable* at the X Beach landings.

Chapter 18: 'Calls for Help From All Around'
1. E. Unwin, The Landing from the River Clyde, a narrative written for W. Wemyss, p.7.
2. ibid.
3. ibid.
4. ibid.
5. ibid.
6. ibid.
7. P.B. Kelly, letter to H. Coke, undated, Holkham archives.
8. E. Unwin, The Landing from the River Clyde, a narrative written for W. Wemyss, p.8.
9. R. Neave, 1st Essex Regiment, attached Staff 88th Brigade, report dated 19 June 1915 in support of Victoria Cross recommendation, Admiralty records, TNA.
10. 'An Officer's Account of the Landing', *Hampshire Regimental Journal*, July 1915, RHRM.
11. G. Geddes, 1st Royal Munster Fusiliers, report dated 16 June 1915 in support of Victoria Cross recommendation, Admiralty records, TNA.
12. A. Sinclair-Thomson, Brigade Major 86th Brigade, report dated 21 June 1915 in support of Victoria Cross recommendation, Admiralty records, TNA.
13. J. Wedgwood, 'With Machine Guns in Gallipoli', *Westminster Gazette*, p.7.
14. ibid.
15. J. Wedgwood, letter to W.S. Churchill, 27 April 1915, IWM.
16. E. Unwin, The Landing from the River Clyde, a narrative written for W. Wemyss, p.8.
17. ibid.
18. ibid.
19. J. Wedgwood, letter to W.S. Churchill, 27 April 1915, IWM.
20. J. Wedgwood, letter to the Rev Dr William St Clair Tisdall, quoted in *Memoir and Poems of A. W. St C. Tisdall, VC*, p.114.
21. A. Illingworth, Case of Sub Lieutenant A. W. St Clair Tisdall, RNVR (Claim for Victoria Cross), Statement dated 10 December 1915, Admiralty records, TNA.
22. J. Malia, Case of Sub Lieut A. W. St Clair Tisdall, RNVR (Claim for Victoria Cross), Statement undated but around December 1915, Admiralty records, TNA.
23. ibid.
24. A. Illingworth, Case of Sub Lieutenant A. W. St Clair Tisdall, RNVR, TNA.
25. Baldwin's Medal Catalogue, Lot 122, 23 June 2015.
26. J. Parkinson, Case of Sub Lieutenant A. W. St Clair Tisdall, RNVR, TNA.
27. J. Wedgwood, 'With Machine Guns in Gallipoli', *Westminster Gazette*, p.7. The story he recalled was Stephen Crane's American Civil War classic, The Red Badge of Courage, a novel first published in 1895.
28. G. Rumming, Case of Sub Lieutenant A. W. St Clair Tisdall, RNVR, TNA. Rumming, who had just undergone 'a somewhat serious operation' for a head wound sustained on 4 June 1915, had no idea who the officer was he had helped until a friend pointed out a brief reference published in *London Opinion*.
29. ibid.
30. J. Parkinson, Case of Sub Lieutenant A. W. St Clair Tisdall, RNVR, TNA.
31. *Official History of The War in the Air*, quoted in Dix Noonan Webb Medal Catalogue, Lot 15, 13 December 2007.

32. J. Wedgwood, letter to W.S. Churchill, 27 April 1915, IWM.
33. ibid.
34. J. Parkinson, Case of Sub Lieutenant A. W. St Clair Tisdall, RNVR, TNA.
35. J. Wedgwood, 'With Machine Guns in Gallipoli', *Westminster Gazette*, p.8.
36. 'An Officer's Account of the Landing', *Hampshire Regimental Journal*, July 1915, RHRM. According to the same record Unwin was 'working in the water with one or two seamen' and 'managed to get about six at one time or another on to a boat and push it back …'
37. G. Samson, 'Scottish Hero's Strange Adventures at the Dardanelles', *The Post Sunday Special*, August 1915.
38. G. Samson, 'Carnoustie's VC: Great Welcome for Seaman Samson', newspaper report, August 1915.
39. G. Samson, 'George Samson's Adventures with Midshipman Drewry', *The Post Sunday Special*, 5 September 1915.
40. H. Weblin, Landing at V Beach, 25 April 1915, Account to the captain of HMS *Cornwallis*, IWM.
41. ibid.
42. ibid.
43. ibid.
44. E. Unwin, The Landing from the River Clyde, a narrative written for W. Wemyss, p.6.
45. P. Kelly, letter to H Coke, undated, Holkham archives. He also stated that 'the 3 Military Doctors were out of it badly hit and one killed …' But it is not clear to whom he was referring. Lieuts Henry de Boer, Harold Atlee and H.J. Panton, medical officers of the 1st Royal Dublin Fusiliers, 1st Royal Munster Fusiliers and 2nd Hampshire Regiment respectively all survived the day's fighting, as did the officers of 89th Field Ambulance on board the *River Clyde*. Of these, the only casualty was de Boer, who was listed among the wounded. He made a full recovery and ended the war with a Military Cross, as did Atlee. Of his own injuries, he commented in a letter to a friend dated 31 August 1915: 'I was very lucky. I got hit early in the right leg – nothing much – and then later they pinked me with one in the left foot.'
46. E. Unwin, The Landing from the River Clyde, a narrative written for W. Wemyss, p.6.
47. G. Davidson, narrative, quoted in *The Incomparable 29th and the River Clyde*.
48. ibid.
49. Information supplied by Lieutenant G. Davidson, in charge of Bearers of B Section, 89th Field Ambulance, on *River Clyde*, contained in unit War Diary, 25 April 1915, TNA.
50. ibid.
51. H. Tizard, The Landing at V Beach, Gallipoli, p.12.

Chapter 19: 'A Good Deal of Wire'
1.   This is based on comments in letters written by Guy Nightingale and Mynors Farmar.
2.   E. Unwin, The Landing from the River Clyde, a narrative written for W. Wemyss, p.8.
3.   P. Hart, *Gallipoli*, p.158.
4.   ibid.
5.   H. Tizard, The Landing at V Beach, Gallipoli, pp.12-3.

6. C. Milward, diary entry, 25 April 1915, TNA.
7. ibid.
8. War Diary, 29th Division, 25 April, 1915, TNA.
9. ibid.
10. C. Milward, diary entry, 25 April 1915, TNA.
11. A. Keyes, *The Fight for Gallipoli*, p.124.
12. ibid.
13. ibid.
14. ibid. p125
15. C. Milward, diary entry, 25 April 1915, TNA.
16. A. Keyes, *The Fight for Gallipoli*, p.125.
17. ibid.
18. C. Aspinall-Oglander, *Official History: Military Operations Gallipoli*, p.247. According to Aspinall-Oglander, the message was signed by Carington Smith, though if Tizard's and Unwin's records are correct he had been dead at least two hours.
19. C. Milward, diary entry, 25 April 1915,T NA.
20. ibid.
21. I. Hamilton, *Gallipoli Diary, Volume I*, p136.
22. ibid.
23. ibid.
24. ibid.
25. C. Aspinall-Oglander, *Official History: Military Operations Gallipoli*, p.229.
26. M. Farmar, letter to Major General Sir S. Hare, 22 May 1915, IWM.
27. ibid.
28. ibid. According to Farmar, they remained there until 4pm. 'Unable to go forward or come back', in Milward's words, they were visible from *Euryalus* on account of having hoisted a 'red screen' in order to point out their position to the Naval gunners'. Frankland never returned, being killed around 0845 'while making a reconnaissance beyond the lighthouse towards V Beach [Official History]'. Farmar wrote: 'He had stood up in order to see, and was shot through the heart, neck and head. We buried him two days afterwards.' Farmar immediately assumed the duties of brigade-major, 86th Brigade.
29. ibid.
30. M. Farmar, The Landing of the 86th Infantry Brigade under Brigadier-General S.W. Hare on the Gallipoli Peninsula and its Subsequent Operations, p.7.
31. ibid.
32. ibid.
33. C. Aspinall-Oglander, *Official History: Military Operations Gallipoli*, p.241.
34. ibid.
35. According to the Official History, he received Farmar's report at 1310, by which time most of the Worcestershires had already landed. But it was not until 1700 that a message from 29th Division HQ fully appraised Wolley-Dod of the situation at V Beach and that the troops there were, in the words of the Official Historian, 'definitely held up, and … could make no headway till an advance from W had cleared the trenches on their western flank'. As a result, Wolley-Dod, who had earlier signalled the Worcestershires telling them to consolidate the captured redoubt on Guezji Baba and to bury their dead, issued revised orders instructing them to continue their advance (p.242).

36. S. Nicholson, Rear Admiral commanding the First Squadron aboard his flagship HMS *Swiftsure*, report, 5 May 1915, TNA.

37. C. Milward, diary entry, 25 April 1915, TNA.

38. ibid.

39. A. Churchill, letter, 25 June 1915, TNA.

40. ibid.

41. H. FitzM Stacke.

42. C. Milward, diary entry, 25 April 1915, TNA.

43. M. Sabri, p.5.

44. ibid.

45. ibid.

46. ibid, p.6.

47. ibid.

48. ibid.

49. H. FitzM Stacke.

50. Ibid.

51. ibid.

52. C. Milward, diary entry, 25 April 1915, TNA.

53. ibid.

54. H. FitzM Stacke.

55. C. Milward, diary entry, 25 April 1915, TNA.

56. ibid.

57. ibid.

58. H. Tizard, *The Landing at V Beach*, Gallipoli, p.12.

59. ibid, p.13.

60. ibid.

61. G. Drewry, letter to his father, 12 May 1915, IWM.

62. G. Nightingale, letter to his mother, 1 May 1915, TNA.

63. ibid, 18 May 1915, TNA.

64. H. Tizard, The Landing at V Beach, Gallipoli, p13, IWM.

65. ibid.

66. War Diary, 29th Division General Staff, 25 April 1915, TNA.

67. A. Churchill, letter, 25 June 1915, TNA.

68. War diary, 29th Division General Staff, 25 April 1915, TNA.

69. ibid.

70. ibid.

71. C. Aspinall-Oglander, *Official History: Military Operations Gallipoli*, p.248.

72. War Diary, 86th Infantry Brigade, 25 April 1915, TNA.

73. ibid. These orders were almost a repetition of the suggestion made to Wolley-Dod more than two hours earlier.

74. ibid.

75. ibid.

Chapter 20: 'Treading on the Dead'

1. War Diary, MEF, General Staff (GHQ), 25 April 1915, TNA.

2. ibid.

3. M. Sabri, p.6.

4. ibid. Despite his brave defence it would appear that Sergeant Yahya's actions went

unrecognised at the time. Sabri stated: 'Sgt Yahya's example should have been honoured in the highest degree. However, owing to the death of the company officers and the evacuation of the battalion commander to hospital wounded, Sgt Yahya's heroism could not be reported.'

5. H. Carr, Additional information about the part played by the 4th Worcestershires at Gallipoli, 25 April–2 May, 1915, in the Official Historian's papers, TNA.
6. H. Tizard, The Landing at V Beach, Gallipoli, p.13.
7. ibid.
8. War Diary, MEF, General Staff (GHQ), 25 April 1915, TNA.
9. H. Tizard, The Landing at V Beach, Gallipoli, pp.13-4.
10. C. Maffett, quoted by H.C. Wylly in *Neill's Blue Caps, Vol III 1914–1922*, p.31.
11. D. French, letter, NAM.
12. War Diary, MEF, General Staff (GHQ), 25 April 1915, TNA.
13. ibid.
14. H. Tizard, The Landing at V Beach, Gallipoli, p.14.
15. ibid.
16. C. T. Atkinson, *History of the Royal Hampshire Regiment, Vol II*, p.73.
17. ibid.
18. R Spencer-Smith, An Account of the Landing on the Beach near Sedd-el-Bahr, Close to the River Clyde, *Hampshire Regimental Journal*, July 1915, RHRM.
19. ibid.
20. ibid.
21. C. Aspinall-Oglander, *Official History: Military Operations Gallipoli*, p.248.
22. G. Geddes, The Landing from the River Clyde at V Beach, 25 April 1915, by a company commander in the 1st Royal Munster Fusiliers, 86th Brigade War Diary, TNA.
23. ibid.
24. Letter by 'A Brother Officer' (Guy Nightingale), quoted in *Stonyhurst War Record: A Memorial of the Part Taken by Stonyhurst Men in the Great War*, p.136.
25. G. Nightingale, letter to his mother, 1 May 1915, TNA.
26. G. Geddes, The landing from the River Clyde at V Beach, 25 April 1915, TNA.
27. ibid.
28. ibid.
29. J. Wedgwood, 'With Machine Guns in Gallipoli', *Westminster Gazette*, p.8.
30. ibid.
31. R. Gillett, transcript of talk given on the BBC in April 1965. According to the Official History, the bridge of boats was 'still incomplete' and linked, in places, by 'single planks'.
32. N. Dewhurst, quoted in *Norman Dewhurst MC* by H.J. Edmonds, p.26.
33. D. Fyffe, diary, quoted by Richard van Emden and Stephen Chambers, p.122.
34. ibid, p.123.
35. ibid.
36. ibid.
37. J. Wedgwood, letter to W.S. Churchill, 27 April 1915, IWM.
38. H. Weblin, Landing at V Beach, 25 April 1915, Account to the captain of HMS *Cornwallis*, IWM.
39. G. Drewry, letter to his father, 12 May 1915, IWM.
40. ibid.

41. G. Davidson, narrative, quoted in *The Incomparable 29th and the River Clyde*.
42. ibid.
43. 'An Officer's Account of the Landing', *Hampshire Regimental Journal*, July 1915, RHRM.
44. ibid. The packs which formed a makeshift jetty to complete the bridge to shore were taken from the bodies of soldiers killed in the earlier failed landing attempts.
45. I. Hamilton, *Gallipoli Diary, Volume I*, p.137.
46. ibid, pp.137-8.
47. ibid, p.137.
48. ibid
49. ibid.
50. ibid.
51. ibid. Hamilton asked him about the state of affairs on Y Beach. The reply was woolly. 'He thought they were now in touch with our troops at X but that they had been through some hard fighting to get there. His last message had been that they were being hard pressed but as he had heard nothing more since then he assumed they were all right!' wrote Hamilton. The next day, after a night and morning of chaos and confusion, Y Beach was evacuated.
52. J. Churchill, letter to his brother Winston Churchill, First Lord of the Admiralty, 27 April 1915, CAC.
53. ibid.
54. ibid.
55. I. Hamilton, *Gallipoli Diary, Volume I*, p.137.
56. C. Milward, diary entry, 25 April 1915, TNA.
57. ibid.
58. ibid.
59. ibid.
60. ibid.
61. ibid.
62. C. Aspinall-Oglander, *Official History: Military Operations Gallipoli*, p.249.
63. E. Unwin, River Clyde narrative, p.7. By then, he said they had got 'nearly every soul on shore'.
64. G. Drewry, letter to his father, 12 May 1915, IWM.
65. G. Smith, narrative of the landing, written twenty years after, LC.
66. ibid.
67. ibid.
68. ibid.
69. C. McCann, quoted by H.C. Wylly in *Neill's Blue Caps, Vol III 1914–1922*, p.33. From memory McCann thought that the order to 'get dressed' and to prepare to leave the *River Clyde* reached them at about 1900. However, most other accounts suggest the time was considerably later.
70. H.D. O'Hara, quoted by H.C. Wylly in *Neill's Blue Caps, Vol III 1914–1922*, p.32.
71. ibid.
72. E. Unwin, The Landing from the River Clyde, a narrative written for W. Wemyss, p.9.
73. E. Unwin, River Clyde narrative, undated, p.7.
74. G. Davidson, narrative, quoted in *The Incomparable 29th and the River Clyde*.
75. ibid.

76. G. Geddes, Extracts from Diary kept in the Dardanelles, 25 April 1915, IWM.
77. G. Geddes, The landing from the River Clyde at V Beach, 25 April 1915, TNA.
78. G. Geddes, typescript diary entry, 25 April 1915, IWM.
79. M. Lloyd, The Landing at V Beach, 25 April 1915, Account to the captain of HMS *Cornwallis*, IWM.
80. M. Farmar, letter to Major General Sir S. Hare, 22 May 1915, IWM.
81. C. Milward, diary entry, 25 April 1915, TNA.
82. ibid.
83. ibid. The officer was Commander John Marriott, executive officer on *Euryalus*. According to Milward, 'he had called up all the boats'.
84. ibid.
85. J. Godfrey, The Naval Memoirs of Admiral J.H. Godfrey, unpublished typescript, p.12, CAC. Hunter-Weston's instincts were proved correct. 'When day broke we saw that the front line had not moved,' wrote Godfrey.
86. G. Davidson, narrative, quoted in *The Incomparable 29th and the River Clyde*.
87. ibid.
88. ibid.
89. H. Tizard, The Landing at V Beach, Gallipoli, p.15, IWM.
90. ibid
91. ibid.

Chapter 21: 'An Awful Snag'
1. R. Gillett, transcript of talk given on the BBC in April 1965.
2. ibid.
3. ibid.
4. ibid.
5. ibid.
6. ibid.
7. G. Nightingale, letter to his sister, quoted by Michael Moynihan in *A Place Called Armageddon*, p.84.
8. ibid.
9. C. Aspinall-Oglander, *Official History: Military Operations Gallipoli*, p.249.
10. ibid.
11. H. Tizard, The Landing at V Beach, Gallipoli, p.15.
12. G. Drewry, letter to his father, 12 May 1915, IWM.
13. J. Wedgwood, 'With Machine Guns in Gallipoli', *Westminster Gazette*, p.9.
14. J. Wedgwood, letter to W.S. Churchill, 27 April 1915, IWM.
15. J. Wedgwood, 'With Machine Guns in Gallipoli', *Westminster Gazette*, p.9.
16. T.C. Genelkurmay Baskanligi, quoted by Edward J. Erickson *in Gallipoli: The Ottoman Campaign*, p.73.
17. M. Sabri, p.8.
18. ibid.
19. ibid.
20. ibid
21. ibid.
22. C. Aspinall-Oglander, *Official History: Military Operations Gallipoli*, p.249.
23. ibid.
24. H. Tizard, The Landing at V Beach, Gallipoli, p.14.

25. ibid.

26. ibid, p.15.

27. D. Fyffe, diary, quoted by Richard van Emden and Stephen Chambers, p.151 and p.153.

28. H. Carr, Additional information about the part played by the 4th Worcestershires at Gallipoli, 25 April–2 May 1915, in the Official Historian's papers, TNA.

29. H. Tizard, The Landing at V Beach, Gallipoli, p16, IWM.

30. ibid.

31. ibid.

32. 'An Officer's Account of the Landing', *Hampshire Regimental Journal*, July 1915, RHRM

33. R. Gillett, transcript of talk given on the BBC in April 1965.

34. ibid.

35. C.J.P. Ball, *The Carthusian*, June, 1916, Journal of Charterhouse School, IWM.

36. H. Tizard, The Landing at V Beach, Gallipoli, p.16.

37. ibid.

38. ibid, pp.16-7.

39. D. Fyffe, diary, quoted by Richard van Emden and Stephen Chambers, p.153.

40. ibid.

41. 'An Officer's Account of the Landing', *Hampshire Regimental Journal*, July 1915, RHRM.

42. G. Nightingale, quoted in the Regimental Records of the Royal Welch Fusiliers, Volume 4, p.15.

43. ibid.

44. ibid.

45. G. Nightingale, letter to his sister Margaret (Meta), May 1915, quoted by Michael Moynihan in *A Place Called Armageddon*, p.84.

46. G. Baker, quoted in *Neill's Blue Caps, Vol III 1914–1922*, p.36.

47. R. Gillett, transcript of talk given on the BBC in April 1965.

48. ibid. Harry Parker was killed in action on April 30, 1915 during the advance on Krithia.

49. ibid.

50. ibid.

51. R. Spencer-Smith, An Account of the Landing on the Beach near Sedd-el-Bahr, Close to the River Clyde, *Hampshire Regimental Journal*, July 1915, RHRM.

52. H.M. Doughty, letter to Walford's widow, 27 November 1915, LC. Doughty was the brother of Lieutenant Colonel 'Dick' Doughty-Wylie and was serving in the Dardanelles as captain of HMS *Abercrombie* from July. His account was based on conversations he had with officers who fought at V Beach.

53. R.H. Tompson, letter to Walford's widow, 22 June 1915, LC.

54. G. Walford, message cited by C. Aspinall-Oglander, *Official History: Military Operations Gallipoli*, p.277.

Chapter 22: 'They Needed a Good Leader'

1. G. Stoney, letter to his brother, 10 May 1915, IWM.

2. ibid.

3. G. Stoney, letter to his brother, 15 April 1915, IWM.

4. ibid.

5. W. de L. Williams, letter to Captain S.H. Pollen, aide-de-camp to Sir Ian Hamilton, 22 May 1915, IWM.

6. ibid.
7. ibid.
8. ibid.
9. ibid.
10. ibid.
11. ibid.
12. ibid.
13. War Diary, 29th Division, 0830, 26 April 191, TNA.
14. ibid.
15. ibid, a report from 'OC Troops V Beach'.
16. ibid.
17. ibid.
18. War Diary, 29th Division, 0900, 26 April, 1915, TNA.
19. E. Unwin, The Landing from the River Clyde, a narrative written for W. Wemyss, p.9.
20. ibid.
21. G. Stoney, letter to his brother, 10 May 1915, IWM.
22. G. Nightingale, quoted in the Regimental Records of the Royal Welch Fusiliers, Volume 4, p.15.
23. Sir Ian Hamilton, quoted in the Regimental Records of the Royal Welch Fusiliers, Volume 4, p.14.
24. G. Nightingale, quoted in the Regimental Records of the Royal Welch Fusiliers, Volume 4, p.16.
25. ibid, p.15. There is some dispute as to when Doughty-Wylie took charge of the advance on the right. Most accounts have him arriving at the commencement of the fight for the village, but Nightingale had him leading the charge into the Castle, 'with the other officers, whom he ordered to form up in line in front of their respective regiments'. In the course of the attack, Nightingale 'saw him pick up a rifle with a bayonet fixed, but he threw it away immediately after the Castle was in our possession. That was the only occasion during the whole day on which I saw him armed in any way'.
26. W. de L. Williams, letter, quoted in *Hampshire Regimental Journal*, June 1915, RHRM.
27. ibid.
28. H.C. Wylly, *Neill's Blue Caps, Vol III 1914–1922*, p.36.
29. M. Sabri, p.9.
30. G. Geddes, The landing from the River Clyde at V Beach, 25 April 1915, by a Company Commander in the 1st Royal Munster Fusiliers, 86th Brigade War Diary, NA. In his diary, Geddes described the *Albion*'s shooting on the first day as 'innocuous'.
31. C. Milward, diary entry, 26 April 1915, TNA.
32. ibid.
33. A Thomson, letter to the historian John North, 20 April 1937, IWM. The incident bears a striking resemblance to the earlier one described by Tizard and another witnessed by Unwin. 'Officers were beginning to form up their men for attack,' he wrote. 'One party of about 30 men started marching up right under the Fort, but the Turks soon spotted them and got a maxim to work on them at once. We signalled to the Cornwallis and she put a 6-inch [shell] right into the casemate they were firing out of and effectively stopped that fellow' (from his River Clyde narrative, undated, p.7, IWM).

34. 'An Officer's Account of the Landing', *Hampshire Regimental Journal*, July 1915, RHRM.
35. ibid.
36. R. Gillett, transcript of a recording made for friends in around 1965, IWM.
37. A. Churchill, letter, June 25 1915, TNA.
38. ibid.
39. ibid. According to Churchill, they remained in their positions 'all the Monday ...'
40. C. Aspinall-Oglander, *Official History: Military Operations Gallipoli*, p.277.
41. War Diary, 29th Division, 0900, 26 April 1915, TNA.
42. The time of this message is taken from the Official History, p.275. However, the 29th Division War Diary gives the time as 1100 and omits any mention of X Beach, the entry stating: 'Instructions sent to troops [at] W Beach to consolidate and reorganise. No further advance to take place until French arrive.' It was followed twenty minutes later by a report from HMS *Dublin* announcing that 'nearly all wounded from Y Beach embarked' and embarkation of the remainder was under way covered by a rear-guard on the 'last ridge'.
43. Message sent by Doughty-Wylie to *River Clyde*, in the Doughty-Wylie Papers, RWFM. Tizard puts the receipt of this signal at 'about 11am', while the 29th Division War Diary makes no mention of it. However, a message timed at 1000 stated: 'V Beach troops reported to have reached NE end of Sedd-el-Bahr village and to be attacking Hill 141.' This was either sent in error or wrongly entered in the war diary.
44. Message sent from OC V Beach to HQ 29th Division, 12 noon, in the Doughty-Wylie Papers, RWFM.
45. H. Tizard, The Landing at V Beach, Gallipoli, p.17.
46. ibid
47. ibid.
48. ibid.
49. ibid.
50. ibid.
51. G. Stoney, letter to his brother, 10 May 1915, IWM.
52. ibid.
53. ibid.
54. H. Tizard, The Landing at V Beach, Gallipoli, p.17.

Chapter 23: 'The Lads Came on Like Devils'

1. Log of HMS *Albion*, 26 April 1915.
2. M. Sabri, p.9.
3. ibid.
4. ibid.
5. ibid.
6. ibid.
7. G. Nightingale, quoted in the Regimental Records of the Royal Welch Fusiliers, Volume 4, p.16.
8. ibid., p.15.
9. *Nuneaton Observer*, 25 June 1915, 'How Major Grimshaw Died: Nuneaton Immortalised', quoted by Chris Holland in *Before Gallipoli*, p.102.
10. ibid.
11. Log of HMS *Albion*, 26 April 1915, TNA.

12. H. Carr, Additional information about the part played by the 4th Worcestershires at Gallipoli, 25 April–2 May 1915, in the Official Historian's papers, TNA.

13. The Official History has the final assault on Hill 141 at 'about 2.30pm', while the 29th Division War Diary reckons the 'actual assault took place just before 2pm', the troops at V Beach having 'worked up through the village and … from the Beach itself …'

14. C. Milward, diary entry, 26 April 1915, TNA.

15. H. Brown, copy of report in War Diary, 1st Royal Munster Fusiliers, 30 April 1915, TNA.

16. E. O'Brien, letter, 1975, IWM.

17. ibid.

18. W. Cosgrove, quoted by M. MacDonagh, in *The Irish at the Front*.

19. H. Brown, copy of report in War Diary, 1st Royal Munster Fusiliers, 30 April 1915, TNA.

20. W. Cosgrove, quoted by M. MacDonagh.

21. Alfred Bennett, from Tralee, has no known grave and is commemorated on the Helles Memorial.

22. W. Cosgrove, quoted by M. MacDonagh.

23. ibid.

24. E. O'Brien, letter, 17 July 1975, IWM.

25. W. Cosgrove, quoted by M. MacDonagh.

26. E. O'Brien, letter, 17 July 1975, IWM.

27. W. Cosgrove, quoted by M. MacDonagh.

28. ibid.

29. G. Nightingale, quoted in the Regimental Records of the Royal Welch Fusiliers, Volume 4, pp.16-7.

30. G. Nightingale, letter to his sister Margaret (Meta), May 1915, quoted by Michael Moynihan in *A Place Called Armageddon*, p.84.

31. W. de L. Williams, letter to Captain S.H. Pollen, aide-de-camp to Sir Ian Hamilton, 22 May 1915, IWM. Williams put the time at 2.30pm, though it was more likely at least half an hour earlier.

32. ibid.

33. ibid.

34. G. Stoney, letter to his brother, 10 May 1915, IWM.

35. W. Cosgrove, quoted by M. MacDonagh.

36. G. Nightingale, quoted in the Regimental Records of the Royal Welch Fusiliers, Volume 4, p.17.

37. C. Milward, diary entry, 26 April 1915, TNA.

38. W. Flynn, sound record 4103, IWM.

39. G. Nightingale, quoted in the Regimental Records of the Royal Welch Fusiliers, Volume 4, p.17.

40. ibid.

41. H.D. O'Hara, letter to Captain D. French, 15 May 1915, quoted by Field Marshal Lord Carver in *The National Army Museum Book of The Turkish Front 1914–1918*, p.46.

42. M. Sabri, p.9.

43. ibid.

44. ibid.

45. ibid.

46. ibid, p.10.

47. ibid.
48. ibid.
49. ibid.
50. ibid.
51. ibid.
52. ibid.
53. F. MacLiesh, diary entry, 26 April 1915, CAC.
54. ibid.
55. M. Sabri, p.10.
56. H. Tizard, The Landing at V Beach, Gallipoli, p.18.
57. ibid.
58. ibid.
59. Message from General Hunter-Weston to W Beach timed at 1435, quoted by C. Aspinall-Oglander in *Official History: Military Operations Gallipoli*, p.277.
60. ibid.
61. H. Tizard, The Landing at V Beach, Gallipoli, p.18.
62. ibid.
63. J. Churchill, letter to his brother Winston Churchill, First Lord of the Admiralty, 27 April 1915, CAC.
64. ibid.
65. I. Hamilton, *Gallipoli Diary, Volume I*, p.155.
66. War Diary, 86th Infantry Brigade, 26 April 1915, TNA. The same entry adds: 'On the authority of Major General Hunter-Weston, Captain Farmar was appointed to act as Brigade Major vice Major Frankland, killed in action on the 25th, and Captain Kane, 1st Royal Munster Fusiliers, took up the duties of Acting Staff Captain.'
67. H. Tizard, The Landing at V Beach, Gallipoli, p.18.
68. D. Fyffe, diary, quoted by Richard van Emden and Stephen Chambers, p.154.
69. ibid.
70. J. Wedgwood, 'With Machine Guns in Gallipoli', p.11.
71. G. Davidson, narrative, quoted in *The Incomparable 29th and the River Clyde*.
72. ibid. It was not until the arrival of the French on the following day that Sedd-el-Bahr was finally cleared of snipers.
73. ibid.
74. Ibid.
75. ibid. The officer was Lieutenant Robert Bernard (see Chapter 21) of Y Company which had landed in Nos 3 and 4 Tows into an inferno of fire the previous morning. Bernard was twenty-three and the son of the Church of Ireland Archbishop of Dublin. He is buried in V Beach Cemetery.
76. W. de L. Williams, letter to Captain S. H. Pollen, aide-de-camp to Sir Ian Hamilton, 22 May 1915, IWM.
77. ibid. Williams added: 'That night when things had quieted down I asked Unwin to have a temporary cross put up to mark his grave. I left next day and was unable to get back to visit the place until about a week ago. I then found the cross had been put up; but the grave wants building up a little …'

Chapter 24: 'We Have Achieved the Impossible'

1. G. Stoney, letter to his brother, 10 May 1915, IWM.
2. H. Tizard, The Landing at V Beach, Gallipoli, p.18.

3. ibid.
4. W. Malleson, account of the landing at V Beach, written on 21 March 1916, via his family.
5. ibid.
6. E. Unwin, The Landing from the River Clyde, a narrative written for W. Wemyss, p.9.
7. E. Unwin, River Clyde narrative, undated, p.7,
8. W. Wemyss, *The Navy in the Dardanelles Campaign*, p.62.
9. G. Stoney, letter to his brother, 10 May 1915, IWM.
10. E. Unwin, River Clyde narrative, undated, pp.7-8.
11. W. Crichton, 'A Few Words', quoted in *The Immortal Gamble*, p.117.
12. ibid.
13. T. Stevens, An Impression, quoted in *The Immortal Gamble*, pp.121-2.
14. W. Crichton, A Few Words, quoted in *The Immortal Gamble*, p.117.
15. ibid.
16. E. Unwin, River Clyde narrative, p.8.
17. H. Weblin, Landing at V Beach, 25 April 1915, Account to the captain of HMS *Cornwallis*, IWM.
18. G. Smith, narrative of the landing, written twenty years after, LC.
19. ibid.
20. G. Nightingale, letter to his mother, 1 May 1915, TNA.
21. ibid.
22. A Hunter-Weston, letter to his wife, 27 April 1915, BL.
23. ibid, letter, 27 April 1915, BL.
24. ibid, letter written to his wife at midnight, 27 April 1915, BL.
25. ibid.
26. ibid.
27. W. Wemyss, letter to his wife, 27 April 1915, CAC.
28. ibid.
29. ibid.
30. ibid.
31. W. Wemyss, letter to his wife, 1 May 1915, CAC.
32. I. Hamilton, letter to Sir John French, 13 May 1915, Hamilton Papers, LHC.
33. ibid.
34. I. Hamilton, letter to Lord Kitchener, 30 April 1915, Hamilton Papers, LHC.
35. ibid. 'Too many of these boats, when they reached land, carried nothing but corpses,' added Hamilton.
36. ibid, letter to his wife, 30 April 1915, Hamilton Papers, LHC.
37. ibid, letter to Sir John French, 13 May 1915, Hamilton Papers, LHC.
38. ibid, letter to his wife, 30 April 1915, Hamilton Papers, LHC.
39. ibid.
40. I. Hamilton, letter to Lord Kitchener, 30 April 1915, Hamilton Papers, LHC. 'The campaign so far has borne no resemblance to any other in the world that I have ever heard of,' added Hamilton. 'Everything has to be improvised to meet conditions quite unexampled.'
41. I. Hamilton, letter to his wife, 30 April 1915, Hamilton Papers, LHC.
42. ibid.
43. ibid.

44. A. Hunter-Weston, letter to his wife, 29 April 1915, BL. Contrary to many of his troops involved in the attack, Hunter-Weston maintained it had been a close-run thing. 'We had not weight enough to get through,' he told his wife. 'But we very nearly did.'

45. H.D. O'Hara, letter quoted by H.C. Wylly in *Neill's Blue Caps, Vol III 1914–1922*, p.39.

46. ibid.

47. H.D. O'Hara, letter dated 1 May 1915, quoted by H.C. Wylly in *Neill's Blue Caps, Vol III 1914–1922*, p.41.

48. ibid.

49. G. Geddes, letter, 30 April 1915, IWM.

50. G. Geddes, letter, 30 April 1915, quoted by Myles Dungan in *Irish Voices From The Great War*, p.41.

51. G. Nightingale, letter to his mother, 1 May 1915, NA. Buller, the Munsters' mascot, was one of at least three dogs that took part in the landings at Gallipoli. According to family legend, Arthur Coke took his Airedale terrier Jack with him on board the *River Clyde* and then on to the peninsula. Following Coke's death on 2 May, Jack was befriended by other members of the armoured car squadron and eventually brought back to Norfolk, where he lived out his days on the Holkham estate, dying in 1918. Another dog, a sheepdog pup called Rags, was carried in a knapsack on to W Beach where its owner, a private soldier in the Lancashire Fusiliers, was killed. Taken across to V Beach and the *River Clyde*, Rags was befriended by Midshipman Haydon Forbes, one of the heroes of the landing. He brought him back to the Cornwallis and Rags, the ribbon of the General Service Medal tied to his collar, later accompanied him to Buckingham Palace when he received his DSC. Rags survived the war, eventually passing away in Malta in 1926. The following year Forbes, who had transferred to the Fleet Air Arm, died in a flying accident and was buried close by his faithful dog.

52. J. Gillam, *Gallipoli Diary*, p.46.

53. ibid.

54. ibid, pp.46-7.

55. G. Nightingale, letter to his mother, 1 May 1915, TNA.

56. ibid.

57. H.D. O'Hara, letter to Captain D French, 15 May 1915, quoted by Field Marshal Lord Carver in *The National Army Museum Book of The Turkish Front 1914–1918*, p.45.

58. C. Aspinall-Oglander, *Official History: Military Operations Gallipoli*, p.284.

59. M. Farmar, letter to Major General Sir S. Hare, 22 May 1915, IWM.

60. ibid. Desmond O'Hara called it 'the day of the big retreat – a most awful show … [when] the whole division simply took to their heels and ran …' He reckoned that 'if the Turks had followed us up we would have been driven into the sea …'

61. C.T. Atkinson, *History of the Royal Hampshire Regiment, Vol II*, p.78. Atkinson added: 'What the weakened and exhausted Twenty-Ninth could not accomplish, a fresh Division might well have achieved, and Achi Baba might have been taken on 28 April.'

62. R. Spencer-Smith, An Account of the Landing on the Beach near Sedd-el-Bahr, Close to the River Clyde, *Hampshire Regimental Journal*, July 1915, RHRM.

63. ibid.

64. M. Farmar, letter to Major General Sir S. Hare, 22 May 1915, IWM.

65. ibid.

66. ibid.

67. E. Unwin, The Landing from the River Clyde, a narrative written for W. Wemyss, p.10.
68. G. Nightingale, letter to his mother, 24 May 1915, TNA.
69. G. Geddes, diary entry, 1 May 1915, IWM. According to Army slang, to be 'Stellenbosched' was to be demoted or sent back to base. It dated back to the South African War of 1899–1902 when incompetent commanders were sent to a holding camp in the Cape town of Stellenbosch after being sacked from their command.

Chapter 25: 'Marvels of Work and Valour'

1. A. Hunter-Weston, report to General Headquarters, MEF, 26 April 1915, War Diary General Staff, 29th Division, TNA.
2. ibid.
3. ibid.
4. ibid. Hunter-Weston stated that the attack was 'excellently carried out and well covered by gunfire of the fleet'.
5. ibid.
6. A. Hunter-Weston, letter to his wife, 27 April 1915, BL.
7. ibid.
8. ibid.
9. ibid.
10. ibid.
11. E. Unwin, The Landing from the River Clyde, a narrative written for W. Wemyss, p.10.
12. G. Nightingale, letter to his mother, 25 August 25 1915, TNA.
13. This is confirmed in a letter O'Hara wrote to Captain D. French on 15 May 1915 in which he stated: 'I sent in his name for gallantry'.
14. E. Unwin, River Clyde narrative, undated, p.7. The reference to Williams as 'the historian' is puzzling. Aspinall, who as Aspinall-Oglander wrote the Official History, was a staff officer with the MEF, but was not aboard the *River Clyde*. Perhaps it was part of Williams' GHQ role to keep a diary of events during the landing.
15. Citation for DSO to Major A.T. Beckwith, quoted in Sir O'Moore Creagh in *The VC and DSO, Vol II*, p.409.
16. ibid.
17. Citation for DSO to Captain G.W. Geddes, quoted in Sir O'Moore Creagh, p.409.
18. I. Hamilton, *Gallipoli Diary, Volume I*, p.157.
19. *Eastern Daily Press*, article headlined 'The Landing: Magnificent Fighting Qualities of the Troops', Press Association War Special, Cairo, 7 May 1915.
20. ibid.
21. *Eastern Daily Press*, article headlined 'Bravest of the Brave: Nameless Hero of Sed-le Bahr: Distinguished Suffolk Officer, Press Association War Special, Cairo, 16 May 1915.
22. ibid.
23. R. Breeks, letter to Betty Walford, 1 May 1915, LC.
24. ibid
25. J. d'Apice, letter passed to Betty Walford,.15 May 1915, LC.
26. Citation for VC to Lieutenant Colonel C.H.M. Doughty-Wylie and Captain G.N. Walford, *The London Gazette*, 23 June 1915, quoted by Sir O'Moore Creagh, p.170.
27. A. Hunter-Weston, Officers recommended for the VC, submitted to GHQ, 10 June 1915, TNA.

28. R. Keyes, *The Fight for Gallipoli*, footnote p.121.
29. A. Sinclair-Thomson, Eyewitness statement, 21 June 1915, TNA.
30. A.T. Beckwith, Eyewitness statement, June 1915, TNA.
31. A. Hunter-Weston, Officers recommended for the VC, submitted to GHQ, 10 June 1915, TNA.
32. ibid.
33. ibid.
34. W. Wemyss, letter to his wife, 29 April 1915, CAC.
35. W. Wemyss, Report on the Southern landing operations on Gallipoli Peninsula on 25 April 1915, dated 5 May 1915, TNA.
36. W. Wemyss, letter to his wife, 5 May 1915, CAC.
37. ibid.
38. J.M. de Robeck, An account of the operations carried out on 25 and 26 April 1915, dated 1 July 1915, TNA.
39. ibid.
40. ibid. Alexander Davidson, captain of the *Cornwallis*, was a notable absentee from the list of honours and promotions compiled by De Robeck. In spite of the ringing praise from the commanding officer of the South Wales Borderers for his support during the landing at S Beach, few awards were made to the men of the *Cornwallis* as her captain's actions became mired in controversy. Lieut (later Commander) Henry Minchin, who led *Cornwallis'* landing party, later wrote: 'When I did get back to the ship, there was a good row brewing up as to why our Gunnery Lt was ashore, instead of firing our guns at the Turks. They were out for my blood and Admiral 'Rosy' Wemyss came on board to investigate. A more charming man you couldn't find anywhere, and he took my side and defended me valiantly. So no further action was taken except that my name was removed from the list for DSC and that did not worry me; I'd seen so many potential VCs knocked over.' (letter to Captain Eric Bush, 7 January 1970, IWM). Davidson was later awarded a DSO (*The London Gazette*, 14 March 1916) for his role 'in charge of [the] Suvla covering force' during the August landings.
41. 'The Navy at Gallipoli', *The Times*, p.7, 17 August 1915.
42. ibid., p.8.
43. M. Moynihan, *Midshipman Drewry VC in A Place Called Armageddon*, p.61.
44. R. Drewry, quoted by M. Moynihan, p.63.
45. E. Unwin, letter to his wife, 20 August 1915, IWM. He was writing from A Beach, Suvla Bay, where he was serving as beachmaster with the acting rank of captain. He added: 'My home is a hole in the ground; I never thought I'd be a rabbit in my old age …'
46. E. Unwin, letter in reply to invitation to unveil a memorial to William Williams VC in Chepstow, 21 September 1921, Chepstow Museum.
47. G. Samson, interview in 'Carnoustie Seaman Hero Tells How He Won the VC' (c.August 1915).
48. ibid.
49. ibid.
50. ibid.
51. Newspaper article headlined 'Modest Irish VC', 25 August 1915.
52. *Cork Holly Bough*, Christmas 1977, article headlined 'From Aghada to Grim Gallipoli', author's VC files.

53. P.B. Kelly, letter to E.L. Gray, 31 August 1915, published in the *Kildare Observer*, 25 September 1915.

54. G. Nightingale, letter to his mother, 29 July 1915, TNA. Nightingale added: 'The whole thing about promotions and awards is much too petty to worry over at present and there are dozens of good fellows who never get a mention even.' On 3 July he had written: 'I am told I have got the Military Cross, but no one seems to know much about it, and it hasn't appeared in any official orders or anything, so I don't count on getting anything. I'm sure no one was able to recommend me till long afterwards, as there was nobody there senior to me ...' And to his sister, he wrote on the same day: 'You needn't count on my getting anything beyond a 'mention' in despatches ... I think it is too late now to expect anything. Anyway there are tons and tons of fellows out here who have done much better than I and just because there was no one there to recommend them they have not even been 'mentioned'. So there's nothing for me to grouse about.'

55 G. Nightingale, letter to his mother, 18 May 1915, TNA. 'You will be glad to hear that I was mentioned in Gen Hunter-Weston's despatches for the night attack of 1 May ... As a fellow called O'Hara [senior surviving officer of the Dublins] and myself organised a counter attack and retook some trenches temporarily occupied by the Turks when they rushed us in the dark. As a matter of fact it was the most natural thing to do and the Turks didn't wait long for us when they saw we meant to retake the trenches ...'

56. G. Geddes, Report on the Services of Captain G.W. Nightingale, 1 November 1915, IWM.

57. ibid.

58. ibid.

59. ibid.

60. Citation for DSO to Captain R.C.K. Lambert, quoted by Sir O'Moore Creagh, Vol III, p.8.

61. War Diary, 89th (Highland Field Ambulance), 16 October 1915, TNA.

62. J. Redmond, letter to Sir I. Hamilton, 22 April 1916, Hamilton Papers, LHC.

63. I. Hamilton, letter to Major Gen A. Hunter-Weston, 28 March 1916, Hamilton Papers, LHC.

64. ibid, 22 April 1916, Hamilton Papers, LHC.

65. A. Hunter-Weston, letter to Sir I. Hamilton, 28 April 1916, Hamilton Papers, LHC.

66. ibid.

67. J. Redmond, letter to Sir I. Hamilton, 13 November 1916, Hamilton Papers, LHC.

68. I. Hamilton, letter to J. Redmond, 15 November 1916, Hamilton Papers, LHC.

69. ibid, 18 November 1916, Hamilton Papers, LHC.

70. ibid.

71. H. Foster, *At Antwerp and the Dardanelles*, p.62. Both keen walkers, they had frequently gone off on 'tours of exploration' together during the division's spell on Lemnos.

72. H. Foster, letter to Mr and Mrs Tisdall, quoted in *Memoir and Poems of A. W. St C. Tisdall VC*, p.114.

73. ibid.

74. M. Tisdall, letter to E. Unwin, 18 August 1915.

75. ibid.

76. ibid.

77. M. Tisdall, letter to Sir I. Hamilton, 24 August 1915, Hamilton Papers, LHC.

78. Ibid.
79. ibid. Mrs Tisdall added: 'We have our two other sons fighting at the Front in France, and our last remaining one is in training: it would be a great encouragement to them and to his large circle of college and military friends if this could be done.'
80. I. Hamilton, letter to M. Tisdall, 15 September 1915, Hamilton Papers, LHC.
81. P. Kelly, letter to Senior Naval Officer Mudros, 13 November 1915, TNA.
82. ibid. The following month, responding to Unwin's enquiries, Kelly wrote: 'In reply to these embarrassing letters and cuttings and copies [presumably collected by Marian Tisdall] I regret I cannot help you very much. I can swear to (1) you, (2) Drewry, (3) Samson, (4) the Petty Officer who was shot who went to your assistance and to (5) Petty Officer Rumming, but then I knew you all. As regards Tisdall, I believe he was the young RND officer who did so well but I cannot swear to it. In the end of June we learned that only one RND officer went in on River Clyde with us and that he was Tisdall. Well then, I suppose the one I saw was this Tisdall. I reported this the other day to SNO after that great bunch of papers reached me. I never saw this RND officer (Tisdall?) help you, others may have, but I saw him picking up wounded, etc, and behaving in a gallant manner. As he disappeared suddenly and I never saw him again I did not find out at [the] time who he was and as I tell you, heard about the end of June that the only RND officer with us was Tisdall. I never knew that he was recommended and I don't know who could have done so. Trusting you are keeping very fit and regretting that I cannot help you except by assuming or surmising re Sub Lieut Tisdall …'
83. J. Wedgwood, letter to Major General A. Paris, 21 December 1915, TNA.
84. A. Paris, letter to the Adjutant General, Royal Marines, Royal Naval Division, 14 December 1915, TNA.
85. C. Walker, letter to HQ Royal Naval Division, 31 January 1916, TNA.
86. ibid.
87. C. Walker, Case of Sub Lieutenant A.W. St Clair Tisdall, RNVR, 15 March 1916, TNA.
88. ibid.
89. ibid.

Chapter 26: 'Too Horrible for Words'

1. A. Tisdall, postcard, 27 April 1915, *Verses, Letters and Remembrances of Arthur Walderne St Clair Tisdall VC*, p.103.
2. A. Tisdall, posted 7 May 1915, ibid, p.104.
3. Unidentified member of the RNAS, letter, 2 May 1915, Holkham archives.
4. ibid. By 5 May, the Inkosi was off Cape Helles and preparing to land another 88 men with more machine-guns and ammunition (letter from Charles Wedgwood).
5. D. Illingworth, letter to his brother, 6 May 1915, via Stephen Chambers.
6. P.B. Kelly, letter to H. Coke, undated, Holkham archives.
7. J. Wedgwood, letter to H. Coke, 5 May 1915, Holkham archives.
8. Unidentified member of the RNAS, letter, 2 May 1915, Holkham archives.
9. ibid.
10. J. Wedgwood, letter to H. Coke, 5 May 1915, Holkham archives.
11. D. Illingworth, letter to his brother, 6 May 1915, via Stephen Chambers.
12. ibid.
13. ibid.
14. J. Wedgwood, quoted in *The Last of the Radicals*, p.108.

15. ibid.
16. J. Wedgwood, letter to his daughter, 8 May 1915, LC.
17. J. Wedgwood, quoted in *The Last of the Radicals*, p.108.
18. ibid, pp.108-9.
19. Letter of an unnamed 'brother officer', quoted in *Verses, Letters and Remembrances of Arthur Walderne St Clair Tisdall VC*, p.112.
20. G. Grant, letter, in *Verses, Letters and Remembrances of Arthur Walderne St Clair Tisdall VC*, p.119.
21. J. Wedgwood, letter to his daughter, 19 May 1915, LC. Wedgwood returned home 'looking eighty, with a white beard', and though promoted 'full commander' returned briefly to civil life. Frustrated by parliamentary wrangling, he managed to wangle himself a position on the staff of General Sir Horace Smith-Dorrien who was appointed to command in East Africa. He then served on the staff of General Jan Smuts before returning to London to join the Commission set up to inquire into the handling of the Mesopotamia campaign. Active service followed with a spell in command of a South African machine gun company after which he was made Assistant Director of Trench Warfare. In 1918, he headed a military mission sent to Siberia to encourage Russia's continued participation in the war. Re-elected a Liberal MP in 1918, he 'crossed the floor' the following year to join the Independent Labour Party. An ardent Zionist and supporter of Indian independence, he served in the first Labour Cabinet and was made a Privy Councillor in 1924. During the 1930s, he was vociferous critic of successive governments' policy of appeasement. The martial parliamentarian donned uniform again in 1940, joining the Home Guard as Britain prepared itself for an invasion that never came. The following year he accepted a peerage from his old friend, Winston Churchill. Baron Wedgwood, sometimes known as Josiah Wedgwood IV, died in 1943.
22. G. Nightingale, letter to his mother, 10 May 1915, TNA.
23. G. Nightingale, ibid, 24 May 1915, TNA.
24. A Hunter-Weston, letter to his wife, 15 May 1915, BL.
25. G Nightingale, letter to his mother, 1 June 1915, TNA.
26. ibid.
27. ibid.
28. ibid.
29. E. Bush, *Gallipoli*, p.202.
30. Frederick Curtiss (DEV/1899C), sometimes spelled Curtis, is commemorated on the Helles Memorial. His death precluded him from being awarded the Conspicuous Gallantry Medal he so richly deserved because of the rules governing the decoration that did not allow for it to be given posthumously. His only recognition was a mention in Arthur Tisdall's VC citation, see Appendix I.
31. F. McLaren, letter, 4 June 1915, IWM.
32. ibid.
33. ibid.
34. F. McLaren, letter, 5 June 1915, IWM.
35. ibid.
36. ibid.
37. ibid.
38. ibid.
39. ibid.

40. H.D. O'Hara, letter to his fiancée, May 1915, quoted by Robert Rhodes James in *Gallipoli*, p.160.
41. G. Nightingale, letter to his mother, 29 July 1915, TNA.
42. H.D. O'Hara, letter to his fiancée, June 1915, quoted by Robert Rhodes James in *Gallipoli*, p.224.
43. ibid, quoted by Robert Rhodes James in *Gallipoli*, p.230.
44. G. Nightingale, letter to his mother, 29 July 1915, TNA.
45. A. Hunter-Weston, letter to his wife, 5 June 1915, BL.
46. ibid, 12 July 1915, BL.
47. A. Hunter-Weston, letter to Major General Callwell, 15 July 1915, BL.
48. ibid.
49. ibid.
50. ibid. After making a full recovery, Hunter-Weston resumed command of VIII Corps, which had been re-established in France. Despite a poor showing during the early stages of the Somme offensive in the summer of 1916, he remained in charge for the duration of a war in which he became the first person to serve as an MP while simultaneously commanding an Army corps in the field. Hunter-Weston resigned from the Army in 1919, but continued to represent his North Ayrshire constituency until 1935. He died five years later, aged seventy-five, following a fall at his ancestral home in Hunterston.
51. Having defended his leadership during the Dardanelles Commission's inquiry into the political and military direction of the campaign, he made repeated attempts to revive his career without success. In retirement, Sir Ian Hamilton busied himself with supporting ex-service organisations and by writing several volumes of memoirs. As well as being Scottish President of the British Legion, he was a founding member and vice-president of the Anglo-German Association and, while not being a Nazi, became an admirer of Adolf Hitler. He served as Lieutenant of the Tower of London and was elected Rector of Edinburgh University. The former Commander-in-Chief of the Mediterranean Expeditionary Force outlived his wife, their adopted son, who was killed during the Second World War, and all of his Gallipoli commanders save for Birdwood, dying in 1947 at the grand old age of ninety-four.
52. A. Shaw, extract from diary, 16 October 1915, IWM.
53. S. Gillon, *The KOSB in the Great War*, p.167.
54. P.B. Kelly, letter to Stoney's brother, November 1915, IWM.
55. ibid, undated but post-December 1915, IWM.
56. ibid.
57. ibid.
58. G. Stoney, letter to his brother, 21 May 1915, IWM.
59. P.B. Kelly, letter to Stoney's brother, November 1915, IWM.
60. J. Peshall, letter to Stoney's brother, 27 October 1915, IWM. Peshall was co-author of *The Immortal Gamble*, a record of the part played in the Dardanelles campaign by HMS *Cornwallis*. He later earned a DSO for his 'strength of character and splendid comradeship' displayed on board HMS *Vindictive* during the raid on Zeebrugge on the night of 22–23 April 1918.
61. Citation for DSO to Captain G.B. Stoney, quoted by Sir O'Moore Creagh, Vol II, p.415.
62. ibid.
63. ibid.
64. ibid.

65. A. Shaw, extract from diary, 16 October 1915, IWM.
66. A. Shaw, letter, 16 October 1915, IWM.

Chapter 27: 'Stealing Away'
1. W. Corbett Williamson, letter to M. Paul Vigroux on behalf of Captain Eric Bush, 10 July 1972, IWM.
2. L. Doughty-Wylie, diary entry, 1 May 1915, quoted by Eric Bush in *Gallipoli*, p.316.
3. C. Doughty-Wylie, letter to his mother-in-law, Mrs H.H. 'Jean' Coe, 20 April 1915, IWM.
4. L. Doughty-Wylie, letter to her mother, 13 May 1915, IWM.
5. B. Doughty-Wylie, letter to Captain Eric Bush, January 29 [1970?], IWM. Brian Doughty-Wylie was born Brian Peirson Thesiger, the son of the Hon Wilfred Gilbert Thesiger, British Minister in Abyssinia. 'Dick' Doughty-Wylie, who was serving as Consul-General, was his godfather. He changed his name by deed poll in 1933 at the request of Lily who had become his unofficial 'godmother'. While serving in her husband's old regiment, the Royal Welch Fusiliers, at Anzio, Brian Doughty-Wylie earned a Military Cross. He retired from the Army in 1957 as an honorary colonel. He died in 1982.
6. ibid.
7. P.B. Kelly, diary, quoted by Sir O'Moore Creagh, Vol I, p.170. In the absence of categorical proof, the identity of the woman at Gallipoli remains a contentious one. Some writers have speculated that the visitor to Helles in November 1915 was not Lily but 'Dick' Doughty-Wylie's lover, Gertrude Bell. They suggest she may have taken a detour during her journey to Cairo to take up a post with British military intelligence. But there is no mention of such a visit in her otherwise copious archive of letters and papers. As one correspondent commented during the late Eric Bush's inconclusive investigation into the matter: 'I think if she had she would have left some written word of this, she wrote a lot and was a very persistent paramour ...' The key to solving the mystery would appear to lie with Lily's diary for the period. But that is missing, the suggestion being that it was buried with her on her instructions following her death in Akrotiri, Cyprus, in 1961. She, however, maintained, according to the hearsay evidence of friends and her own subsequent diary references, that she had visited 'Dick's' grave on at least two occasions, the first being in November 1915. For an alternative version read John Howell's The Only Woman at Gallipoli.
8. R. Keyes, letter to his wife, 5 January 1916, quoted in *The Keyes Papers Vol I*, p.306.
9. ibid.
10. R. Keyes, diary extract for 3 January 1916, quoted in *The Fight for Gallipoli*, p.335.
11. ibid, p.334.
12. R. Keyes, report on demolition of blockships off Helles to Vice-Admiral Commanding, Eastern Mediterranean, 2 January 1916, CAC.
13. ibid.
14. J. Murray, sound record 8201, IWM.
15. J. Murray, diary 8 January 1916, quoted in *Gallipoli As I Saw It*, p.191.
16. R.R. Thompson, *The Fifty-Second (Lowland) Division 1914–1918*, p.232.
17. J. Young, quoted in *The Fifty-Second (Lowland) Division 1914–1918*, p.236.
18. J. Murray, diary January 8, 1916, quoted in *Gallipoli As I Saw It*, p.192.
19. R. Keyes, *The Fight for Gallipoli*, p.341.

20. ibid.
21. R. Thompson, ibid, p.238.
22. ibid.

Chapter 28: 'One Almighty Might-Have-Been'
1. Writing home on 1 May 1915 after his first trip ashore following the landings at Cape Helles, Wemyss had commented: 'We are in hopes that the Turk may get sick of it. I don't think his heart is in the job – of course they are led by German officers.'
2. W. Wemyss, letter to Sir David Beatty, 14 November 1918, quoted in *The Life and Letters of Lord Wester Wemyss GCB, Admiral of the Fleet*, p.398.
3. W. Wemyss, The Life and Letters of Lord Wester Wemyss GCB, Admiral of the Fleet, p.395. Wemyss went on to attend the Paris Peace Conference as Britain's senior naval representative. He resigned as Admiral of the Fleet in November 1919 and was raised to the peerage the same month as Baron Wester Wemyss of Wemyss. Having devoted his considerable energy to chronicling the navy's part in the Dardanelles campaign, he enjoyed a full and active retirement, serving as director of a number of companies. The man who sanctioned the *River Clyde* operation died at his villa on the French Riviera on Empire Day, 1933. After a funeral service at Westminster Abbey, 'Rosy' Wemyss, the 29th Division's 'special admiral', was laid to rest at Wemyss Castle, within sight and sound of the sea.
4. Exning Remembers website, Sub-Lieutenant Maurice Charles Humphrey Lloyd, DSC and Bar.
5. ibid.
6. ibid.
7. ibid.
8. R. Keyes, *The Naval Memoirs 1916–1918*, p.291.
9. Newmarket-born Maurice Lloyd died on 24 April 1918. The citation for the Bar to his DSC stated: 'Showed great coolness under heavy fire, and by his bravery and devotion to duty set a fine example to his men. On abandoning ship, after she had been sunk [scuttled], Sub-Lieut Lloyd was severely wounded. This very gallant young officer has since died of his wounds.'
10. George Drewry was not forgotten by his friends and colleagues in the Northern Patrol. They contributed to a memorial window in All Saints' Church, Forest Gate.
11. P.B. Kelly, letter to E.L. Gray, 31 August 1915, published in the *Kildare Observer*, 25 September 1915.
12. ibid.
13. ibid.
14. ibid.
15. ibid.
16. ibid.
17. Obituary published in *The British Medical Journal*, 22 May 1920.
18. P.B. Kelly, diary, quoted by Sir O'Moore Creagh, Vol I, p.184.
19. ibid.
20. The words on a wreath laid on his grave by the Leinster Old Comrades Association.
21. G. Nightingale, letter to his mother, 1 June 1915, TNA.
22. ibid, 4 June 1915, TNA.
23. G. Geddes, The landing from the River Clyde at V Beach, 25 April 1915, TNA.
24. J. Morse, letter to E. Unwin, 4 May 1926, IWM.

25. R. Keyes, *The Fight for Gallipoli*, p.125.
26. H. Malleson, letter to the author, September 1991. Commander Hugh Malleson had by then retired after twenty-five years' service in the Royal Navy.
27. J. Macintyre, in conversation with the author, 20 August 1991. Commander J.P. Macintyre (Retd.) was a colleague of Malleson's from their time together on the China Station in the 1930s.
28. ibid.
29. J. McWilliam, Malleson's daughter, letter to the author, 9 September 1991.
30. E. Unwin, quoted in the *Morning Post*, 26 April 1926.
31. E. Unwin, quoted in the *East Anglian Daily Times*, 25 April 1938.
32. ibid.
33. ibid.
34. E. Unwin, The Landing from the River Clyde, a narrative written for W. Wemyss, undated, p.10, IWM.
The *River Clyde*'s engineer, William Rowntree Horend, had a regret of his own so far as the landing was concerned. In a letter to Sir Ian Hamilton in 1924 that was inspired by newspaper reports about the Dardanelles campaign, he declared: 'Had time permitted I believe other openings could have been cut in the hull of the 'River Clyde' in such positions as to have ensured 50% further safety [*sic*] to the troops when landing and although one hesitates to discuss what might have been yet the time is never too late to place on record what may be a helpful object lesson for the future'. Hamilton replied on 16 April 1924. 'I am greatly interested in what you say about the other openings,' he wrote. 'Had we really ensured 50% further safety to the troops when landing we should have carried V Beach right off, just as W and X were carried.' Hamilton Papers, LHC.
35. E. Unwin, letter to Sir Ian Hamilton, 22 July 1943, Hamilton Papers, LHC.
36. E. Unwin, letter to Captain Hughes Lockyer, 21 June 1936, IWM. Lockyer commanded the pre-dreadnought HMS *Implacable* at the X Beach landings.

Chapter 29: 'Something Sacred'
1. L. Doughty-Wylie, letter to her mother, 13 May 1915, IWM.
2. ibid, diary, 12 November 1918, IWM.
3. ibid, 7 January 1919, IWM.
4. ibid, 9 January 1919, IWM.
5. ibid.
6. 'Dick' Doughty-Wylie's grave was never moved. In 1923 an engineer, A. E. Cooke, arrived on the peninsula to restore and reinforce the grave from subsidence as part of a wider commission to construct a series of war cemeteries. In a record of his efforts, Cooke later wrote: 'The grave was located on a small knoll just outside of the village. I was requested by the IWGC [Imperial War Graves Commission] to make the site more permanent as his widow had in view building a monument over it. We went to the spot & I instructed my men to make a trench down to solid ground around it, then to pour concrete in it and to cap the whole grave with a 6' slab of concrete. We got started first by removing the tangle of barbed wire over it and then carefully to remove the top-soil. Within a few inches his body became visible – enveloped in a ragged uniform with belt huddled in a crouched position. I marked off the location of the foundation I wanted. I then mounted 'Harry' [his horse] to visit the other cemeteries on my morning round. I got back as soon as I could and

looked. I did not know whether to laugh or to cry. What had obviously happened is that the trench in the soft soil had collapsed so that my men removed the body from the grave and finished the excavations. Then they had placed his skull at the top of the grave and made a geometric pattern of his bones – even to his finger bones! I hurried to get the foundations around the bones and waited to put the concrete slab over him. I hope he now rests in peace [IWM].' The crusader-like tomb today stands in splendid isolation on the summit of Hill 141, the only original wartime British grave on the peninsula and a much-visited memorial to the gallant struggle to secure V Beach.

7. *Tell England: A Study in a Generation* was published in 1922 and nine years' later was made into a highly successful film. The original novel, which was inspired by Raymond's own experiences at Gallipoli, places its fictional characters at the bloody landing on V Beach. Raymond himself took no part in the operation, going ashore on W Beach in the summer of 1915 as a chaplain attached to the 42nd (East Lancashire) Division.

8. E. Raymond, *The Story of My Days*: An Autobiography 1888–1922, p.162.

9. ibid.

10. A. Pearman, quoted by Denis Stonham in 'Steamship River Clyde – How Britain Failed to Save a Hero of Gallipoli', *World Ship Review* No.40, June 2005, p.11.

11. ibid.

12. ibid, p.12.

13. *The Times*, 18 November 1919.

14. *Hansard*, debate in the House of Commons, 18 December 1919.

15. ibid.

16. ibid.

17. ibid.

18. Ibid.

19. ibid.

20. *The Times*, 29 January 1920.

21. ibid, 31 January 1920.

22. ibid.

23. ibid, 12 February 1920.

24. *Hansard*, debate in the House of Commons, 18 February 1919. The question was posed by Lieutenant Commander Joseph Kenworthy, later 10th Baron Strabolgi, Labour MP for Central Hull.

25. ibid.

26. *Hansard*, 10 March 1919, quoted by Denis Stonham, p.12.

27. ibid.

28. ibid.

29. C, Mackenzie, *Gallipoli Memories*, p.175.

30. ibid.

31. W. Stanton Hope, *Gallipoli Revisited*, p.18-9.

32. D. Stonham, p.13.

33. E. Raymond, *The Story of My Days: An Autobiography 1888–1922*, p.127.

34. E. Raymond, *The Daily Telegraph*, 24 April 1965.

35. ibid.

36. ibid.

37. L. Raymond, 'The End of the River Clyde', *The Gallipolian*, No.62, Spring 1990.

38. E. Raymond, *The Daily Telegraph*, 24 April 1965.
39. ibid.
40. R. Allanson, *The Daily Telegraph*, 29 April 1965.
41. ibid.
42. L. Raymond, 'The End of the River Clyde', *The Gallipolian*, No.62, Spring 1990.
43. R. Allanson, quoted by Lella Raymond in 'The End of the River Clyde', *The Gallipolian*, No.62, Spring 1990.
44. L. Raymond, 'The End of the River Clyde', *The Gallipolian*, No.62, Spring 1990.
45. E. Raymond, *The Daily Telegraph*, 24 April 1965.
46. E. Raymond, *The Daily Telegraph*, 6 May 1965.

Appendix 4
1. Commander Isham Worsley Gibson was *Albion*'s gunnery officer on 25 April.

Bibliography

Ashmead-Bartlett, E., *The Uncensored Dardanelles*, Hutchinsons, 1928.

Aspinall-Oglander, Brig-Gen C.F., *Official History of the War: Military Operations Gallipoli, Vols 1 and 2*, Heinemann, 1929 and 1932.

Atkinson, C.T., *History of the Royal Hampshire Regiment, Vol II*, Gale & Polden, 1950.

Boyle, W.H.D., *Gallant Deeds*, Gieves, 1919.

Brodie, C.G., *Forlorn Hope 1915*, Frederick Books, 1956.

Bush, Capt E.W., *Gallipoli*, George Allen & Unwin, 1975.

Carroll, T., *The Dodger*, Mainstream Publishing, 2012.

Carver, Field Marshal Lord., *The National Army Museum Book of the Turkish Front 1914–1918*, Sidgwick & Jackson, 2003.

Chatterton, E.K., *Dardanelles Dilemma*, Rich & Cowan, 1935.

Corbett, Sir J.S. *Official History of the War: Naval Operations, Vols I and II*, Longmans, 1921.

Creagh, Sir O'M. and Humphris, E. M., *The VC and DSO, The Standard Art Book Co, Vols I-III*, n.d.

Creghton, The Rev. O., *With the 29th Division in Gallipoli*, Longmans, Green & Co, 1916.

Davidson, Major G., *The Incomparable 29th and the River Clyde*, James Gordon Bisset, 1919.

Dungan, M., *Irish Voices From the Great War*, Irish Academic Press, 1995.

Edmonds, H.J., *Norman Dewhurst, MC*, H. J. Edmonds, 1968.

Emden, R. van and Chambers, S., *Gallipoli*, Bloomsbury, 2015.

Erickson, E.J., *Gallipoli: The Ottoman Campaign*, Pen & Sword, 2010.

Farmar, H.M.,*The Landing of the 86th Infantry Brigade*, Sackville Press, n.d.

Forrest, M., *The Defence of the Dardanelles: From Bombards to Battleships*, Pen & Sword, 2012.

Foster, The Rev H.C., *At Antwerp and the Dardanelles*, Mills & Boon, 1918.

Gillam, J., *Gallipoli Diary* (reprint), Strong Oak Press with Tom Donovan Publishing, 1989.

Gillon, Capt S., *The KOSB in the Great War*, Thos Nelson, 1930.

Halpern, P.G., *The Keyes Papers 1914–1918, Vol 1*, Navy Records Society, 1972.

Hamilton, Sir Ian, *Gallipoli Diary, Vols 1 and 2*, Arnold, 1920.

Hart, P., *Gallipoli*, Profile Books, 2011.

Holland, C., *Before Gallipoli: The 29th Division in Warwickshire and north Oxfordshire, December 1914–March 1915*, Warwickshire Great War Publications, 2014.

Howell, G., *Daughter of the Desert: The Remarkable Life of Gertrude Bell*, Macmillan, 2006.

Irwin, the Rev F., *Stonyhurst War Record: A Memorial of the Part Taken by Stonyhurst Men in the Great War*, 1927.

James R. Rhodes. *Gallipoli*, Batsford, 1965.

Jerrold, D., *The Royal Naval Division*, Hutchinson, 1923.

Johnstone, T., *Orange Green & Khaki: The Story of the Irish Regiments in the Great War 1914–18*, Gill and Macmillan, 1992.

Keyes, Admiral of the Fleet Sir R., *The Fight for Gallipoli*, Eyre & Spottiswoode, 1941.

Lecane, P., *Beneath a Turkish Sky: The Royal Dublin Fusiliers and the Assault on Gallipoli*, The History Press, 2015.

Liddle, P., *Men of Gallipoli*, Allen Lane, 1976.

Mackenzie, C., *Gallipoli Memories*, Cassell, 1929.

McCance, Capt S., *History of the Royal Munster Fusiliers, Vol II 1861–1922*, Gale & Polden, 1927.

McGilvray, E., *Hamilton & Gallipoli*, Pen & Sword, 2015.

Moorehead, A., *Gallipoli*, Hamish Hamilton, 1956.

Moynihan, M., *A Place Called Armageddon*, David & Charles, 1975.

Murray, J., *Gallipoli As I Saw It*, William Kimber, 1965.

Nevinson, H.W., *The Dardanelles Campaign*, Nisbet, 1918.

Potter, A., *Torquay in the Great War*, Pen & Sword, 2015.

Prior, R., *Gallipoli: The End of the Myth*, Yale University Press, 2009.

Raymond, E., *The Story of My Days: An Autobiography 1888–1922*, Cassell, 1968.

Rodge, H. and J., *Battleground Europe: Helles Landing*, Gallipoli, Pen & Sword, 2003.

Rudenno, V., *Gallipoli: Attack from the Sea*, Yale University Press, 2008.

Samson, Air Commodore C.R., *Fights and Flights*, Ernest Benn, 1930.

Snelling, S., *VCs of the First World War: Gallipoli*, The History Press, 2010.

_____. *VCs of the First World War: The Naval VCs*, The History Press, 2013.

Stacke, Capt H. FitzM. *The Worcestershire Regiment in the Great War*, G. T. Cheshire & Sons, n.d.

Steel, N., *The Battlefields of Gallipoli: Then and Now*, Leo Cooper, 1990.

_____ and Hart, P. *Defeat at Gallipoli*, Macmillan, 1994.

Stewart, A.T. and Peshall, *The Rev C. J. E. The Immortal Gamble*, A & C Black, 1917.

Thompson, Lt Col R.R., *The Fifty-Second (Lowland) Division 1914–1918*, Maclehose, Jackson & Co, 1923.

Tisdall, A. W. St. C., *Verses, Letters and Remembrances of Arthur Walderne St Clair Tisdall VC*, Sidgwick & Jackson, 1916.

Travers, T., *Gallipoli 1915*, Tempus, 2001.

Usborne, C.V., *Smoke on the Horizon*, Hodder & Stoughton, 1933.

Walker, R.W., *To What End Did They Die?*, R W Walker Publishing, 1985.

Wallach, J., *Desert Queen*, Weidenfeld & Nicolson, 1996.

Wedgwood, J.C., *With Machine guns to Gallipoli*, Westminster Gazette, Darling & Son Ltd, 1915.

_____, *Memoirs of a Fighting Life*, Hutchinson, 1940.

Wemyss, Lady Wester, *The Life and Letters of Lord Wester Wemyss, Admiral of the Fleet*, Eyre & Spottiswoode, 1935.

_____, *The Navy in the Dardanelles Campaign*, Hodder & Stoughton, 1924.

Williams, W.A., *The VCs of Wales and the Welsh Regiments*, Bridge Books, 1984.

_____. *Heart of the Dragon: The VCs of Wales and the Welsh Regiments 1914–1982*, Bridge Books, 2008.

Willis, C.J. and Rogers, D.F., *For Valour: HMS Conway & HMS Worcester*, Conway Club & Assn of Old Worcesters, 1984.

Winton, J., *The Victoria Cross at Sea*, Michael Joseph, 1979.

Wylly, Colonel H.C., *Neill's Blue Caps, Vol III 1914–1922*, Gale & Polden, 1924.

Index